A SILENCE FROM HITCHCOCK

THE HITCHCOCK QUARTET

I. *An Eye for Hitchcock*
II. *A Dream of Hitchcock*
III. *A Voyage with Hitchcock*
IV. *A Silence from Hitchcock*

A SILENCE FROM HITCHCOCK

MURRAY POMERANCE

SUNY
PRESS

COVER ART: Still from *The Trouble with Harry* (Alfred Hitchcock, Paramount, 1955). Digital frame enlargement.

Published by State University of New York Press, Albany

© 2023 State University of New York

All rights reserved

Printed in the United States of America

No part of this book may be used or reproduced in any manner whatsoever without written permission. No part of this book may be stored in a retrieval system or transmitted in any form or by any means including electronic, electrostatic, magnetic tape, mechanical, photocopying, recording, or otherwise without the prior permission in writing of the publisher.

For information, contact State University of New York Press, Albany, NY
www.sunypress.edu

Library of Congress Cataloging-in-Publication Data

Names: Pomerance, Murray, 1946- author.
Title: A silence from Hitchcock / Murray Pomerance.
Description: Albany : State University of New York Press, [2023] | Series: The Hitchcock quartet | Includes bibliographical references.
Identifiers: LCCN 2022023826 | ISBN 9781438491875 (hardcover) | ISBN 9781438491899 (ebook) | ISBN 781438491882 (paperback)
Subjects: LCSH: Hitchcock, Alfred, 1899-1980—Criticism and interpretation. | Silence in motion pictures.
Classification: LCC PN1998.3.H58 P667 2023 | DDC 791.4302/33092—dc23/20221121
LC record available at https://lccn.loc.gov/2022023826

10 9 8 7 6 5 4 3 2 1

to
NELLIE

A strangely feelable, prickling silence, as if a wound were healing.

It was a silence which, a moment before, no one would have thought possible.

He knows who is standing there; he realizes that everything has become silent, without any transition: absolute silence. Now the voice will come that he recognizes from long ago . . .

—Rainer Maria Rilke, *The Notebooks of Malte Laurids Brigge*

CONTENTS

Acknowledgments, ix

Introduction: What Is Given, What Is Not Given, 3

1. A *Notorious* Way to Live, 12
2. How a Lady Vanishes, 64
3. Our Frenzied Life, 120
4. For the Grace of God: The Wrong Men, 172
5. The Trouble and Harry, 218
6. The Dirty Truth of *Topaz*, 270

Notes, 325

Works Cited, 337

Index, 349

ACKNOWLEDGMENTS

To Kate Barrett (Greensboro), Linda Barrett (New York), Julia Basin (Toronto), the late Kenneth Boulding (Ann Arbor), the late Henry Bumstead (Los Angeles), Alex Clayton (Bristol), the late Herbert Coleman (Los Angeles), Dirk Crockaert (London), the late C. W. 'Doc' Erickson (Los Angeles), the late Leslie Fiedler (Buffalo), Elliott Gould (Los Angeles), the late Harvey Roy Greenberg (New York), Will Hole (Firle), the late Norman Holland (Miami), Christopher Husted (Los Angeles), Jason Jacobs (Brisbane), the late Abraham Kaplan (Ann Arbor), Ann Kaplan (New York), the late Carleton Kelsey (Amagansett), Mark Kermode (London), the late Norman Lloyd (Los Angeles), Hailey MacInnes, MD (Toronto), Douglas Messerli (Los Angeles), Mark Crispin Miller (New York), Stephen Miller (New York), Laura Mulvey (London), R. Barton Palmer (Atlanta), Stephen Rebello (Pasadena), Mercedes Haziot Ribicoff (New York) and the late Peter Ribicoff (New York), William Rothman (Miami), Bob Rubin (Los Angeles), Dan Sacco (Toronto), John Sakeris (Toronto and Santa Barbara), Jonathan Soja (Schöneberg), Matthew Solomon (Ann Arbor), Carol Tavris (Los Angeles), Daniel Varndell (Southampton), the late Eugene Weiner (Haifa), Linda Ruth Williams (Southampton), and Jonathan Wright (Asheville), my sincere gratitude for invaluable help quite frequently given freely and without self-regard. I am also in debt to Linda Harris Mehr, former director of the Margaret Herrick Library (Beverly Hills) and her committed staff, especially Barbara Hall, Louise Hilton, and Jenny Romero; and to Ned Comstock at the Cinema-Television Library, University of Southern California (Los Angeles), along with the staff at the Warner Bros. Archive there.

My colleagues, nay friends, at SUNY Press have been unfailingly giving and unfailingly true, especially Michael Campochiaro, Aimee

Harrison, Ryan Morris, and James Peltz. A copyeditor's copyeditor, Eric Schramm has worked every word of this entire Quartet with me.

Ariel Pomerance and Nellie Perret live through my strange and always deepening faith with Hitchcock and his work, for which devotion no payment of gratitude is enough.

A SILENCE FROM HITCHCOCK

INTRODUCTION
WHAT IS GIVEN, WHAT IS NOT GIVEN

In his masterful defense of poetry, Paul Goodman considers silence:

> There is a silence beyond speech, an accord closer than verbal communication and where the situation is unproblematic. In one of the scriptural lives of Buddha there is a remarkable sentence, at the conversion of Anathapindika: "The Lord consented by becoming silent." I take it that this means that the silence of the Lord creates accord, *is* accord; and from the human point of view, if the *Lord* consents, what further is to be said?

He writes out, too, this pithy thought: "Very close friends often do not speak, because they do not have to" (4). I might go further: the intensity and extent of the silence will indicate the closeness, although only to the silent ones. There are surely many kinds of silence, friendly and otherwise, many paths along which silence can step as, without sounding, it speaks.

We know how Alfred Hitchcock's cinematic mastery is often thought both lordly and Lordly, that he is a "supreme creative being standing over his work"; or that, analogous to the way the Divine Being is figured in Genesis as a creative artist ("He made ... ; and He saw that it was good"), so Hitchcock behind, above, beyond, and underneath his films is a creative artist indisputable, too. Silently, in his work, he makes consent.

Still more important than the idea of elevating the Silent One, the artist, to the position of Lordly being, is the quality, meaning, and range of implication contained in the artistic silences: the silence itself, for Goodman a matter of astonishing importance and fascination to be only gestured to by way of the tale of Buddha. The silence of the compassionate, comprehending, concurring divinity, perhaps; or sanctified one; or seeker who would find the unexpressed charm. Or, again, that silence of close friends, which for each can be the same silence.

If any one silence can be the same as any other...

Let us work on the assumption, shared by many millions of people around the globe, I believe, that if friends do not need to speak it is because they can see, feel, and imagine the conditions in which they find themselves, or which they recall or hope for, and verbal articulation simply does not add anything meaningful to the moment. Indeed, it might obstruct. Not only that: potential speech is foreknown and fully accepted as an addition that would be of no value; hence no energy is expended engaging in it. Or perhaps more stunningly: things are happening far too fully and far too swiftly for words to find a way in bearing the necessary torch—as regards film and film watching, the insuperable ekphrastic problem of being given so much so rapidly that the language is overwhelmed.

Having spent considerable time watching, rewatching, and again rewatching his work, and examining much correspondence about its production, and speaking to people who worked with him, I believe I can know the Alfred Hitchcock behind the Hitchcock film as one with whom silence surpasses understanding. While the film is unfolding through my breathing, I am experiencing a chain of moments being shared with me by a friend, a friend to the viewer in general but—as I feel it (and I think I am not alone)—especially to me, a loyal viewer who sees always in memory. Even during the screening, every sight is a memory. Very often spoken sound is not required, the simplest reason being that both Hitchcock and his viewer know that everything of necessity is already on the screen. The look on a face. The movement of a hand. The signal gesture of character or camera. The color. The design. The decoration of the room. A little boy's open-necked white shirt, or puppy. The pins a woman puts in her hair. The depth of field. The architecture of the moment, among moments. Think of the very, very famous extreme long shot from a high position that initiates the cropduster sequence in *North by Northwest* (1959)[1] and now imagine that gazing at it we could be obliged to hear an off-camera voice, if gentle still ineradicable: "Here, all alone in a vast and empty countryside, Roger stands expectantly and isolated and open to the elements." What a ruination, what a destruction of the temple that—or any other monotone—would produce! Or think how, at that very, very famous concert scene at the Albert Hall in *The Man Who Knew Too Much* (1956), Ben (Jimmy Stewart) arrives to find Jo (Doris Day) in a climactic dialogue-free passage, a little mime, albeit a whole conversation was written for them to deliver but on the set, as they prepared to shoot, Hitchcock summarily decided no, the Arthur Benjamin music was enough.

The silence of knowing when enough is enough...

A particularly elegant silence—because most complex as the dramatic situation goes—lies between, under, or around uttered words, in short what an openly heard statement *does not say*, for one reason or another: timidity, shyness, modesty, tact, strategy, ineffable awe. In the galvanizing parlor chat scene of *Psycho* (1960), Norman Bates utters a great many profound and intriguing things, energizes and moves our speculation not only about him but about life—"A boy's best friend is his mother"—but as lovers of the film know (too) well, what this young man is saying in this scene is not all of what he is meaning. This gap between utterance and meaning is a root of poetry, of course, and Goodman discusses it. I say, but not what I mean; this *not* because I wish to be cagey or cute but because *that which I mean* is not expressible in the language as we have it. T. S. Eliot had this idea when he used Dante in "The Waste Land": *Poi s'ascose nel foco che gli affina.* (Then he hid himself in the fire which purifies.)

In *The Trouble with Harry* (1955, discussed in this book) a hyperopic medical practitioner holding a (presumably attention-grabbing) book very close to his eyes stumbles across a corpse while taking a walk in the woods. It's a sweet little moment for comedy, and never fails to provoke a laugh. But something true and provocative is not being said, in order to adduce which, if adducing is valuable at all—and exactly because onscreen there is a silence about this matter—I must now spell it out: here we have a doctor so absorbed in matters of "theory" (fiction is also theory) he cannot see what's real. And this could raise for any or all of us the question: Does anyone escape the confines of some theory to have a direct relation with the reality around? Or: in *The Lady Vanishes* (1938, discussed here, too) a nun sitting in a private train compartment next to a bandaged patient laid out on the seats maintains strict silence when spoken to by some travelers. Is she a person who does not speak or comprehend English? Is she a person who had reasons for *not revealing* that she does in fact speak and comprehend English—that she is, in fact, English herself? Is the silence malevolent or benevolent, and can it morph as the film winds on from one state to another? In this latter case, the suspension of our knowledge about the character depends securely on her remaining speechless when we might hope for speech.

It would be straightforward enough, and perhaps interesting—yet it is not interesting to me here—to go through Hitchcock's oeuvre and tease out telling moments of silence like the two I have just mentioned. It need hardly be said (!) that they are all over the place, these hushes, from the cryptic failure of utterance in the protagonist of *The Lodger* (1927) onward. Silence here, silence there, silence, silence everywhere. But narrative silence is not exactly the "thing" I hope to point to in framing this book around the idea of a silence from Hitchcock. There is a greater, far more troubling and ultimately far more uplifting silence in his films, particularly, perhaps, in the six films to be found here. This is a silence involving a certain compact of belief and corresponding engagement, that the filmmaker and his eager viewer share; an experience; a breath.

A compact between the filmmaker and the viewer? The Italian producer Goffredo Lombardo (1920–2006) gave an interview to discuss the making of Luchino Visconti's *Il Gattopardo* (1963). The cast and crew, he said, and the audience, firmly believed in the conditions of the story—that is to say, they shared a belief about what was to be realized, and what was realized, on the screen. It is this kind of utterly silent conviction that not only attracts the viewer toward a Hitchcock film but binds her frame of attention and the passion of her interest as the film progresses. When one speaks of Hitchcock knowing his audience, one refers to his knowing his own belief, which they share. One is not only standing outside to witness a situation in which dramatic activity unfolds; one is embedded within the situation, one is *there*. And because one is there, one is among friends—the filmmaking team, also there—friends with whom a great deal need not be said. No matter how much is said, then, a great deal remains unsaid. Far more than restrictions in dialogue, this creative silence bears upon the filmmaker's ability to show a fictional world infinitely more detailed, more complex, and more moving than can be referenced—that actually is referenced—in language. What Hitchcockian characters say is only part of a grander construction, just in the way that the story contained in the film, the "plot," is only part of the grander construction that is the film. Do not, with Hitchcock, fall into the trap of focusing on, worrying about, querying, or trying to unravel the plot. Look at the film. The film, not as a package securing the plot for shipping but an aesthetic entity with a coherence, a touch, and a pulse.

In *Notorious* (1946), on the many occasions when Devlin (Cary Grant) holds his tongue in conversation with Alicia (Ingrid Bergman), holds his tongue because the present moment is too ambiguous for words, note how we can virtually hear the tongue being held; that Grant manages to give off two signals at once, first that this is a moment not to answer a question—part of the unfolding plot; and second that he does not know this better than we do. We are in on the scene; the devious complexity into which Alicia tumbles, and which will almost destroy her, is one we have watched in construction, watched put in place. When Devlin begins to worry about her, seriously to worry, we already know why he should do, and have been wondering what on earth took him so long... and that is another thing he keeps mum about.

The silence of the audience's agreeable companionship with Hitchcock is our willingness to go along and make the best of even the sloppiest situations. Our tendency to wish, and to hope that he will sense our wishing and gratify it, a tendency of which he is aware and which he can jiggle. The silence of language that cannot fully speak its conditions, or that can only circumlocute, or that answers questions with words that are themselves also questions.

Hitchcock very often fashions a space in which objects and object relations "speak" not by sounding but by their own particular presence. Many routes: through the design of a locale—a room, a corridor, a building, a street—its general shape, its relation to the magnitude and extent of the movement and behavior to occur in it, its historical period, its completeness or incompleteness; or the way specialized objects sit or move within a space to give it both character and moment—a painting on a wall, a cushion, a coffee cup; or the way the camera shows the area it gazes at, with multiple planes of focus or only a few or only one, and away from or close to the grounding, and stretching or elongating space; and with the color films—Hitchcock was a supreme colorist—not only the way color is used to accent and balance the frame but the way different colors work with or against one another while something done by an actor's body is seen at the same time. Music cues can certainly fill behind these kinds of silence, but need not necessarily do so: Manny Balestrero (Henry Fonda) trapped overnight in his jail cell in *The Wrong Man* (1956).

If places speak in Hitchcock's films so do bodies, although, to be sure, the fashion has spread for talking about characters in Hitchcock films as though by and large they do not have bodies, only narratological or celebrity fame. When one casts for a film one must collaborate with the cinematographer to some degree beforehand or afterward, but in any case the framing and the lens in play will work according to the size and shape of the body being filmed. Michael Redgrave is rather tall, May Whitty is rather short. Cary Grant is somewhat tall, Claude Rains is considerably not so. Jerry Mathers is tiny compared with all the other characters around him in *Harry*. A body can have more than height. It can have girth, it can have a certain palpable tenderness or toughness. It has shape, color, presence; and it carries clothing in one way or another. This last is one of the reasons why the actor in a film is wearing clothing designed for the job, not just lifted off the rack according to personal taste. What, we can ask, does a character speak about him- or herself by dressing one way or another, or by dressing (or failing to dress) for a circumstance? The secret "speech" of social class is everywhere evident in Hitchcock to those who know its "tongue."

But in Hitchcock's films there are also what might be called Great Questions, the objects after which questing philosophers seek, very much notwithstanding the storylines that so many watchers take as The Treasure. There are no available answers to great questions, and yet great questions perturb and annoy and motivate and inspire us. The problem of death, for one: what it is in human relations and what it is in nature and whether these two are one. The problem of loyalty: what is the proper focus of faith, the nation-state, the political structure, or the human soul? How is it that we can be certain? Can we trust our perceptions, and can we trust our ideas, and in the end, what is it, if anything at all, that *can be* trusted? Or the problem of systems: that the social aggregation of the many requires some address far out of proportion with the individual, so that, in one interesting case, the system of order and justice can exist quite outside human experience, outside innocence, outside even witness testimony. This means no less than a questioning of the very perceptual act viewers commit in watching a film, since if perceptual lapses and flaws are possible, if one can swear to having seen something (even swear on a bible) and be wrong, how fraught, indeed, is the experience of seeing and digesting a film? And the issue of power: that machine power and social power can be related but are not the same, that the power of a machine will be opened by, yet limited to, its design, but the power of high-placed individuals can be executed through secrecy or public diplomacy, two very different possibilities, and power can play equally well in false dramatization or in life-and-death reality. Hitchcock uses his story material to work through issues of this kind. How did Harry die, where is Miss Froy, will Alicia succumb, will Manny go to prison, why is Richard Blaney so lost in London, who is "Topaz" really?

A comment about writing in general, about writing on Hitchcock, and about this writing. A dear friend of mine was told by the master, "Film is all music." I have been inspired by Hitchcock's études to write études of my own, perhaps vaguely in the manner of Claude Debussy or in the manner of Frédéric Chopin, both of whose strict grammar matches Hitchcock's accurately, or riffingly as in Bill Evans. Musical études are shorter than most filmic ones, surely shorter than the explorations in this book and shorter than the Hitchcock film, which is structurally symphonic. Always preparation for the statement, always careful treatment of the cadence. I have found that the more one watches Hitchcock's films, losing one's sense of everyday rationality or at least putting it aside, finally "drowning our book" of quotidian rational considerations, the more evident it becomes that, as he was far from conventional in setting his works on the screen one must be far from conventional in finding words to address them. For the Hitchcockian scene, nothing but a poetic approach will do finally, because there is so very much to apprehend, to feel, to wonder about, and to try to say, *all at once*. As a trifling exercise, I thought of a sentence describing Cary Grant and Eva Marie Saint's characters in the dining car of *North by Northwest*—not an inappropriate focus, perhaps, because this Quartet began with that film. But having written it, I began to play with *other* ways of wording that one sentence, and then other sentences that would do the job differently but just as well, each of them framing the reader's attention on a different aspect of the scene while opening the gates for a discussion of all of it. Easily more than three dozen possibilities emerged, almost on the instant, so that in suffering through the challenge of writing about the scene it became mandatory to imagine how all the sentences could be articulated simultaneously. An impossibility, of course, but the challenge begins to get at the complexity of what's onscreen with Hitchcock and the poverty of plain language to even half-fully come to terms with it. "A man meets a woman in the dining car of a train." "In the dining car of a train a man meets a woman who, unknown to him, has been waiting for his arrival"...

This book, which attempts to offer the reader opportunities for "hearing" the speech of dramatized silences in Hitchcock, for assessing different kinds of silence and different kinds of speech, does not propose itself as an exhaustive study, either of the problems it nods to or of Hitchcock's work. Many other authors have written brilliantly of this filmmaker, and the reader who finds interest here will be happy to explore them; and is surely encouraged to explore the films. From Richard Allen to Charles Barr to Lesley Brill to Tom Cohen to Bill Krohn to James Naremore to William Rothman to Slavoj Žižek and many, many more, the probes go on. But the chapters here would claim to be idiosyncratic in one special way: that they seek beneath the obvious surface of the films—that much canonized surface—for the truly profound. In Hitchcock, the latent becomes manifest.

Watch the six films discussed in these pages, if you will, one by one before reading the appropriate chapter; or else afterward at leisure; but watch in relaxation from the dictate to follow along, and in surrender to the image. A case in point. In *Rear Window*, a film more or less universally addressed as posing for its central protagonist a number of "miniature" films in the windows of the various apartments over which he watches, it is true that we find a debilitated soul seeking a "story," call it coherence, in his world. But what is far less often talked about is another issue, similarly blaringly present yet somehow out of view, and that is the fact that in every apartment Jeff looks at he sees action without a beginning and without an end, as it were only the middle of a scene or a story. And, too, that every time he picks one window to look at he must perforce not see what is apparent somewhere else. Hitchcock gives the audience a very direct hint of this with the Miss Lonelyhearts episode, yet it applies across the board. To see what is before one in *Rear Window*, then, one must try to grasp what is not given to be seen.

A Silence from Hitchcock is the fourth, and culminating, volume in a series, the Hitchcock Quartet. *An Eye for Hitchcock* (2004) discussed *North by Northwest*, *Spellbound* (1945), *Torn Curtain* (1966), *Marnie* (1964), *I Confess* (1953), and *Vertigo* (1958). *A Dream of Hitchcock* (2019) included *Strangers on a Train* (1951), *Rear Window* (1954), *Saboteur* (1942), *Rebecca* (1940), *To Catch a Thief* (1955), and *Family Plot* (1976). In *A Voyage with Hitchcock* (2021) one could find *Psycho* (1960), *The 39 Steps* (1935), *The Birds* (1963), *Dial M for Murder* (1954), *Rich and Strange* (1932), and *Suspicion* (1941). With the six films in this book, *Notorious*, *The Lady Vanishes*, *Frenzy*, *The Wrong Man*, *The Trouble with Harry*, and *Topaz*, one fails wondrously to fill one's basket, since so many fruitful Hitchcockian orchards go without a visit.[2] This is sad in one way, since there is a great deal more that bears consideration, but it is proper in another: since this writing comes out of a person whose eyes gaze upon many things, that is, from life, it finally proposes a living—a fully living—response to the films of the master. The essence of the thing: one never quite has it; one never stops reaching.

CHAPTER ONE

A *NOTORIOUS* WAY TO LIVE

> When the dead weep, it means that
> they do not want to die.
> —Carlo Collodi

Not very far into *Notorious* (1946), Alicia Huberman (Ingrid Bergman), daughter of a disgraced (and now suicided) American traitor who worked for the Nazis, is horseback riding in Rio de Janeiro with Devlin (Cary Grant), a CIA operative who has beckoned her help in an undercover operation there. A long, pleasant corridor between rows of lush trees, the lure of dappled sunshine. A man has passed by on his horse, looking peculiarly at Alicia but continuing his pace. When this fellow has reached a distance Devlin, eyes on the prize, subtly prods Alicia's horse so that it races away with her, leaving the man to nobly catch it. Savior. Hero. A bond of sympathy, on the instant.

The man is Alex Sebastian (Claude Rains), leader of the local Nazi cadre that Devlin is in South America to find and ferret out, the man he has asked Alicia to help him corner. This is an "accidental moment" designed to elicit the *europäisch* Sebastian's dignified courtesy, his extending

the hand. From Sebastian's point of view a sudden delight, as he knew the father (of course) and remembers the daughter (!). *Poor* Sebastian's point of view, as we will come to feel in one of Hitchcock's strange and marvelous twists since although this is a bad man to be sure, involved with other men substantially worse, we never stop liking his graciousness. When much later he gets "what's coming to him" we will think, How sad! while at the same time realizing that our heroes can be saved only if Sebastian is not. *Poor* Sebastian. Poor malevolent Sebastian. In Rains's elegant performance, poor somewhat diminutive Sebastian, a small man with grand pretenses and ambitions, invoker of the grand avatar so many Hitlerians continued to admire after his suicide whilst they planned to reincarnate Der Führer. Alex is ambitious in that *nostalgisch* kind of way, but to Alicia he is unfailingly sweet (even as, summatively, he collaborates to murder her).

To shine bright light is to open shadowy depths. Sebastian is not held up by Hitchcock as morally admirable; in his actions he is morally scurrilous. But the film offers him as both a man and an agent, both a warm heart who longs for this love from his youth and a heartless operative of a dastardly regime. Both a man and an agent: doppelgangers. In order that the agent who deserves an unhappy end should have that unhappy end, the charming man who shares his body must have an unhappy end, too.

Meanwhile, to Alicia it is hardly fully clear that in "bumping into" Sebastian she is being positioned by her puppeteer for something as stringent as marriage; nor even, as is essential with this kind of puppeteering, that she is a puppet and he her puppeteer. A great deal confounds the proposition. She is *done with* Sebastian, for one thing, whatever that relationship or pretense to relationship ever was way back in the glory days, and while it is possible for her to see him socially she is hardly thrown back into a romantic frame of mind. A cultivated woman like Alicia knows how to be pleasant, engaging, and interesting without committing herself. Further, she has been growing attached to Devlin, quickly and earnestly. If she could have her way, he and not Sebastian would be coupling with her. Hitchcock makes this plain in a way I will discuss (but knows, too, that since we have Grant and Bergman there is no great need to make it plain). Worse for Alicia, the counterintelligence scheme, moved forward by Devlin on the instructions of his rather cold-blooded superior Paul Prescott (Louis Calhern), places her ideally close to Sebastian and his Nazi cadre, as though after the debacle with her father, the public embarrassment, and her ensuing depression she could possibly still be eager to be reminded that Nazis exist. To signal this bitterness, Hitchcock arranges that we should meet Alicia in a kind of flight from the world her father created.

She trundles out of a courtroom (into which we have peeked just in time to hear the twenty-year sentence pronounced), hounded by reporters whose shrill voices act as projectiles aimed at her heart. We find her next at a party she is throwing for her "closest friends": pour enough down your throat, dance a little, shake the past away. Very drunk, she goes for a car ride with Devlin who—at this point inexplicably—was at the party, too. She drives them through the Florida night, giant palms shuddering in the velvet gloom on either side of the road, and picks up far too much speed. Things are getting dangerous (a cute Hitchcockian clue, very early on, that "things are going to get dangerous" in this story) when she is pulled aside by a no-nonsense highway patrolman on his motorcycle. As he stands by Alicia's side of the car and asks for identification, Devlin quietly reaches over her and hands him a little wallet something inside of which produces telltale astonishment. Oh, yes sir. All right, then. And a courteous salute before hopping on the cycle and zooming away. Alicia is sufficiently half-sober now to be alive to these circumstances. She wonders aloud who this man is, that the police should give deference and obedience. A lousy copper! Wrestling her for the wheel, he drives them safely back to her house. We next see Alicia profoundly hung over in bed and Devlin, magically appearing out of nowhere, positioned in the doorway to her bedroom. Simulating her consciousness as, fixating on a glass of orange juice that has been set down beside her face she struggles to twist herself awake, the image rotates (in a move that inspired Nicholas Ray)[1] so that Devlin walking toward her flips upside down in a powerful torsion before he is righted again. He must go to South America, says he (turn the world upside-down), to help track a swindler. Will she come? It would be helpful. She scorns him, has no time for coppers! Clearly, she also wants nothing more to do with the kind of sordidness her father bequeathed her. But Devlin has something for her to hear. This is a 33 1/3 rpm vinyl recording, made through surveillance, of a telephone call between Alicia and her father in which the man tries to importune her understanding and cooperation and she makes a noble speech deploring him and everything he does. When she hears herself making that speech, with Devlin standing at her bedside as witness, she feels the gravity of reality, and agrees.

On board an aircraft now, descending over Rio de Janeiro. They are a "team" of some kind, Devlin with the information and the skills to guide the mission, Alicia as his clandestine operative. By their postures in seats side by side, her slightly leaning over him to see out the window, the expressions on their faces, and their handsome good looks it is evident that these two are already on warm terms of friendship. Not only will Devlin be her guide in Rio, he will be exactly the guide she would most wish to have. She is enchanted, and perhaps he is, too.

But he is in hiding...

GAMES

...Hiding and showing being one of the notorious silent games of *Notorious*. First, consider mimicry, identified in the late 1950s by Roger Caillois as one of four elemental game forms:

> Mimicry is incessant invention. The rule of the game is unique: it consists in the actor's fascinating the spectator, while avoiding an error that might lead the spectator to break the spell. The spectator must lend himself to the illusion without first challenging the décor, mask, or artifice which for a given time he is asked to believe in as more real than reality itself. (23)

It is too easy to think of this form only in terms of the professional (official) stage or screen: actors in a drama working to convince the hyper-observant audience of a truth that is not, patently, there. More deeply, mimicry lies in the universality of performance, that every social setting has "wings" behind or outside of which perceivable elements of interaction are kept out of sight lest the fantasy dissolve.² When a drama tends toward realism, the characters are not only mimicries put on *for an audience* by actors striving to avoid glitches; the characters as fictive beings are miming *to one another* as we so often do in real life with other people. *Notorious* is replete with such carefully guarded presentations. Devlin, obviously, an agent hiding as a party guest and then as a friend on tour. Sebastian, a conniving butcher hiding as a socialite. Sebastian's aging mother (about whom more to follow), whose maternal etiquettes cover deathly malice and fear. The Sebastian cohort, loyal and manipulative Nazi collaborators pretending to be upright businessmen. And Alicia herself, by command: a grieving and confused young woman now pressed into service for her country, finally a spy pretending to be a loyal wife. As with mimicry in general there is no fleeting instant when by happenstantial carelessness the game might not be given away: here, once the show gets rolling we suspend breath while under mortal peril a little act is put on for carefully probing disguised villains sufficiently paranoid to regard almost anything as a conspiracy to unmask them. With Devlin and Alicia, the fakery of presentation is made immediately evident so that the film's suspense lies in our having to wait until some character puts together the puzzle we have already completed. Devlin and Alicia are the characters we are led to care most fervently about, and the characters whose clarity of perception is most seriously compromised.

Caillois is careful to note that mimicry "exhibits all the characteristics of play: liberty, convention, suspension of reality, and delimitation of space and time" (22). Masquers are playing consistently as regards their masks. Sanford Meisner holds up for students of acting the principle of "living truthfully under imaginary circumstances" (87).

As we are in a spinning delirium note another principal form detailed by Caillois, *ilinx*, games

> which are based on the pursuit of vertigo and which consist of an attempt to momentarily destroy the stability of perception and inflict a kind of *voluptuous panic* upon an *otherwise lucid mind*. In all

cases, it is a question of surrendering to a kind of spasm, seizure, or shock which destroys reality *with sovereign brusqueness*. (23; emphasis added)

Reexamine the camera-rotation shot in Alicia's Miami bedroom through the agency of *ilinx*. The *otherwise lucid mind* is Alicia's by attribution, emphasis on the adverb, and while Devlin remains stable we share her sense of the rotation. For us as for her, the stable perception of reality is wholly deranged *with sovereign brusqueness*. And for the instant during which the camera rotation patiently extends, there is a feeling of *voluptuous panic*. In this vertiginous experience Devlin is turned upside-down, morphed into the opposite of what he seemed, and all the world seems turned on its head. For making this image Grant's unexpressive poise was required: it is not Devlin doing this flip, it is Alicia's perception as, working to escape the past (and a hangover), she confronts her morning orange juice. Rotation of this kind would have been easier to produce through the optical printer than by spinning the camera on set. Through this little device, Alicia gets a wake-up cue to a stunning transposition of circumstance, one identification sharply converted to another, negative feelings turned positive, the whole social situation quickly pressed toward remolding. The rotation is no "entertaining" fillip of decoration inserted to make Devlin's early relationship to Alicia seem eerie; it is preparation for a different eeriness and strangeness he must sense, involving the identity she will choose to claim when the chips are down and the survival of freedom is at stake. She is attached to an eerie and strange past, but he is going to flip her regard for it. Here she is, in the privacy of her bedroom, in her own personal bubble, and Devlin is about to make it plain that outsiders have been listening to her conversations, have been committing them to hard vinyl so that her voice can be played back to her should the need arise.

However the many lines of action in this film resolve, and, having resolved, evaporate from our thought, the provocation of games and gaming, the uplifting, separation, and conjoining of one consciousness to another, will remain as a kind of silent phantom.

It is intriguing to watch the narrational weave in which character-beings are directed and controlled by one another in this film, the abject thingness of the spiritual body before it is brought to life and activated by the desire of another. Old Huberman is cast into prison by the fiat and decree of the judge we see in the opening scene, the nature of his crimes unrevealed; criminal destruction is one thing, the idea of punishment still another, but enacting punishment in daily life hangs upon a command from without and above. Or, on the airplane to Brazil we see Devlin conferring with a man at the rear and, as though on this man's instigation, coming back to his seat and letting Alicia in on the news that her father suicided in prison, this voiced information finding a passage into her deep being. But that man in the plane, Devlin's superior Prescott, is able to go considerably beyond merely influencing his employee; he gives instructions that are to be followed to the letter, and Devlin follows them scrupulously, until a redeeming moment of freedom at film's end when he acts of his own volition. We will come to see how Sebastian is controlled, directed, shaped, and navigated by his mother. And how even she is subject to the control and direction of a dominating member of the Nazi cadre, Mathis (Ivan Triesault). No doubt this puppeteer is being puppeted by a foreign source, on very long strings. We are entertained, as are Devlin and Alicia (at least superficially, because they are in mask) at a horse race, where the energy of splendid creatures is marshaled and funneled by the controlling jockeys who ride them—even the background of a scene speaks. In her riding sequence, Alicia is in control of her horse until Devlin takes over the control by jabbing the creature. In the Sebastian mansion, as Alicia uses Alex's keys (that he has dropped on a dressing table) to try all the doors of the place in search of whatever the Nazis have hidden, she is confounded by one door to which only the master has access: the wine cellar. Here, by agency of a special key—special to him because of its supreme power as a magical tool; but also special to Hitchcock, as we will see—Alex mobilizes the motoring force that keeps the house and its operation going. These puppetings are silent.

At issue in the extrinsic controlling is considerably more than the free will of the independent human. We are looking at a limited and expressly situated determinism, not something cosmic or eternal. Determined action and determined flow are set by a source figure we are to take as being in some special way "in the know" of what another hitherto passive figure will do, feel, think, and achieve. The film is thus a kind of dumb show, in which a great many splendid (and splendidly acted) displays of emotion and intent have been initiated from and propagated by sources outside the person who displays. *Unschuldige!* We certainly know that in all his films, Hitchcock invisibly performs as the mobilizing agent causing his characters to behave as we see them do. The controlling arrangements by which characters come to be here rather than there, doing this rather than that—all come from the invisible, thus silent directive force. In *Notorious,* Hitchcock makes the process of control from without explicitly tangible by means of this narrative filled with persons who observe, monitor, direct, and measure each other. The puppet show is given a kind of "proscenium," within the clear bounds of which it will seem nothing other than a puppet show.

PUPPETS / PUPPETEERS

Kenneth Gross writes,

> The hand of the manipulator travels from puppet to puppet, stuck inside one and now another form of cloth, or picking up and putting down the strings or rods of many different figures. It is the closest thing we have in the ordinary human world to the transmigration of the soul from one body to another, or from one creature to another.

And, too, "The puppet artist is likely to be himself or herself a wanderer" (7).[3] Note the anxious uncertainty etched on the wanderer Prescott's face as he "enters" his game players. Note, too, Devlin's struggles with being controlled. For him the film's finale gesture is a summative and very grand liberation, even as he liberates Alicia.

Alicia could at any moment give up her masquerade, leaving Devlin in serious trouble and Prescott out of luck. Devlin might suddenly give up his refusal to show Alicia how much he loves her, thus frustrating Prescott and Alicia in two different ways, with two different kinds of pain. Some embroidered cushion or velvet curtain in the Sebastian house might fall out of place, any tiny revealing thing, leaving Madame at the mercy of her German controllers: on the staircase at the finale watch her very carefully. And Alex might blunder into an error, not exactly a bumbler, just a wannabee juggler who hasn't learned yet how to keep more than one piece in the air at a time. His error will prove lethal—at the instant a car door is not made accessible to his groping hand. Perhaps Alex's error will be so gross, so boldly proportioned that no one would reasonably believe an intelligent man like him could have taken such action intentionally. As his mother whispers to him in her sunny bedroom, with desperate hope, "We are protected by the enormity of your stupidity."

Alicia is a special case. At the film's outset she has been stirring and stretching under the lashing corset of her father's strictures and commitments, and the first scene we attend, her party, is a kind of stripping of the corset. Under the aegis of a Nazi she has not had time or space to grow naturally, and even in her twenties has not yet formed a gyroscope of her own. Ingrid Bergman was just emerging from her twenties when shooting commenced. At the party we see her only flickering attention as one guest after another implores her assent or promise or agreement or at least understanding. Alicia's attention shifts across not only this room but also her sense of being. The Commodore (Sir Charles Mendl) asks her to come yachting with him in the morning and she does not have the self-command to say no, although she finds him far from appealing.[4] There is only one figure at her impromptu house party who neither beckons to her nor expects anything of her nor takes the liberty of proposing an action to her, and with him there is magnetism.

That solitary figure—shall we imagine him Alicia's guest?—is a well-built male with a dark suit and dark hair. We see him—we see him *only*—from behind as, crossing in front of him she wonders, "Haven't I seen you somewhere?": Ingrid Bergman recognizing Cary Grant sharing her shot, a Hitchcockian joke since the viewer knows instantly, through a magic only cinema can convey, that this "nobody" viewed from behind is Cary; we know the actor and know nothing about the character he is playing. Palpably Grant is both player and character at this point. He will let Alicia take him for a ride into the night. The guests she invited she doesn't want; him she wants and didn't invite.

Initially Devlin is careful about making an approach to her, but with the recording he calls up an unseen and shocking cadre. There are agents working for some unspecified government agency;[5] they have recorded her and stored the recording on orders from "someone" above. "They" are puppeting Devlin and now, if she will agree to come aboard his "yacht," they will puppet her, too, by way of his delicacies. He is never deceitful about that, although because he is so glamorous we might hope that he is beckoning Alicia to a private and wonderous tryst. As Alex Sebastian tries to make nice to her in Rio, phase by phase in a conventionally *gemütlich* High German style, very proper, very very very proper, first this and then that, it is under Devlin's charm that she falls, if perhaps only in a carefully modulated and fully conscious performance. *Perhaps*, a Giant Perhaps. "We are what we pretend to be," Kurt Vonnegut said, "so we must be careful about what we pretend to be" (v).

We are shown nothing to suggest Alicia is aware she is a puppet. She acts out of the allegiance Dev has fostered. Awareness will be possible for her only much later when she is far too ill to have clear perception of anything. None of the others under control are naïve about it, and every one of them bridles or puts up a posture to cover disaffection and discomfort. Alicia is a glorious empty vessel ready to be filled with redeeming purpose. The other characters in this film are Pinocchios in a curious way, Pinocchio being the *exemple par excellence* of the puppet conscious of being a puppet, and who through this consciousness exercises his yearning to be a human being. Alicia does not model him but is caught, horribly caught, between a kind of "life" and a kind of "death." As Collodi wrote, dreaming, perhaps, of some Alicia later to come,

> The Crow, moving forward first, felt Pinocchio's pulse, then he felt his nose and then his little toe. When he had felt them thoroughly, he solemnly pronounced these words, "In my belief the puppet is quite dead; but if by some mischance he is not dead, that would be a sure sign that he is still alive!"
>
> "I regret," said the Little Owl, "to have to contradict my illustrious friend and colleague, the Crow. In my view, on the contrary, the puppet is still alive; but if by some mischance he is not alive, that would be a sign that he is really dead."
>
> . . .
>
> "When a corpse weeps, it's a sign that he is beginning to recover," the Crow said solemnly.

"I regret to have to contradict my illustrious friend and colleague," remarked the Little Owl, "but in my opinion, when a corpse weeps, it's a sign that he is sorry to die." (51; 52)

But even as she lies abed on the edge of actual death our Alicia has no tears; that is, offers no sign of emergence. When to Devlin (who has intruded on the upstairs bedroom) she whispers the word "poison," her voice is so very unarticulated we can believe she does not believe it. The viewer's hope is that after Devlin drives Alicia away in the film's penultimate vision (Alex will have to be seen wandering back into the limbo of his home), she will begin to be whole:

"But how did you manage to grow so fast?"

"It's a secret."

"Teach me the secret; I wish I could grow a bit too. Have you noticed? I've always stayed knee-high to a cricket."

"But you can't grow," replied the Fairy.

"Why not?"

"Because puppets don't ever grow. They are born puppets, live as puppets and die puppets."

"Oh, I'm tired of being nothing but a puppet!" exclaimed Pinocchio, giving himself a slap. (90)

CONNUBIAL

Flying down to Rio heats and tickles Alicia's emotional response to Devlin. By the time they are consorting together—we have a splendid aerial view of Floriano Peixoto Square and swiftly the two of them at the Brasserie Antarctica—she is growing ever more to hope that he might love her, this American at work. For do not disattend that Devlin is on assignment. He has always been on assignment, as far as we learn. Sitting at Alicia's party he was on assignment. Coaxing her to Brazil he was on assignment. Shepherding her around Rio he is on assignment still. Not that there is any good reason why the two of them should not enjoy as pleasant a time as possible under the circumstances, sitting and smiling and lingering and breathing each other's air. Nevertheless, enjoyment is not paramount for him. It will be Alicia who has to pull the trigger, and we can sense her doing this at a scene in her apartment.

Beginning on a balcony that overlooks the sea and progressing all the way across the long living room, she locks herself with him in an uninterrupted clinch. This little scene is legendary and I will discuss it further below. Hitchcock told Truffaut he was inspired by something he saw from a train, a boy urinating at the side of the tracks with his girlfriend attached to his arm throughout. The kiss was surely not an entirely innocent gesture on Hitchcock's part. The Production Code (from 1933) having stipulated bluntly that "lustful and prolonged kissing" was expressly tabooed, Hitchcock was thumbing his nose at the Breen Office in directing the scene to show "prolonged" and "lustful" going hand in hand (or lip on lip). Though it was scripted as "at least two shots" (Krohn 84), Hitchcock made the inspired call on set to make for one extended take, in which he asked Grant and Bergman to begin on the balcony by simply talking about whatever they liked (97), a way of setting up an atmosphere of easy affection between them that reads powerfully onscreen. Alicia has let go her guard, and is fully given over to Dev, a young woman of the 1940s modestly enough offering herself. Offering, it is impossible to avoid noticing, in an expressly calculated use of her upper body, somehow more noticeable in aspect than his: Joe McElhaney reminds us that at 5′ 9″ Bergman was comparatively tall for a star female and therefore she was shot often in medium- and close shots:

> The bulk of Bergman's expressive power as an actress, then, is forced to occur from the waist up. In this regard, we may think of her as the purest of Hitchcock's actors in that the movements of her body, by the very limitations imposed upon it, must often be repressed or controlled, resulting in the face becoming the primary expressive tool. (73)

Devlin suavely keeps her involved, drawing out the moment at least as much to confirm her position vis-à-vis the Agency as for his pleasure. He is not crestfallen when a requirement to telephone his boss makes interruption:

DEVLIN: Do you mind if I have dinner with you tonight?

Alicia kisses him again. Devlin starts to move away toward the apartment.

ALICIA: Where are you going?

DEVLIN: If we aren't going out, I must call the hotel to see if there are any messages.

Alicia doesn't let go of his arm as they walk into the living room and to the phone.

INT. LIVING ROOM

Alicia and Devlin, very close, walk to the phone. Devlin takes the receiver from the cradle with one hand but, since his other arm is close around Alicia, has no free hand with which to dial. Alicia takes the receiver from him, holds it while he dials. They are gazing at each other all the time. Devlin takes the receiver back from Alicia, and they kiss again while waiting for an answer. They pull apart only enough for Alicia to murmur:

ALICIA: This is really a very strange love affair.

The romantic truth, or romantic anticipation, between Dev and Alicia is a crux of the film, the giant star faces glowing together on the screen and the giant character presences breathing fast for what is—what is possibly—to come.

Answering a later summons to Prescott's office Devlin learns something of Alicia's past... with Sebastian. That he and her father had been friends and in that *freundlich* way he met her the first time. Met, we are led to know, and fell for, since these two were real or would-be lovers, but in the end Sebastian was rejected. Setting up the encounter at the bridle path, probably on Prescott's instructions, Devlin did not know he was working to rekindle an old flame, to bring to life at least a friendship, a happy memory of an interrupted past.

We can reflect that the "past" is how and why Sebastian would pay more than momentary heed to this girl (without that "past" he is merely—as Devlin presumably thinks—a roué here); how the past could suddenly come alive for him again, subtle radiance of a Hitchcockian silent invocation: that Sebastian's calling up soothing memory of a glowing yesteryear—a time when Aryan superiority produced a culture of "such supreme beatitude" it "should reasonably be preserved" with violence against the incursion of destructive forces—makes his personal act of gallantry a "looking back" to a golden time.

Devlin thinks he has a plan, but what he has is Prescott's plan.

She is to infiltrate the Nazi cabal somehow and he is to assist, by setting her up properly to meet Sebastian, by preparing her in whatever arcane ways are demanded by circumstance, and by being her support on the outside, a person to whom she can convey what she learns in the household and who can keep her ship on course. When he sees—as we can have no doubt he does see, since Grant telegraphs Devlin's gazes very articulately—that her emotions are warming toward him, he is caught in a bind, Alicia being nothing if not friendly, nothing if not attractive, and his instructions about her being nothing if not serious if also, as we are learning, not terribly clear. Devlin's "bind" he did not make, Preston did, the silent, the invisible, the string-twitching Preston. After all, Preston knew how alluring Alicia Huberman was and that his agent Devlin would be attracted. And he knew his agent Devlin would attract her. And he also knew the intimate bonding with Sebastian would be required. We hear him say in a private meeting with his team that Devlin is unaware of the *actual* plan. As the long kiss-clinch is tenderly ended, two matched residues linger: a woman hungering to bond with a noble man; a noble man guarded about losing his purpose in bonding to a powerfully attractive woman. It is not the kiss as kiss that counts in this scene, it is the manner: that he is poised and she is released.

Devlin's feelings surface not long later when in Prescott's office it is announced that Alicia is about to enter the room:

PRESCOTT (wary): I don't like that. I don't like her coming here.

BEARDSLEY (one of Prescott's associates): She's had me worried for some time, a woman of that sort!

Devlin turns from the window for the first time.

DEVLIN (quietly): What sort is that, Mr. Beardsley?

BEARDSLEY: Oh, I don't think any of us have any illusions about her character, have we, Devlin?

DEVLIN (angry): Not at all—not the slightest. Miss Huberman is first, last and always not a lady. She may be risking her life, may end up with a knife in her back working for her country—but when it comes to being a lady—she doesn't hold a candle to your wife, sir—sitting in Washington playing bridge with three other ladies of great honor and virtue... No, let us make no mistakes about Miss Huberman!

PRESCOTT (quietly): Lay off, Dev.

This little moment could have come off without Devlin bringing in the word "wife." And given that his comeback is structured here as a balance to Beardsley's sniping, we can reason Devlin's reading: that Alicia may be thought to stand with him in the role of a wife; or a wife-to-be. *You have maligned my wife; I malign yours.* Turnabout as fair play; lunge and parry.

BEARDSLEY: I think those remarks about my wife are uncalled for.

DEVLIN: Withdrawn. Apologize, sir.

(Without the "I" of affirmation.)

Only after this tête-à-tête does Alicia make clear her purpose in visiting: to deliver some information, principally to Prescott but incidentally to Devlin: "Something rather confusing. Mr. Sebastian has asked me to marry him":

DEVLIN (to Alicia): May I ask what inspired Mr. Sebastian—to go this far?

ALICIA: He's in love with me.

DEVLIN (reflecting): I see. And he thinks you're in love with him.

ALICIA: Yes—that's what he thinks.

Grant unmistakably shows secreted chagrin—that she could read as snideness. He directs his words toward romantically aggressive Sebastian but also, we can feel, at romantically inspiring—and aspiring?—Alicia. At any rate she has chosen to accept a marriage—I think we can see Devlin thinking with some distaste—"of true minds," to which no impediment should be introduced (Shakespeare, Sonnet 116). Has she managed getting into the Sebastian camp with a little too much speed and efficacy? Dev's "I see" has two meanings, only one of which is typically interpreted by viewers: (1) that by this engagement and the thought that Alicia could have serious feelings for the other man in lieu of him Devlin's romantic hopes are dashed, thrown in his face, or at least depreciated: some narcissism on Devlin's part, and a sad prospect for his future in love (a disappointment for the viewer, too, who wishes to construct the Bergman-Grant bond). Or (2) that Devlin is astutely on the job, detecting not just Alicia's route in passing from the Nazi-detester to the eager mistress ready to marry in, but also the rapidity of her movement as a technical performance. Could Alicia be a clandestine Nazi collaborator? And if so, has he fallen for her masquerade as well as for her? That would match Devlin's current position with Alex's position later, confessing to his mother that his wife is an American spy. Alicia has given no explicit evidence of her political preference in Rio; Devlin has been presuming it, as have we. But Dev doesn't fail to notice things and surmise what they might mean.

Hitchcock emphasized to Truffaut how in this scene, although many figures are present or alluded to in their placement out of frame, he shot the action between single images of Alicia and single images of Dev, so that the "he" who has proposed is transposed visually into the "he" we see onscreen (see Truffaut 170–71; and Krohn 86–87). (A perfect illustration of why following Hitchcock's dialogue alone won't work.)

To ice the cake, Alicia's announcement comes in the face—literally, bluntly—of the vapid bureaucrat Beardsley who abused her behind her back, thus echoing Devlin's angry riposte (that she didn't hear) even as it shows Beardsley something of a fool.

She will marry Alex Sebastian, and they will go off to do what married couples do. Prescott and team can hardly be anything but "overjoyed" since she will be in an exclusive interior position, from which virtually no limit can be placed on the information she obtains—obtains, they are confident, for the United States of America. Whether in their "agent" guises Prescott and Devlin seem distinctively American is a matter for debate. Crucial to our understanding of the film: Devlin at the moment of Alicia's wedding is far from overjoyed, although he can see with depressing clarity how opportune this marriage is. He is concerned; and demoralized if she is showing disdain for his love, which until now has been a very silent one indeed; and it would worry him even more were she riding into a swift adoption by the Nazis of not only her own accord but also her own will. Seeing the many angles of perturbation that Devlin suffers, we can understand his being notably assiduous in his meetings with her, his continuously watching every detail she presents as lover and spy. Devlin the riddle; the discarded; the pro. Sebastian sweetly invites his mother to the ceremony but, in a gesture that gives away her suspicion and her churlishness at once, she declines.

TWO HOUSES IN RIO

It was in *Shadow of a Doubt* (1943) that Hitchcock highlighted the act of looking into other people's homes. "Do you know the world is a foul sty?" Uncle Charlie (Joseph Cotten) confronts his innocent niece Charlie (Teresa Wright). "Do you know if you ripped the fronts off houses, you'd find swine?" Here is the too-piquant thought of looking past the pleasing facades people put up for social integration, sniffing out their "realer" and more disgusting inside world. To a considerable degree, by the time of *Notorious* Hollywood's imagination of domestic interiors was mimicking its depiction of exteriors, grandiose palaces having palatial insides, lowly hovels having shabby and decrepit ones. But Hitchcock's insinuation is that the world we keep away from view is *incoherent* with the world we display. Once there is incoherence there can be revealing or startling incoherence, carefully designed.

The modernist Sebastian house sits on the outskirts of Rio, near a sheltered beach where laps the tempting sea. We will need to think always of this as a royal house, and remember the dictum elaborated by Mircea Eliade—

> Every temple or palace—and, by extension, every sacred city or royal residence—is a Sacred Mountain, thus becoming a Center.
>
> Being an *axis mundi*, the sacred city or temple is regarded as the meeting point of heaven, earth, and hell. (12; emphasis original)

—nor fail to notice one curious, sweet invitation that will be issued Alicia by Dr. Anderson (Reinhold Schünzel), who would have her visit his headquarters on another sacred mountain. The road leading to Sebastian's residence has a shallow curvature, pleasing to the eye but also contrasting with the Florida road Alicia and Devlin drove earlier; in Florida the road seemed endless, here it seems possessed by the house. While the structure itself, partly hiding behind a row of dark trees by night, is Italianate, its status as what Steven Jacobs calls a "villa" is perhaps compromised by notable length and relative lowness, its vague California modern style (as Jacobs informs us, a building in Beverly Hills was used).[6] Regardless of label, the house gives a feeling, as we visit, of sleek and puissant modernity, a design pared down for streamlined, even unconscious movement. Ornament qualifies the scene as authentically European; empty space and sleekness of line make for *lebensraum*. Money, even untold money, lies behind putting up and decorating such a place, a haven of business and bustle, progress and change, curtness and flashing light: a magnate's world by moonlight. The moonlight is reflecting off the waters of the beach.

Inside the Sebastian home, however, a second world waits. The two Sebastians, mother and son, are converted to the Sebastian trio, mother, son, and wife, hosting their august (apparently permanent) guests in decorous and sentimental luxury. While Hitchcock himself is always modernist in his filmmaking, here he has selected characters who live ornate lives, who fill their daily experience with one or another form of ornament—good wine, the decorous smile. Jacobs is brilliant in description, and here is his presentation of the interior of the Sebastian mansion, that "evokes the atmosphere of a castle of a fairy tale":

> Having passed the impressive doorway, the visitor ends up in a stately hall with a grandiose curving stairway, which would not be out of place in an opera house. The hall, as well as most rooms of the house, is richly furnished. Set decorator Darrell Silvera, head of the RKO prop department, could give free vent to his talents: crystal chandeliers, numerous paintings, antique furniture, ornate mantlepieces, doors with classical moldings, clocks, and vases adorn the interiors of the mansion. (226)

Adorn, but without cramping, as though the objects have all the world to inhabit. If the house interior suggests a fairytale castle, perhaps the reigning personality is that of a wicked queen. That curving stair, never present in Hitchcock without springing to function, may be from an opera house but no one is singing. The "numerous paintings" will be found in gilded frames, made not so much to set them off from the walls as to blend with them. Moldings and skirtings are in general a direct index of social class.[7] The very idea of using a vase in and for itself to fill and decorate a space indicates a classical attitude, borrowed from the universe of Weenix and Ruysch, whose vases hold flowers less enthusiastically than they hold themselves. The space is all gracile distractions for the eye: capacious runways for posing and repositioning, arching standards of dignity, lush surfaces, coffee cups in the thinnest porcelain. We may think that the Sebastian domestic world is a celebration of what was for Kracauer that great threat to truth, "the naïve affirmation of cultural values that have become unreal" (326).

No character *speaks of* the inner and outer prospects of the Sebastian home. "Oh, what lovely furnishings!" "Oh my, what a grand façade!" Yet without explicitly pointing to it, Hitchcock contrives a dramatic world in which a particular dualism never stops evidencing itself. This is the two-faced pairing of orientations: one that looks back to a glorious, culturally resplendent past and one that looks forward to escaping the torments of a poverty-afflicted present; pre-1933 and post-1933 Germany. As these expatriates believe, Germany now is poorer for the loss of its Führer: halted on its path, denuded and bankrupted by invading victors. Postwar German pretense, configured in *Notorious*, through the gestures and actions of Sebastian and his crowd, reflects the impotence that Wolfgang Schivelbusch finds in Germany after its defeat in World War I. Our figures seem to be

> heirs to and prisoners of a heroic past that they sought to emulate with gestures and rhetoric. [They] used modern technology to develop a highly romanticized style of public presentation and ... lost any sense of realistic political proportion in the process.... The memories of centuries of national inferiority, supposedly relegated to the past ... now reappeared like an unwelcome guest on Germany's doorstep.... People reacted not with manly composure, as the heroic

vision would have it, but with everything from bewilderment to literal paralysis and nervous breakdown. (*Culture* 196–97)

Aside from Alicia, all those present in the Sebastian household must be at a loss to fathom how the Germany of Goethe and Schiller, of Scheler, of Wiene and Lang and Gropius and the Bauhaus, like the Austria of Musil and Klimt and Hofmann and Schiele, could have been transmogrified into the Nazi horror. Or how German Expressionism (studied up close by Hitchcock, "swept away by the controlling style and pictorial mood" [McGilligan 63]) could be so utterly degraded by the Hitlerian storm. The Sebastian home has to stand for this radical transformation somehow, since it will be haven to the Nazi cadre who are planning something totalitarian and apocalyptic as a memorial to a golden past.

Looking back to more beautiful times, Alex may show a besmirching of *ressentiment*. It crosses his face whenever he does not labor to produce his (movie star) smile. Max Scheler had written about *ressentiment* already in 1914:

> an incurable, persistent feeling of hating and despising which occurs in certain individuals and groups. It takes its root in equally incurable *impotencies* or weaknesses that those subjects constantly suffer from. These impotencies generate either individual or collective, but always negative, emotive attitudes. *They can permeate a whole culture, era, and an entire moral system.* The feeling of ressentiment leads to false moral judgments made on other people who are devoid of this feeling. Such judgments are not infrequently accompanied by rash, at times fanatical claims of truth generated by the impotency this feeling comes from. (5; emphasis mine)

In *ressentiment*, a central cause and feature is self-comparison with others (Hitchcock not only does not attempt to conceal but indeed plays upon—and with—Claude Rains's diminutive stature; in one scene he had a ramp built so that approaching Alicia in the bedroom Sebastian could ascend in height), even with heroic others, leading to jealousy and ambition (for many postwar Nazi clingers, who could not handle the shock of Hitler's suicide, he remained a hero). Prior to the thirteenth century, notes Scheler, comparison of the self with others at a remote distance was inconceivable: "Each group had its exclusive task in life, its objective unity of purpose. Thus every comparison took place within a strictly circumscribed frame of reference" (33), one that by the time of Weimar Germany's mid-phase, prior to 1929, had rotted. Mobility, capitally enhanced mercantilism, the omnipresence of the stranger collaborated to make comparison of the self a more free-floating and tendentious procedure. If now one could feel smaller than one's neighbor, brought close enough to be viewed for measurement, one could form a personality founded upon *ressentiment*. Under these conditions, an economic collapse could pave the way for a dictatorial lunatic to take power.

Peter Gay shows how early Weimar, 1918 to 1924,

> with its revolution, civil war, foreign occupation, political murder, and fantastic inflation, was a time of experimentation in the arts; Expressionism dominated politics as much as painting or the stage. Between 1924 and 1929, when Germany enjoyed fiscal stabilization, relaxation of political violence, renewed prestige abroad, and widespread prosperity, the arts moved into the phase of *Neue Sachlichkeit*—of objectivity, matter-of-factness, sobriety. And then, between 1929 and 1933, the years of disastrously rising unemployment, government by decree, decay of middle-class parties, and resumption of violence, culture became less the critic than the mirror of events; the newspaper and film industries ground out right-wing propaganda, the best among architects, novelists, or playwrights were subdued or silent, and the country was inundated by the rising tide of *Kitsch*, much of it politically inspired. (*Weimar* 120)

Madame Sebastian's rejection of Kitsch is a haughty rejection of the *Volk*, a harkening back to the cultural atmosphere of imperial times that her disoriented, somewhat confused son has tried hard to breathe. But look at the fool!: capable of falling for a girl of whom he knows almost nothing; certainly a girl from *below*, and surely not a girl truly acceptable.[8] Robert Musil comments in 1936, and not without nostalgia for an absolute, "In the Biedermeier period you still held open house; today we merely imitate the custom" (59). In some ways, through its furniture and décor the Sebastian home looks back to that period of open houses, certainly does not put forward cheap imitation, yet of course for the best *technische* reasons it is anything but an open house. And an overweening nostalgia for glorious living is of course a mainstay of the Nazi argument: that a penetrating infection has crept through the borders, has killed authenticity, has compromised, poisoned, diluted, and evacuated the labor of loyal *Landsleute*.

Hitchcock is making this film before World War II is over, not to forget, and in the immediate postwar period after Japan's surrender. He knows that all these undertones riddling the Sebastian world are entirely taken for granted by his audience (as ideally they would still be today, were history not so zestfully forgotten) and that he therefore has no need to overdramatize by accentuating them on the screen. The word "Nazi" does the trick, and with thoroughness. Bill Krohn reports that Hitchcock and screenwriter Ben Hecht together wanted to "say, precisely, that the Nazis were not old hat" (102).

But if, adventurous and nostalgic, decorous and malevolent, the Sebastian home is experienced by Alicia, vicariously it can be experienced by Devlin and friends. The interior decoration will reek of nostalgic fever. In every chamber is a tone of the lingering past, a yearning for the unrecoverable that might fuel its own kind of violence.

As part of the courting ritual Alicia has been invited to dinner. She steps from her limousine into the Sebastian home as an especially valued guest, a possible inheritor, and is introduced there, in the grand atrium beneath the swooping stairs, to the serene and generally taciturn mother, now giving a polished, perfectly cultivated smile. *Perfectly* cultivated: the curled lips of the monarch before the cameras. The old lady has climbed down like royalty, and also like a movie star. She does want to know, however—and that smile is a command to answer—why it is that Alicia didn't testify at her father's trial. A razor edge: the loyal daughter of a Nazi friend of this family would have made some declarative attempt to save Huberman from American justice. But Alicia is deft. Letting Madame know her father did not wish her to be involved allows her to hold up a child's respect for and responsibility to the parent, that is, to honor the past as transcendent. Introductions proceed, as the princess meets some of Alex's "close friends," including Anderson, who at first holds himself loftily away from the others, shifty-eyed gaunt-faced Eric Mathis, nervous Emil Hupka (Eberhard Krumschmidt), and two who bathe in grisly silence, Herr Knerr (Friedrich von Ledebur) and Herr Rossner (Peter von Zerneck). Each comes forward, bows, and gives a formal, as well as somewhat antiquated *küss die Hand* in a movement that is shown, notes Bill Krohn, in an "unbroken subjective shot" from Alicia's point of view, so as to add "yet another unsettling touch to the endangered heroine's first visit to the Sebastian house" (96). At table, a jarring moment. Hupka sees a bottle of wine on the sideboard—wine bottles are the holy relics in this house, and blackest secret—and acts with dramatic alarm: gaping eyes and horrible silence all round. Hupka's reaction, far too pointed, too off-key, is instantly perceived by the other men as seriously inappropriate in front of this guest. His abject apology to Mathis and the others comes too late for him. Alicia catches all this, as—Hitchcock ensures—do we; a social gaffe, to be sure, and one of many to follow.

When she recounts the event to Devlin and Prescott it becomes clear that gaining access to Sebastian's wine supply is of key importance. A business plan is concocted. If Alicia can persuade her husband to throw a gala soirée with plenty of high-ranking guests Dev can attend, and if they are lucky enough to purloin the key he can slip away to the wine cellar and hunt around. The soirée and the wine cellar will receive attention below, but the dramatic movement is powered by Alicia's difficulties with keys inside this house. Already we have seen her secretly trying Alex's closets, her wanting to find the "key to Sebastian," and seen, too, how the wine-cellar key is not kept with the others. Where is this special key except in his possession! And how to filch it in such a way that he isn't aware it's gone? For Alicia the *key* key is now an iconic *objet d'être*, and we must see not just her behavior in stealing it but the way she clutches it, gleamy in her alabaster hand.

When Dev is in the basement area, Sebastian is hardly so slow he would fail to catch it. The American makes a hasty and proper excuse, kissing ("pretending to kiss") Mrs. Sebastian, and darts away (leaving Alicia in his wake), but the German's suspicion sets him upon a hunt that will lead, not long later—and after Alicia has slipped the key back to his dressing table where it belongs—to Sebastian entering the cellar, fingering the wine bottles, and discovering the telltale evidence of intrusion. Now he knows that he has been goosed. But the mortal question for him is, who can share in this knowledge? For Hitchcock, then, the evil husband's discovery of his wife's perfidy is *not the crux of the story*. Sebastian must make confession *to mother*.

In that premarital dinner sequence, then, we sense the toxic atmosphere we will soon be breathing: old-style, even gracile mid-European (specifically German) etiquette, handsome formalities, gentle aestheticism, regal design, austere matriarchy, and the art of socializing mixed with a scathingly cunning violence, a bent for retribution, aching suspicion, and pervasive anxiety. The anxiety is an undertone of all the scenes with Alex—courting Alicia with a broad but unconfident smile; demanding to know about her relationship to Devlin—especially when he is with his demanding mother, with whom his staunch duty of respect is never exercised with ease. "Victorian bourgeois seem to have been more alert to symptoms of apprehensiveness than their fellows in other epochs," writes Gay again, discussing the world that would have produced Madame Sebastian, embedding its tissues deep in the fabric of her intelligence:

> All ages are ages of anxiety, but it seemed appropriate somehow for the Victorians to diagnose anxiety as a modern disease and to give it a technical name: neurasthenia. That was in 1880 [the old lady is at least in her sixties in the mid-1940s]. Several decades before that, popular usage had already converted a familiar epithet for high spirits and energy—nervousness—into an ailment, a timid, tremulous sense of agitation. (*Schnitzler* 129)[9]

The dramatic effect of the cloud of agitation is to alarm the viewer into a subterranean tremulousness, too, so that at each moment, not only here in Rio but through the film, present moments, glittering, smooth, and alluring—the kiss that will never end—make one wary of what is to come. "Understanding, in Hitchcock's films, means acknowledging the limits of understanding," writes William Rothman, "understanding that there is something all-important—something wonderful? Something frightful?—that we cannot understand" (265). For the wary viewer Sebastian's wariness is yet collegial, understandable, normal. This man is a monster, but he moves us to a sense of pleasing relationship. His personhood eclipses his politics—or at least our sympathies take him this way.

HEART OF AN ATOM

While Devlin fiddles with them and, in yet another gaffe, lets one slip out of his fingers and smash on the cement floor, we see that the mysterious and special wine bottles in Alex Sebastian's closely guarded sepulcher contain no liquid at all, but a dark gray powder instead. Dev works feverishly to sweep the mess under the shelving and shift the wine bottles above so as to camouflage the missing one. But what comes to light only much later is that this gray powder, coming from and being refined in a special part of Brazil where "Dr. Anderson" has been at work, is... uranium. Laying aside the requirement for dramatic simplicity—spieling the events, that is, notwithstanding that uranium has a half-life, is being kept in wine bottles and without protective cladding—we must consider what it could have meant, to Devlin and associates but much more broadly to the world at large, had these slick ragtag remnants of the Nazi Party, alive and plotting in South America, made uranium their possession. Uranium of all things, easily sloughed off as only a simple MacGuffin.

The US project to develop fissionable atomic materials (notably uranium) and to embed an explosive device with atomic power, later on named the Manhattan Project, had begun in 1939, but by the middle of 1945 it was on the cusp of success. The United States performed the Trinity Test of their bomb on 16 July. Roughly three weeks later such devices were exploded at Hiroshima and then Nagasaki, producing untold death and destruction, images of which and rumors about which were so inconceivable they riddled the human imagination for decades without decay. On 15 October, Hitchcock commenced filming *Notorious*, but as public access to information about the bomb construction was still blocked—the Manhattan Project was highly classified—he had no special access to information. He had "invented" something much as did American scientists (Robert Oppenheimer et al.), but rather than awarding explosive possibility to the Americans he gave it to the Nazis.[10] If, reborn, the Nazis had made, prepared, and exploded an atomic device, how would the world have changed! When we watch *Notorious* seventy-five years later, thinking ourselves securely distant, the presence of fictive "uranium" in the wine bottles seems only a dramatic ploy without the gravest political, historical, ecological, and social import.

In light of that dramatic and historical weight, Hecht, a man beset by sensitivities about Nazi antisemitism, wrote for Alex a seductive little speech that did not make the final cut. As Krohn reports it, here is the speech Hitchcock wanted, to show that the Nazis were "not old hat," a yearning on his part especially intriguing given David O. Selznick's prediction that the critics would find Nazism "outmoded and tiresome" (mere months after the end of the war!):

> SEBASTIAN: The Nazi dream will never be removed from the world. It will only go underground—for a while. Do you remember the fairytales of the underground kingdoms? We are such a kingdom now—and I am such a king. (102)

Patrick McGilligan's opinion was that the Hiroshima and Nagasaki bombs laid to rest any lingering doubts about Hitchcock's uranium trope, but also that

> after Japan surrendered on August 14, ending the war, the script seemed all the more propitious, as it anticipated the fears—suddenly pervasive in the press—that diehard fascists would hide out and conspire after the peace. (375)

The balance of the story rides a precarious perch, between the personal and politically trivial on one side (Alex's delight to meet Alicia after all these years, now that she has grown!) and the quintessentially perilous on the other (John Huberman's loyalties and actions before the film began; his daughter's infiltration of the Nazi cadre). Hitchcock allows this quality of precariousness, this nervous frenzy, to permeate the film at all levels and far below the Nazi plotting story, so that in every respect as we become absorbed with observing the characters, we find them teeter on the edge of chaos. The brutal mechanism of the Sebastian inner world hidden behind a glittering façade; the nefarious German intent hidden beneath the gloss of dignified politeness, *würdige Höflichkeit*; Devlin and Alicia's caching their desires behind flirtatious banter and equivocally silent smiles. To point to a culmination: Alicia has walked into Prescott's office and announced that Alex wishes to marry her, *and soon*. She seeks from Devlin's face some indication of disapproval, anything to show definitively that he loves (and wants) her. But professional that he is (Cary Grant is always used by Hitchcock to show off some exceptionally well-honed deftness of manner) Dev holds his peace, locks away whatever feeling has grown for her. Perhaps she is taunting him, after all, earnestly in love with Alex and not, as he ordered, pretending.

Here is Alicia forced by circumstance into uncertainty about Dev's true motive—Hitchcock is a master of such bedeviling circumstances. And Dev is forced under Prescott's gaze to show only a wavering hesitation about Alicia's astonishing progress with Alex (far beyond expectation). In her apartment when she could barely separate her lips and face from his, was she only toying? Is she actually as morally lax as Beardsley thinks, and was he himself picked up purely and merely for entertainment, a playboy of the moment? Devlin has never once gazed Alicia's way without untold seriousness and sincerity of purpose but he has also given no express commitment. In that kiss, for example, his poise is casual and comfortable—*comfortable* as in "experienced," not "at home."

That kiss—part embrace, part cuddle, part *frisson*, and always an endless sense of gliding into an undefined future. Diffuse, evenly spread, low-contrast interior mid-day light from a bright balcony above the long stretch of Copacabana beach and its lapping waves under a sunny sky: harmony, unity, amity. Two heads intimately together: a formidable figure-ground relation. If the body moves suggest contact and even *frottage*, the conversation is about as mundane as can be: She would love to cook—but she hates cooking, doesn't she?—yes, she hates cooking but she would love to cook, but she hates doing dishes, maybe they'll eat with their fingers (in an earlier scene at the brasserie she has demanded the government provide her with a maid to do the cooking). May I stay for dinner?, but I must call to see if there are messages for me. All of it like a couple's trying out a *pied-à-terre*. Touch, fondling—surely; but can we eat? If she is faking all this, Devlin has to think, she is not only a very good faker but also, since he can feel the touch of her apparent desire, a somewhat insatiable young woman whose drive for him is fully performed, if it is not just full. If she is faking, her true personality is that of a ravenous sybarite. He has caught a fish he wasn't fishing for. And if her hunger is boundless—her sexual hunger explicitly—Alicia may have caught Alex (hoodwinked into believing Devlin is not her lover).

For her part, Alicia may well think that although she has to go off and play in the Sebastian mansion, she will reserve for Dev and Dev alone her honest love, because in that kiss she yielded to him (the man who wrestled her for a steering wheel and knocked her out when she wouldn't relent; that lousy copper). Because he is feeling now, not merely observing—every professional is at heart a human being—Dev needs true reassurance about her. And because she has given herself over to feeling instead of mocking and teasing, Alicia needs to be sure of him, a man who is cryptic. Of course he taught himself to be cryptic, it helped with his work: even smiling her way with what we read as sincerity he may be covering. The Miami bedroom: I've been bugging your bungalow *for three weeks now*. Playing a systematic and complex masquerade.

Out of honor, Alex has accepted Alicia's assurance that Devlin is not to be taken seriously as a suitor—he is a "pest"—and doesn't doubt her affection for himself; the honorable Gentleman—*der ehrenwerte Herr*—does not require a lavish show of desire, only an honest promise. But we must see that until Alicia happens upon him on that riding path Alex Sebastian has been leading a perfectly well contained, carefully designed life, in which all his contacts are vetted, in which he lives with a loyal mother (!) and in the company of associates who share his political alignment and his trust. He is not seeking love. His importing an outsider into this exclusive company, even attributing the move to connubial desire (and who would deny Alex this?) is hardly typical. He is overjoyed to have Alicia as wife in this house, yet if he is not keeping a beady eye on her himself, he cannot fail to notice the beady eyes being trained by the others. The more Alicia becomes his, the more he can discern a kind of surveillance circling him but not, of course, directed his way. This is an extraordinarily artful way for Hitchcock, with Hecht's aid, to make an open show of the strange awkwardness that accompanies a typical new marriage where partners' individual lives, in all their complexity, are now stretched to incorporate each other's. In this case, of course, Alicia has basically no one of substance in the world—beyond her "pest."

Perhaps, Devlin thinks to himself (loudly), she could have declined Alex's kind proposal, employing one of her patented gracious and ambiguous smiles and out of some lingering memory of That Kiss, if not out of a love still pulsing. Perhaps she could do the job I have asked her to do without quite so much enthusiasm, without having Dionysus rob her of rationality. Or more bluntly: without having that damned Alex within her spirit, instead of his peaceable self. The politics of love; the love of politics. And for Alicia: must not the acousmatic speaker be whispering, from behind the curtain of her consciousness, "Why does he not say just two words?"[11]

To save our Dev from damnation—he *is* too damned silent!—it should be emphasized that he is not a bus driver or medical practitioner or art gallery owner on holiday here, afraid to let go his business in the face of the power of love. He is an operative of the intelligence arm of the United States Government, on a mission to catch and if possible destroy enemy agents who fully intend to bring havoc on the world. In close focus the enemy is just little Sebastian, charming little Sebastian, poor Alex with his pompous martinet mother. But through him we can spy a vast spreading cadre of cold-hearted myrmidons, plotting in their wine cellars.

So close, those two faces, those mouths, giants filling the academy-ratio screen (1.33: 1)—a really marvelous experience for the viewer who had the privilege of seeing a proper projection—real movie stars as spies; spies as movie stars—that during the kiss we would need to lip read. One particular interchange (which I pick up from where I left it, above):

ALICIA (reflecting): This is a very strange love affair.

DEVLIN (curious): Why?

ALICIA (as he holds the phone): Maybe the fact that you don't love me.

DEVLIN: When I don't love you I'll let you know.

ALICIA: You haven't said anything...

DEVLIN: Actions speak louder than words.

"People," write Ekman and Friesen, "are held more accountable for their words than for their facial expression. There is more comment on what you say than on what you show on your face" (135). In the everyday, no doubt. But in cinema, what you show on your face is the final frontier. But Alicia is in "the everyday."

Let us note some of the Hechtian verbal ambiguities in the ambiguous face-à-face:

[A] a *strange* love affair: the word emerges from the same root, *extraneus > estrange*, as extraneous, and dates from the early thirteenth century. Does she mean to suggest she finds their affair bizarre, or that she finds it inexplicable, or that it is tangential (extraneous) to the hard business at hand in Rio?

[B] *Maybe* the fact that you don't love me: is she proclaiming a bald fact, that (from her point of view) he actually *does not* love her, and using the word "maybe" as a conversational softener? "You do not love me and possibly that is the reason this 'love affair' is strange." Or by *you* is she referring to Devlin the spy, Devlin the master of this spy business, and intimating that she can see how *you the spy* couldn't be in love, haven't emerged from behind your mask? Or, more simply, is she petulant? "I want you to love me, I want you to love me, and I put up this straw-man statement only to beg your contradiction of it." Tell me, tell me, tell me you love me.

[C] *When* I don't love you I'll let you know: *when*, as in *if ever?*; or *when* as in, *at that future point we both know will come*; or *when* as to invoke the subjunctive world of conceivability but not actuality? And, from her point of view, *how* is he going to let her know, since he hasn't, at least by her claim, let her know anything yet? Therefore

[D] You haven't *said* anything, meaning *anything yet*, or *anything right here now as we are smooching*. This last is a tiny Hitchcockian joke, cinematographer Ted Tetzlaff framing these two so tightly we can actually discern the sound of lips touching. He hasn't *said anything*—anything pertinent to love or to anything else—because her mouth has been upon his mouth, or she has been inviting his mouth to inhabit hers. Not that two people should choose to have a conversation while lipping, but here are two people choosing to discuss whether they love each other at such a time, every yummy instant ironic. (Imagine, too, O ye of mini-screens, what in a 1946 projection thirty feet high and forty feet long, in close up, those mouths and lips would have been!)

When the lips part, so they can talk about how they're going to finger dinner, her complaint that he hasn't said anything is residue.

To be so close to these souls burning with concern or frustration is to approach the heart of the atom; which is like approaching the inside of that wine bottle; which is like approaching the deep interior of the Nazi plan and, of course, the cavern of *Notorious*. Other atomic nuclei are penetrated in the film, too. We will see Sebastian in Mama's bedroom, the birth bedroom, the bed of lies and of truth. We will see the cabal plotting Hupka's murder—in a silence within the atom of action. We see Prescott and his Brazilian cohorts muttering over the plan to penetrate Sebastian's home, a plan of which Devlin is still innocent; we are even further inside the strategy than he is. At her party, we saw the comparatively louche private life of the woman who nobly strode out of the Miami courtroom. Watching Devlin rotate into her bedroom we are given a nuclear view of her regard, not only a view from within Alicia but a view from within her deepest (most inebriated) consciousness. The film is a relentless tease, offering us cardiac glimpses but blocking belief while throwing up vivid, sparkling, extensive, even interior-decorated displays of the atomic surfaces that hide away a nucleus of truth.

In positing his Uncertainty Principle (1927) by which it is impossible to know both the position and the velocity of a particle at the same time, Werner Heisenberg reaches outside of physics and mathematics, writing, "Any use of the words 'position' and 'velocity' with...accuracy...is just as meaningless as the use of words whose sense is not defined" (15). Alicia and Devlin are Heisenbergian particles undefined to each another. As the film ends we are given only a reasonable hope each might pause to discover where the other one is. Their challenge—it hits each of them in a different way, and also both of them in the same way—is to act without Sartrean bad faith. When Hamlet announces, "I have that within which passeth show" (I.ii.85), who, after all, knowing Hamlet is being played upon a stage, is to believe him?

KAFFEEKLATSCH

The high priestess of the drama has taken confession from her chastened son, who admits in horror that he married an American spy. He creeps into her bedroom, *unschuldige!*, while she sleeps, puts himself onto her very handsome chair beside her lambent window. Now her eyes open. *Unschuldige, unschuldige!* She is sitting up, thinking on what he has said with her lofty cigarette, and we may be sure that her wordlessness notwithstanding, Madame Sebastian is devising a plan.

Alicia will have to go, and in such a way, such a silence, that she will not be perceived going. A woman's method. Poison.

We are present in the salon as the participants play out the rather conventional scene of dividing up the coffee cups, care being taken to be sure the new wife gets the right one. The chemistry begins. After some of the poison is in her, even if Alicia discovers the ruse there will be nothing much she can do to keep herself alive. In a much-celebrated vision we are given the family on their expensively upholstered chairs and sofa, with, in the extreme foreground, Alicia's Brobdingnagian coffee cup on a side table. To aid the cinematography, Hitchcock asked for the cup to be made in gigantic size for one of these shots, so that positioned at the front of the focal field it would be, more than even a looming sign, a looming presence. Alicia herself is made queenly in this company, seated in a fabulously elaborate Louis XV-style nineteenth-century wingbacked and gilded grand *fauteuil*. Over a period of time not so very lengthy, our young queen progressively weakens, suffers, and is finally laid abed on the cusp of death.

The silence of the Empress drowns out the silence of the victim. The Empress holds in all kenning, all speculation, all regret, all intentionality, all connivance, all of medical knowledge, all of choreography, all of what is to come. Hair up in an impudent bun. The long flowing gown (that trails all the way into Hell). The eyes detached from the face. One version of an origin tale, crisply sanitized:

> "I do not wish to set eyes on her again. And bring me the girl's heart in this box as proof that you have done as I have ordered."
>
> The huntsman then led Snow White deep into the forest. But as he was drawing his hunting knife to kill her, Snow White cried,

"Please spare my life! Let me run away into the forest and I will never come home again!" (Grimm 12)

In *Schneewittchen* (*Schneeweiszchen*, 1812), the Brothers Grimm cause the beautiful young girl's *mother*, not her stepmother, to condemn her and demand that her lungs and liver be brought home as food.

The political stakes of this drama-within-the-drama are not without importance characterologically. Madame has been posing in front of the German cabal as a caring mother, a wise matriarch and head of the household, a woman who has been keeping order in an excessively tidy, utterly *richtig* fashion, and, supremely, a model of silence. This is the *femme définitive* of mid-century European culture, minister to the needs of men, accomplished in all the arts of homekeeping and nurture, a never-failing, never-lapsing, never-weakened heroine, Resistor Queen to the onslaught of alien cultures and barbaric (uncivilized, *schmutzig*) hordes. Poison, we may remember, derives from culinary creation. Leopoldine Konstantin, born in 1886 in Austria and a film actor since 1910, exhibits a model's poise and grace of movement as she floats through space, as she ascends and descends the regal staircase, as she sits in absorbed witness. This palace by the sea is utterly and entirely her domain, yet she never pronounces herself its doyenne. Her commands are in whispers. These "associates" (in flight from postwar Germany, presumably) easily take advantage of her splendid hospitality and constitute for Madame the Nazi controlling force in Brazil. Maintaining her castle as a bastion against all things anti-Nazi is her sacred and fearsome trust. Within these walls a great, inestimably dark secret is kept. The grinning son, with his far too sincere bonhomie in the wrong places at the wrong times, is a continuing danger; yet he is blood. It is because of Madame Sebastian's importance, her hushed power in the house, and her awesome responsibility in preservation of the undertakings at hand, that her telltale coffee cup must loom gigantic before us.

But to reexamine that cup, with cognizance of its capacity to hold coffee:

The Josiah Wedgwood pottery was making glazed porcelain coffeeware from the late 1860s—coffee, friend of the tobacco we find with Madame abed as she smokes in her son's face. A smoker, then a coffee maker. Poisoned coffee: *kaffee mit Gift*. By dramatizing the bedroom scene so emphatically and then by magnifying the coffee cup soon later, Hitchcock links tobacco and coffee with both the Sebastians and the Nazi cadre more generally. A *kaffeeklatsch*, richly prepared in Madame Sebastian's care, will coldly illuminate Alicia and Sebastian's marriage, but also ignite Alicia and Devlin's love.

Wolfgang Schivelbusch comments that the

> female passion for coffee is to be seen as compensation for women's exclusion from another, more public domain. Thus the afternoon coffee party functions as a sort of anticoffeehouse, a surrogate for the original coffeehouse created for male society. And yet the attempt to set up *Kaffeekränzchen* as domestic, feminine counterparts to men's coffeehouses lent itself to ridicule precisely because they became mere caricatures of their prototype. In the same way the Kaffeeklatsch or "ladies' gossip circle" became the butt of men's jokes in the eighteenth and nineteenth centuries, being viewed as a parodic debasement of coffeehouse talk. (*Tastes* 69)

The giant cup is both a Hitchcockian emphasis in purely visual terms and a joke about Madame and her style. As to the Sebastians' alienation from England, France, and the civilized West that had been enemies of the Nazis in combat, coffee played another role:

> The German relationship to coffee was [from the start] an index of Germany's relationship to the advanced nations of the West. Coffee, in fact, would never have attained the eminent position it did in German middle-class life [Madame Sebastian is high-middle class] had it not already been a beverage that symbolized the power England and France had assumed in the world at that time [in the eighteenth century]. (Schivelbusch, *Tastes* 72)

Schivelbusch emphasizes that coffee, very like tobacco, was a rationalizing, sobering drug, something that compelled sharp (and sharply critical) thought, serene reflection, a businesslike attitude, the very opposite of alcohol.

Poisoning Alicia with coffee is an act of supreme devotion to rational calculation, to withdrawal from emotional involvement, and to sober employment of a productive machination. Alicia has infiltrated the family in order to gain intelligence, and it will be through an application of intelligence, not passion, that she is terminated. Notably, she meets Devlin in a commitment to alcohol—hard liquor and not beer, so that she can "get drunk with one-tenth the quantity of liquor, or in one-tenth the time it had formerly [in the era of beer drinking alone] taken" (Schivelbusch, *Tastes* 153). Dev matches her, glass for glass. And the two of them are either drunk on attraction or faking it and rationally conducting business—anyone's guess. As to the grand *Hausfrau*'s use of tobacco to stimulate her *kaffeeklatsch* plan, the dry reaction of the body to tobacco makes the nose "ultimately insensitive to smell" (146), this accounting for the old lady's palpable inability to "smell something foul" in her son's marriage, once she is convinced of his (unanticipated) happiness.

SEPARATIONS

Rational Alicia is a separate creature from intoxicated Alicia. We can consider *Notorious* a treatise on separation and its silences, even beyond the arch distance a person must strike from another to label them *notorious* in the first place. Alicia separated from her father with deep and genuine distaste: "I know what you stand for. You and your murdering swine. I've hated you ever since I found out.... Don't ever come near me or speak to me again about your rotten schemes." And, airborne, having been told he administered himself a toxic capsule this morning:

> ALICIA: I don't know why I should feel so bad. (*Devlin gives a smile of sympathetic intimacy.*) When he told me a few years ago what he was, everything went to pot. I didn't care what happened to me—

—a distancing not only from paternity but from herself, a sloughing off of a self that had been Huberman's little girl, with all the concomitant confusion and aloneness—

> ALICIA: —But now I remember how nice he once was. How nice we both were. Very nice. It's a very curious feeling—as if something had happened to me and not to him. You see, I don't have to hate him anymore. Or myself.

There is a queer silence in Bergman's hazy half-aware, half-voyaging stare as she looks out the plane window but does not see, or looks at the present and sees the past gone far away, long ago.

The primal separation between Alicia and Devlin—unsureness about trust, maladeptness about belief and commitment, skirting danger by twisting through desire. It may be that these two lovers are never further apart than when they are locked in a passionate embrace, extending that kiss.

Sebastian: so cloven from his mother that he dare not reveal his eager affection for Alicia until the deal has been signed and there is no dignified way out. Here is a mother who obviously pampered him in childhood, kept him inside, doted on his every whim, denied him social bonds with other people. He lives in an oversized, stuffy world, sealed in a cell. He never leaves the bubble of his mother's protection. And his belief in the Nazi cause is his separating withdrawal into fantasy.

Prescott the smooth operator faces a political abyss, because he can act only insofar as his Latin counterparts choose to agreeably cooperate. Proud American in a strange land. Between him and Devlin is another separation, icy cold and flat as memorandum paper: Alicia is a pawn on his chessboard, as Alex is a pawn on his mother's.

And then, in the terrifying conclusion, with Alicia on a deathbed and cut off from communication with the outside, the house interior seems to have swollen into a malignant edema of malice so that the bedroom shrinks in relation. The Sebastian home is her new universe, and it is fading. Devlin has heard nothing from her for far too long—he is her *superior;* she *reports to* him—and he has no luck trying to reach out. Is it professional caution or feeling the pang of separation, as never before, that leads him now to step forward?

The film renders separations palpable. Consider the magnitude of the Sebastian living spaces, the distance between one piece of elegant furniture and another, the way that bodies are kept distinctively apart in the physical dance of social relation there. Or at the race course the distance between panicky, observant Sebastian with his mother and, a long squint away, confabulating Devlin with Alicia. In the riding scene, Sebastian's galloping horse closing the separation between him and Alicia with no sound beyond the hoofbeats—closing a separation that has been with him for so long, trapped as he is. On the airplane, the cozy cuddle of Devlin and Alicia looking down on a Rio that floats in a separate universe outside, a great city of the world rendered (pictorial and) silent.

But Hitchcock goes beyond this to tease the viewer with a different kind of separation. Rio was not to be used for most of the principal photography, yet the characters would have to seem to be there. This is often achieved in composites that induce a cold but elusive sense of separation. Sometimes the key problem was setting a scene without bringing Grant, Bergman, Rains, or any principal actor to Brazil. Sometimes it was setting a foreground action "away" from a background that could now seem both linked to action and separate from it.

Some key special-effects separations:

- *Night drive in Florida*. A conventional establishing shot begins it, made by a second unit team in Los Angeles where the palm trees are key to establishing the place as Miami. The lambency suggests that curious and evocative moment before the sunrise, when the sky is diffusely bright with sleep—the spectacular, eerie effect of black-and-white film shot day-for-night (the camera is pointed anywhere but up into the sky; and the film is overexposed in development by four stops). The shots that follow, of Alicia and Devlin in the car looking forward with us seeing their faces, are all done on a car rig in the studio with a rear-projected highway background (on rear projection problems and techniques see Fielding; and Pomerance "Bells"). That the protagonists are in crisper focus than the background is entirely appropriate to Hitchcock's intent: the car is moving quickly so if from the dashboard we magically looked past the riders through the rear, the environment would not be in sharp focus; but more importantly, it is the faces of the two conversants we are guided to watch in detail, not the territory. These repeated rear-projection facial portraits are intercut with a few live-action shots taken from a moving car driving forward on a similar road.

  Some of the rear-projection footage has been carefully arranged to include an advancing cop on a motorcycle with his headbeam on. Alicia checks her rear-view mirror and we see the cop not far behind: this mirror image is a separate piece of film matted in during optical printing. As the car slows and the cop pulls alongside we have a studio profile shot with a different rear-projected ground. In the sequence as a whole, we have a slight sensation of being *with* Alicia and Devlin and thus cut away from the world around. That world intercedes along with the policeman, who is seen in tighter framing so that he takes over the screen (for a reprise of which, see *Psycho* [1960]).

o *Airplane*. As Devlin informs Alicia about her father we are looking at them in their seats on the aircraft from slightly in front and on the aisle side so that the view outside is angled. Between their heads we look through the separation between the seats to the passenger behind with a view of the landscape exterior; this sixty-degree angle shot requires for the Rio exterior some rear-projection film photographed while the camera vehicle (in this case a helicopter, likely) flies at a speed slightly lower than what is used to let us look directly laterally out Alicia's window and the window across the aisle. The introductory and concluding aerial tourist views of Rio de Janeiro are stock footage, as is the single shot of the aircraft above an unidentifiable urban zone: all this is used by permission. Very meticulous design of the aircraft interior and of the clothing enforces our sense of actually being on the plane with Devlin and Alicia, and the brevity of the shots out the window helps give the feeling that here in this filmic moment we are no more separated from actual Brazil, down there, than we would be if we were really coming in for a landing (in the company of two people who are more interesting to us than the world outside).

o *Brasserie*. The Brasserie Antarctica will appear in several scenes. The set-up long shot is from across the road, with a passing tram, in broad daylight, and would have been made by a traveling second-unit team. There are visual ties between this place and other Rio locations in the story but the brasserie is not used to remind us where we are geographically in the city. The close-up action here is filmed in two ways. As Dev and Alicia occupy an outside table, the shiny vitrine behind them, copiously filled with reflections of street action, is a second piece of film matted in, and the entire composite is made on a soundstage. When the conversation progresses and we move to facial portrait shots of Alicia, then Dev, we find each of them in front of rear-projection plates showing many more relaxed diners or drinkers and white-jacketed waiters moving around in perfect synchrony with the foreground action. This waiter movement is choreographed in advance for the rear-projection plates so that in the cross-cutting of the facial portraits the space around Alicia will seem to be circular and homogeneous. In the medium-close portrait shots of Dev we see another diner's back behind him—this is live on the soundstage. Both main characters seem ensconced in a world full of lateral action from which their static poses and quiet conversation suggest pleasant withdrawal. To be in Rio, but also not in Rio.

- *Hilltop.* We see a car drive up and park on a hilltop overlooking the city. The two figures are stand-ins, likely shot in or around Los Angeles, the foreground matted into a shot made earlier of the Rio panorama background. Cutting in, we are in a studio shot with Devlin embracing Alicia on a little knot of studio grass with a splendid rear-projected panorama backing them. The focus of a rear projection can be controlled minutely, and throwing his rear-projected backgrounds a little out of focus is sometimes a trick used by Hitchcock to pull his viewer away from being distracted by stupendous views. Most importantly, studio lighting and sound control make it much easier to shoot acceptable star portrait shots than could be the case on location (even if a location were not prohibitive for financial and insurance reasons).

- *Prescott Office.* A street scene in hot daylight of a large building—second-unit footage again—from which we jump to the office where Prescott is working with his associates. The office interior is a studio set, with the view through the window—seen through the slats of Venetian blinds—a rear-projected exterior with passing pedestrian traffic.

- *Beach approach.* Devlin and Alicia are driving to her apartment in Rio, and the car passes along the side of Copacabana Beach, with legion sunbathers and swimmers, bright sky, happy waves, a curling line of tall palms. This is a location shot by the second unit. As the car approaches and turns a corner near us we can think to see Devlin and Alicia inside it, but we don't. Then in a studio mock-up of her apartment building exterior we see them, in medium shot, exit the car and enter. The long beach shot fixes our attention on this tropical locale—there is nothing to attend to in the shot except its power of rendering a luxurious location. This will make the apartment the United States Government has secured for Alicia seem impressively plush.

- *Apartment.* There follow now two apartment scenes, the first in daylight and the second after the sun has set. Between them Devlin will take a meeting with Prescott. In Scene A, beginning on the balcony with a matted aerial view of the beach and city below, Devlin is seen from above, beginning to embrace Alicia. They shuffle inside to continue the cuddling for several more screen minutes. The point of going to the cost of arranging for the matte and its optical printing, for only the brief balcony portion, is to establish the optics of "romantic setting" and "wealth": there must be a quotidian world away from which these two are lifting themselves, emotionally and literally. Hitchcock uses a rear-projected background for a medium shot of the kiss taken straight on; here the background could have been made in LA.

    As Devlin drives to Prescott's we see the same building as earlier, shot in the same way, but we are now on a Los Angeles soundstage with this shot as a rear-projected ground against which Devlin's car pulls up in live action. He is abstracted, pulled away from a make-out session for this, and may have some fears about what is in the offing. If we compare the view of him entering this building now with the view of him entering the apartment building with Alicia, we can sense the emotional withdrawal here.

    The nocturnal reprise in the apartment is stiffer. Outside the balcony doors we see a night rear projection that includes a distant beacon. To bring some warmth to the emotional effect of the scene (a chill is on its way) there are glowing table lamps lit to contrast against the night sky. The tête-à-tête here will be of vital importance to the ongoing events—events neither Dev nor Alicia will be positioned to fully interpret: they stand more or less on the same level of awareness as we do. Rear projection is used to effect the exterior zone, but mostly we are in portrait or conversation shots, with the background dropping away.

- *Riding.* The horseback scene requires very deft image construction. A riding path in Arcadia, California (near Pasadena) works as setting. Shots taken from behind any of the protagonists here use doubles on horseback. Facial portraits of Alicia and Dev, showing the horses' heads and ears in part, are made with them astride real horses walking a treadmill in studio, with the background rear projected. These are, after all, star portrait shots for which exquisite control of lighting is needed. A scheme of Devlin's is in effect here, and he is more interested in the work coming up than the pretty glade in which they ride; so we concentrate our focus on Alicia and him. A shot of them passing Sebastian and his companion—that is, four bodies on four horses—is taken from slightly behind at an angle, thus with stand-ins. A brilliant profile composition now shows Grant clearly with Rains slightly less crisply focused behind him, and behind Rains the companion of the moment. Here the companion is in rear projection, Sebastian near Devlin but only "near" the companion (who must disappear from his attention). This scene has us flicking around mentally between the crisp "reality" of live action, most especially the horse flight and catch, and the vaguer psychological reality of Devlin and Alicia thrown into relation with Sebastian.

- *Restaurant.* An expensive restaurant is the setting for Alicia's first romantic encounter with Sebastian. Very large studio set, with glass walls and a rear area for mimed action of waiters and diners to fill in the "reality" of the moment. A great deal of choreography of the extras in the background—the work of the assistant director—supports the twosome in the foreground. We transpose to portrait closeups, where star lighting is used to create character allure and support the viewer's affiliation with known performers.

- *Dinner party.* A limousine delivering Alicia to Sebastian's house for dinner is seen at twilight pulling along a curved road and stopping at a mansion. The curling beach inlet, with moonlight and waves, is a second shot matted in behind the foreground.

- *Racecourse.* Sebastian and his mother carp at one another in a studio set. Devlin finds Alicia on a soundstage, backed by rear-projected crowd movement nearby. The crowd must be visible enough to make the meeting seem real and present, but there should not be enough clarity to distract the viewer for one instant from Devlin and Alicia conversing, to allow, for instance, that any one stranger shuffling behind might suddenly capture attention. Here as so often in the film, much trouble is taken to build and/or establish authentic grounding, but the attention of the viewer is abstracted away so as to swim in the emotional mist that encloses the principal duo.

- *Sebastian home.* After the racecourse sequence there is a quick meeting in Prescott's office where we learn of the Sebastian proposal. Soon we are inside the Sebastian home with the newlyweds. Almost all of the remainder of the picture takes place here, a set of connected built rooms on a large soundstage, including an ascending practical (that is, useable) staircase, a view of the upstairs landing, and numerous locations intended to be seen as linked: the wine cellar and basement; the bedrooms upstairs. The decoration of the Sebastian home is, as Jacobs says, a tour de force, with marble (that is, marbleized) columns and stairs, thickly upholstered furniture, urns on pedestals, a grand piano, chandeliers as though everywhere. As rendered in the imagery, the opulence of this space makes for a neat contrast against the rear-projected scenes in which Alicia meets Devlin on a palpably underdesigned public bench in the city. That bench screams, "Where we really are!" while the Sebastian home is that "fairytale castle," cousin to Hohenschwangau. Interior design in the Sebastian home withdraws Alicia, and us, from a "real" world that is progressively sliding into oblivion elsewhere.

- *Poison.* Ingrid Bergman will now use performance technique to show Alicia's feeling and thought systematically drawn away from the fairytale castle after Madame Sebastian takes to poisoning her. We have a number of shots of coffee cups, and Bergman's slowed speech and awkward balance to suggest she has been separated from her own body. Meeting with Devlin at the city bench she uses a silent gaze, a turndown of the eyes, and especially a weakened voice, but he mistakes all this physical withdrawal for emotional withdrawal. We see her going for a walk alone in the city, almost stumbling against a cement abutment (which margins a rear-projection screen). In a revelation scene, when Dr. Anderson almost picks up her coffee cup by mistake and is sharply corrected by Sebastian and his mother together, Alicia realizes what has been happening to her and jumps sharply to her feet. So do the Sebastians. But the two Sebastians are photographed against a rear-projected view of the room space behind them, so that the lighting in both background and foreground can be manipulated to extremes until there is finally very high contrast between two shadowy figures and a blaringly bright ground. This warped vision, now accompanied by an optically printed background wavering, is given as Alicia's severely affected, severed sense of the space.

- *Exit.* After Devlin has rescued Alicia and walked her down the perilous staircase, as he moves with her and with Sebastian and the Mother to the door that will lead to freedom—"Note that during the descent of the group, the camera will follow them down in *all* the shots," writes Stefan Scharff, "until they come to the hall" (83)—we see outside a distant view of the city: city as redemption. But there is no movement of any kind in that vision—it is a painted backing. The three principals move through a physical space toward less a future than a picture of a future. Finally, of course, Sebastian is locked out of the car and his tomorrow.

NO REPRODUCTIONS

Alicia's first glimpse of Devlin (at the party) makes her think she has seen him somewhere before: as an agent he has perhaps been on her trail. At the brasserie in Rio she will tease, cajole, and poke at him to see if she can discover who he really is. We meet him, however, in what can only be thought a peculiar way: from behind. An image to inspire musing, and wonder.

Whilst he owned many paintings (and had Albert Whitlock render copies of them for hanging so that the originals could be kept in safe deposit [Krohn correspondence]), there is no recorded connection between Hitchcock and his contemporary René Magritte (1898–1967), whose *Réproduction interdite* (1937) bears so startling a resemblance to the opening

Florida party shot where we see the interloper, back to camera. A moment later the man will become Devlin, tumble with this dream woman into a dream zone of lasting uncertainty and concern, love and trepidation. In the Magritte the subject appears to be in a dream zone of another kind, standing before a mirror in which he sees yet another image of himself from behind. In the Magritte, but also in some sense in *Notorious*, this man seems to exist *a tergo:* seen from behind as he looks into a mirror, at least temporarily he does not have a face; yet in this painting the "temporary" is also eternal. Devlin has no face, either—not one Alicia, or we, can feel certain about although ironically the actor's is one of the most celebrated faces in cinema. A cipher, bait for curiosity, and object of beauty we would wish to reach out and touch. And it goes without saying that with Cary Grant, reproduction is out of the question. And the "CaryGrantness" of Cary Grant: nothing at all.

Beside Magritte's faceless man, on his mantel, rests Edgar Allan Poe's 1838 novel, *The Narrative of Arthur Gordon Pym of Nantucket*. Pym meets a chain of horrors and life-threatening dangers aboard a ship that is not his home. Devlin is never absolutely certain Alicia is not a life-threatening danger, even as he saves her life.

Why does this stranger pique Alicia's nerves? Not that she has been drinking too much and is wobbly. And the blazing black-and-white striped blouse she wears at her party is a sign of her inner vibration.[12] The moment on the highway where Devlin's ID wallet frees them from the policeman's critical gaze is a genuinely perturbing one for her, nerve-wracking, not only because she is not sober. How can this man sharing the front seat of her car have a relationship with a motorcycle cop out of nowhere in the middle of the night while being so supremely attractive? She lives already in the hope of falling in love, and also in abject fear that love will never come along; in Rio we begin to see this fear take shape with the doubt and insecurity in her eyes.

But in the marriage proposal scene at Prescott's, Devlin does turn away.

She is waiting at that moment to know what he thinks. That is, she is waiting for him to carry her off forever. She needs at least for him to show he loves her, and here and now the way to show it would be to stand in the way of that marriage. To openly declare that he would place impediments to this proposed marriage of minds that are not "true"—*true* as a carpenter would use the word, *in alignment, matching*. She wants at least to see his face collapse in regret. But he gives her a *tabula rasa*, decisively expressionless, tantamount communicationally to the back of a head.

The rear view of Devlin's head also foregrounds his indecipherable thought process, makes us wonder whether he thinks at all since his movements are so fluid, his obedience so unquestioning. If for a great part of the film Alicia should take this Devlin to have no inner life; if the inner spirit she so eagerly seeks seems gone, or never yet born; then she has come to feel about him precisely what we were led to feel when first we saw him: sculptural form without energy. She shares our state of mind, a state created by Hitchcock with his strange camera position. Alicia of course does not see the back of this man's head literally; she speaks of Devlin as though he shows her the back of his head. We see; she comments. As Darwin taught, "The face is the part of the body which is most regarded" (327). For Alicia, most regarded and unintelligible; for us, regarded as unregardable. When Devlin goes to the wine cellar with her, however, they will know each other.

A SOIRÉE TO WATCH

Hitchcock has a strategy for giving us access to the Sebastian soirée that Devlin intends to crash in order to have a go at the wine cellar. One can point to the sumptuousness of the interior architecture, the breadth of the echoey spaces, the grand height of the atrium, the guests in their nappy tuxedoes and long gowns holding champagne and whispering to one another about whatever it is that in-crowds like this convey in whispers. And the frictionless gliding around. And the servants trucking trays of champagne, like living delivery vans. Alex shuffling around to be certain everything continues as he would have it be. Every personage showing off in "best light," whatever that is. The chatter sounds like so much tinkling glass in a billion chandeliers. But what does Hitchcock do beyond giving a few perfunctory sweeping shots of such action? He leaps away to a high balcony and gazes down, quite as though following a dream. "I looked and observed a great deal," Hitchcock is quoted by his biographer Donald Spoto as saying in adulthood. "I've always been that way and still am. I was anything but expansive. I was a loner—can't even remember having had a playmate.

I played by myself, inventing my own games" (19). Now, from outside the inside, and from inside the peculiar outside one can inhabit looking down on a social gathering, he watches the movement of the many living pieces of the puzzle of life.

The black and white tiled floor. The guests in their black and their white.

Is it the child's point of view, when he has been scuttled off to bed early so that he will not be a disturbance to the grown-ups' many important guests? Regardless that this party is in his house (RKO Studios), he is not of this party; the space is divided, there is a zone down there to which he is forbidden access but which fascinates. He observes the characters flashing their sparkly drinks, this one, that one. He does not taste the wine, catch the perfume, hear the illicit sentiment curdling on painted lips: he sees and speculates and imagines. And when will all these be sent home so that I can go to bed? Let us say that Alicia has never looked more glamorous in all her life and that, crashing the scene, Devlin is distinctly aware of this, sharply aware, a man who cannot take his eyes off her. But we gaze from a high silence.

A technical matter rivets Dev's eyes, that she holds the wine cellar's magical key. He is planning a pickup. But Hitchcock's need is to deliver the key *as informative object* at the same time as he indicates his own withdrawal to that balcony. It is through his agency, outsider on the inside, insider outside, that we detect Alicia's special gift. Any other filmmaker would avoid the balcony altogether, or start there but jump down to a neutral, third-person narrative stance for displaying her holding the prize in such a way that Devlin would see it. Bill Krohn reveals the fascinating fact that this sort of visual jump was exactly what was in the script, with the shift from a downward-gazing long shot to a tight close-up being "accomplished with a cut" (84). In the event, Hitchcock opted to have built a mechanism that would make possible a fluid, almost intoxicated slow descent through vertical space—this not only a way of showing us each fraction of a moment but also of explicitly announcing the moving camera. The massive wooden crane/elevator-dolly apparatus, "camera and technicians suspended in a wooden cage from rails attached to the ceiling" (98), built especially and only for the purpose of making this one shot, allows for wafting down from the balcony in a straight diagonal line, slowly, like a bird coming to rest on a jungle gym or an aircraft preparing to land at Rio, down, down, the noise louder, louder, and down, down, down, and Alicia there before us, and Alicia's head, and Alicia's shoulder beside her neck—Alicia growing on the screen as we watch, Alicia becoming enormous—and her long long long arm, all the way down and down her arm, down and down, to her fist, but still traveling, closer now into her fist, closer and still closer, so that her fist is a giant fist filling the screen with its slightly fiddly fingers and the dark moist nook they make. Then, an optically printed join to a macro-close-up (98), moving even closer, closer, and yet closer to the shiny key. From the high balcony through the moving world to the fist, in one (apparently) uncut unblemished transposition. We devour the key.

And Devlin receives it. After *we* find the key.

It is not the party that interests Hitchcock, it is the key. *Der prächtige schlüssel.* For Dev and Alicia the party exists only for the key, after all. Even more, *possession of the key.* Sartre writes,

> The possessor is the reason for being (*raison d'être*) of the possessed object.... The object possessed is inserted by me into the total form of *my* environment; its existence is determined by my situation and by its integration in that same situation.... It is animated, colored, defined by the use which I make of it; it *is* that use and exists only through it. ("Meaning" 144, 145)

The "total form" of an environment into which that key fit when it was Sebastian's, *his* world, is altogether different from the form of environment it gains coming to Alicia and then to Dev. Dev will integrate that key into *his* situation, which is to say, his project of getting information. Everything about that key, once he touches it, will be an animation of his definition. And once the key is returned to Sebastian's dressing table it will retain traces of Dev's use, just as while Dev handles it, it retains traces of what Sebastian used it for beforehand: plumbing that wine cellar. The ambiguous key, then, changing its face and its purpose from hand to hand. Julio Cortázar's "Daily Daily":

> A man clambers onto the streetcar after having bought the daily paper and tucking it under his arm. Half an hour later he gets off, the same newspaper under the same arm.

> Only now it's not the same newspaper, now it's a pile of printed sheets which the man drops on a bench in the plaza.
> It hardly stays alone a minute on the bench, the pile of printed sheets is converted into a newspaper again when a young boy sees it, reads it, and leaves it converted into a pile of printed sheets.
> It sits alone on the bench hardly a minute, the pile of printed sheets converts again into a newspaper when an old woman finds it, reads it, and leaves it changed into a pile of printed sheets. But then she carries it home and on the way home uses it to wrap up a pound of beets, which is what newspapers are fit for after all these exciting metamorphoses. (67)

One could say Sebastian's purpose in the film is to be master of that special key. The challenge to Dev: find it; overcome the master's mastery; possess it. This key is not the tool for opening up this film; this key *is* the film. Will Devlin find the key to Alicia, Alicia find the key to Devlin, America find the key to the lingering Nazis, Madame find the key to save her son, Alex find the key to Alicia's heart or at least to promoting his own nefarious success? Can any outsider really find the key that opens the gate? The key is also, of course, *le clef*, the "musical key," which means the organizer of tonalities registered in range and in juxtaposition to make the composition resonate with feeling. "No one knows how language began," writes R. Murray Schafer, "but one theory is that it originated as an echo of the soundscape" (*Sound Education* 67). And, "By assembling words or forms," writes Jacques Rancière,

> people define not merely various forms of art, but certain configurations of what can be seen and what can be thought, certain forms of inhabiting the material world. These configurations, which are at once symbolic and material, cross the boundaries between arts, genres and epochs. They cut across the categories of an autonomous history of technique, art or politics. (91)

Keys can be conceived as assemblages; assemblages as keys. Is this film in the Key of Romance, or is it in the Key of Espionage Intrigue; the Key of Travel and Exploration or the Key of Militant Patriotism? When in that Second District Courtroom, "Miami. Florida. Three-Twenty P.M., April the

24th, Nineteen Hundred and Forty-Six...," John Huberman standing before the judge tries to offer his final words, "Next time we'll w—," is he (a) uttering despair; (b) expressing hope; (c) revealing strategy already in place; (d) bluffing fearlessness before the enemy; (e) committing a conviction to words? In what key is he making this utterance (which as we listen is our overture)?

Given that Alex's soirée is exclusive, that in its space there are many souls transmigrating, we are of course quite petrified with fear the moment that key comes into Dev's hand. (•) How soon will it be before Sebastian realizes he doesn't have his key? Because (•) now a steward is warning him they are running out of champagne and it may be necessary to go down to the wine cellar. (•) How efficient can Devlin be finding the spot, opening the door, looking around, coming to some conclusion? Or in (•) searching the wine cellar when he does not have the first idea what he is looking for? Something about a wine bottle. Well, yes—in the wine cellar there are wine bottles. There are only wine bottles. Uncounted wine bottles. Which one or ones should he find? (•) And won't some of the many shufflers in tuxedoes upstairs be mobilized to find him, catch him, bind him, torture him, rip him to shreds, perhaps down here, in the secrecy of the wine cellar? (•) And what will happen to dear Alicia if it is discovered that she took the key? What is she doing with this "pest" Devlin anyway? All of the soirée in order to frame the key; the key in order to free Devlin to search, but also the key that may drop Alicia from Alex's cloistered world. Once Dev has the key we think not of what he might find but of what could be lost.

Everything onscreen goes precisely right so as to make us fear that something is soon to go precisely wrong.

CALL IT SLEEP

"I went away without my head," he said apologetically.
—Henry Roth, *Call It Sleep*

In the film's powerful conclusion—beginning with a pillow exchange of whispered syllables that couldn't be further from the chatting tease at the brasserie when Rio was new—as Alicia stumbles down the grand staircase with support from Devlin on one side (caching his pistol) and sheepish, terrified Sebastian on the other, and the Mother just behind, a signal problem is created for the German cabal. Three of the plotters stand in formal dress on the checkerboard floor, staring up. *What is wrong, Alex?*

They do not realize Devlin is rescuing the poisoned Alicia, not yet. (She is poisoned?!? If she is poisoned, then who poisoned her... and to what end?) And their awakening must be kept off as long as possible. Madame Sebastian, following one step behind like a petrified geisha, is aware how carefully she and Alex must act to save their lives. "Devlin *knows!*" the son has confessed, almost in silence. The spies below are on the cusp of realizing the door has been opened to a spy, but only on the cusp. All this while Alicia nearly collapses from the effects to her body. On Madame's face we can see that, brains of the household, she surely does know what the cabal sees gazing up, what even we see, since we are "with" the cabal, and knows, too, that her doltish son is too besotted with terror to understand. Stand down there on the cool marble floor and look up (antithesis of the gliding descent at the soirée) and ask yourself, indeed: *What... is... wrong?*

Not what the audience knows is "wrong."

Not what Sebastian knows and his mother knows that he knows.

Not even what Alicia dimly knows is wrong, in her stupor: "They are poisoning me. I couldn't get away."

But what these smartly dressed outsiders, who do not mingle in the family's sanctum, would think could be wrong, so that they would use that word. Scharff asks us to note "that the size of the image of the group of Germans is, in a sense, a measure of our protagonists' progress in their descent, since we see them only in close shots; the larger the Germans, the closer our four are to reaching the hallway" (84). Their interrogative mood augmented with each cut to them, not merely the forms of their bodies but the forms of their swelling doubts. What could be *wrong* swells, too, until, for them, a very great WRONG is in the offing.

All they need do now is just what they are doing now: look; and look as if being roused from a colossal daydream of power. Alicia nestled with her husband, feeling unwell—this much is understandable. Alicia being escorted by her husband, under the mother's eye, away to a hospital—this much is understandable, too. But:

This man Devlin holding Alicia...

What is this man Devlin doing *in this house* holding Alicia? Holding her the way her husband holds her on the other side? Acting on this staircase as though he belongs on this staircase (surely the feeling we have about him, mercifully). What is this embrace of sorts between this man and this woman? For the Germans, Alex and his mother evaporate out of the picture while in alarm they see Devlin bonded to Alicia and guiding her away.

The bonding of this American and the new wife they helped welcome into the *gemütlich* family—almost into the cabal!

Step...step...step...step...

In its final moments of tension the film resolves into the iconic image of Man and Woman Entwined, a virtual sculpture, and into what may reasonably be read from such an icon. That all along, through whatever masquerades, This Man has been entwined with This Woman. All along, notwithstanding Alicia's tears and recriminations and notwithstanding Devlin's silences and professional equivocations. All along, love. Unshakable, undilutable love. We can sigh with realization of what these formal men have not *quite* gathered, that what this woman most desperately yearned for was what this man most desperately yearned for, too, and forever. But because actions speak louder than words, no words were used to say what might have been said. And the ambiguity of action has been resolved.

The Nazis will have the words to say, however.

Hitchcock always prepares his cadences. Alicia's house party in Miami, at the point when our hostess has become tired of straining for sociability (with people she neither knows very well nor cares for especially): she says, "It's been a perfectly hideous party," and tells everyone to go. And everyone does go, save Devlin. Save Devlin and—

And one couple.

A man and a woman are lost with, and in, one another, it appears without end. We pass by them as they lie together upon one of Alicia's chairs, the man with his head thrown back, and dressed in a tidy pin-stripe suit (such as Devlin will wear when he saves Alicia). Spread laterally across his lap is a woman in a casual gown, and his hand is on her thigh. They are both away in the land of sleep. There is no separation between them, yet they are in two separate bubbles of privacy. They share a bond of intimacy given off now for public show, a neo-modern pose that could be called "The Lovers," such as Devlin and Alicia finally give without trying, and while the enemy is watching,[13] as *Notorious* ends.

CHAPTER TWO

HOW A LADY VANISHES

> All the intellectual value for us of a state of mind
> depends on our after-memory of it.
> —William James

MEMORY OF A PRELUDE

Mary Ann Doane reads in Freud's *Beyond the Pleasure Principle* (1920) an assertion of "the incompatibility of memory and consciousness" (45). For Freud, "becoming conscious and leaving behind a memory-trace are processes incompatible with each other within one and the same system" (Freud, *Beyond* 25, qtd. in Doane 45). We do not look back and look forward at the same time. As Doane proceeds she goes further and asserts how "time is antithetical to the notions of storage and retention of traces," a conclusion or proposition if entirely enticing in itself still not an accurate indicator of the route I would wish to follow here, along which I hope to suggest that it is presence, not time, that exhibits this antithetical bent. What strikes me about Freud's assertion, and makes me grateful for Doane's recapitulation of it, is the recognition of temporal positioning at an elemental level,

a recognition that depends upon a conception of time as a dimension of "space" in which what has already happened and what is happening now, indeed the past and the present tenses of language, are embedded, perhaps on a line but certainly in some undefined ether open to movement and passage, a flow just sufficiently primordial as to make the conceptualization of time possible. Freud is suggesting that what we experience now, and sense ourselves now to be experiencing now, cannot be reached by us if we instead attempt to access past experience, indeed The Past, *and this whilst both present and past experience are potentially to be accessed in the same zone.* Or: if we happen to try bringing to experience now, still again, something of an experience of the not-now, we cannot simultaneously bring forth an experience of the now in accompaniment.[1] As we cannot be in two places at the same time, we can also not be in two "places" at the same time. William James put it this way: "There is before the mind at no time a plurality of ideas, properly so called" (405). This "plurality" of ideas that is not present *can be imagined to be present but not realized as presence.*

Impossible to be alive to the moment and remembering, at once.

But even more weighty than this putative dichotomization between "now" and "then" is the thought of experience and the thought of memory, two thoughts, or ideas, in relation to each other. How destabilizing is uncertainty about memory altogether! Uncertainty about memory's distance from, memory's relation to, the Now.

If I tell you I went to the corner store to buy some raisins one day when I was a little boy, I cannot be certain—and am plagued at being unable to be certain—whether this happened as other things happen—a bus drives past—or is only a present invention of mine, set grammatically in the past tense for the purposes of recounting. Not a real past but only a false "past," a purely narrative "past." If I had a deeply interiorized personal, even visual memory of it all, could it be only a "memory"? That is, if I say to myself that I remember, do I only "remember"? And if I think I do not remember, if I think I forget, do I actually "forget"? That (hilarious) opening of *David Copperfield:* Chapter One. I AM BORN. Yes, well...

Hang onto these thoughts, Dear Reader, or consign them to memory.

CHOO CHOO

Before he was ten years old, at home in London's east end, Alfred Hitchcock studied timetables, "and astonished his family by reciting from memory the schedules of most of England's train lines" (Spoto 19). He was obsessed by route maps and schedules, but especially by trains themselves (like so many other little boys, including me). Might he not have fantasized his own toy train set, running along an elaborate twist of routes around and among snow-capped mountains, kissing little villages, saluted by friendly folk? The beginning of *The Lady Vanishes* (1938) envisions traffic, especially train traffic, of just this kind in just such a place. We are transported by the camera to the high wintry climes of a substitute for Switzerland, Mandrika, where in a tiny village a pack of guests are trapped at an inn. The credit shots depict what resembles a child's train set-up, as they ought, indeed, because that is what they actually show, the whole arrangement poised so that a hovering camera will define it as an exotic reality. All around is pandemonium (the daemonic is everywhere) because, the train route being blocked, all the travelers are obliged to take rooms for an extra night: but are there enough rooms? Chaos, telephone calls, panic, hubbub, variations on a theme of consternation.

In a move he would not repeat until the elaborate overture/opening of *Rear Window* sixteen years later, Hitchcock begins *The Lady Vanishes* with an extended cadenza, as elaborate a set piece as any he ever made and running, at twenty-four and a half minutes, a full quarter of the length of the film as a whole. The credits flashing over the decidedly picturesque mountain landscape, with majestic snow-capped peaks hovering over a lush and peaceable valley, we slide rightward and downward, passing over snow-laden railway tracks at a snow-laden station with a snow-laden platform upon which three tiny male figures converse, epitomes of artifice (the mountain background taking on the character of a handsomely painted flat) except that as the camera clears the railway platform, at the last possible moment, one of the tiny men moves his arms.

A toy world, then, or an unspeakable reality. There is surely the galvanizing charm of a toy. Remember your toys?

We are gliding rightward past a number of chalet-style buildings, all fronted in decorative wooden boarding to suggest the style of the high Alps. Zooming slowly into the doorway of an inn we find an assembly of mechanisms—toy action. Every transition from one "performer" or "act" to the next—this is like Vaudeville—seems inevitable when one thinks back to what preceded, whilst at each juncture what comes next won't be obvious or predictable at all. Here is the line-up:

[A] *Lobby*. A vaulted chamber with at least a dozen despondent travelers waiting for a train that may never come, suitcases by their feet: very Pirandello; and precedent for Tennessee Williams:

> JACQUES: There's a rumor of something called The Fugitivo but—
>
> MARGUERITE: The What!!!?
>
> JACQUES: The Fugitivo. It's one of those non-scheduled things that—
>
> MARGUERITE: When, when, when?
>
> JACQUES: I told you it was non-scheduled. Non-scheduled means it comes and goes at no predictable—
>
> MARGUERITE: Don't give me the dictionary! I want to know how does one get on it? Did you bribe them?
>
> (*Camino Real* Block 7, 173)

For the moment, peace. Down the stairway comes:

[B] *Seniority*. Moving toward the reception desk (toward the camera), a letter in one hand and her purse in the other, is an elderly lady (May

Whitty: b. 1865; Dame Commander of the Order of the British Empire as of 1918; d. 1948). A courteous nod for the manager, occupied with a phone at his ear. She places the letter down indicatively, opens her purse, and pays for a postage stamp he mechanically hands over.[2] Four passengers have looked this way to observe (even evaluate): two men with elbows touching; a proud young woman in a shoulder wrap of lush fur; and her well-suited male friend, clearly agitated. The old lady heads for the door. But a fierce wind has blasted it open and the two Elbows who rose to shove it closed only have to open it again to let her out (decorum decorum decorum): what an irritation people can be! She offers them a gracious smile, dressed practicably, wearing "sensible" shoes, and bearing one of those open and wholly unconcealing but also instantly forgettable faces: a doting grandmother type but nobody's grandmother. The Elbows have re-seated themselves, one with a telltale cigarette and one with a telltale pipe. As two workers barge in, schlepping skis and suitcases, an ornate clock chimes. Much shouting, so that—

[C] *Exasperation!:* —the innkeeper, a fluent speaker of at least five languages as well as a Master of Gesticulation, is wholly unable to hear what is being said to him on the phone. Arms flying around, hand anxiously covering face. He hangs up abruptly. To the gatherers a mini-sermon: "Signiorini signiore..." (ladies and gentlemen)... But this clown of expressivity, babbling, barking, fluttering, spluttering, twisting, and insisting cannot find, in the mélée of his consciousness with the storm wind blowing, the words to say what he must. Hands flying out everywhere. Obsequiousness nonpareil. Emile Boreo's extremely emphatic vowel extensions and glottal spasms making him a Master of Ceremonies holding court in the center ring.[3] He squeaks out in Italian and three men run to the desk. He switches to French, and we cut to the two Elbows, one demanding of the other what this is all about (Do Not and Would Never speak...French). Now, German. Soon, as everyone but the four individuals we noted before has rushed the desk, the two Elbows who don't speak French, the svelte woman, and the anxious man, the manager segues into English. "I'm very sorry, the train is little bit uphold, and if you wish to stay in my hotel you have to register immediately." The pipe smoker, outraged: "Why the deuce didn't he say so in the first place!"

Looking their way as they march toward him, the manager gives a welcoming grin and a pleasing "Ahhh!"—but now they see it isn't them he's looking at. He's looking beyond, to what he's more than overjoyed to see:

[D] *Three little maids (from school).* Three young ladies, Hungry, Hungry, and Hungry are lavishing him with movie-star smiles and flashing their casual, quite summery clothing. "It's a *great hono*r to have you with us again!" with one of his trademark kowtows. They were staying here with Boris last Friday, these three; obviously trundled off somewhere on a lark, and have returned for a reprise. Plenty of personal jokes—they know the staff by name and are frequent guests in this "private country club." He guides them up the staircase, leaving the crowd lonely at the desk downstairs. Soon we will know these women as Iris, Blanche, and Julie. "How you said it? Is a bad wind that blow nowhere no good." They ask for dinner in their room, some chicken nuggets and a magnum of champagne. Most of the crowd watch this Ascension in speechless wonder. However:

[E] *Authority.* Our two British blokes are culture critics. Nappy Bowtie (Charters [Basil Radford]): "Meanwhile I suppose we have to stand here cooling our heels. Confounded impudent." The other disdainful, cigarette in hand (Caldicott [Naunton Wayne]): "Third-rate country." The three women must be Americans—plenty of money. (Even well before World War II when so many fought bravely in England, but so many were not welcomed, the American type was regarded through a dubious squint.) Charters and Caldicott missed their train at Budapest (because Charters dawdled over what he'd thought was the national anthem but was actually *The Hungarian Rhapsody*). Politics squeeze in: "England on the brink," mutters Charters, and Caldicott rejoins, oddly because of his British accent, "Your country's been on the brink before." Charters turns to a passing gentleman and asks what time the train leaves Basle, and gets the confounding reply, "Ich sprech kein Anglisch." How can humans who don't speak English exist?

[F] *Hubbub.* The manager is being thronged at his desk, seizes the phone: "Champagne, Miss Anderson." Charters and Caldicott settle themselves into wondering what 21:20 means in English time, since they have just read a train is leaving Basle at that hour.[4] The manager regrets he can offer the young woman and her nervous beau only two single rooms or else a "little dubble room at de back." The man opts for the two singles, outraging her. We track left to follow them into privacy. "At least you might have asked me which I preferred!" His hunger for propriety could not be more evident, nor hers for something else.

[G] *Anna.* It is Charters and Caldicott's turn with the manager. All he's got for them is the maid's room: "Don't get excited—I'll remove the maid out." No, maybe we'll go sleep in the train. The manager instantly goes haywire: "There's no eating in the train!" Eating, what? "No, 'eating!" with a demonstrative shiver. Anna will have to come and remove her wardrobe. "Anna!..."

[H] *A promising introduction.* Anna the maid is introduced (Kathleen Tremaine). Plumpish, blondish, grinning with...eagerness? "She's a good girl." Her hair is braided in Nordic style. A managerial instruction: "*La tratta la sitta...,*"[5] making Anna spread a grin from ear to ear. "Pity he couldn't have given us one each," says Caldicott. —"Huh?" —"A room apiece." A man like Caldicott always has something crisp ready on the tongue.

[I] *"Have no regrets."* Iris (Margaret Lockwood) has been awarded an enormous chamber. While Blanche (Googie Withers) and Julie (Sally Stewart) lounge casually in their slips she perches on a table making a solemn renunciation of her maidenly past. Thursday next, she shall "take the veil (and the orange blossom)" and change her name to Lady Charles Fotheringale. Charles Barr argues reasonably that she is a woman "who is traveling toward a doomed marriage" [194], yet at this point in the film—indeed until later in the film—I see no signals of "doom."[6] She has certainly been very proud of herself, and has raised The Fotheringale as a pennant of victory, if victory somehow hollow. The food and drink are delivered by Rudolf the waiter (John Miller), ogling Iris's legs. She drops the information that arrangements have already been made at St George's Hanover Square (posher than posh) and her friends toast to the "blue-blooded check-chaser she's dashing to London to marry." A macro-close-up on Iris. "I've no regrets. I've been everywhere and . . . done everything. . . . What is there left for me but marriage?" Closing the girls' door, Rudolf runs into Anna in the corridor. They have an unintelligible few words in somewhat readable mime: he is surprised, then mildly outraged at her boundless excitement. Who is Rudolf to Anna, and what adventure in disloyalty has been promised her?

[J] *On the beam.* Anna's room is low-beamed. Charters and Caldicott dress for dinner,[7] thoroughly miffed at not knowing "what's happening in England." Anna enters, a grin splashed across her face. The men politely turn their backs so that she can dress, but from under the bed she withdraws a large hat and puts it on. They try to explain that she shouldn't change here: "Outside," whereupon with a pleasing grin she begins to strip off her dress. As the men retreat to the hallway outside, Charters smacks his head on the beam. And on a second beam, marching downstairs. The Elbows can never bring themselves to believe they aren't in England, where the beams reach the sky. "Reach the sky" in Hollywood fictions of England, to be sure.

[K] *Cricket.* Striding through the lobby in full evening dress, Charters and Caldicott take a breather to flip through old newspapers at the desk while Boris is taking an incoming call from London. Shhhhh! "You want Mr. Seltzer? Yes. Hold on. I'm going right to—." He lays the receiver down and rushes off, whereupon Charters boldly picks it up. "Hello, hello, you in London—" Several seconds of decorous babbling to the idiot at the other end: "Tell me: what's happening to England? . . . Blowing a gale? . . . You don't follow me, sir. I'm inquiring about the test match in Manchester. Cricket, sir, CRICKET!!! What, you don't know?! *You can't be in England and not know the test score!*" He slams down the receiver, killing Boris's call. The two Englishmen slink into the dining room unable to comprehend how any person ignorant about cricket could be alive in England.

[L] *Cheese.* Plenty of smoke in the dining-room air, every booth jam-packed. Fighting off some Europeans our two arbiters squeeze into one where the old postage-stamp hunter sits finishing her dinner. They cannot make the waiter understand they're ravenous for a beefsteak, so she helpfully intercedes to interpret. Regrettably, owing to the crowd of visitors, there is no food left in the kitchen. "What sort of place is this?... Is that hospitality? Is that organization?... What a country, I don't wonder they have a revolution!" But she offers to share her remaining morsel of cheese, "awfully rich in vitamins."

The polite thing is some helpful conversation, too, so she tells them the story of her life.

Babble babble, twinkly eyes, babble babble. More twinkle than face. "Mandrika is one of Europe's few undiscovered corners." She knows it well and is feeling miserable at the thought of going home. Her little charges are quite grown up. She's a governess and a music teacher. She's lived here six years and loves the country, "especially the mountains. I sometimes think they're like very friendly neighbors. You know, the big father and mother mountains with their white snow hats and their nephews and nieces not quite so big with smaller hats right down to the tiniest hillocks without any hats at all." Every night she watches the mountains from her bedroom. Dimly in the background, perhaps from outside, a folksong. "Do you hear that music? Everyone sings here! The people are just like happy children, with laughter on their lips and music in their hearts." She doesn't think one should judge any country by its politics. After all, "We English are quite honest by nature, aren't we." Babble, twinkle, babble.

[M] *Wedding dance.* Meanwhile Iris is in the upstairs corridor, bidding her two friends good night, the folksong still audible outside. "Nothing to keep me awake." Turning back to her room she notices the old lady giving a polite nod as she ascends. Nod from a stranger, mm-hmm. We enter the old lady's room. She opens the French doors to the balcony, the song louder, a thrumming without lyrics. Cut to the patio just below, the guitar-playing singer. But from above, like thunder, loud clumping sounds that make the lady look up in surprise. She goes into the corridor along with her neighbor Iris, also disturbed. Iris takes action. Seizing the phone, she demands that Boris march upstairs and stop all this.[8] The old lady: "Some people have so little consideration for others, which makes things so much more difficult than it need be."

[N] *Unwelcome.* Boris discovers Rudolf and two other locals stomping around in a little circle, while on the bed a young man accompanies them on his clarinet, occasionally making them pause to jot down some notes. He gives Boris's imprecations no attention and the dancers start up again. "You dare to call it a noise? The ancient music with which your ancestors celebrated every wedding for countless generations?" Boris is sent packing.

[O] *Bribe.* At Iris's bedside, Boris makes report: "He say, 'Who does she think she is, the Queen of Sheba?'" She bribes him to move the fellow upstairs to an Elsewhere.

[P] *Gutte nacht!* Caldicott is in bed with a paper spread open, muttering about baseball: children's play done with a rubber ball and a stick. It's the *Herald Tribune:* "Not a word about cricket!" Knock on the door. Paper drops down. Charters and Caldicott are side by side in bed, we see now, Caldicott with no shirt, Charters with a pajama top. Anna enters, grinning approvingly. She must put back the hat in its box under the bed. (Where did she go in that hat?—Not our business.) Into the wardrobe to fetch some nightclothes. Out the door. Grinning. But popping back: *Gutte nacht!* Charters hops out of bed, passing a full pair of pajamas hanging to dry.[9] As soon as he gets to the door to lock it, in comes Anna again and he bumps his head on that low beam. She goes into the dresser for something else but this time, singing another *Gutte nacht!,* steals a glance at his bare legs. Stiff and Brittle seem to be obvious dolts, scene after scene, but be cautious in downgrading them because in Hitchcock nothing is all of, or only, what it seems.

[Q] *Stinkers.* Iris sleeps. Her door opens to a strange dark shadow and the light is turned on. The clarinet player (Michael Redgrave), evicted from his room and now moving in here! Not at all happy to meet one another. "Who are you? What do you want?" brings only a clarinet riff. He approves of the room, daintily moves some of her things from the bedposts, asks which side she prefers to sleep on (tiny tip of the hat to *The 39 Steps* [1935]). Removes pajamas from his suitcase. He will "sleep in the middle." Goes to the bathroom to change: "Smart of you to bribe the manager. An eye for an eye, and a tooth for a toothbrush"—She seizes the phone—"Oh, I shouldn't if I were you. I'll only tell everyone you invited me here." Behind the closed door he is singing the Colonel Bogey March. She is onto Boris, whispering, "I was thinking I might change my mind." The stranger emerges—fully dressed—and catches her eye: "You might have my things taken upstairs," with a triumphant smirk. As he exits she cannot desist: "You're the most contemptible person I've ever met in all my life!" to which he smilingly whispers, "Confidentially, I think you're a bit of a stinker, too!" Dissolve to:

[R] *Death by moonlight.* A long shot of the village by night, with the singer humming somewhere outside and below: essentially a waltz structure, but la-la'ed very slowly and in a minor key so as to render it a dirge. The old lady lingering in her balcony doorway, nodding along, even trying to sing (reminding us she's a music teacher). We cut to the singer, portrait close-up, mouth wide open in "happy" singing. On the plaster wall behind him the shadow of two approaching hands[10] that reach his neck and strangle him. Hearing the music suddenly stop, the enchanted old lady comes to the balcony and tosses over a coin, and we see it hit the cobbles below. She draws her curtains as we gaze briefly at the lonely coin.

* * *

This complex overture runs a little like Rossini, beginning tranquilly, a bucolic idyll, then suddenly erupting into an unimaginable vivacity, with figures running off in all directions in rhythmic emphasis. Beyond Boris the manager, whose racing and flailing lace the many elements together in a believable coherence but who will not be continuing on the voyage of the film, we are left with introduction to persons and themes, all to resonate later if not declaring importance now. For Hitchcock, an escapade of comedic, dramatic, and musical opportunities. The English blokes will be comic relief of a peculiar sort—the world stops at Britain. Iris will be the femme. Perhaps the clarinetist will head her way. A whimsical old lady fond of Mandrika. A pair of trysters, Miss Daring and Mr Shy. In the background, interrupting and surrounding these markers both acoustically and visually (and relentlessly), the "foreign element": many languages; contradictory desires; puzzling gazes; competition for limited prizes. All of this is set in a charming little no-place in the middle of nowhere, "one of Europe's few undiscovered corners." The murder victim is a singer, killed like Cock Robin mainly because he sings, as far as we can tell. Sings without lyrics, even.

And finally an invisible train, stalled until an avalanche is cleared.

HEAD INJURY[11]

A bright and cheery Mandrika morning. While the train, soon to reveal itself as a time capsule, energetically huffs and puffs at the platform, our new friends ready themselves to board, each in characteristic fashion: Charters and Caldicott, showing off their tweeds and hoping good weather for the Manchester test match[12]; Mr and "Mrs" Todhunter, he urging that she hurry or they won't get a compartment to themselves and she sneering back, "Does it matter?"; the three girls in marching step, Julie and Blanche to bid farewell to Iris, who this morning doesn't seem overjoyed at looking forward to Hanover Square; and the old governess, searching for a lost bag. "Would you know?—" She marches to the side of the hotel, rummaging among some bags there. Iris's eyes drop. Here! "Gran" has dropped her eyeglasses. She rushes over with them, at which exact moment someone in an upstairs window pushes away a windowsill flower box that sails down and smashes Iris on the back of the head. But the train must leave, everyone must scurry aboard. The trip is begun. The governess (whom we have never seen with eyeglasses) gratefully helps Iris to go forward.

Fascinating to be wrapped up in these many story fragments, knowing virtually nothing about the protagonists.[13] Charters and Caldicott: why go on tour if you so deeply cherish England, England and only England?

Iris and friends: are they present to help ease her into a new life or to bask vicariously in her limelight? The "lovers": heading home, no doubt, but to whom? And the governess: her mind focused elsewhere, eyes peering constantly through the fog of the social charade.

Wounded Iris does require attention. Looking out of the train she collapses as her waving chums rotate before her eyes in a glary haze. When she wakes she is cornered in a compartment, the governess seated opposite. Next, a dull-faced goggle-eyed man in a beret and a personage draped in a black mantilla, proudly turning her face to the window. Adjacent Iris a woman with a small child. The governess urges a little eau de cologne for the forehead. And leads Iris out—wobbly, wobbly—for a cup of tea. They pass the lovers' compartment, he racing to draw the blind down. The dining car, a quiet paradise. Cozy table for two, with the mountain scenery whizzing by outside. A marvel to be settled and in rapid motion, simultaneously. Across the aisle, Charters is trying to show Caldicott a curious cricket move by mapping it on their tabletop with sugar cubes. The governess introduces herself to Iris, "My name's Froy," but the train whistle rudely blocks her voice. "Did you say Freud?" "No, O-Y, not E-U-D. Froy." Finally she fingers it onto the window: F R O Y. Because a dark train is swiftly passing on the other track the letters are momentarily blazingly visible.[14] "Rhymes with joy!"

Our Miss Froy has her own teabags, drawn from her clutch: Harriman's Herbal Tea, a million Mexicans can't be wrong! They must importune the cricket fiends to surrender some of their sugar treasure: irritated grumping. More old-lady babble now: governess, getting married is lovely, have children, I love children... a nice little cuppa.

In a truly splendid moving matte, the train crosses a high Roman aqueduct over a gorgeous valley. Roman aqueduct: the country has been here like this for a very, very long time. A lateral, symmetrical, extensive structure modeling *time*. History (not the events of history) is stable; a young country like Mandrika is inherently unstable. And the beauty of the shot distracts us nicely from the tea chatter.

Now, back in the compartment, Iris should "try and get a little sleep. It'll make you feel quite well again. There's a most intriguing acrostic in *The Needle Woman*. I'm going to try to unravel it before you wake up." Wake up >> awaken >> acrostic, mystery >> unraveling... the words are melding. Hitchcock demonstrates the difference between hearing something and seeing something: watching the old lady's lips move, with so much floating away from short-term memory, we do not really hear. But: we do not erase that F R O Y on the window and neither, one presumes, does Iris, dream-mapping it now.

Notice Hitchcock's classical preparation for this drama—every happening is a drop from a rise:

- He prepared us for the window scrawl *as sight* back on the railway platform when, her girlfriends blathering, Iris looked down and saw the eyeglasses. Returning the eyeglasses → her being wounded (and Miss Froy not). All this portentous consequentiality shown in silence.

- Iris's compartment mates as they regard her: glaring bug-eyed interest, squinting suspicion, sagacious or tactical withdrawal, all coded in a kind of expressionistic cipher. Of these others, beyond their appearance and *pronounced optical gestures* we know nothing. Optical gestures, positioned gazes—always important in Hitchcock, here especially. Who is looking? And at what?

- Delivering sugar cubes to Miss Froy, blithering Charters and Caldicott cast glances that can be regarded only as judgmental (a Hitchcockian comment on critics). These men know Miss Froy only by her generosity at "dinner," but feel entitled to Blimpish disapproval.

- Miss Froy's constant nattering about seeming trivia could lead to our mistaken surmise that she doesn't see much. By convention, characters' eye gestures indicate the world as they take it in, and Miss Froy may see a lot, but acutely? As a retired governess what else has she to do but look around? Iris is her new charge, but is the governess competent?

The train scuttles on.

A shrill whistle awakens Iris from her nap (sound cuing sight). Beret still gorps at her, Señora still stares out the window, but as the camera slowly jogs left simulating Iris's stumbling perception we find... an empty seat, an antimacassar doily glaring emptily. As a steward comes into the compartment to see about luncheon bookings, Iris thinks her "friend" has managed one but, concerned, peers into the corridor after her. No one. Then, to Beret, "Have you seen my friend?" Curtly, no. "My friend, where is she?" An amicable but hopeless gesture of raising the arms and opening the hands. "La signiora Inglese. The English lady." The Señora in black turns from her window to speak most clearly. "There has been no English lady here."

"What?"

Close-up now on two cold, javelin eyes: "There has been no ... English lady ... here." An insistence that, from the dining car Iris came back alone.

"I mean the lady who looked after me when I was knocked out."

Beret speaks!: "Ahhh, perhaps it's making you forget, ehh?"

Yes, it is powerfully difficult to tell remembering from forgetting; or remembering from thinking; or remembering from saying "I remember." In forgetting one fails at thinking because the object of thought has become a blank—here in the present. Does one ever remember the experience of forgetting?

Iris moves down the corridor, checking compartments one by one. In the dining car the steward sits with paperwork, alone. She turns to go back. Here is the white-jacketed waiter who served the tea, insisting no, no, you were alone. The steward comes up: no, you are making a mistake. But, "You must remember ... she ordered the tea and paid for it." — "No, it was *you* who paid!" Iris insists the waiter was given a *special* packet of tea, but no, no, "The tea was ours, Madame." The steward has found the bill. "Tea ... *for one.*"

She proceeds, into a car with raucous music and dancing and the air full of smoke. She stops to ask a man his help—mercifully, our clarinetist: "Oh well, if it isn't old Stinker!" But when he sees her holding her head he tenderly helps her sit and asks what's the trouble. (The chivalry we have been hoping for.)

"If you must know, something fell on my head."

"When, infancy?" mockery of an entirely affectionate sort. "My father always taught me, never desert a lady in trouble." Did he see a little lady in the hotel last night, in tweeds? And now we may suddenly reflect—now, in fact, may be the first time we do reflect—that in all that spinning

Rossiniesque opening there was no moment in which the clarinetist and the old lady appeared together. "She's still on the train." But who says she isn't, he asks blithely, the moment being somewhat fictional for him. He agrees to help, however, and they return toward her compartment arm in arm, coming upon Beret anxiously conversing with a tall mustachioed man. When Clarinet explains that "this lady seems to have lost her friend," the tall one speaks with cultivated eloquence, an Actor on a Stage: "Yes, I have heard!... I think under the circumstances we shall all introduce ourselves." An important moment for the story in some ways, but also a convenient moment for the narration, since the clarinetist hasn't been introduced either (and perhaps we've failed to notice that). Beret is an Italian citizen, and these are his wife and child. "And the lady in the corner—," who will be announced as a Baroness.

"And I am Dr. Egon Hartz of Prague. You may have heard of me."

"Not the brain specialist!"

But oh yes! And he is picking up a surgical case at the next station. "I shall operate at the national hospital tonight. Among other things, a cranial fracture with compression. You understand?" We don't, Iris doesn't, but we all pretend we do: standard operating procedure. Neither this doctor nor Beret, nor Beret's wife, nor the Baroness have seen a little English lady, even with Iris's meticulous description. (She's an imaginative one, this!) She recollects how some fellow diners passed sugar at the tea, so Clarinet will take her to find them. Doctor finds this all "most interesting." He will join, scientist, student of life.

FORGET SEEING PEOPLE

But wait—memory again: Iris suddenly remembers a couple in a compartment along the way. Her new friend slides open the door and out comes Todhunter, too poised. "Do you happen to remember this young lady passing the compartment with a... little English woman?"

Disturbed, hesitating: "I'm afraid not."

Iris intends to find her even if she has to stop the train! But at corridor's end Charters has overheard this proposition. Girl "has lost her friend," he whispers to Caldicott, and "point is, she threatens to stop the train! If we miss our connection in Basle we'll never make Manchester in time." (All of the previous cricket nonsense with C & C a preparation for their cadence at this moment.) They hide together in the lav (memory tweak of the shared pajamas), as Clarinet concludes that Todhunter "obviously doesn't remember." ("Todhunter" = *seeker of death*.) Well, is the man remembering and saying he doesn't remember? Is he not remembering and wondering if he should? When an actor remembers his lines and speaks them, does he also say, "I am remembering these lines"? And does everyone who claims not to remember always everywhere actually not remember?

Finally, to clumsy Charters and Caldicott. "I wonder if you could help." No, no, Charters *doesn't remember*. Caldicott *does remember* passing sugar (he says he does remember: character minds are in character assertion). But as we were discussing cricket, you see, we noticed nothing else. Here, cricket and the cricket obsession are not Charters and Caldicott's excuse for tuning the world around them completely out as much as they are Hitchcock's mechanism for establishing a completely innocent disavowal of witnessing. In the same vein, C & C are disputing Iris and Clarinet much less than they are disputing *our* conviction that the lady who has vanished was visible to us.

"Well, I don't see how a thing like cricket can make you forget seeing people!"

"Oh, don't you! Obviously there's nothing more to be said."

Iris is sure there must be *some* explanation, whereupon the esteemed doctor interrupts. He has known cases where "a sudden shock or blow has induced the most vivid impressions." Such vivid impressions would not seem like (only) impressions to the suddenly shocked mind (albeit we are all beneficiaries of nothing so much as impressions). Compared with the world outside the theater, is cinema a "sudden blow"? And, tranquilly, "It's not a question of belief. Even a simple concussion may have serious effects upon an imaginative person." We saw when she announced her intention to join the aristocracy how Iris is "an imaginative person." And we saw the windowbox strike: no kiss. Concussion + imagination = effects. This diagnostic patter is of course pointing to our own absorption with cinema.

There is much to be noted about the disappearance of Miss Froy as part of this narrative, or, better, much about Iris's conviction that there was a Miss Froy who disappeared. I would suggest that the viewer who is utterly convinced Iris is right, at this exact point in the film, is not treating their own processing of the filmic moment very thoroughly, because this "Miss Froy" as person or idea is now, and wholly, only in the fast-receding wake of the past. Consider:

- Iris discovers an empty seat where she imagines the lady was sitting, this only after awakening from a sleep, which will have "[made] her feel quite well again." Quite well = quite different. Still, she may feel herself to be the person she was before. A journey to Before. Last night at the inn, she only perfunctorily glanced at Miss Froy. We glanced at her doing this, and also at the old lady who was in her glance, but Iris is not us at any rate.

- Iris's compartment-mates are splendidly equivocal. Beret mimes, but then suddenly speaks. The wife and child are without language. The Baroness is more than fluent, but her sharp reserve makes her seem hostile, generally. Are we seeing quirks or secrecy?

- Look at the idiosyncrasies—each floating in vacuum space: the various denials of Miss Froy, each personal and authoritative, down to the steward riffling through his bill receipts or Beret's gregarious introduction of his family and his child (born in 1934!). Though we gain no useful information about Miss Froy—who seems at this moment to be a hypothesis—we amass a deal of useless information, that here and now merely fills time and mental storage space. Our thought is stimulated, our memory vexed. The doctor regaling his listeners *in detail* about the operation he will perform tonight. Read William James's excellent essay "The Perception of Reality" to find that a telltale signal inducing us to take things as "real" is the presence of replete and/or confirming information, the small details: "Among other things a cranial fracture with compression."

And then watch Hitchcock's preparation for the simple unfolding of this "reality," while a train moves:

Iris Henderson. As, certainly concussed, she leans out of the train to wave goodbye to her pals she has a delirious vision. We have special access to her perception and state of mind: blurry, weak, circling, and begging help. A perceptive, evaluating, ascertaining mind has been wounded, perhaps severely.

Miss Froy. A giver of the little handkerchief soaked in cologne to put to the forehead for balm; then a shepherd to guide Iris for an invigorating cup of tea; then producer of pleasant, in no way painful conversational distraction, like a living music box. When a person is concussed, mental focus is difficult (Dr Hartz will testify to this), so distraction is a comfort. This kind lady is not someone to be carefully examined, more like dainty lace to be worn at the neckline.

Gilbert Redman. The clarinetist (it will be some time still before we know his name) picks up on his encounter with Iris the night before, much as a musician might restate a theme to make a variation. Unsurprisingly, he is very good with language and his language will help: as he takes over questioning people on Iris's behalf he is articulate and precise in his questions, and also courteous. Because of his articulateness, well established before the moments when it will be necessary, there is never an ambiguity in the interrogations; never a chance for us to wonder whether the question came through clearly enough. And he is also multilingual, able to interview the Baroness in her mother tongue. Since he is never churlish we will not be shocked if he becomes affectionate.

Todhunter. A nervous man disavows having seen Iris and Miss Froy together: less fact than posture, we may be thinking, since he did see them, didn't he?! and didn't we see him seeing? (How well, as we watch a shot in a film, do we remember shots that came before? That is: do we remember better or worse than Iris does?) Why put forward a lie? Were he an abject liar, or a man with bad eyesight or a faulty memory, he would be tedious; but a man with a secret is interesting, even if we do not really learn much about the secret. Perhaps he fears to be caught in his liaison, will refuse to be caught up as witness. Todhunter's secret will turn out to be charged enough to believably panic him, yet conventional enough not to gain too much attention from us. We do not—and must not—care about him.

Tea. The waiter disavows Iris's claim that Miss Froy gave him special tea: he used the train's own supply. Since the claim of the special tea resides upon the existence of a woman who could have offered it, and since for the waiter that woman is apparently in question, there is no particular reason for believing in the special tea. As to the steward: he would surely not find a bill for "tea for two" if there were in fact no Miss Froy and if, therefore, Iris had drunk tea by herself. The more doubt seems to attach itself to Iris's claims, the more we doubt her as the claimer; else the more elaborate must be other people's duplicity. Not to forget that the little tea party was a therapy for a young woman in mental distress. With brain injury, you can look perfectly fine while being entirely out of the picture.

Father's boy. Gilbert comes to believe Iris. Why? Because his father taught him never to deny help to a lady in distress. If at the moment Iris is a lady in distress, after next Thursday she is going to be a Lady, perhaps also in distress. Without his father's lessons in propriety Gilbert has no reason to go out of his way for this young woman unless, of course, he finds her attractive, and at first that twist is not even hinted at.

Hunting. Iris carries on her search for Miss Froy—someone *now* who will seem like someone from *back then*—in two zones at once. She searches on this train, back and forth, in and out as it shuttles down the track; and she searches in her memory, for the face, the voice, the telltale evidence. As she navigates the train she must be a thinker to navigate, and so she is managing thinking and remembering both, *not together*, and all this challenge for a brain that has had a shock.

Dr Hartz. Egon Hartz (Paul Lukas) gives expert testimony in the court of public opinion as to Iris's state of mind. He has been recognized by Gilbert as having just returned from saving a politician's life in England, thus as being internationally eminent; and has advertised himself further as expert in neurological matters through a discussion, however brief, of a surgery he will perform this evening. When he lectures Iris that he has known many cases of concussion that have led victims to imagine things, he is planting a seed—not only in her but also in the viewer, who must now begin to wonder, trying hard to look back to the movie that has gone by so far (and with speed) about whether there really was a little old English lady at all. As movies are always moving forward, one cannot really look back. Under the musical tone of the name "Froy," sounded over and over, is there, was there a person?

What we could possibly remember: (a) humming a folk song; (b) offering cheese, "awfully rich in vitamins"; (c) rapture about glorious Mandrika and the mountains; (d) tossing a coin down as tip; (e) having lost a suitcase.

But the plummeting windowbox that hits Iris escorts us away from Miss Froy, rudely, notwithstanding (f) perfectly charming tea-time stories that are also perfectly forgettable—only the sing-song voice, floating away; and (g) fingering a name onto the window, like inscribing a manifesto in sand before the tide; and (h) the ditty, FROY rhymes with "joy": cute... but does it prove anything? What if Miss Froy really isn't on the train, and wasn't, and won't be? And is an invention... FROY rhymes with toy.

She is not presently present to the eyes.

And if we cannot participate somehow in Iris's conundrum, cannot actually wonder about this Miss Froy, even just a little, the whole film finally collapses as thin parody. We must, we do, we cannot but participate.

Let's try for details of a potential memory and proof—keeping in mind that *memory* is one thing and current stipulation of detail another and that they are perhaps incompatible:

- Do we remember the folksong the old lady was humming? Could we hum it as she did? Or have we already generalized it in our thinking (and memory) as "only some folksong-type-thing"?
- Can we be sure she offered Charters and Caldicott cheese? There isn't any now. Why would she offer two ravenously hungry men a morsel of cheese? (You may surely claim she did because I am telling you she did; but beyond that I am giving you a word voyage to trip along with, why would you believe me?)
- Her little speech to Iris—have children, children are wonderful—is a lullaby-bore. So many people preach this, can we really be sure we heard it from those old lips, if old lips existed?
- The coin tossed to the ground could have sprung from anywhere. Whose coin? Thrown why?
- The suitcase Miss Froy purportedly "lost" on the platform: we never saw her with any suitcase if we saw her at all. If we saw what I said earlier we saw (earlier at a point you have probably now forgotten) she had a purse and a letter. It might be worth noting that this suitcase now vanishes from the story.

- Iris woozy on the train: might not a concussive blow produce hallucination? She would not be the first person to hallucinate what she desires.

- The glyph on the window, visible only because another train was passing. So far she has not returned to seek it. And other trains have not passed. Was it there?

- And if she remembers much about her chafe last night with Gilbert he might cause her some mistrust, just enough to doubt him when he says he trusts her. Who is he anyway?

Hitchcock has arranged that if we are to believe in Charters, in Caldicott, in Todhunter, in the girlfriend, in Boris, in Anna, in Julie, in Blanche, in Signior Beret, in his wife, in his child (born in 1934!), in the Baroness, in the waiter, in the steward, and in the doctor, not to say in Gilbert and Iris herself, we have no rational reason for not believing in Miss Froy. Yet of all these characters she is the one whose presence is most doubtful. Perhaps she was a sweet little lady, so sweet as to melt in the air.

About denials:

Charters, Caldicott, Todhunter (and by implication his "Mrs") all deny the existence of Miss Froy and, having known them longer we feel somewhat closer to their observations than to those of the new folk we meet on the train. All the newcomers—even Dr Hartz—are relatively oblique, even eccentric and hard to read. Given that they seem to come out of nowhere, on what reason could we conclude they are lying about this "Miss Froy" or about anything? So, we have some reason for suspecting they speak the truth about a figure who either doesn't exist or has never been seen. Beret looked glazed to begin with, perhaps he doesn't see well; the Señora haughty and disattentive. The steward and the waiter were caught up with their jobs. The doctor is so full of what he knows he cannot see what is in front of him. And as to our old friends who were at the inn, the film is structured very tightly to show how each has a very definite and practical reason for either (1) not wanting the train delayed or (2) not wanting their names and faces brought into public light; in short, each has every good reason for refusing to feed Iris the answers she is so hungry for, and indeed more: every good reason for not bringing themselves to believe they did see the lady (whom we will be likely to persist in claiming we did see, too). Whenever we claim we did see someone or something, we have brought ourselves to believe in that remembrance. The folks from the inn are reasonable to themselves, even if lying; so may the new folk on the train be reasonable to themselves, too. A number of disconnected arrangements may be in place at once, intersecting on the presumable face of Miss Froy.

Reader: If you are thinking you remember Miss Froy, and therefore that you know the true dispensation of every playing card on the table, so be it; but could you be influenced by the fact that in these many pages past you have seen the word "Froy" many times asserted in print and thus believe she must not be invented? (Miss Froy is of course wholly invented.) The problem we face in the middle of a film is that while perceiving the hunt action of the present we do not and cannot simultaneously remember the creatures of the long-gone forest. Dante sings it:

> Midway in the journey of our life I found myself in a dark wood,
> for the straight way was lost.
> (*Inferno* I)

Plenty of discussions of *The Lady Vanishes* pursue intricacies of the narrative from this juncture onward. But the issue is not what happens or does not happen to the presumed Miss Froy, or as a result of the presumed Miss Froy, or around the presumed Miss Froy; or even whether Iris is correct in her belief in the existence of Miss Froy; but *the fact that agonies of memory can be established in relation to her,* that she is at once both memorable and forgettable, and that in order to think about her one must accept the impossibility of remembering a fleeting past as one reflects upon a fleeting present. On top of this conundrum, the film proceeds down the hardly straightforward pathway of implicating its viewer in the throes of head trauma. It points to a concussion discursively; but in its form it offers the viewer a virtual concussion in direct experience.[15] Yet does not film always somehow do this as we watch?

LOOKING BACK

Hitchcock makes every backward gaze through the narrative—what came just before this, leading this way?—seem natural and undeniable and every forward gaze as obscure as British fog, but in doing so produces something else. There are constant, subtle allusions to an extra-diegetic world that *we are never given to see* but are obliged to presume exists. The extradiegetic Hitchcockian world that is never a fantasy: a real social environment with a class structure, a history of biography and event, a climate in evidence, a scale of probability in regards to happening... and all not explicitly on the screen. Hitchcock is not the only filmmaker to do this, but his way of doing it is notably replete, sophisticated, subtle, involved, and expressly elegant.

[1] *Chime.* The wall clock chimes in the opening scene, a tiny door opening upon a soldier who steps out and salutes before retiring. Soldier time:

   [a] Theater and narrative time will pass during this sequence anyway, there is no stop-time, so an explicit temporal reference is neither surprising nor, for the case of the opening of this film, necessary. Nothing in the action calls for a character to know the time. Explicit time is not in the scene. As well,

   [b] had Hitchcock wanted to signal only time passing, the fact that seconds are flying away, any clock would have done as long as it were audible or visible. This clock entertains, but also:

   [c] notably alludes to the military. The time passing here in this inn, if not also in Mandrika, is military time. Or: the military has more to do with what is going on in this country than we are being told. Military force will have its place in the film, signaled early, here, through a symbolic notation of its absence.

[2] *The Baroness and the Lady.* The Baroness (Mary Clare) stares directly at Iris (directly into the lens) to assert that there is "no English lady here." On one level she refers (categorically) to the (absent) personage about whom Iris has been asking, described by Iris as an "English lady." (The Baroness was staring out the window as Miss Froy offered Iris the eau

de cologne.) "English lady," as in female and adult. But what we are seeing as we hear these words is a blunt portrait of the Baroness, who is not merely an adult female but, pointedly, a Lady. A Lady speaks of a missing lady. Or of a missing Lady? "There is no English lady here" also means "There is no English Lady here," this conceivably a pointer not to some "imagined person" but to Iris herself, the girl who is about to become, but *has not become yet*, an English Lady. Is the Baroness giving a warning? ... Or is the Baroness asserting, "There *is* certainly a Lady here (me), but she is not English!"

[3] *Signor Doppo, Magician.* Doppo, the man in the beret (Philip Leaver), shows that he is a magician by entertaining his child with a little trick. We will soon witness his magic in a more nefarious vein. But there is a silent overtone: that the "disappearance of Miss Froy" could be another of Doppo's "disappearings," a trick on a higher order—yet not so high as the trick directed by Hitchcock, who makes characters appear and disappear at will, in the case of Miss Froy with a simple edit. This wonder of cinema, that a creature can vibrate before our eyes and suddenly not be there, goes all the way back to Georges Méliès and before him to a Buatier de Kolta 1886 stage trick, "The Vanishing Lady." Hitchcock's is the subtler magic.

Regarding disappearance (and Miss Froy) we may reflect on Laurent Mannoni's teaching: an impression "lasts for some time after the disappearance of [an] object" and "does not itself disappear instantaneously; it is more probable that it decreases gradually to nothing" and thus we cannot "assign to it a precise duration" (208). Nothing is unnatural about Iris's retention of a strong impression of Miss Froy after the person herself is no longer present to stimulate her senses; or at least about Iris's conviction that she has such a retention. Perhaps the impression was started in the inn, and she is retaining it from there.... In failing to adduce this fact as part of his "diagnostic" discourse the doctor makes something of a faux pas. Do we also retain impressions of what (of whom) we imagine we saw? Are such impressions the same as visions, or are they more like dreams?

Hitchcock is fully aware that a trace memory of Miss Froy may be resting with his viewers, too—she was carefully introduced before vanishing, but even the vanishing may vanish if our attention is redirected to something present and engaging. To make a case: note how in the elaborate chain of opening sequences, every one of the characters introduced is dancing in a kind of circus, surrounded by desperate action, comedy, strain, strangeness; and no one character, not even an old English governess if she is there, is framed to stand out. Hitchcock uses all his skills of narrative construction to confound persistence of vision enough that Iris's conundrum will be felt, that is, experienced by us as we watch her experiencing it. Dramatically the emphasis must shift from the old lady to the young one, to her insistence upon a claim; from manifest presence to proposition. How certain can we be about Iris's claim? How certain is she?

[4] *Caldicott (and Charters).* Who is this man who does not regard England as his country yet sounds so British? What, beneath the addiction to cricket, is his bond to Charters, to journeying through Europe, to his own presence on this train? These two never stop thinking of a test match that is alive in their frustrated minds, but nonexistent for us.

[5] *Fear.* Todhunter's incomparable clumsiness suggests he has not had extramarital affairs before. But his girlfriend has, and cannot quite grasp what so daunts him. His continual panic at being "caught out" is that of the amateur criminal who after thieving is positive someone will point to him. No one this man is likely to run into in Mandrika will care a whit whether he's sleeping in the young woman's bed or not. Her knowing this is what peeves her at his prurience. And some gender politique in 1938: the eagerness for casual sex is hers, not his. We may begin to wonder if his motive for the *liaison dangereuse* is freeing himself from an imprisoner elsewhere, of whom we see nothing, whereas she intends to divorce someone named Robert, similarly invisible.

[6] *The Doctoral Manifestation.* Along with other people, including Doppo, his wife, his child, and the Baroness, Dr Hartz seems vivaciously present, yet we did not see him climb aboard. He was not at the inn, nor were the others. Did they sleep on the train with "no 'eat"? Rabbits out of a hat.

[7] *A cuppa.* Miss Froy shares a widespread British assumption, that foreigners do not know how to brew a proper cup of tea: "Make sure

the water is *really* boiling!" A special tea when one is away from home, but where is home? Where did Miss Froy learn her unimpeachable manners? Not Mandrika. Nor would we imagine Mandrika to be the origin of Harriman's Herbal.

[8] *Rule, Britannia.* A beautiful, but fleeting, portrait of British snobbery is given as we watch Charters and Caldicott sharing Anna's small bed and being wrapped up in the *Herald Tribune.* This American paper, published in the 1930s with offices in Paris, is an English-language daily aimed at American tourists across Europe, who want to "keep up" with home. But these two Brits aren't reading about home; they are trapped in an article—that we do not see—about baseball, inferior to the sport of their dreams. Everything resonates "cricket," even what isn't cricket. And cricket isn't here.

[9] *Creation.* Dr Hartz attributes to Iris a "creative" personality, suggests that under sufficient stress from a head wound she might create an imaginary world, including, perhaps, a "friend." Such a world is offscreen, in Iris's head and heart.

The viewer will shriek: *"But I saw!!!"* Yes, but as far as the characters go, *who are you?*

Albeit all these seeds of wonder and seeds of doubt will grow, it is vital to see that Hitchcock arranges his moments instead of merely presenting them. Iris, Gilbert by her side, is forced to remember everything she can about her interactions with, her perception and experience of this non-visible English lady as she tries to convince not only other people but also—perhaps principally—herself that the person was truly there. If she is to remember, there must be a past to ground a memory. Nothing and no one can vanish, after all, without being here in the first place.[16] And even if remembering it we look *back* to the past, the past occurred *before* our looking back. And what is *looking back?*

One further comment about viewer "certainty." In film, all film, all of the characters we meet we only "meet"; not a one of them is truly there. The state of mind which is occupying dazed Iris is very similar to the moviegoer's, beset by "encounters" that seem like encounters, "concussed" by the phenomenon of cinema. It can be enlightening to think how, when we look back fondly on a film that we were happy to see, so much of what we would claim to remember we only "remember"; how much as we reinhabit that magical space *"there"* was never there in the first place.[17] The intrusion of a tiny poetic mantra like "FROY rhymes with joy" penetrates consciousness, more lyrical than plain statement and more indubitable than visual presence. But a mantra, like a melody, isn't quite there, either.

PROOF OF LIFE

Insufficient attention has been paid Iris Henderson's state of mind at the moment she begins her train voyage. That is, one easily presumes her to be as sharp-minded, astute, eagerly perceptive, and sensible as we think we are watching her. I have tried above to detail some of the equivocations built into the film's structure about (a) the way and circumstances in which Iris came to Miss Froy's particular attention and Miss Froy to hers: an attenuated, even inconsequential mutual sighting in a corridor; a half hello on a train platform; a brutally interrupted thought of handing over eyeglasses; (b) Iris's multiply focused attention as, preparing to leave her friends (old friends? recent friends?) and make passage into a new life, she sees those eyeglasses and darts off with them (spontaneously to be sure, yet so perspicaciously that later in the baggage car, on the instant, she can recognize them); and (c) the concussion she sustains, in itself, its weakening effects; not to mention (d) her demonstrated perceptual trouble as the train pulls out (a special optical process to convey it) and then (e) the rather quirky experience she has of the old lady when she pops awake, drinks some tea, and drops asleep again—rather like Alice in Wonderland. The overall encounter could well be described as fragmentary and flighty at once; fragmentary because no single meeting is rounded to any fulness, flighty because Miss Froy has a very charming little babble, a country brook in the sunshine, and is full of wisdoms, reflections, meanderings, and general goodnesses that lack a coherent design as they ramble away. (Compare the doctor's definitiveness; or Gilbert's sharp teasing.) Concussed, she has more than just a sore head; she has perceptual, balance, and memory trouble to some degree and has had her logical powers assailed. For Iris reflecting back, then, could not Miss Froy be part of a dream, like the White Queen?

> The White Queen only looked at her in a helpless frightened sort of way and kept repeating something in a whisper to herself that sounded like "bread-and-butter, bread-and-butter" and Alice felt that if there was to be any conversation at all, she must manage it herself. (Carroll 120)

Managing a conversation oneself! Supplying both sides of a conversation! Iris's strange sensory impairment reflects the true condition of the viewing audience (who love to think they are watching the film but, given a very great deal to see at every moment, cannot take it all in):

[1] *Sight.* In cinema the power of sight is primary (and primal), so that seeing and knowing are indistinguishable. This, albeit one chooses what to make prominent in one's consideration, thus sees in a limited way. Jonathan Crary reflects John Dewey:

> In attention we focus the mind, as the lens takes all the light coming to it, and instead of allowing it to distribute itself evenly concentrates it in a point of great light and heat. So the mind, instead of diffusing consciousness over all the elements presented to it, brings it all to bear upon *some one selected point* which stands out with unusual *brilliancy and distinctness*. (Dewey 134, qtd. in Crary, *Suspensions* 24, my emphases)

For Dewey, Crary shows, the mental faculties of the mind are, precisely, focused, so that the analogy with the photographic lens can be made apt. If the mind seeks focus, surely the focal act seeks mental resonance. And the target of mental concentration, *some one selected point or plane*, is qualified not by importance or weight or richness but, specifically, by *brilliancy and distinctness*, again purely visual qualities. The mind sees. Mentality is visual. But also, seeing is mental. And so optical disempowerment, such as Iris suffers, makes for cloudiness of thought. And cloudiness of thought may similarly produce cloudy vision.

Let me give an example. When in the film's concluding sequence the train comes to a stop in a forest, we are given to concentrate on the remaining passengers—Iris, Gilbert, the "Todhunters"—as they are confronted by Hartz, the Baroness, and a uniformed battalion outside. Shooting is taking place. We are concentrating on the action, eager to see what happens to each of the bodies we recognize. But at the same time, it is made evident outside the train that the *forest is filled with pines*. This is the second great reference in the work to the northern setting, say (as Fiedler does in *Vanishing American*) its gothic quality. We are far from the slumbering lassitudes of the Mediterranean, and the quick temper, and the burning passion. This is the evergreen land of rationality, calculation, investigation, even, as with Hartz, brain surgery. And a central motif that has turned our action has been memory, brain power itself. But to think along these lines, and here I forego any further development because I simply want to point to the vision, one would have to look *past* the active protagonists in and outside the railway car, and note a particular feature of the "background" that has gained foreground pertinence. Typically we don't do that here. The forest itself is not apprehended as *brilliant and distinct*. Memory played a central role, too, in another of Hitchcock's "northerns," *The 39 Steps* (1935).

[2] *Hearing.* When there is no sound, writes R. Murray Schafer,

> it is said that there is no hearing, but that does not mean that hearing has lost its preparedness. Indeed, when there is no sound, hearing is most alert, and when there is sound the hearing nature is least developed. (*Tuning* 259)

The empty seat confronting Iris as she awakens from her slumber is an index of soundlessness, the absent sound being the prattling voice of Miss Froy, especially at the tea. Such a lullaby, diddle-de-da; the up-and-down nature of her organic melody a bird's chirrup. But can we remember what she said?! She was making a good-hearted attempt to soothe and refresh her new young friend. But for Iris, the overabundance of sound—exacerbated by the roar of the passing train—reduces the development of her hearing, makes her operatively deaf. The more Miss Froy says, the less one can hear her, so that memory finally attaches to her little mantra about Froy and joy, very tidy and pointed and abrupt, thus audible. But audible is not memorable.

[3] *Touch.* As to touch, we can think on Ortega's observation about proximate vision, that it "has a tactile quality":

> We shall not now attempt to violate this mystery. It is enough that we recognize this quasi-tactile density possessed by the ocular ray, and which permits it, in effect, to embrace, to touch the earthen jar. As the object is withdrawn, sight loses its tactile power and gradually becomes pure vision.... An age-old habit, founded in vital necessity, causes men to consider as "things," in the strict sense, only such objects solid enough to offer resistance to their hands. The rest is more or less illusion. (111)

Let us say Miss Froy has gone outside the bounds of touch. But a second reflection brings us to realize that in social relations, most especially with strangers, touch is almost exclusively replaced by language formation. We speak our intentions of intimacy until climactic points when touch is possible and desirable, but this is far from what is happening between Iris and Miss Froy. Miss Froy is not to be touched, ever; "more or less illusion." When we discover that she *has* been touched, in fact that the medical plan is to *touch her further, and soon*, we are chilled.

[4] *Smell.* And of course Iris will not be tasting Miss Froy in any way; suffice it to say that in human relations outside of cannibalism and rapt sexuality, the sense of taste plays only a negligible role. We taste instead the culinary preparations offered to us in generosity. Tasting one's friend's cooking is tasting one's friend.

In sight, hearing, touch, and taste, then, Iris is in a very weakened state if not utterly disempowered. We see her experiencing sensory deprivation much more clearly than she sees Miss Froy. But there is one sensual contact that, curiously, is undiluted for Iris and entirely impossible for us, and that is smell. Miss Froy offers a handkerchief soaked in eau de cologne, to apply to the girl's forehead as a reviver. There is a long history to the use of eau de cologne and other fragrances for purposes such as this, and whilst parfumerie began culturally for, and among, the upper classes it quickly spread; so that a governess and music teacher like Miss Froy can as easily by 1900 own perfume as can the Baroness. Here is Alain Corbin:

> The majority of [early fragrance] names were connected with the aristocracy and the ruling families. Haute parfumerie thereby acknowledged its close links with European courts. Its spread was partly due to the immense popularity of royal couples in the middle years of the Third Republic.... Over the decades, the aesthetics of the sense of smell became commonplace; the moderate price of perfumed soaps, the industrial manufacture of eau de cologne, the expansion of the network of drapers who distributed the products of perfumery enlarged the range of the clientele.... The downward social mobility of eau de cologne was evidence that the poor man too had joined the battle against the putrid odor of his secretions. (199)

With an application of scent, eradicating and enriching, reviving and mysterious—yet also entirely forgettable—Miss Froy can make herself intelligible, tangible, visible, distinct, and brilliant for Iris, and swiftly, too, as in the breath of a wind; although we must take all of this under advisement, since in gazing at the screen we are without smell. The screen is without smell and the script is without reference to it, too.

HALLUCINATIONS

The reflection of Stanislaw Lem's narrator in *Tales of Pirx the Pilot*, that if he should chance to see a dead acquaintance in public he would sooner believe in a resurrection than admit to his own insanity, is a cogent reflection on the massive change in attitudes toward visual perception begun in the nineteenth century. The new vision is discussed by Jonathan Crary who, in *Techniques of the Observer*, adduces Johannes Müller's *Handbuch der Physiologie des Menschen* (1833) and the signal importance of this work in raising consideration of "a body with an innate capacity, one might even say a transcendental faculty, to *misperceive*—of an eye that renders differences equivalent" (*Techniques* 90). Crary discerns how "vision [has been] redefined as a capacity for being affected by sensations that have no necessary link to a reference, thus imperiling any coherent system of meaning" (91). Almost a decade later Crary is addressing "the idea of subjective vision," namely, "a severing (or liberation) of perceptual experience from a necessary relation to an exterior world" (*Suspensions* 12). As Paul Cézanne told Joachim Gasquet, "Everything we look at disperses and disappears, doesn't it? Nature is always the same, but nothing remains of it, of what appears to us" (in Cachin et al. 52).

Complications upon complications in *The Lady Vanishes*. The good doctor is of the professional opinion that Iris has had a hallucination. "You know, there is no Miss Froy. There never was a Miss Froy. Merely a vivid subjective image." He is thinking back to Alfred Binet's "disease of external perception." And of course, to give this medical school graduate (another one who is not really there) his proper due, there really is no Miss Froy, but like Iris (who is also not there) we will decline vigorously to accept that fact while we are watching the film.

A vivid subjective image, merely.

"I met her last night at the hotel.—"

"You thought you did."

It need not be elaborated how the passionate subjective feeling of attachment to an object of esteem or beauty can aggrandize it in our minds; seeing someone we feel at the instant we would like to meet can cause us to come into the belief that we are meeting, that we have met, them. Spectators have this sense about figures of the screen all the time: the fan's "knowledge" of the adored one.

Yet: at the hotel the extended Rossiniesque overture had so many flighty characters, so many expostulations, arms stretching, faces growling—who is to abstract a single *brilliant and distinct* figure to remember her?

The benevolent smile on Dr Hartz's avuncular, ingratiating face as, sweetly, he speaks to Iris: it can be registered, from the exact angle at which Hitchcock gives it, as being directed our way just as well, and we can relax to some degree into an assurance the man is at least trying to be helpful in regards to this vanished woman we never saw him see: this woman who, for him, "never did exist." We met her last night at the hotel too, didn't we. Or did we meet her? (The woman's name doesn't come out until the tea party on the train.) Last night she was associated with a morsel of cheese and a melody. Now the doctor gives reassurance that we only thought we met her, indeed that we only think it now: we met her in our thoughts. Again, for exactness: we cherish the illusion of having met a woman *in the past, here now* as we conjure our own history. Is Hartz perhaps describing to Iris with excruciating exactness what has been happening to us? His statement, "There is no Miss Froy," could not be more apt, although it flies in the face of our attachment to the narrative. This contraposition of viewer belief and narrative construction is one of Hitchcock's favorite dances. When we see a picture of an apple are we seeing an apple? The rattling of the brain can produce a conundrum like this, in regard to so-called reality. When a lady sits before us on a train and offers eau de cologne (that we cannot smell), how accurate can our befuddled perception be?

But the doctor must excuse himself because the train is now pulling into the station where his patient will come aboard. A tiny village station. The man takes long-legged strides along the platform to meet bearers holding a stretcher with a fully bandaged figure. A fully cloaked nun stands by. The patient is loaded aboard while from a pair of matching side windows Gilbert and Iris search the exterior on either side for Miss Froy, to no avail. What, here, are we paying attention to? There are so many things to watch it is difficult while watching also to *watch for*.

An argument heats up in Todhunter's compartment. He (Cecil Parker) wants promotion to the bench—a lawyer, of course!—and will not be involved in any scandal (a judge's purity, Hitchcock's joke; see on judges *The Paradine Case* [1947]). Thus, he explains to his grilling girlfriend (Linden Travers), he denied having seen Miss Froy. She wants a divorce and he shuns the scandal of being involved with that, too. And his own wife will never divorce him. Awareness is dawning on her. She goes out and confronts Iris. "I saw your friend." Bolstered, relieved, excited, Iris now confronts the doctor who says no, his theory is not defective but the facts are wrong (a good, solid medical analysis). And now, with gusto, here is Signor Doppo, excited to announce, in his (signally useful) fractured English, that "your friend" has returned and is in the compartment! The bliss of resolution . . .

At the door to the compartment, however, Iris and Gilbert see a very strange woman slowly turn to look up at them. Dressed in Froyish tweeds, with a perky little hat and a flat Germanic face. This one is certainly not Miss Froy, she is Madame Kummer (Josephine Wilson). *She* is the person Iris saw. The doctor has come to watch. Yes, Madame Kummer did meet Miss Henderson at the hotel, "I, not Miss Froy." Oh, she must be the wrong person entirely! Or must she? Could we swear absolutely that Madame Kummer didn't meet Iris at the hotel? To go back to the hotel in memory how very much must we traverse! And memory is the only vehicle, because in cinema there is no going back.

Multilingual Gilbert translates. Madame Kummer is pleased to accompany Iris and him to the Todhunter compartment where the girlfriend is presented to her. When "Mrs Todhunter" is asked if this is the woman she saw, she looks up with calculation behind her eyes and says it is. A purely self-centered act on her part: if she can't marry this man there is nothing to be gained for her by shoving him into the middle of the kind of authentic scandal a missing person would bring on; but also, if he won't marry her he is a cur, and now she can make him into a liar. As in repeated other examples, side characters are shown to have the very best of reasons for making statements that will throw Iris off the track. This woman is fed up with the whole business, we may surmise with the trip to Europe also, with Todhunter, with herself for being his "wife." Back in the compartment now, troubled Iris sees the image of Miss Froy gazing at her exactly where Madame Kummer is sitting. (The bedevilment of a Hitchcock image, in this case an optically printed double exposure!) The same face over Doppo's wife, too. And over the Baroness. And over Doppo himself, now grinning slyly. Madame Kummer glares and frowns. Why are so many people going to the trouble of convincing Iris that Miss Froy is not there? Or: why after such a flurry of action are we convinced that many people are going to trouble, and that there was a Miss Froy?

But for the eau de cologne, were Iris to question herself in a rigorous Cartesian mode she would doubtless discover that it is only because she believes in what she sees and hears, and because she believes she can remember what she saw and heard—remember while concussed—that she concludes there was a Miss Froy. And in the face of all things living and dead, all things past and to come, all things here and in the universe, would her own conviction in her own sight and hearing, now and then, be sufficient? Yet, would God deceive her? And that relieving aroma...(forbidden)...

Hitchcock's narrational predicament at the moment: he knows that should his audience leap too swiftly and irrevocably to the conclusion that, indisputably, Iris is correct, then he would be left with no more than a whodunit in which an action has been committed for reasons as yet unknown upon a little English lady who is gone. This is the kind of architectural model that would be far less likely to fascinate Hitchcock than it would his many incompetent imitators. He wants to bring us to much more alarming territory, and "Miss Froy" is the gamepiece to jog us. We are to wonder about hallucination, in Iris's case one that turns every living person around her into a phantasmal reprise of an invented personage with a life wholly bounded by her own imagination. The viewer's ultimate need to eclipse Iris for a test upon Miss Froy is Hitchcock's reason for introducing the scenes at the inn where Miss Froy is seen but not with Iris—except that we find people she was with all denying her. Only the viewer remains.

Iris leaps up in defeat and confronts Gilbert who has been standing in the corridor. "The doctor is right. You're all right.... I'm afraid it didn't happen. I know now." And we wonder, of course, if she is just resigned to defeat; or if she believes what she is saying. If she has been deluded how is Iris signally different from any of us, who actually hold a belief in what we think we see? To put this more sharply: when we think we see the wind blowing through the sunny leaves, and when we think we see Miss Froy having tea with Iris, are these two thoughts about seeing, different kinds of thoughts? With Miss Froy, *we know* we are looking at a moving picture but we do not *see* that we are looking at a moving picture; and with the leaves, we know that *we are not looking at a picture of leaves* but we do not *see* that we are not looking.

Her "watchdog" Gilbert takes her to the dining car for something to eat (in this way reprising earlier action).

They place themselves at the same little table we visited earlier and with which we are now cozy: an imperative of the staging. Before anything happens, we are to remember that table, and think that Iris will do the same. And what is it here that provokes our memory, since this is, after all, a table like many other tables in this dining car? This moment of recognition: oh! I know this!

He lowers the window, but as he sits back down and she reflects unconsciously we find ourselves looking past the two of them and seeing, without mistake, F R O Y fingered upon the window. Again, a trick: the glyphs of the letters make, we are certain, indication of a finger that etched them; the finger pointing to a person. The problem of worrying about when characters we admire will catch up with us and know what we already know is a frequent Hitchcock imposition, too.[18] Still not having looked over at that window, Iris says she doesn't want to make her fiancé a nervous wreck. Suddenly Gilbert is crestfallen—oh, she's getting married. But his wit remains: "Quite sure you haven't imagined that?" Is he wishing she were (just) imagining that and not really about to do it—that is, is he murmuring to himself, "I think I am falling for you"? He begins to prate about his father, "a very colorful character," as she declines a bowl of soup and asks for tea, looking down morosely. Looking down in thought. Looking down in time travel.

"Harriman's Herbal Tea," she mumbles, "a million Mexicans drink it." As he looks up at her, with soup spoon in hand she recalls, "Miss Froy gave the waiter a packet of it."

"Packet of what?"

"Harriman's Herbal Tea. She said it was the only sort she liked."

He has told her to try to make her mind a complete blank, and encourages again now. She relents, abandons Harriman's tea and Miss Froy, and lets him go on about his father. His father was a "very remarkable man" and he couldn't help inheriting his love of music. These two are surely growing on each other, his smile is distinctly less cynical that it was before—in truth he's ineffably shy—and her eyes are shining. Right now he's writing a book on folk dancing, "Would you like to buy a copy?" In a natural way, an unreflected way, almost as though she is a living creature moving to gain the blessing of a ray of sun, she shifts her eyes window-ward and her head a little, too. "Do you know why you fascinate me? . . . You're always seeing things. . . ."

She is staring hard now. Seeing things?

"Well, what's the matter?"

Nodding firmly. "Look!" And as the train sounds its whistle shrilly (to wake the audience up), we see the code name scrawled on the window, plain as day, but instantly the train enters a tunnel. Quickly in the gloom they are without sight, and afterward the name is gone. "Miss Froy's name on the window! You saw it, you must have seen it! She's on the train!!" She gets up, strides to the end of the car, swivels, and orates to the multitude. "Listen, everybody: There's a woman on this train, some of you must have seen her, they're hiding her from me." The doctor has stood from his table and is rushing forward as she finishes, "I appeal to you, all of you, to stop the train." To the doctor, imploring: "Please help me, please make them stop the train. . . . Do you hear? Why don't you do something before it's too late?" To Gilbert, over her shoulder, "For heaven's sake, stop this train!!!!" Again the whistle sounds a long shrill call—the sound of Iris's true heart—and she tears away from Gilbert and the Doctor, rushes to where the emergency brake pull hangs, and tugs down hard on it. A portrait shot of her, hand clutching the brake pull, fierce and grim resolve on her face. She collapses into the camera's welcoming pit of darkness.

TRICKS

How cooperative is the engineer driving this train for those who would wish to engage with the film's adventure, since at every critical instant, every instant of special, piercing crisis he whistles. The train is an inherent contradiction. It supplies, supports, houses, and promotes the villains who have hidden Miss Froy away (do not fear) but at the same time whistles us cheerily along, and with so precise an intelligence. Every Hitchcock film has some indication of his "authorial" presence—I mean not a cameo but some stand-in as his openly declared agent. Here the stand-in is the train.

The train is a kind of magical cabinet for "disappearing lady" tricks.

The collapse into darkness as she stops the vehicle is a convenient point of transition for Iris, who is now, in her own mind at least, certain beyond certainty that Miss Froy is real and somehow present. Audiences can find it tedious to watch a character who is genuinely—realistically—insane because in their own logic characters must always be sane. Should Iris rant without fading to darkness we would have to follow the neutral or negative effects of the rant, and this would be cumbersome and inefficacious. Too much attention to Iris herself, Iris as one who might have interesting defects and is, if she does have them, only flawed as we are. What we need is a figurehead leading the hunt through the story. A pleasing, youthful, innocent, well-meaning, attractive, and not unintelligent figurehead in attending to whom we can feel noble but who does not act in such a way as to seem superior or disappoint our most fervent expectations. Whatever Miss Froy is, was, or will be, Iris must be real.

If not yet descend to it, the film must show recognition that there is a ground and that Iris is standing on it, perhaps with Gilbert's help.

Cut bluntly to Charters and Caldicott, pipe in mouth/newspaper in hand, lounging in their privacy, a sunny landscape gliding by outside:

CHARTERS: If she gets up to any more of these tricks I'll be too late for the last day of the match.

CALDICOTT: I suppose you couldn't put it to her in some way.

CHARTERS: What.

CALDICOTT: Well. People...just don't...vanish and so forth.

CHARTERS (looking up): She has!

CALDICOTT: What.

CHARTERS (removing pipe): Vanished.

CALDICOTT: Who.

CHARTERS: The young dame.

CALDICOTT: Well, how could she?

CHARTERS: What.

CALDICOTT: Vanish.

CHARTERS (pipe in mouth again): I d'know.

CALDICOTT: That just explains my point. People don't just disappear into thin air.

CHARTERS: It's done in India.

CALDICOTT: What.

CHARTERS (pipe in hand): The rope trick.

CALDICOTT: Oh that! Well, it never comes out in the photographs.

With Gilbert standing watch, the doctor is comforting—"comforting"—Iris in his compartment. At the upcoming station, just before the border, he will leave the train with his patient, and she could come and have a private room in the hospital. "You need peace and rest."

"Nothing doing."

Gilbert: "Is there anything I can do?"

"Yes. Find Miss Froy."

Giving him the "knowing" eye, the doctor rises to confabulate with Gilbert. "I tell you, my friend, if she does not rest I will not answer for her. It would be best if you persuade her. She likes you."

"I'm just about as popular as a dose of strychnine."

With a professional smile: "If you coat it with sugar she may swallow it."

As Gilbert takes a few steps away to puff on his pipe he sees the train's chef emerge from the kitchen with a large tub of garbage to hurl. Some paper flies back and sticks to the outside of the window next to him. Gobsmacked, he stares. Part of a packet for Harriman's Herbal Tea. And now in the wind it blows away. Was this fate? Was this nature (gravity)? Was this random accident? It was surely dramatic design.

Clarinet has seated himself beside Iris now, Doppo and the Baroness across the compartment, the former dozy and the latter puffing on a cigarette far too conscientiously. "Cosmopolitan train," he mutters: her ears only, "People of all nations. I've just seen at least a million Mexicans in the corridor." Her eyes pop as their two jittering personalities arrive at a meeting place. They exit to the vestibule. "You're right! Miss Froy is on this train!" Iris is more than miffed; he's a trifle late; she might be dead by now. But they search. Through a third-class car and into the baggage. A familiar Hitchcockian set piece for nouveau commedia dell'arte. Piled wooden crates. A huge bound wicker basket vibrating to a low-toned moo. They race to open it, only to find a curious (and adorable) calf. Joint release of laughter, urgent for the audience's sense of release. As they hunt behind a trunk, a masking cover slides away, presenting a larger than life-sized cardboard maquette of Doppo in top hat and tuxedo,[19] with a poster Gilbert must translate: "The Great Doppo, magician, illusionist, mind-reader... impersonating act... the vanishing... Lady."

"The vanishing lady!!"

A crate opens and a crew of pigeons fly out.

Gilbert gently pries back the curtain covering the cabinet of Il Grande Doppo. Darkness. He touches something, revolves into darkness himself. "Where are you?"—"I'm here..."—"I can't see you"—she steps in and disappears and he emerges, "Here I am! Where are you?" — "I don't know!" He taps the outside and a platform spins revealing a little black and white bunny. The baggage car is something of a shambles now, with pigeons crawling around and cases upset and Iris on the floor. "In magic you call it a disappearing cabinet: you get inside and vanish." Gilbert has a theory to expound (dressed for the moment in a Holmes deerstalker with curly pipe):

> GILBERT: In the first place a little old lady disappears. Everyone that saw her promptly insists that she was never there at all.... We know that she was. Therefore they did see her. Therefore they are deliberately lying. Why?
>
> IRIS: I don't know, I'm only Watson.
>
> GILBERT: I'll tell you why. Because they daren't face an inquiry. Because Miss Froy is probably still somewhere on this train.
>
> IRIS (holding her own): I told you that hours ago.

What if they were to search the train in disguise? Gilbert tries on a mortarboard and a pair of specs, transforming himself into a "headmaster."[20] But she seizes the glasses from his nose. "They're Miss Froy's!"

Those eyeglasses to which Miss Froy showed no allegiance but that Iris instantly knew as belonging to her. The eyeglasses she held in her hand, and holds in her hand now.

Bend down to search the slatted floor. In macro-close-up, from behind them, come the long curling fingers of another hand (the hand we saw approaching the neck of the singer). Trying for the glasses and failing is Doppo, now roughly confronted. "Will you please give me those spectacles! They belong to me! My spectacles, please!!" With pigeons fluttering around them and Iris in assistance, Gilbert overcomes Doppo as the calf peeks out of its basket to watch. See if the cabinet has a false bottom, he calls, as three little bunnies cuddling in a hat peek out to watch. The three bodies wrestling make a kind of multi-limbed creature, grunting, squealing, and groaning. Now Doppo has pulled out a switchblade, held up high in the air. To reach it, Iris stands on a suitcase, bites his hand. Gilbert throws him into the revolving cabinet and when he emerges on the other side Iris smacks his head with a small club. They have to hide the woozy magician somewhere. Gilbert opens a chest. They pile him inside and tie it shut...

But Doppo has the glasses!

When they reopen the chest, he is gone.

Unable to battle the whole train, they must trust someone. The decision is "that Dr Hartz person." But no answer when they knock at his compartment. They gingerly open the door with, again, another cue from the train audibly rattling along its track. Inside: a somewhat chilling image. Lying supine at left, entirely swathed in white, the doctor's patient, still as a mummy. Keeping vigil beside, and seen from behind, the nun. But Gilbert does a double take. "I've just had a particularly idiotic idea.... Supposing that patient in there is Miss Froy...!"

His thought is a fearsome one, since it draws our attention to the passive vulnerability and nominal neutrality of this figure inside the bandages, this thing who could be anybody, after all, and who if it were Miss Froy would alarm any observer by its deathly silence, not to mention the surgical treatment planned at the doctor's hands. The figure is sarcophagal, wrapped for preservation not only in the face of a quotidian death but in the context of deep mortality, that is, the ages. Dead forever, dead in time, a resident of time, a timeless presence. And sheathed in a positively forbidding medical white. They have stepped back into the corridor.

"But it didn't come onto the train until after Miss Froy disappeared," Iris recalls. And more: "Did you see something wrong about that nun?... I don't think she's a nun at all. They don't wear high heels." Gently Gilbert pries the door open again and peers down the nun's figure, all the way to the svelte legs and new-polished high heels.

Then he realizes that no one actually saw Madame Kummer get onto the train. What if they took Miss Froy into the luggage van to hide her. The patient came onto the train; the patient was Madame Kummer. Madame Kummer became Miss Froy. Miss Froy has become the patient. (Echo of the magic cabinet revealing a bunny.)

And now, the question aimed to illuminate that Sacred Chamber all audiences wish to enter, and are prohibited from entering upon pain of disenchantment: "But why should they go to all this trouble to kidnap a harmless little governess?" Not how, not who, but why. The purpose. The direction in which they wished to take "the train." If—our heroic clarinetist is surmising—Miss Froy is the patient under those bandages, and if Hartz manages to have her escorted off the train at the next station, she will be imperiled. That body wrapped in white has become a chilling icon of diabolical possibilities, as well as a graphically composed reminder of the "invisible man" as sketched in 1933 by James Whale for Universal. That "invisible man," novelized in 1897, was H. G. Wells's creation of a scientist researching in optics who fiddles with the refractive index of light, in short, the sort of figure who could easily have been a pioneer of early cinema. We now see Miss Froy's large, observant eyes again, as she gazes in phantom traces at Iris; the eyes of an optical expert now made invisible to sight.

DIA/GNOSIS

Our friend the doctor will assume a certain diagnostic centrality in what follows, and what follows will be a rapid-fire action motoring the story toward its culmination. Without the deftest care, this action story will gain such prominence, or seem to have such likelihood, as to easily distract attention by focusing on outcomes moral and logical at the expense of a view of the landscape of principles, including the caves of mystery. The distraction-avoidance trick is produced by a tightly knit surface, that holds:

[1]   Gilbert and Iris revisiting the compartment where the body lies, bypassing the apparently mute nun, beginning to tease at the bandages on the face. The doctor coming in behind them outraged, outraged,

and doubly outraged that they wish to see the face. From his mouth a vision of hell: "Are you out of your senses? There is no face there, nothing but lumps of raw flesh. What do you want me to do, murder my patient?"[21]

[2] After the hunters' departure Hartz confronting the nun, who now blurts in Cockney English that someone must have tipped them off (in short, for the viewer the plot turner: Iris and Gilbert have been right!). But *Cockney English!* Who is this creature?

[3] The doctor giving the nun heavy sedatives to sneak to the waiter, then inviting Gilbert and Iris for a drink. His will be green Chartreuse (made by the diligent and kindly monks! And by name an exotic essence!) but he watches them like a hawk as they hold, then sip their wine. Trustingly they ask, has he actually seen the patient's face? They have worked it all out, they tell him: Signor Doppo being a music-hall artist is touring Mandrika and the Baroness's husband, Minister of Propaganda, will close down his act on one word from her, so he's lured into cooperation. The doctor genially listens. "To our health," he raises a toast, "and may our enemies if they exist be unconscious of our purpose." 1938: *our enemies if they exist....!* And worse: *be unconscious of our purpose...* A prayer for unconsciousness, both what the so-called "patient" experiences; and what the buried-away Miss Froy is experiencing should she happen not to be this patient; and what poor Iris has experienced in a way, with her consciousness wounded. Not to mention a piquant unconsciousness that is ours to enjoy, as we wait for happenings to unfold.

[4] The doctor sitting Gilbert and Iris down in his compartment and cordially informing them they have both been drugged and will soon be asleep. (Cordiality, always.) A heavier dose, which he has forborne to give, would have driven them mad. (He has taken pains, this doctor, to protect their sanity!) The patient is indeed Miss Froy. She will be taken off the train to hospital at the next station, in three minutes, and there she will be operated on. (Technically speaking, operated *upon*; and medically speaking, too.) "Unfortunately the operation will not be successful—Oh, I should perhaps have explained—the operation will

be performed (a gracious bow) by me. Need I say how sorry I am having to take, how shall I say, such a melodramatic course?" (Hitchcock "speaking." Even in the marriage-bound *Mr. & Mrs. Smith* [1941] he avoids melodrama.)

[5] Upon his exit, the two hunters awakening somehow, in an act of pure dramaturgy: if they stay asleep, the plot goes on without them and we need to wonder why they've been in our way all along. Gilbert clambers out the window and narrowly avoids an oncoming train as he shifts to the adjoining compartment and lets himself in. The nun, in an English accent now *no longer* Cockney: "You needn't be afraid. You haven't been drugged, he told me to put something in your drink but I didn't do it." (Don't let the viewer wander down any false trails.) If the silent nun was being performed for Hartz by a "Cockney Englishwoman" and the Cockney Englishwoman is performed for Iris and Gilbert by an Englishwoman not Cockney, who performs that Englishwoman-not-Cockney? (How many of these nuns seem to be present but don't exist?) Madame Kummer saunters down the corridor and steps in. Gilbert and the nun seize her and knock her out.

[6] Gilbert returning to Iris and pretending with her to be asleep, while the doctor arranges their bodies together in a sweet embrace. (The romantic embrace being a signal melodramatic touch, and coming from the creative hands of the villain! Hitchcock "speaking" again, with what might be called an "anti-melodramatic" accent.)

[7] When the bandaged body on its stretcher is inside the ambulance, the doctor peeling away the bandages and discovering...Madame Kummer! Racing back onto the platform, persuading officials to uncouple the rear of the train. Confrontation with the confederate nun who gives a neat moral assessment: "This was murder, and she's English! You were going to butcher her in cold blood."

[8] Gilbert and Iris reunited with Miss Froy, imploring her to trust them and explain what is going on. But the old lady is as reticent as earlier she was garrulous.

[9] The half-train chugging off and slowing to a halt in a woods where two vehicles await, with Hartz and the Baroness accompanied by a group of armed soldiers. On board, general consternation of various sorts, Charters and Caldicott refusing to believe what they are told is happening; Todhunter refusing in cowardice to participate, as his girlfriend screams at him; and Miss Froy becoming increasingly agitated.

[10] When gunfire begins the old lady drawing Gilbert and Iris into privacy and quickly confiding: "I want you to take back a message for Mr Callendar at the Foreign Office in Whitehall."

> IRIS: You are a spy!
>
> FROY: I always think that's such a grim word.

The message isn't words, it's a tune containing, "in code of course, the vital clause of a secret pact between two European countries . . . I want you to memorize it." And here, of course (of course!) the "happy" but dour melody from Mandrika, la-la'ed by the old lady quite precisely, and calling it back to us in full form. Gilbert promises he has musical training, and he won't stop whistling it. Miss Froy escapes into the forest: "I do hope and pray that no harm will come to you, and that we shall all meet again one day." We should also refuse to stop whistling it, if we wish to remember, but that is a severe challenge in the face of the extreme flurry now presented onscreen.

Anxious Todhunter insisting on walking outside with a white handkerchief, being shot dead on sight. Barrister to the end.

Gilbert and Caldicott managing to get themselves to the engine and start up the train, which they drive backward to the crossing point. The nun rushes out, throws off her veil—the veil she once apparently "took up" to vanish the lady she was and would now become again—and throws the switch for them. The train rolls away to safety.

Charing Cross Station, London. The clarinetist and Iris standing together, preparing to leave their train.

> IRIS: Well we're home, Gilbert (the first time his name is mentioned).

GILBERT: Charles be here to meet you?

IRIS (looking past him): I expect so. *(They are outside near a taxi.)*

GILBERT: You'll be very busy between now and Thursday.

IRIS: I could meet you for lunch or dinner.

Well, he plans to go up to Yorkshire to finish his book. We cut to Charters and Caldicott happy that they can catch the 6:50 to Manchester after all, but then gobsmacked to see a news hawker's billboard: TEST MATCH ABANDONED FLOODS.

GILBERT (humming the tune): Any sign of Charles yet?

IRIS (looking at a slender toff who is searching for someone): No, I can't see him.

GILBERT: Well—this is where we say goodbye.

(But she leaps into the cab with him.)

GILBERT (with a knowing smile): Charles?

IRIS: Yes, you heartless, callous, selfish...

and they collapse together into the kiss that has been a long time coming.

Whitehall. In a sumptuous lobby Iris and Gilbert sitting in wait, but though he didn't for the last several screen minutes stop humming it our poor musician has now forgotten the melody (a second poor musician, living shadow of a corpse)! The melody has simply vanished. Vanished, shall we say, like Miss Froy. He tries some notes but that's the wedding march, Iris says (archly). Then from somewhere off, from some *au-delà*, the strains of a piano, on which the melody is being played in full four-part harmony. The door opens to Callendar's office and when they walk in, there sits darling Miss Froy at the keyboard, overjoyed to take their hands. Charles Barr sagaciously observes Hitchcock's "long take of over a minute" at this vital moment:

> The camera is placed behind the couple as they sit, follows them forward as they go toward the door, pauses as Gilbert frantically tries to recall the tune, and then follows—or sweeps—them in, to find Miss Froy at the piano, at the apex of the familiar kind of triangle composition. As she joyfully rises to meet them, it moves into a close-up of her looking lovingly out of frame at both of them in turn. (201)

The film spins through something of a vortical wrap up, escalating with each scene graciously if tersely punching out the action amid numerous melodic courtesies, most of them from the villain, of course. We must find Miss Froy, somewhat haggard but in no way wounded, must realize what a great mobilization was in place to put this lady down, must watch her athletic escape from the railway car into the forest, and must witness in jubilance her triumph and the new young lovers uniting all in a (musical) breath.

Yet:

There linger two intriguing issues and one captivating shadow.

The shadow first. Film is an extraordinarily complex art in the nature, delicacy, variability, and internal organicism of its form, needing at each screened instant the collaborative labor of dozens of professional artists and artisans whose will to labor and create is tickled and encouraged by not only the promise of cash payment but also spirit. Further, it is a medium in which things can happen very, very swiftly with a great profundity. At Charing Cross there is a single instant, it flashes by in less than three seconds of screen time, in which we are to take Iris as noticing, there on the bustling platform, and stretching himself too too eagerly to find her, Charles Fotheringale. He is too too preening, too too polished, too too self-possessed, a man far too expectant of finding in the crowd shuffle the treasure that he thinks expressly his to have. In short, a smart Upper, arrogantly uncouth, the sort of man who wants his woman waiting at the door. And now, *for the very first time* Iris Matilda Henderson sees all this—sees not the person but the qualities, because we are seeing them, too—and for our first time (he has not appeared before). As a man, how repulsive he is! (Repulsive in a vision so swiftly presented.) The man accompanying Iris is a very different creature, so here is a young girl's education as to how all men are not the same. Again, all this in a flash. The gates opening for Gilbert, in a flash. The dreamed marriage an empty yearning for class ascension: our Iris has been looking up to Charles and his family, just as he is now looking out to find her. He is the explorer in the jungle, she is the prey. All in a flash, managed for us by showing Charles, not showing Iris: an uncredited extra fitted perfectly into a tailored suit and coat that instantly express position; the perfect camera angle for revealing his gestures and the moving crowd in a single vision; the performer's exquisite use of poise and position to show off a festering eagerness; the lighting dappled enough to give us a sense of the flicker of the platform and the spotlit moment; the speed of the man's movements and that of the crowd around—all this worked together so that instantaneously upon catching sight of him we recoil from this man. We recoil, in fact, first; and then we see Iris recoiling. In this way, with a light touch, as a kind of fillip, Hitchcock conveys a whole rumbling theme of class division and class consciousness under the straining pains of the film. Class was always there for us to see, it was always a halo of trouble around Iris, but only at Charing Cross, and, as it were, effortlessly, is it made plain.

This Charles: the spot of cement upon which he stands is his fiefdom, he lords over the space, his bearing is heavy with privilege. Indeed, the whole presentation for all its glimmering and energy strikes as a dull weight, an anchor dragging us down and away from all that we now cherish because it is dragging Iris, too. It is Hitchcock's careful exclusion of the Charles figure from the film *as a visible figure* coupled with his abrupt insinuation of the figure here and now that serve together to take us for a moment whither we never remembered to think to go, albeit Iris has been indicating hesitation about the unyielding, if officially blessed, bond this man will insist upon, the "reality" after her adventure is over. "Oh no!" we feel because she feels; "Oh no, I don't want to go there!"

A reflection is engendered: that social class was everywhere here, from the obsequious hotel manager in Mandrika and the pompous British couple, the utterly middle-class Charters and Caldicott, the professional class Doctor and his slumgirl nun, the authentic high-European contessa, the itinerant showman, and the intrepid utterly classless old lady who lives in the moment and will sacrifice all for England.

Now, the two issues. First a lingering one: *The Lady Vanishes* encapsulates a somewhat conventional spy story, in which an agent penetrates a sacred space, retrieves a vital secret (to aid political forces we esteem and/or affiliate with), and returns safely "home," summing up a battle the true proportions of which are always, by convention, only hinted at. In the present case: *The Lady Vanishes* having opened in London on 7 October 1938, almost seven months to the day after Hitler annexed Austria, and with Hitler's concentration camps in existence already for five years, it is hard to understand how the British and American audience could have failed to grasp that in Hartz they were watching a full-fledged Nazi substitute. The concentration-camp surgeon figure, epitomized by Josef Mengele, was on the way; Mengele started at Auschwitz in 1943, having joined the party in 1937, and was a—if not *the*—central figure "operating on" human beings for "the benefit of science." By 1938 Britain was well into the throes of war. Two days after the Nazi annexation of Poland, Mollie Panter-Downes wrote to *The New Yorker*:

> Yesterday, people were saying that if there wasn't a war today it would be a bloody shame. Now that there is a war, the English, slow to start, have already in spirit started and are comfortably two laps ahead of the official war machine, which had to await the drop of somebody's handkerchief.... On the stretch of green turf by Knightsbridge Barracks, which used to be the scampering ground for the smartest terriers in London, has appeared a row of steam shovels that bite out mouthfuls of earth, hoist it aloft, and dump it into lorries; it is then carried away to fill sandbags. The eye has now become accustomed to sandbags everywhere. (3)

Miss Froy is an English spy messing about in charming Mandrika to cache some all-important European affairs just on the cusp of Hitler's moves. One can chuckle at the unlikelihood of her cover, the brilliance of choosing her: a spy with a musical turn of phrase (go back and listen to her lilting sentences) and the military secret being encoded with the melody.

The first time I saw this film, certainly more than four decades ago, I found the idea of coding information in a musical syntax arcane as a narrative ploy.[22] Yet the idea of musical encoding was not sui generis to Hitchcock (his literary source, Ethel Lina White's *The Wheel Spins*, has a very chirpy Miss Froy but of course no music) but floated somehow in the ether of culture at the time, Edmund Wilson employing the word "song" as a substitute for "cash," for example, in his descriptive comments about

Los Angeles of the time. The musical secret as form makes possible not only the introduction of the fated singer but also sonorous musical recapitulation as, in the opening sequence, the song is heard over and over at different volumes in different locations by different people. The repetitive rotation, turning from a beginning to an end and then all the way back to the beginning, in a way analogizes cinema. Miss Froy's dream (and canny) reception finds an easy match in her projection of the people of Mandrika as happy folk who like to sing. The spy listening for a melody, then. The fated guitarist warbling it so she can put it to use. And for use, the vital importance of remembering...

A second lingering issue is both more complex and more daunting, and requires that we consider once again that problem of memory, our inability to experience and remember experiencing at the same time. Memory's uncertainty is Iris's problem on the train. Just as anyone might struggle now to recall exactly what was said on these pages before (without turning back, as in cinema we cannot do). And struggle to recall with a certain energy or desperation. Just in that way, Iris is pressed into the conundrum of trying very hard to convince herself of Miss Froy's present existence by remembering, by conceiving, a past one.

How challenging to gain a complete, fulsome, detailed, exact, and balanced vision of something that happened or of a place one visited or of a person one met long, long ago. The faces melt, the landscapes shift psychotectonically, the order of the happening is scrambled. Because the ear is an auditorium, the sounds one heard then reverberate and echo now, dissolving their identity. When we are utterly convinced we remember some little detail that was confided to us we can double-think that the detail is being invented, since in listening to other people's stories, as we know too well, we are all of us storytellers.

Even if no flowerbox fell from a high window to smack Iris in the head, she would be having trouble, then, just as any viewer has trouble as a film progresses remembering exactly what happened before. Remembering fully. But imagine the peculiar, chilling consternation that must befall someone who cannot be certain she has not been hallucinating. For all of what one "knows" of one's past may be regarded as hallucination—just as Dr Hartz says—especially if one is creative. The uncertainty persists, even intensifies as one gazes steadily into the present moment: for the filmgoer, gazes at the scene being played now. If the flickering upon the screen is continuous in itself, one is subject to the effect of an enduring image at the expense of being subject to other images not projected now. The more we gaze at Iris, the more Iris gazes into the faces—now—of the others who are not Miss Froy. Froy that rhymes with joy. That rhymes with toy. That rhymes with coy.

Obversely, the more certain Iris grows about *the Miss Froy who was*, the more dubious she becomes in comprehending the reality around her now—who these figures are, what they intend, where events are heading, and to what purpose. Miss Froy generalizes for Iris into her past as a whole, so that when the girl is reunited with her old friend her past can finally be liberated. Miss Froy here now is the real one; the Miss Froy as was is in question. But this is always, everywhere the case. One has a sense of having done something, seen something, felt something, but the more intensely one cultivates that sense the more the present moment of cultivation is dissolved in one's focus backward. And as the present moment gains in clarity, it becomes harder to grasp where we came from.

Like film frames, sensations are fleeting. To remember sensation with any fidelity at all one must retire from present circumstance, and this withdrawal, this abstraction, is what the doctor is noticing of Iris in his diagnostic comment. A glaring mistake in viewing the film is to pay no attention to what the doctor says except as a calculated misdirection; with Iris he is not misdirecting, he is telling the blunt truth (albeit a truth that benefits him). And he speaks as a neurosurgeon, someone who knows how to delve into the perceptual mechanism and produce an effect. Iris, he can see, is not really here as she searches for Miss Froy.

It is a nightmare to be told—or worse, convinced—that one has been fabricating a world one firmly believed was really there. All of the architecture of the film is designed to lead Iris to this horrible suspicion about herself; and to lead the viewer, too—without leading too far (which is why very shortly after she surrenders, Gilbert must find the tea package on the window—a second window sign).

At stake is far more than a single case of espionage, one melody, a little old lady, and whether or not the secret message gets through to its intended destination. Our presence is our experience; and our memory is our identity, or at least the basis of it. We move toward the future bringing an ever-growing repository of memory traces: not experiences but, as it were, pictures of experiences that bear some—only some—of the qualities of the experiences to which they relate but all—all—of the qualities of pictures, especially of mental pictures. "As a rule," writes William James,

> sensations outlast for some little time the objective stimulus which occasioned them. This phenomenon is the ground of those 'after-images' which are familiar in the physiology of the sense-organs. If we open our eyes instantaneously upon a scene, and then shroud them in complete darkness, it will be as if we saw the scene in ghostly light through the dark screen. We can *read off details* in it which were unnoticed whilst the eyes were open. (645; my emphasis)

Because we can map our memories we can be the persons we would claim to be. But our mapping can only be imperfect.

THE VANISHING LADY

Iris is about to be swept away into the aristocracy. To resolve the film's eccentric "melodrama" in a pleasing way, that must not happen. Perhaps the wise old companion may somehow, herself, be a key. Miss Froy's name rhymes with joy, yes, but is also homonymous with *freu*, the (in this case significantly) German word for *happy*. The returning Miss Froy not only produces happiness in Iris, she stands for happiness all along, perhaps most notably when she swoons with pleasure at the happy citizens of Mandrika she must now leave after being with them for six years. Let us say that when Iris loses Miss Froy she loses her happiness, not figuratively but literally; that losing her happiness is of paramount significance to this girl at this time in her life; and that perhaps the so-stressed relevance of her happiness is one reason at least for her being so obdurate in her search. If happiness sadly lost is found again, or reborn, we can look for transformation on a deeper, more mythical level than is made accessible by the information economy of espionage.

Iris is not the only loser of happiness in this story, nor is Miss Froy the only happiness Iris loses. Our clarinetist Gilbert possesses Miss Froy in two ways, by accretion. First, he finds himself attached to this girl, and we see clearly and hear as well, by his vocal manner, the way his chiding morphs into tenderness, the way his marginal doubt morphs into supportive belief, against all odds. He is in truth her partner. Her belief in and search for Miss Froy become his belief and search. But then, once the old lady has given them her confidence, just before escaping into the forest, he absorbs that precious little tune and doesn't stop niggling it over in his head. (How unpleasant that tune eventually becomes!) The tune is his Miss Froy, a living substitute and, indeed, all the value of whatever secret treasure Miss Froy bears and represents. Therefore, when he forgets the tune at the worst possible moment he loses his Miss Froy, his *Freulichkeit*. But as to his losing the melody, losing his Miss Froy, we must ask (with as sharp a memory as we can draw up) when exactly this loss occurs. With Iris, loss is very clearly indicated. With Gilbert indication is perhaps a little coyer. He loses his Miss Froy at the moment in the taxicab when it becomes obvious to him and to Iris that they should fall into a kiss; obvious, in short, that there is a loving bond. In the chemistry of that bond the ditty from Mandrika dissolves.

But back to our *freuliche* (if expressly not *Freudische*) Froy:

In any conventional filmic representation of the source novel, the sine qua non would be a character described at first in a distinctly memorable way disappearing without a trace and without reason, from the company of others. When Hitchcock makes the film, however, it becomes crucial to have an elaborate expository first movement in which the old woman, seen again and again, her circumstances variant, *quietly*—and only quietly—fits in. It is later that she announces (pronounces) *a name*. And once she is gone, someone is endlessly invoking her—"Where is Miss Froy?"—bringing responses of whatever kind that invoke the name, too: "Miss Froy???" The name replaces the person to fill dramatic space. Every utterance is directly or indirectly about this non-present but nameable form. The lady. The lady. The lady.

Iris Henderson was introduced to us as especially self-assured and convicted of her pathway in life—she is a forebear of Joan Webster (Wendy Hiller) in Michael Powell and Emeric Pressburger's *I Know Where I'm Going!* (1945). She wanted chicken nuggets and champagne, even traipsing through a crowd of anxious and forlorn travelers, even when she heard (as we did) how improbable it would be for them all to be settled. She imperiously commanded the service of now-familiar servants. She showed off to her girlfriends. She was not only aggrieved at being disturbed from above the ceiling but, in her arrogance, self-avowingly demanded that something be done (bribing the manager). To the gentle, doddering stranger with the clarinet she was impolite, if not downright offensive. To the old lady she was blithely inattentive. And through the hunt on the train she was never for an instant less than utilitarian in her way of listening to other people's admissions or denials, other people's lives. She had her purpose, her future, and ears shut to all and sundry if they didn't march along. Garrulous, sharp-witted Iris is climbing, and whether or not she can seem delighted about it, she is on track to become Lady Charles Fotheringale, in her mind a Lady on a train.

But now, thanks to the accident of a plummeting windowbox, she has fallen into the care of someone—say, a mother figure—and worse, someone suddenly gone out of her life (too soon) and mysteriously, so that the logic of the grieving hunt makes sense. In becoming devoted to the Miss Froy she seeks, she is believing that an answer to her query exists, and she is coming slowly, through trials and mistrusts and dangers, to believe in the arcane existence of her friend the clarinetist, too. She is on the platform at Charing Cross, musing about lunching or dining with this handsome young fellow, and looking around. There!, point blank!, is Charles, the vaunted Charles, also looking around, and, not seeing her, gawking off. A Charles, she suddenly realizes, who is of no interest at all; or worse. Iris Henderson has just discovered what interest is. And she is in Gilbert's taxi even before him. So she is not with Charles: not now, not next Thursday in Hanover Square, not ever.

She is not going to become a Lady.

(In late-1930s England the word "Lady" had a very specific usage and was not used generically to mean "woman" as in some contexts it is today. Miss Froy surely behaves like a Lady, but we are given no indication whatsoever that she is one; that is, no indication of her class. Whereas with Iris, the plan to enter the aristocracy by wedding is boldly announced.)

Class dominance is toppled here through an act of desire and commitment. Nor is this toppling marginal to Hitchcock's concern. What easily goes undetected is that Iris's abandonment of Charles, though it happens almost too rapidly for us to catch and notably without expressive gesture from her, is not only the turning point for her but the central act of the film. For making a story about a kidnapping aboard a train and the heroism of a young woman, after all, there is no call for an anticipated marriage, especially not a marriage into aristocracy. Iris's "passion" about finding Miss Froy exemplifies her determination in general, her plans for a future, her abandonment of a past. That she and Charles were to be an "ideal couple" marked her intended class attainment as supreme, yet now it is Gilbert and Iris waiting together outside Mr Callendar's Whitehall office who make the "ideal couple." It becomes clear that Miss Froy's function, as we see here but didn't presume from the start, is to wed them. Owing to a magic more powerful, more elusive, and more touching than any trick Signor Doppo knows how to perform, and celebrated at the vital moment our missing spy holds out her hands to join the children in that blessed triangle, a Lady vanishes.

CHAPTER THREE
OUR FRENZIED LIFE

PROLOGUE

Uninformed and full of gaudy imaginations, I visited London for the first time in May 1972, literally days before the première there of *Frenzy*, a show of London life in particular, British life in general, and modern life more generally still. Hitchcock thought the film comedic. The source material, Arthur La Bern's postwar *Goodbye Piccadilly, Farewell Leicester Square* (1966), was an invocation of the late 1940s, when the pulse of Piccadilly Circus reverberated through all corners of the Empire, and Leicester Square, a major hub of movie entertainment in London, so crucial just after the war, shone bravely with gaiety and light. Echoing Jack Judge and Harry Williams's "It's a Long Way to Tipperary" (1912)—"Goodbye, Piccadilly, / Farewell, Leicester Square! / It's a long long way to Tipperary, / But my heart's right there"—the La Bern title immediately announced the energized hum of wartime London. But Hitchcock points to a London tellingly squalid, entrenched in the scurrying Everyday of 1970s capitalism, where "everything is in life and motion" (Ackroyd, *London* 333). Explicit attention is given to working-class roughness and the metre of business, the everyday ramble

among characters who, in the English form, always mean more than they say (communicating through implication and nuance) and are patently untouched by the velvety electricity of Royalty that to this day charges anglophiles around the globe. The England of *Frenzy* has no monarch, only the staunch uprightness and brittle etiquette that holds the line, even among costers and lorrymen. The vivid red, white, and blue of the Union Jack (amalgamating the banners of St George, St Andrew, and St Patrick) is unavailable for salutes.

To say a character might "communicate through implication and nuance" is not to suggest only pretty things would be said. Through their bright faces, all of the characters in this film express, in fact, darkness.

Two principals hold the center: Bob Rusk (Barry Foster, from the London stage), a purveyor of fresh fruit at Covent Garden market and serial murderer (his deep identity, The Necktie Killer, will not long remain unknown to us, as it does to the police) and Richard Blaney (Jon Finch, star of Roman Polanski's *Macbeth* [1971]), an "angry young man," to pick up John Osborne's theme about a resentful stratum of young postwar British masculinity (Hitchcock, Raymond Foery claims, had wanted Michael Caine [59]—possibly because of *Alfie*, I would surmise: he often screened actors' previous work). What the "angry young man" is angry about is . . . well, England altogether, his ostensibly dim prospects there, the turgidly brittle class structure, and the fact that his education has not saved him from wallowing in a seething marketplace of discontent. Rusk inhabits one of the truly famous London centers of business (of its day; Covent Garden was moved to Battersea two years after the filming and the old market has since been gentrified). He wholesales fruit to grocers,[1] being himself a relishing consumer of his own merchandise. Peter Ackroyd quotes John Timbs's

121

Curiosities of London in regard to Covent Garden: "There is more certainty of purchasing a pineapple here, every day in the year, than in Jamaica and Calcutta, where pines are indigenous" (*Biography* 333). For Rusk in his killer stance, there is something altogether fruity about the bodies he devours. The fruit of life, the fruiterer with the trained hand.

It is in connection with either Rusk or Blaney that other characters take their positions, all save, at least for the time being, Chief Inspector Tim Oxford (Alec McCowen), our intrepid detective, who flips between calm professional devotion to finding the murderer and not-quite-so-calm domestic devotion to his fiendishly experimental wife (Vivien Merchant). Like so many eager (female) Londoners of the time, she has decided to take up something like a Cordon Bleu cooking course—Cordon Bleu came to London in 1933—and *improve* the style of her cuisine, dear Tim being her guinea pig, save him. (Yes, he will be saved.)[2]

Just as Chief Inspector Oxford will show himself duteous, Rusk will be diabolical; his objectivity will show no more regard for a female than for a grape. Richard Blaney is another case altogether, descendant, perhaps, of D. H. Lawrence's Oliver Mellors in that he is plausibly immigrant to London from a gamekeeping position in the midlands (where he knew how to make love, and certainly how to read the territory).[3] Blaney is far from urbane, it is fields and streams he knows; London's air is never fresh enough. Rusk inhabits the underground, one of the city's "mole men" who build their passage "at the expense of much cost and suffering" (Ackroyd, *Under* 100).

In his anger Blaney hails straightaway from a contemporary trend born in the theater, expressly the Royal Court at Sloane Square. David Kynaston quotes Anthony Heap's review of the first night (8 May 1956) of Osborne's *Look Back in Anger*:

> What we had inflicted on us tonight was, in fact, not so much a play as one long mortifyingly monotonous monologue by one of the most insidiously and insufferably boring characters it has ever been my misfortune to encounter as a playgoer—a too awfully bitter and so terribly cynical young neurotic with an outsize chip on his shoulder and a pathological hatred of everything and everybody. He begins ranting, railing and raving in the most pretentiously puerile manner

as soon as the curtain goes up and...never—or hardly ever—lets up to the bitter end. (*Family* 622)

Like the Osborne prototype, our Blaney is fashionably discontented, sneering in his beer at everyone he meets—yet at the same time never mounting to coarseness. Perhaps he lost (or was robbed of) his couth as well as his youth. The contented population might find him off-putting and surly; brutish in a too aggressively heterosexual way. If he doesn't mean his ugly bearing, he can't erase it. When Blaney essays politeness his rage punctures it. Rusk will appear the more refined, *the more to attract you, my dears!* (although he will be patently unattractive every time we see him).

All the characters in this film must seem realistic, with social position, prospects, history, and attitude instantly appreciable. But rather than giving any single character a full highlight, Hitchcock surrounds them with a dense circus, London tightly packed. If in 1972 (and now) nowhere near the world's most jam-packed cities, still the Greater London area is cramped: social classes rub elbows (as happened, for example, at Raneleigh in the late eighteenth century), criminals crawl and lurk upon the public high streets. Every person dresses and behaves to perform a condition, and the performed conditions are constantly read and monitored by those who pass.[4] All of London life is theater. *Who are you to stand so close to me?* Since necktie murders are increasing and the police are apparently helpless, public fear is worked up to a feeding frenzy for information, a panic to decode—devour—others swiftly if without full knowledge. We are being shown England not as fiction but as truth.

Alfred Hitchcock was English before all else, of course. He crossed the Atlantic in March of 1939, *en famille*, with plans to set up home and shop in Los Angeles, David Selznick's New York agent Dorothy "Dottie" Brown having made the arrival arrangements and hosting the newly landed Hitchcocks at her place in Long Island. He had finished working in England with *Jamaica Inn* (1939), indeed in a tortuous *contretemps* with Charles Laughton, and would soon be at work on Selznick's *Rebecca* (1940), in a *contretemps* with him. In America he became an established figure without delay, but it wasn't until 1955 that Henry Bumstead drove him to a Los Angeles courtroom to swear citizenship to the USA. Before this he returned to England to direct parts of *Under Capricorn* (1949) at Borehamwood and then for *Stage Fright*, filmed 1 June 1949 through August of that year at Elstree and released in New York 23 February 1950 and in London 26 May.[5] Both *Rebecca* (1940) and *Suspicion* (1941) are set in England but were not filmed there. *Stage Fright* showed more toffiness, with scenes in Mayfair, Belgravia, Fitzrovia, and Bloomsbury, a "London" with which American adepts would have been familiar as postwar viewers of British period drama. For *Dial M for Murder* (1954) a few short location shots were taken in London, by a second-unit crew. For *The Man Who Knew Too Much*, over an hour of the film is set in London and several weeks of location shooting took place there in the spring of 1955 including, of course, the Albert Hall sequence. But in Hitchcock's "English" settings after *Rebecca*, story dominated scene, England being only a background (however fabulous). In *Frenzy*, the English ground becomes the subject; and the human subjects are unified with that ground: the cautious panic of the middle class, the sharp emptiness of normality, the scramble upward under the complacent Royal gaze. In Richard Blaney's England the most offensive violence is the most civilized, the stuff of the invisible.

PLEASURED INNOCENCE

I jump to that violence at its bleak worst, a high-contrast version of the civilized violence all around. Rusk lets himself into Brenda Blaney's (Richard's ex-wife) dating service at lunchtime, commits rape (as he would like to think, on her provocation) in her private sanctum, then strangles her to death. But Hitchcock contrives the scene to summon and reflect the watcher's own watching, the camera drawing us to see a vision offered explicitly to us. The viewer's (macabre) desire to approach, stimulated and echoed by the camera stand-in, is Hitchcock's true subject, more than the grisliness, extensivity, vulgarity, remorselessness, pity, horror, and abjectness of Brenda's victimization. ("I can't watch it, I'm turning away!" one would love to cry, and also, *"You* tell me when it's over...," while staring coldly as Brenda herself comes to do.)

Graphically, the murder of Brenda Blaney (Barbara Leigh-Hunt) is a grotesquerie—appropriate for a grotto, one of those purposely ornamented private spaces for pleasurable reflection very often carved out of a cave (and usually related to rocky formations) and set with fantastic gargoyles and beasts unimaginable in the world at large. Manifestation of withheld fears, projected into Nature. Naomi Miller recounts an ogre in the Orsini park at Bomarzo,

> the upper lip of whose gaping jaws bears the inscription 'Ogni pensiero vo...' ('Every thought flies'), surely inspired by Dante's telling words in his *Divine Comedy*, 'All hope abandon ye who enter here.' The word Ogre itself is a variation of Orcus, one of the names of the King of Hell (and of a river associated with the orc, that most voracious of cetaceans, the killer whale). Here, the entry leads to no garden but to a large subterranean world. (51)

Dead and discarded in her office, the remains of Brenda do make "every thought fly": eyes bulging open to a field of vast and incalculable invisibility, tongue dolloping out of her mouth (as though sickened by some ineffable flavor), her blouse and bra torn away to reveal the breasts Rusk surely thinks inflamed his docile passion (when it is promise of brutal domination that inflames him). Rusk himself is never grotesque. He is apparently sociotypical, ordinary, even civil, one of the bustling urban minions covering amoral ugliness with a mask of nappy fashion. When he discovers Brenda's half-eaten apple and cheerily munches it beside the corpse, he is at once outlandish and a man of the everyday: a supremely ironic subject.

In staging the rape as prelude to the killing—"Lovely!...Lovely!! ...Lovely!!!!"—Hitchcock teases his viewer's curiosity-become-rage with a calculated objectification of Brenda's partial nudity. Seeing her at a respectful distance in the office conversation, as does Rusk, the viewer tries to lean in, see her face. And seeing her face, to come closer and see past the face. Always closer and closer, and soon we see the frightful necktie tightening. These are all medium or medium-close shots, *nothing left to the imagination*, so that our conventional nosiness hiding under a mask of sweet civil propriety can redound upon itself. Stefan Scharff gives a shot-by-shot discussion of the strangling, coming even closer to the density of the affair than the most curious of innocent viewers. His conclusion is blunt: "The act of strangling is horrific in itself; Hitchcock arrives at a reality of a peculiar kind that does not beg for more elaboration of naturalistic details. Its veracity is indisputable and what we see is the essence of the thing." But then, as in a frenzied defense, his mind pulls a step back in conclusion: "Devastating as it is, it represents some sort of an extract, a stylized rendition" (192). Aside from the fact that all cinematic renditions can only be extracts of something that no camera can wholly digest, this sequence is not experienced as an extract.

Yet (to lean into the leaning in!), what can it mean to say that Hitchcock *leaves nothing to the imagination*?

Not, surely, that he denies his viewers opportunity to imagine, or that he monopolizes the "conversation," or that he presents every conceivable detail (because no one could do that), or that he stymies, flummoxes, stuns, or otherwise renders his audience powerless to express. It can mean, instead, that he senses the quality and magnitude of his viewer's hunger to see further, see more, see onward, see again, see with more light. What can be seen is less than *the desire to see*. Here and always.

Screen murder can offer a visual "vacuum," into which we interpose our own expression or, more "virtuously," from which we cast away an already gelded—that is, previously flaccid—gaze. In casting away, the disembodiment of the victim becomes our daydream, and every daydream is created, always our poetry (see Freud, "Type"). In the daydream whereby we construct what we are not looking at we devise our own torsions and pressures, delicious points of contact, in short play out an erotic fantasy that brings its own rhythms and hiatuses, its own rush to judgment as we tell a generalized Someone—a version of the telling self—the horror of what was watched. Such a self-directed response would be masturbatory.

Not that in other circumstances, in this film and others, we are loath to participate in a masturbatory way, involving ourselves in order to touch ourselves involved, speaking of ourselves involved in order to hear the forms of our own reminiscent breath. As the modern viewer is anything but unhappy for the masturbatory moment, *Frenzy* distinguishes itself in not providing time for one. Thomas Laqueur's claim in *Solitary Sex* is that around the mid-eighteenth century, the masturbation that had brought pleasure *became problematic*—at some points, as people claimed, anti-feminine but surely against the "laws of nature." Masturbation made its appearance precisely when a major reconfiguration of masculinity was in full swing. The old sorts of male friendships—eroticized, physically intimate, perhaps even consummated—had become suspect or worse. The secret vice thus seemed to track new anxieties about the collapse of decent heterosexuality; or, more accurate, it became a matter for serious concern at the same time that new standards of heterosexual masculinity appeared. (255)

Blaney and Rusk, say. Better still: Rusk and Blaney.

Hitchcock does know how to invite us to play with his material and play with ourselves playing (the hike after Jeff Jefferies's visions in *Rear Window* [1954] is a good case). But in the Blaney murder we are given to visualize not fantasize, witness an execution, the incessant forward rhythm systematized for the production of death and nothing more. The thing and only the thing; the thing unified with our reaction to the thing.[6] "No discordant note disturbed the work of the machine": Kafka (14). The "guilty criminal" is central to the operation of the penal/penile system—"Crime is an attack on society and the criminal is a social enemy" (Foucault, *Punitive* 62)—and here guilt is transferred onto Brenda, once arrogant Rusk has stolen the authority to undo her. After his orgasm cools, a sententious denouncement: "Women! You're all the same! I'll show you...!"

And yes, Brenda is shown, and shown being shown.

Brenda, whom we don't meet very well, is decorous and intelligent, self-possessed and dignified, but Rusk collapses her into an epitomizing depravity to contrast with his own self-purified image. He has carefully choreographed all the moves he will make to force her moves. And their dance is leached of sincere spontaneity, staged systematically: the knot must go just precisely here; the tension must be like so, from this angle; the timing of the noosing must be right. If there is latent pleasure for the killer in reducing life to death it is impertinent in a system. Let the killer/executioner find some obscure erotism at work but pay it no heed! It is only in a *person* that one could register such a thrill and Rusk is only a functionary, like every other executioner. *Nothing personal!*

Hitchcock will ensure we do not *only imagine* the killing action, and finally, relievingly, our (Sadistic) pleasures will be erased in the face of a legal presence. Hitchcock wishes to make this killing educational. "Not only must people know, they must see with their own eyes" (Foucault, *Discipline* 58). That in this case punishment is directed against a female is no accident for London or for England.[7] Yet: how is Brenda's dating service a "criminal case"? Ah, but she's at work making money, a taboo for properly passive women who ought to stay home and cook for hubby (Brenda as a dramatic foil for the Chief Inspector's wife, who labors in the kitchen without pay). Convicted, tried, caught (as in Wonderland)—we see Richard's jealousy of her success as they dine; we see Rusk's impotent loathing—she is to ascend the scaffold. In screen executions the disintegrating body is virtually invisible for the glare of the equipment, but not here.

Its call for sombre invocation suggests the killing is sublime. If one can snatch a breath one searches in vain for language adequate to utterance, some full affirmation of denial, a way of saying "No!" as though negation could make the event disappear. Even if one closes the eyes, one is *closing the eyes upon this undeniable act*. Unable to say no, we must, in some revolting way, say yes, and saying yes we must see the importance of affixing blame to what we assented to see while wallowing in blame ourselves. Call the villain Rusk. Call him Hitchcock. As long as we do not append our own name. The audience is born innocent.

Moral defacement of a victim is frequently made to seem part of a normal coherence, as Harold Garfinkel pointed out in his 1956 paper, "Conditions of Successful Degradation Ceremonies." The one to be tortured and maimed is first lowered in status—Brenda is nonchalantly stripped of her dignity, her modesty, and her professionalism in a blink. More than a mere change of status, suggests Garfinkel, degradation was a material feature of the moral indignation to which audiences must be aroused, before any narrative, filmic or otherwise, can support "public denunciation." "Denunciation": *not approving but* willfully following the action logic; not thinking how right it is that Brenda should be lowered, because we do not think that at all—but this is too late: she is lowered already, her new condition matches her new fate. She is already a "person like that," one to whom "things like this" happen. The point isn't that we agree with Rusk's attitude toward Brenda and toward women; it's that we comprehend fully how it *is conceivable that somebody somewhere might agree*, in short, that his attitude is agree-able. He may be vile, but he is not a mystery.

Foucault helpfully advises that "the 'pain' at the heart of punishment is not the actual sensation of pain, but the idea of pain, displeasure, inconvenience—the 'pain' of the idea of 'pain.' Punishment has to make use not of the body, but of representation" (*Discipline* 94). This will be difficult to grasp if one insists on thinking of narrative cinema as a privileged window on the world, when it is anything but.

SCOPIC

As we see him onscreen, Bob Rusk epitomizes male visual pleasure as Laura Mulvey once noted it, "enjoying the freedom of action and control over the diegetic world," although for him it is not, of course, diegetic but as real as real can be for any character. *We* have the opportunity to share that pleasure, men and women viewers alike (see Mulvey 29ff.).[8] We should consider the Blaney murder and scopophilia. Regarding the term "scopophilia" itself, Freud's use more or less strictly connected the "pleasure of looking" with the child's eagerness to see the parents' sex, in short, to be "allowed to see everything" (*Lectures* 220).[9] In neurosis, the "everything" is often converted to a formal presentation, such as the theater or the cinema (my scopophilic take on *Frenzy*, for example). In some forms of scopophilia the would-be lookers are "content merely to *imagine* [the] satisfaction" and "need no real object at all, but can replace it by their phantasies" (*Lectures* 306). What the scopophilic "sees" in an event is manifestly acceptable for some others if perhaps not for him or her, peeping in on an act of intimacy that for the intimates is neither outlandish nor naughty as they commit it, only private (a nod to courtesy and convention). Against the act itself there is no injunction; the injunction is against the seer observing. In *Frenzy*, however, there are two important catches:

- The Rusk-Blaney sex is not *de facto* juridical, it is criminal, notwithstanding that the script characterizes Rusk as a male normal in his sexuality (in the single sense adduced by Freud, that his castigation of Brenda shows he has chosen one of two typical object formations, "love for a harlot" ["Type" 194]). (For a woman *he can call and think of as* a harlot, not a woman who would call herself one.) The "hidden" aspect of the relation (Brenda's closed office, lunch time, that Rusk uses an alias on entry) applies not to a couple's modest secreting of private pleasure but to a covering, against rightful condemnation, of behavior that even the participants, Rusk especially, can know as illicit. This sex—one is not certain it should be called that—ought not be in progress *even if we don't watch*; and it should not lead to murder.

- As we are not witnessing something that could reasonably be made visible but out of propriety is not, we probe instead into the anti-social, cross the boundary, and not under the mask of our idiosyncratic selves but as the Public Anyone from whom crime is cached. The peeper in scopophilia is trying to catch a glimpse—even "with the most minute details" (Freud, *Lectures* 369)—of something that promises the peeker visual pleasure explicitly because it can be taken in advance to offer pleasure (read, sensitivity and sensibility) to the enactors; one gains pleasure by seeing their secret pleasuring, by invading their legitimate secrecy. *That* would be scopophilia. But it is not a viewer's scopophilia Hitchcock plays with here, not the audience's eagerness for a sexuality sublimated through watching an "actual" one, but the audience's willingness to stand by a vision of abject cruelty, a spying upon a crime: upon not only what I myself should not see happening but what all of us agree should not happen. With this scene the filmmaker is posing one of the limiting conditions of looking in, an action that is essential to film watching (and filmmaking).

TABLE FRENZY

Perhaps we have gained an appetite. Move to Chief Inspector Oxford's table, where violence and submission occur regularly and on a less explicit order. Mrs O. lives in a frenzy of creativity, and her husband, should we take him at his word, is almost starving. With this chef's *haute cuisine*, there are a number of simultaneous jokes working, although the Oxford dinner table is not depicted as a joke.

- *Stereotypy.* For working- and middle-class British spectators, the dining scenes present rhythmically repetitive stereotypy, something North American viewers would have learned to appreciate from Monty

Python's antics.[10] In this case the caricature of a hen-pecked, timid, bourgeois husband being tortured by dishes he cannot bring himself to eat (or even look at: another form of turning away) whilst at the same time being too discrete to state his aversion. It is a constant challenge for him to make food disappear. (The wife has been making living things disappear in a systematic way, of course.) For the comedy to work, Mrs O. must appear to have no awareness at all of the circumstances she imposes or her husband's agonies. She glides into the kitchen to fetch her next course (the torturer selects a new tool), and behind her back he can take action. This routine is stated and given variation, a standard comedic form. A comedy of metrical misfit.

o *Taste.* The British kitchen, I can assure readers, had not yet in 1972 widely benefited from the infusion of European techniques and preferences, or Californian coffee, and purveyed instead a stolid, boring, overcooked, colorless, and starch-heavy cooking bruited around the world. This notwithstanding that the sunlight of change was beginning to appear, and that in the year of the filming the career of Elizabeth David as a revolutionary of English cuisine was at its peak. But she didn't have a lot of company, and she wasn't cooking in The Globe pub or the Coburg Hotel, Bayswater. It may be that the upper class ate with relative sophistication, at least sometimes (see Grosvenor) but middlers like the Oxfords, nestled into their cozy little domestications, normally ate beef and suet; bangers and mash maybe done up with peas; bubble and squeak; plump pork pies; kippers and black pudding; mushy veg, sticky toffee pudding, and the omnipresent cuppa tea. Not to forget the Potato in a thousand thousand forms, "that marvel of insipidity" (David 135). To savor the silent delight of a curry was to voyage outside the home (and away from one's pub) to an exclusively Indian restaurant (such as, in 1972, Akash Tandoori on Irving Street behind the National Gallery, where it was possible to eat gold foil for dessert). Much ahead of her time, our Mrs Oxford is a modern woman who knows there is a world outside Piccadilly, an entertainment beyond Leicester Square, and who dares to take lessons for, and practice at home—albeit upon her beleaguered husband, captive audience—dishes he has never dreamed of. The script conjures possibilities no living soul has ever dreamed of either, making the wife's attempts not only likely to be futile but comically preposterous at the outset, mockeries at once of the English diner who would never have the first clue and of the ridiculous *chefs de cuisine* across the channel whose taste and invention are as hideous as *nonpareil*. Is the Chief Inspector more beleaguered by the mystery of the multiple killings or by his forced servitude to this *saucier*-dictator? The wife is very particular in announcing all the little frills and adjustments she has added to dish after dish; she broadcasts her learning experience as a prelude to torture. If Tim Oxford sits to table in a frenzy of hunger—and he is working hard enough to have developed one—that frenzy is being blanketed. There is no way to see the dining room scenes other than as sketch comedy (see Clayton) in which an instrumentalist performs an étude of sorts upon the Chief Inspector's trim little body.

○ *Nexus*. But eating is alimentary, beginning with the mouth and proceeding through a tube. Much of English working-class wit of the time had to do with ingestion and excretion, or with reproduction, so that, for example, the unclothed bum in a radical public setting or men's eyes popping at extra-large female breasts unconsciously bared, or foods that resemble genitalia—all this kind of word and image play, often denigrated as being "utterly" juvenile—is in the early 1970s virtually everywhere to be found.[11] But the digestion motif is actually a cover for gender differentiation, eating a mask for genital intercourse, body parts made to appeal to not only genitally based erotic life but an expanded eroticism, localized in the nexus between mouth and lower region. Here at the table are two people no longer quite so young who dine instead of screwing, and dine with purpose—perhaps more accurately, with two purposes. The table etiquette can be read as referential to something far away from the table—or at least far away from *this* table, beneath mention.

○ *Ethnos*. And there is pointed reference, in both celebratory and mocking terms, to long-lived British ethnocentrism, the blimpishness we see heralded by Charters and Caldicott in *The Lady Vanishes* (1938): not only that there needn't be thought a world outside the Isles but that whatever space does happen to be out there can be home to only enemies who would cheerfully invade if they could.[12] And if they invaded, they would plunge down our throats and ultimately clog up our toilets just as likely as skim over the Channel to bomb London. Foreign cooking as poison. Ethnocentrism does not mean only a preference for the local and the recognizable over the unknown and untasted, it is a pungent terror of strangeness, especially at table. Further, an ethnocentrism stronger, more tenacious, and more vitriolic—also more preposterous—can hardly be found than English attitudes toward the French in general and French culture in particular. Here, Mrs Oxford not only cooks French cuisine—and with copper pots—but verbalizes it, giving her prefatory announcements a schoolmarm's twinge of pronunciatory precision. Impeccable French, as spoken by a British person who would like to seem impeccable. But oh my! French altogether!

Let me summarize these germ layers of the laughable (in a group of scenes that Hitchcock invented for the film, since they are not in the source material). The oddity of broadcasting strange words (in meaning and in sound) as though in the present circumstance they make coherent sense. The treatment of physical material in terms notably different from conventional use. Specialized attention to buttocks, breasts, groins, apertures, prods. Novelty of experience, or importation into England of techniques of mastery that seem to come from indiscernible origin. And then domination and control, since when our chef carries out her newest creation the diner is under her spell in so many ways: What will this be? Will it be a delight finally, or another kind of pain? How can I behave with propriety in the face of this cataclysm?

Dart back now and apply all these humorous keys to the murder of Brenda Blaney: the strange language ("I'll show you!")...the torture born out of a promise of pleasure...the domination...the focus of attention upon specific (forbidden) body parts...and a novelty tactical and situational that makes the entire event seem like an unfolding surprise. Do not get carried away laughing while the Chief Inspector tries to eat. As Shakespeare did so many times, Hitchcock creates his comedic relief not as a pathway away from the painful territory of the crimes but as an inversion of the same awkward principles that ground them. When Oxford goes home for dinner, it is as though the victimization he is calmly studying has been flipped on its head.

WASTE

Hitchcock's opening passages are invariably constructed to offer, beyond thrilling engagement, crucial contextual information. Over Ron Goodwin's Malcolm Arnoldian main theme, *Frenzy* begins with an extended helicopter shot westbound over the Thames, with Tower Bridge approaching. On the far right of the screen, just on the cusp of the frame, is Leytonstone where at 519 High Street Hitchcock was born in 1899. We do not see this part of London directly, but the point of beginning this far to the east, and just west of Canary Wharf, is to signal that we are in Hitchcock's territory, definitively and memorably—he has never taken us there before, directly.[13] Territorialism will become a silent enunciation in this film. As to the bridge, certainly until at least the end of the 1970s if not much later, this was *the* preeminent symbol of London seized and carried away in tourists' memories. Passing, we see at right the Horror That Was Inculcated In Our History Lessons, namely, the Tower of London, where the headsman's axe fell and the Crown Jewels rest. Death and fabulous wealth. Holding to the river with history gliding by, we come to County Hall, on the South Bank just opposite Westminster, where a crowd has gathered, including the Lord Mayor and his spouse, to hear an eager urban planner make a brave speech.

> When I was a lad, a journey on the rivers of England was a truly blithe experience. "Bliss was it in that dawn to be alive," as Wordsworth has it. Brook lime and flag iris, plantain and marsh marigolds rioted on the banks. And kingfishers swooped and darted about, their shadows racing over the brown trout. Well, ladies and gentlemen, I'm happy to be able to tell you that these ravishing sights will be restored to us again in the near future, thanks to the diligent efforts of your government and your local authority (*portrait shot of Lord Mayor blushing with a squint and his wife closing her eyes in the blissful imagination of bliss*). Alllll the water above this point

(*stretching out an arm, a new Moses*) will soon be clear. Clear of industrial effluent. Clear of detergents. (*Young man with camera snapping.*) Clear of the waste products of our society with which for so long we have poisoned our rivers and canals. (*Some applause. We look down on part of the crowd standing near the parapet over the river, including one gentleman in a dark suit and tie and bowler hat, who bears a remarkable resemblance to Alfred Hitchcock: he does not join in the applause.*) Let us rejoice that pollution will soon be banished from the waters of this river, and that there will soon be no foreign—

No Shakespearean actor but a snowy-haired knight who has developed some splendidly rolled r's. However, he's being disattended. One watcher has turned to the water and spies what quickly gains general attention: a naked female body, floating prone, with a necktie laced around her neck. "Another necktie murder," murmurs in the crowd. A wife coos to a man nearby about "another Jack the Ripper" and "Not on yer life," says he, "'e used to carve 'em up."

A Lord of the Realm is being drawn away from the "danger" by an aide:

LORD: "I say, that's not my club tie, is it?"

A club tie possibly stained in the river's age-old pollution, surely stained by contagion with this body that does not belong:

> According to the system which it was sought to improve, the London Main Sewers fell into the valley of the Thames, and most of them, passing under the low grounds on the margin of the river before they reached it, discharged their contents into that river at or about the level, and at the time of low water only. As the tide rose it closed the outlets, and ponded back the sewage flowing from the high grounds; this accumulated in the low-lying portions of the sewers, where it remained stagnant in many cases for eighteen out of every twenty-four hours. During that period the heavier ingredients were deposited, and from day to day accumulated in the sewers: beside which, in times of heavy and long-continued rains, and more particularly when these occurred at the time of high water in the

> river, the closed sewers were unable to store the increased volume of sewage, which then rose through the house drains and flooded the basements of the houses.
>
> The effect upon the Thames, of thus discharging the sewage into it at the time of low water, was most injurious, because not only was it carried by the rising tide up the river, to be brought back to London by the following ebb tide, there to mix with each day's fresh supply,—the process of many days' accumulation towards the sea being almost imperceptible,—but the volume of the pure water in the river, being at that time at its minimum, rendered it quite incapable of diluting and disinfecting such vast masses of sewage. (Bazalgette 10)

Already by arrangement at this early point, two strains of thought are invoked because the orator's discourse has been interrupted in two ways at once:

[1] The words coming out of his mouth have been interfered with by the talk of "the people," then by amplification of the crowd's attention river-wise; but, more signally I think,

[2] The man's openly declared dream of renewal, his enthusiastic delight in a New Purity that will evacuate the Thames of the "waste products of our society," is marred by the appearance of a bona fide taxpayer now become a waste product herself.

The speaker's plans confront a very long history. Peter Ackroyd notes how undersheriff Thomas More "knew the malodorous and insanitary conditions of London at first hand" and "decided that in his *Utopia* (1516) anything *sordidum* (dirty) or *morbum* (diseased) should be forbidden within the walls," which is to say, deposited in the river. River as sewer to the sea. Indeed, as Ackroyd writes:

> The very houses of London are built upon refuse. Discarded and forgotten objects, left among old foundations, help to support the weight of the modern city, so that beneath our feet are copper brooches and crucibles, leather shoes and lead tokens, belts and buckles, broken pottery and sandals and figurines, tools and

gloves, jars and pieces of bone, shoes and oyster shells, knives and toys, locks and candlesticks, coins and combs, plates and pipes, a child's ball and a pilgrim's amulet, all spreading their silent ministry through the earth. (*Biography* 339)

But just as we live with waste we are prone to becoming waste—waste, an ultimate silence.

CLUB TIES

Hitchcock's inclusion of the toffy query about the club tie is no mere quippy put-down of the Upper who issued it. One must take interest in what a club tie is in London. The game is social-class claims and consequent legitimation in public discourse; the corridors of power. Still by the 1970s this was all a boys' competition. If one was to end up in the House of Lords (being identified this way as one of the major landholders in the United Kingdom) one began in late childhood by attending a public school, of which Winchester is the oldest in England. The school tie signaled the school as presence, foundation, and altar of anointment. One wore the school tie with secret pride and outward haughty carelessness, since the point was not to make oneself look proper but to make it evident that one possessed the means of doing so. By the late nineteenth century it was well established that one's school tie was an index of one's class, an index that would lead to either Oxford or Cambridge (ruefully, perhaps, Durham instead), and Oxbridge would lead to the Establishment. On the way, one joined an appropriate London club and took a new tie. Our genteel Lord on the embankment is outraged not only that someone may have used his club tie as a murder weapon but also that the someone so debased as to commit raw murder would have the cheek to show off that he possessed it. Memberships are of no value if they are open to anyone; and the claim of social superiority cannot be upheld if one has been seen to consort with riff-raff.

Public schools predated Dr Johnson's tenure in London. But they were given a critical view. Jonathan Swift, for example, "saw clearly enough the mischiefs which often accompanied education in rich homes, the inefficient tutors, the lack of discipline, the spoiling and coddling of boys 'taught from the nursery' that they were to inherit a great estate, the folly of supposing that accomplishments were all that a gentleman needed and that the study of Greek and Latin was a loss of time" (Mallet 215). But such "mischief" could be remedied: cold showers, hard outdoor activity, assiduous study that was extended to the point of painfulness, the hazards of bumping into upper form boys. Thinking of even a middling school, George Orwell could remember how "The Sixth Form was a group of older boys who were selected as having 'character' and were empowered to beat smaller boys" ("Joys" 417). The school would stand for one's special and particular "gentleman" status, for one's "great estate." As to the London club itself, thus the London club tie, it goes back to Samuel Johnson's late eighteenth-century days, and was an offshoot of something older, distinctly rarefied and very established in the city: to remain "above," one had to find a systematic way to stay clear of the "thronging crowds and ceaseless traffic" that were London already in the 1780s (George 170) and the formal club developed out of first the pub and subsequently the coffee houses, in which young and old men met to drink their favorite exotic beverage and discuss politics. White's in St James's Street "had been a resort of men of fashion for high play since the end of the seventeenth century" (177–78). Addison claimed that "Man is a sociable animal and we take all occasions and pretences of forming ourselves into those little nocturnal assemblies which are commonly known as *clubs*" (qtd. in Ackroyd, *Biography* 360). One can see how latterly the gentleman's club could be imitated, at least in function, in the working man's "local," a focus of social gathering—and setting for two of the telling early scenes in *Frenzy*. The invocation of the club tie is an open suggestion that social-class distinction may be at play in the happenings of this tale, and signally. If by the 1970s the gentleman's club is cloistered in Piccadilly, the pub is anywhere and everywhere, surely in Covent Garden. He who frequents the club may drop into the pub, but it's not a two-way street. Our Sir George is afeard not just that a lowlife might be clowning in his territory but that his own elite coterie might house a sordid murderer (people speculated that Jack the Ripper was a member of the House of Lords). A club tie is here besmirched through murder, but worse, letting down the team: the killer is in *my club!* Hitchcock is not himself suggesting this about Rusk, merely raising "team spirit" for consideration, placing cutlery on the table, as it were. Lining up the plates. Positioning the fruit fork.

Cut briskly to Richard Blaney in his little barman's abode above The Globe, tying his necktie at his mirror. Not every necktie is a club necktie. Nice and spanking neat, but old clothing. Presentable, not exemplary. And not particularly urban, as we shall see. He goes down and pours himself a double shot before opening. But now pounces Felix Forsythe the manager (Bernard Cribbins), irate and arrogant, firing him on the spot notwithstanding that Babs the barmaid (Anna Massey) protests strongly how Richard always pays for his drinks. Drinks aren't the problem, though. Forsythe plainly thinks Blaney has been pawing Babs too much. Out strides our loner, along Drury Lane, then Russell Street to approach the fruit market. Head high, expecting nothing. Finch "subtly avoided the temptation to be sympathetic" (Bergan). A ginger in a nappy jacket and tie welcomes him in friendship: Bob Rusk, proprietor of a fresh fruit wholesale—couldn't be more amicable, a warning, perhaps, since in the city friendliness may have a purpose. Have a muscat grape, in just this morning! Have a tip on a horse this afternoon, twenty-to-one! Dick extricates himself. Rusk is just a little on the elegant side with his pretty green tie and diamond tie pin and swank dark maroon jacket. Exemplary, not just presentable.

Exemplary as people are when they intend to make an impression.

A nearby hostelry, Nell of Old Drury, and a brandy too small (Blaney complains). The jovial barmaid serves two toffy regulars, a solicitor (Gerald Sim) and a doctor (Noel Johnson)—two pints and a quick nosh, lunchtime in the market. The necktie murderer is obviously their subject. Adjacent at the bar, Dick can't avoid swallowing every irritating syllable. The doctor is an authentic expert on perverse behavior, no less: the killer could have a serious sexual psychopathology. No hesitation, either, in tossing the barmaid a ribald suggestion: wink wink wink, the killer rapes his victims before slaying them. Smirk, giggle, pull back the head—Sim and Johnson play all the tonalities and gestures of repression traditional in British character acting onscreen through the 1950s and 1960s. No viewer will find it difficult interpreting these two smarmy rats, eager to show off while feigning a circumspect air.

Blaney heads up Oxford Street way, to his ex-wife Brenda's dating and friendship bureau. He is grumpy with Monica the "new" receptionist (been here a year) and surly to Brenda. Sparks of displaced anger fly off when he closets himself in her office and shuts the door. She wants to know why he's so aggressive and slamming his hand on her desk he affirms that he is not—this heard by Monica and witnessed through the warping bubble glass in the door. Not a particularly sociable type, this Richard Blaney. He seems to have a low regard for the idea of "fixing people up together," creating marriages of the sort that patently didn't work for Brenda and him and, as he estimates it, probably won't work for anyone else either.

So far, then, a tidy essay encompassing (A) detritus and civilization; (B) class resentment; (C) unfulfilled hungers; and (D) emotional masquerade. We must always show politesse, no matter what we feel (offended Monica being oh-so-correct with blunt Richard; the Nell barmaid pretending [but only pretending] to chuckle with her smarmy toffs [who know her name while she doesn't know theirs]). Do not lose control. Stiff upper lip and carry on and God bless the Queen.

[a] And this necktie chappie, well!—he sometimes rapes 'em before he kills 'em, and there's a giggle for you! Have your pleasure before you go to work, and hip hip hurrah.

[b] The blaggard has the cheek to use my club tie for his killings?! Who *does* he think he is! And then

[c] The river: all the way from here to what, Rotherhithe? It will be diamond clear! Purity reborn. Not to mention:

[d] We are in the throes of modern London, able to observe the continual movement of strangers who if they do not collide at least leave traces of their steps.[14] In this general throng are tiny communities of familiars—bar cohorts—who have gathered, as they gather now, for what seem centuries, their language curt and implicating and full of discreet abbreviation. Of course all the key values of civic life, however barbaric, are shared and accepted. This is the camaraderie Richard is outside and Rusk is not; and Richard's pretense of not caring is his way of holding back his rage.

A recipe for London and London life. Eighteenth- and nineteenth-century London, the cultural historians show, were pretty much the same if less slick, less electronic. The decorative forms differ; the substance continues.

As to Britain and British personalities, Dick Blaney is a curious one to center a Hitchcock film. Hitchcock has plenty of Britishers, or British transatlantics, including Julia Rainbird (Kathleen Nesbitt) in *Family Plot*; Sarah Armstrong (Julie Andrews) in *Torn Curtain*; Old and Young Rutland (Alan Napier; Sean Connery) in *Marnie*; Vandamm (James Mason) in *North by Northwest*; Gavin Elster (Tom Helmore) in *Vertigo*; O'Connor (Anthony Quayle) in *The Wrong Man*; the Draytons (Brenda de Banzie; Bernard Miles) and many others in *The Man Who Knew Too Much*; the old Captain (Edmund Gwenn) in *The Trouble with Harry*; and on and on. Needless to say, the paramount case is Cary Grant, with his four appearances (*Suspicion, Notorious, To Catch a Thief, North by Northwest*). Note the modest gracility in the way he hands the valet his clothing to press at the Ambassador Hotel by contrast with Blaney's abrupt stripping in the corridor of the Coburg Hotel, Bayswater, so that the nosey busboy can get the stench of the Sally Ann out of his clothes. Hitchcock's Brit is generally tidy, honorable, somewhat airy of consciousness, smart, graceful if not also gracious, mannered, well- or at least very cleanly bred, and not vulgar. But Blaney is nothing if not vulgar. Vulgar, as in "of the gutter," *vernacular:* this doesn't mean dirty, malodorous, or repulsive as much as what in 1950s America was called "beat"; of the streets; a Street Dick. He steps through the traffic of life; he tumbles from job to job; he is down where the objects of the day are dropped, butts, condoms, yesterday's newspaper, apple cores, not lingering in the sedate and aromatic chambers of a club. Bob Rusk is low, too, but higher than he once was. He has burnished his surface, Blaney would say, "tarted himself up," has gained a few tastes to show off and an air of blitheness to feign. What irritates Rusk, what prods the bruise of his fundamental lowness, has been cravenly swallowed and roils in his gut— and below his gut—along with the muscat grapes. Blaney does not repress. He doesn't mind showing resentment, anger, and displeasure. What he will seem to be is what he knows himself to be, directly, presently, feelingfully, authentically. Like other aristocrats he cannot behave but as himself.

To Brenda, Richard is neither rude nor angry, and their no longer being together has left him no bitterness. About the end of their marriage we will learn; but it's clear he was as content as she to stop it, grounds, perhaps, for his ironic humor about the Blaney Marriage and Friendship Bureau. The institutionalized "friendship" that Brenda's advertising sells isn't his cuppa. Bluntly, he doesn't *care* about all the things one is supposed to uphold in order to be seemly in the City. 'E's a live one's wot 'e is. Don't fool yourself that because he hangs out in the market he's uneducated: his language is flawless, even sophisticated albeit not florid. Not to forget that it was a direct cut from the lord expostulating about his club tie to Blaney before the mirror. *Necktie* means Blaney—a fellow tied by the neck. Soon we will learn *necktie* also means Rusk. To the telltale lesson it is no great leap: Rusk means (imports) Blaney.

A MASCULINITY

In a class society like Great Britain, every character's identity is bounded by a class position, exemplifies a class. Felix's hyperaggressive panic about profit and loss and its match, hyperactive sexual jealousy, suggest that he comes from a world in which goods both profitable and pleasurable are scarce. Babs's ease in openly contradicting him about Blaney shows a confidence based in a more secure background: perhaps she left her lower middle-class home to strike out on her own, and that is why we find her here. Or the two toffs at Nell of Old Drury: quite happy to share a conversational tidbit with the barmaid but the abruptness with which they turn away from her to continue their schmoozing shows she couldn't matter less to them; she is one of the servants who don't really exist. Blaney detects all this, with some loathing. There are no filmmakers whose portrayal of class relations is as knowing or as thoroughgoing as Hitchcock's. What can easily read as personality quirk is almost always a given of the character's class position, a blueprint of the jail in which he or she is silently celled.

Blaney resents not having had better pickings in the feeding frenzy of life. Like a working man he blames the problem where he also pins his hopes—luck. "The very thought of luck is sufficient to dazzle," comments Roger Caillois. "This illusory expectation causes the lowly to be more tolerant of a mediocre status that they have no practical means of ever improving" (115). He lets Brenda know, dining at her club, that his friend Bob Rusk offered a tip on a horse who came in at twenty-to-one and *for all his rotten luck* he didn't have money to back it. But, though he's been "done by," luck is the thing he has found to live for, as Dostoevsky would put it. The genuineness of Brenda's sympathy heats to a boil his sense of persecution and his loathing of the successful. He loses self-control, loudly accusing all the diners sitting around, in their furs and pretty hats and with their lovely cutlery sliding across their fancy plates, of being so very good at *business* (ostensibly a despicable concentration) that they all typify an abject whoredom. And she, spits Richard, has been successful with her ridiculous clientele because though she can't make love she can sell it—a slap she takes with dignified poise. But then her poise is another superiority: Brenda may have married Richard from above, what should have been a definite stroke of luck for him but it didn't pan out. We sense from Leigh-Hunt's performance that the graciousness springs from an authentic affection for her husband of ten years. He is wallowing in self-pity now because under her brolly, even temporarily, he has the security to let his feelings out.

In the late morning we find Brenda at her desk when a man lets himself in. "Oh, it's you again, Mr Robinson!"

Rusk wears a brown suede jacket (expensive) with a blue and beige tartan tie, very spiffy and drawing our thoughts back to Blaney's costume yesterday, that worn gray gamekeeper's jacket with leather at the shoulders against which Brenda's evening attire of stylish black dress, large single strand of pearls, and pink and black overcoat seemed so true a contradiction. Rusk has been trying a little too hard for his look, but not without conviction: looks matter to him. We pick up Brenda's carefully polished manners, fruitful in her business success.

"I'm having my lunch."

"*You're the one* I wanted to see." (Her eyes open wide in a direct gaze. Her absent companion Monica's gaze has a tendency to seem shifty.)

Slowly across the chamber he glides, as we see from her position at the desk, then, to imitate his reciprocating view, we dolly right, across a medium shot of her. The snake in her eyes; the morsel in his.

She has "already explained" that they cannot help with his odd demands.

"Oh, I know that you can be *most helpful!*" Read between the lines.

Mr Robinson needs women of a certain type, she is aware. "Certain peculiarities" appeal to him and he needs females to submit to them. (Note the artistic circumlocution.) She, however, serves "a very normal *clientèle*" (pronounced with dignity, as educated English people pronounce the French to which they have been educated; Mrs Oxford's pronunciations are more striven for).

He explodes in blushing rage. "If you can fix up a lot of idiots, then why not me?" (*I am preferable to those other men.*) He takes his lack of success in her *clientèle* as a mark upon himself. He is surely not having the run of luck with Mrs Blaney's services that he has with the horses, and as Dick apparently did, but in his sly way he is sharing with Brenda angry resentment against the "lucky" ones. In short, Dick Blaney curses bad luck itself; Rusk curses those whose luck is good. Luck is out there, a material presence: *what is the sufficient reason why it should not drop upon me?* For Rusk luck is delice; for Blaney it is survival. Rusk is not to be disparaged: "I like flowers. And fruit. People . . . like . . . me." Approaching the camera (the desk) with menace. She coaxes him to go elsewhere, "not that any reputable agency would service you." A glance from her, upward at his angry but well-tended face—Hitchcock uses the Dutch angle, always, to pronounced effect—and from Rusk, looking down at her increasingly anxious one. This is the *best agency*, he says (Brenda has closed her eyes), because . . . "I like you. You're my . . . type of woman."

Brenda's eyes, now seen very close up, are opening to the dawn of an unthinkable unpleasantness.

Here is a typifier of women, assembler of an exclusive set. As to Rusk's *type*, we could consider moveable type, the multiple placements and usages any one piece can have as contexts shift; the replicability (see Benjamin) of pieces and usages;[15] type as residue of an operation of categorization, equalization, and commodification; the human "type" not merely a fruit of taste but a certificate of ownership. Typification in sexual partnership is inherently depersonalizing. Bob's denoting "his type" is his calling card.

And, Rusk is happy to inform Brenda, *we're in the same trade.* They put it on the fruit, after all: "Don't squeeze the goods 'till they're yours." At the corners of his eyes there is uncontrolled twitching, and his face, phallic substitute, has been steadily engorging. "Squeezing goods" serves as a gentrifying hyperbole, since Brenda is going to be squeezed much more than she can imagine, pulped even.

A bouquet of purple anemones sits behind her as he clamps down on the telephone she has tried to raise. "What made you think I was going to call the police?" she tries, one could say *fruitlessly.*

With a smile too amicable for the circumstances he seizes her half-eaten apple: "Oh! English? 'Course it is!"—more than two thousand varieties of apple are grown in England[16]—a commendation for consuming local, flair of national pride, the whole package. Also a blunt signal of Rusk's own preparation to consume local, Hitchcock invariably gesturing an upbeat before every downbeat. Gnawing, he notes her "frugal" lunch, "certainly not enough to support a lady with your opulent figure"—a comment about her weight and self-attention that trounces the boundary of intimacy. *Opulent*, of all conceivable words. Rusk the salesman has the lexicon.

We move on, not only because Rusk is randy but because the viewer is eager to bind with the forward process of cinema, which carries us on in any event. Onward, and somehow believing that nothing to follow in this scene will be surprising, in short previsualizing it: his offer to give her the best lunch in town, her demurral then clever second thought that it might be an escape, her coming around the desk, him seizing her, the forced kiss, the push against the wall, her affirmation, "All right I know what you want, let's go back to my place" (self-preservation in the face of severe violence, learned perhaps in a seminar), her advising that the secretary will be back any minute, his refusal to buy, "You know what happens to wicked girls who tell wicked lies...," her wincing agony as he wrenches her arms from behind, her fainting and being laid into the client's chair, his insatiable hunger as he leans atop her and the camera takes her place, making him so *very* close, perspiration streaming on his rose-pink brow, "Don't worry," whisper from Eden, "you've got nothing to worry about," her head dropping back. Brenda "awakens," lifts her feet to kick him away. She runs. He chases, grabs her leg. Throws her back into the chair. "Take the money! In the bag!" Diabolical heat burning his muscles and breathlessness taking her away. Macro-close on the two faces, Brenda's insistently rational, Rusk's far past reason. He could use the money to buy any woman he wants but "I don't buy women! It's *you* I want. *You're my type!*" Pencil lips planted hard upon her. Phone jangling in pathetic fallacy. In profile now, his legs forcing themselves between hers. She gives assurance she won't struggle ("Preserve yourself! Preserve yourself!"). "Oh, I like you to struggle!" (He took the seminar, too, and learned the evasive tactics.) "Please, don't tear my dress!" as he tears her dress. The bra glaring white and lacey with a tiny pink noisette rose at its center (find that noisette in white at the center of Lina Aysgarth's black mourning dress in *Suspicion* [1941] and, pink, in Madeleine's nosegay in *Vertigo* [1958]). Brenda's bared breasts, a situation cold as medicine, her legs thrown up. "Lovely!"

Consider, reader, how one's attitude toward this progression is self-generated.

Then the rape. "The humiliation she anticipated is undergone in fact" (Beauvoir 405). And to cap it the necktie gesture, something we've been waiting for as it's rumored all over town. Insatiable, goading, endless.

My reading is that Rusk, who claims desire, believes in his claim: thinks he generally desires to have, possess, employ, and enjoy his victims; and that after the release, desire spent entirely, they will be nothing but waste, the apple core after the apple. Any number of rape or violation scenarios could be played out without culminating in murder. Yet, reflecting back as we watch the noose tighten we can sense the present brutal moment eventuating logically, coherently, forthrightly from what we were cued before—by his display of mounting desire—would be likely to happen now. Following from it so "logically," then, the murder *is* the sex, is certainly part of it for him, all the prototypical sexual moves only an inversion of foreplay. As to us sitting to witness this execution, we can claim to watch *without desire*... because our watching *is* our desire:

> O, for shame, for shame,
> Lie not, to say mine eyes are murderers.
> *As You Like It*, III.5

We strangle the story, watching the story strangled.

Hitchcock never tries to spell out the fabulous secret of Rusk's motive, how it is that he's dangerous as a wounded tiger who before charging has a special way of opening the eyes. One reacts without deliberating. There is even a sense in which, not understanding him (not being given to understand), we perform rejection; rejection that joins Rusk and Blaney: they both suffer it, *directly inside the film,* Rusk from the affronted viewer, Blaney everywhere he goes and as long as he can remember, except, ironically, from his friend Rusk.

ANNIHILATING THE FUTURE

The Salvation Army doss house where Blaney sleeps the night—or half-sleeps; he's awake enough to snag the arm of a neighbor trying to filch the money Brenda gave him—brings to mind George Orwell's *Down and Out in Paris and London* and its careful description of the English life of the very poor. The guests here having been allocated smart-looking, uniform, rose-pink-and-white blankets—a vague hint of recuperation and redemption—staying one night would only hint at the abysmal position Orwell describes:

> At eight the porter came along the passage unlocking the doors and shouting "All out!" The doors opened, letting out a stale, fetid stink. At once the passage was full of squalid, grey-shirted figures, each chamber-pot in hand, scrambling for the bathroom. It appeared that in the morning only one tub of water was allowed for the lot of us, and when I arrived twenty tramps had already washed their faces; I took one glance at the black scum floating on the water, and went unwashed. (147)

In order to attract a suitable middle-class patronship for Universal, Hitchcock has made the natural choice of not letting Blaney seem unwashed. He's been a presentable tramper, a mover from cadge to cadge, now in jangling 1970s London eager to spend what few coins he has on a pint or a brandy rather than, as with the tramps of the 1920s, on some tea while searching the city for cigarette stubs. Blaney depends on the kind good fortune of others, poor Brenda being one of the saviors most sympathetic to his condition. Unlike Rusk, he cannot fancy himself proprietor of an established business—*he is not established*—and in his state of modest but presentable destitution cannot seem even modestly empowered. He's a person to whom things happen, not one who makes things happen. Perhaps he has come to recognize "the great redeeming feature of poverty," in Orwell's words; "the fact that it annihilates the future" (20).

Blaney, Rusk, Forsythe, Brenda: all of them born in the mid-1930s. When they were about four, the world they were beginning to taste was being withdrawn from beneath their feet. 3 September 1939:

> The evacuation of London, which is to be spaced over three days, began yesterday and was apparently a triumph for all concerned.... The railways, whose workers had been on the verge of going out on strike when the crisis came, played their part nobly, and the London stations, accustomed to receiving trainloads of child

> refugees form the Third Reich, got down to the job of dispatching trainload after trainload of children the other way—this time, cheerful little cockneys who ordinarily get to the country perhaps once a year on the local church outing and could hardly believe the luck that was sending them now. Left behind, the mothers stood around rather listlessly at street corners waiting for the telegrams that were to be posted up at the various schools to tell them where their children were. (Panter-Downes 4–5)

Note how this journalist, reporting on England for the American reader, cannily points to "luck," a word she would have heard coming out of the mouths of these relocated babes. They were having, yes, all the luck in the world, but when they were back in the city, some sooner than others but virtually all by the mid-1940s, things would be ugly and rough and the world they would have to inhabit would be neither amenable to the touch of creativity nor charged with the sparks of hope. Much of victorious postwar Britain was unrepaired, waiting for reconstruction, waiting for glory. It isn't hard to see the birth in Forsythe of not only jealousy but seething jealousy, in Rusk of not only self-loathing but boundless self-loathing, in Blaney of not only hunger but unremitting hunger, in Brenda of not only assiduity but zealous assiduity; or to understand how by the early 1970s (1972 was the year the Duke of Windsor died) their habits and personalities had congealed into form. And jealousy, self-loathing, and hunger: these are not badges wondrous and glowing.

ON THE STREET

Wearing a face that she keeps in a jar by the door.
—Paul McCartney, "Eleanor Rigby"

Frenzy has a unique place in Hitchcock's oeuvre in its striking, meticulously observed banality, as if this very emptiness is the world and no other is possible. Typically some enchanting tissue—quirky, coincidental, wild, exaggerated, glamorous—dominates Hitchcock's organization; the viewer's attention moves to it often. In *North by Northwest* (1959), adorable and goofy Roger; in *Vertigo* (1958), intoxicating, unforgettable Madeleine; in

Rear Window the fabulous apartment complex; in *Notorious* (1946) the Nazi plot.... A "flavoring" of one kind or another, essential to the film, relieves us from the banal something that resides in every story. In *Frenzy*, everything that could be poetic becomes mundane, not glamorous. One has to see mundanity as antithetical to "the Hitchcock film" in order to understand what is profoundly Hitchcockian about this one: shuffling movement in everyday London; sameness of structures and experiences, as with the different pubs that are not so very different; repetition in the killer's method; standard police questioning; misevaluation, as with the incorrect readings of the Blaney divorce settlement that lead to his accusation; characters persistently blending in with circumstance rather than appealing as personalities—look at all the lonely people. Lonely and direct. Is Dick Blaney couth, charming, and honey-toned?—not at all. Here he is at Brenda's bureau with Monica (flagged phrases discussed below):

> BLANEY (straightforward): You're new here, aren't you?
>
> MONICA (self-affirming): I've been here for over a year now. What can I do for you?
>
> BLANEY: You can inform Mrs Blaney that one of her less successful exercises in matrimony is here.
>
> MONICA (with a mask of tone): And who shall I say is calling?
>
> BLANEY: Mr Blaney. Or if you preferred it, (*a) ex-Squadron Leader Blaney, late of the RAF and Mrs Blaney's (*b) matrimonial bed.
>
> MONICA (perhaps too properly): I see. Is Mrs Blaney expecting you?
>
> BLANEY (sporting): She must be. Everybody expects (*c) a bad penny to turn up sooner or later.

If she is catching him raptly, Monica can pick up several clues from Blaney in this tête-à-tête:

[a] That he is out of the military and, given his surliness, perhaps not for the most sanguine of reasons. Was he tossed out? At best, did the military rough up his manners?

[b] That he not only gives indication of who he is, but also invokes, of all things, her employer's matrimonial bed. He was "bedding" Mrs Blaney (obvious; but something one doesn't say to prim and proper Monica).

[c] If he does not see himself as a bad penny, he is predicting that his wife will. (Although when we see them together, she seems not to.)

When, later, Monica recalls this talk she might take pause to consider the grace in his etiquette—take pause if consideration is her main purpose. But Monica, talking through clenched teeth, will not take pause:

[aa] She is a passive-aggressive, whose politeness covers hostility. "Puts on her face." Flagging passive aggressiveness in this lonely witness is crucial because when Rusk converses with Brenda before killing her he is distinctly not that way, does not cover either desire or loathing with couth. Monica also does not pause to consider Blaney as a person because she has urged herself to feel rubbed the wrong way by him and is resentful and vengeful already. She has spent a whole year here, spotlessly careful, dedicated, good at her job, and he treats her without recognition, without a seemly bow; moreover, he is sneering at her for not realizing instantly that he is the ex-husband. She misinterprets him, of course. He is being wry, knowing she does not know and could not know who he is, and that at this moment he is informing her; but also anxious about the awkwardness of that, and covering his anxiousness with wit.

[bb] Monica takes it as an aggressive insult that to her face he refers to the "bed of sex." He is perverse. He is a jungle beast here, now, instantly, always: hungry.

[cc] Clearly, he presumes she would take him for a "bad penny" *and in fact she does*, so he has violated the privacy of her thoughts, and been a lowlife, too.

All this careful elaboration of Hitchcock's, the careful writing by Anthony Shaffer, the precise use of lighting and angles by Gil Taylor, the careful rehearsal of Finch and Jean Marsh (cast for the smallish role of Monica at a time when in Great Britain, because of *Upstairs, Downstairs* [1971], she was a household name [playing Rose, a household name]), the eloquent timing of the scene, the tonality, the view of Brenda's well-lit office through the ripple-glass door, alluring but inaccessible (or alluring *because* inaccessible—watch what Rusk will do with that), all this preparation, and especially the facial expressions of this young woman sealing up her swelling vat of poison so that the world will sense only flowers——all this in order to prepare a conversation that will ensue not very long later:

Chief Inspector Oxford comes on the scene with, "Good morning, one and all." With the gentlest gentility he begins to question Monica. She claims she saw Mrs Blaney's ex-husband coming out of the premises just as she got back from her lunch, during which the murder occurred: is she absolutely sure that was Richard Blaney? Then, can you describe what the man looked like? With this comforting interlocutor, Monica can relax her guard (flagged phrases discussed below):

> MONICA (obedient, meticulous, ravaging her memory): He came in yesterday afternoon and was (*a) perfectly horrid. (*b) He'd been drinking and (*c) insisted on seeing Mrs Blaney.
>
> OXFORD (plainly): Did he see her?
>
> MONICA: Oh yes, she'd never turn anyone away, (*d) not even him!... Mr Blaney was becoming (*e) very violent both in his language and his behavior.
>
> OXFORD: Did he strike Mrs Blaney?
>
> MONICA: Yes, (*f) I think so. There was the sound of a blow.

Now, could you describe the man?

> MONICA: He was wearing a rather old-fashioned jacket with leather patches on the shoulders and at the elbows, in my opinion it was (*g) quite unsuitable for London.

The rhythmic forward thrust of complaint, phrase after phrase after phrase, is a kind of unconscious (on Monica's part) mimicry of Rusk's raping motions. It is so easy to be caught up in the brilliance of direction and actorial performance yet miss the payoff of a moment—Monica is tidily setting Blaney up for the hangman.[17]

[*a] *Perfectly horrid.* This is "perfectly" + "horrid." Two idiosyncratic estimations joined: that his behavior was scurrilous and that in scurrilousness it achieved a limiting position, because it's one thing to call something horrid and quite another to add the word "perfectly." Perfectly, as in "nothing on earth could be worse." (We see clearly in this film how wrong she is about that. If she is using speech merely to dramatize—"perfectly" a lovely three-syllable beat—still she is speaking to The Law.)

[*b] *He'd been drinking.* Likely enough with Blaney, who began his day with a shot. Dick Blaney has pretty much always *been drinking.* But Monica means suggestion by implication (she has the uptightness of a teetotal moral entrepreneur).[18] He drank enough not to be sober (sober as I proudly am: her pose), his drinking puts him in the gutter compared to me. Being low, he can of course be thought guilty of so low an act as murdering my employer, his estranged wife. And also, *I surely would never have married a man like this, drunk all the time.* But how does she know he's been drinking, was she whiffing him?

[*c] *Insisted on seeing.* Some people come in here and request an opportunity to see Mrs Blaney, and some are even in extremis. This one, however, *insisted.* Would not take no for an answer. Thought himself above our clean and serene routine. I could sense his violence from the very start because he lived it. (She was out at lunch while Rusk wasn't taking no for an answer.)

[*d] *Not even him.* "Even" as keyword. Kindly and responsible Mrs Blaney didn't turn people away. She loved people, all people, *even this one.* She wouldn't have shunned *even a person who merited shunning*—who indeed should well have been shunned, he was so disgraceful and so rude. Brenda taking *even this one* in is rationale for the marriage Monica has so much trouble comprehending (and blessing retroactively).

[*e] *Violent in his language.* "Language," not "speaking" or "tone." Not: the melody coming out of a speaker's mouth, that riff; what it is he deeply

means—no, not that. Like all good English children who paid attention to their teachers, Monica knows the different between "language" and "speaking" and she means only, and exclusively, the words and phrasings in Blaney's lexicon. Literally, if you typed out what he said you would find the script violent. Yet if we listen to Blaney actually speaking to Monica we find no violence whatsoever. Insistence, sharp (even snide) wit, precision—but not violence. She is casting him for the police, likely in her case normal practice.

[*f] *I think so. There was the sound of a blow.* Two comments melded into one, again. If he is accomplished and serious, the Chief Inspector will hear them as disconnected though she conflates. Having turned away at the instant, she was not in fact looking (as we were) through the ripple glass in the door, and therefore cannot possibly *think* that he struck Mrs Blaney; he struck the desk. The blow was to a sheet of wood. But the phrase "sound of a blow" is so evocative—we quickly fill in a victimized body.

[*g] *Quite unsuitable for London.* A moral evaluation and a fashion statement, Monica dubbing herself arbiter of suitabilities. When we saw Blaney talking with her, this man who had been walking the streets of Covent Garden didn't seem unsuitable for London. A person's dress is always less an index of personal taste (*à chacun son goût*) than a resultant of economic power (of which we already know Blaney has little) and geographical origins. Rusk, who dresses nappily, is a proprietor of a burgeoning business; Blaney has been working as a barman on hourly wages (some of which have paid for his Scotch). Monica judges, absent all this information. This is also, of course, a proud burgher's social-climbing dismissal and disavowal of those "country folk": he's not dressed *for the city* (as Milord recognizing his club tie is).

We can wonder, too: did she recognize in him a gamekeeper, and did he "talk of country matters"?[19] And for what *London* is his dress unsuitable?—the fruit market? the stock exchange? Lincoln's Inn?

Biased and opinionated if not altogether off the mark, Monica speaks with a crisply articulated poise—severely elevated Received Pronunciation useful, as she would think, for giving her words weight. Like a polished little grammar-school student perched in front of the class, she is "in the witness stand," virtually fingering a killer in the act of his killing; but objectively her "observations" are slight and hard to verify. Her glorious diction is a shining embellishment.

Still, our Monica has kicked the switch of the machinery of justice.

A DARKENING PATH

...through foggy London Town
The sun was shining everywhere.

—Ira Gershwin

Eager and happy, Babs is fetching Blaney's things from The Globe to Leicester Square ticket booth, where he lurks in wait (the film's only touch upon Leicester Square). They taxi to the Coburg Hotel in Bayswater (a decent enough district, nearby Kensington Palace) for the beginning of what will be a long, twisting, strange, perilous flight from the police, who have been helped by Monica to think Dick the Necktie Murderer. He is also in flight from himself, his personality having become his own best enemy. Perhaps only in the modern world can a man's personality wage war against his honor. A darkening path:

[1] Confrontation at the hotel with an imperious and hyperjudgmental desk clerk who sneers at the obvious disingenuousness of these "marrieds" (as though liaisons are something new). Her nosy bellman chum escorts them up and is summarily handed Blaney's clothes to have sprayed and cleaned because they reek of the doss house. Dick slept at the Salvation Army:

BABS: With all the old men?

BLANEY: Yes, that's it. Oh, we had a high old time. The conversation was mature, the red biddy flowed down the odd throats, and the good fellowship of the open road prevailed.

BABS: Red biddy—what's that?

BLANEY: Blended red wine. Half vino, half methylated spirits.

The bellman sights an alarming newspaper announcement of police searching for someone whose attire matches what he's just been asked to clean. *We have the Necktie Murderer upstairs in Room 322* (the Cupid Room)! He rings the police, who arrive almost instantaneously. A race upstairs. The door thrown open. The room has been used but is entirely empty.

[2] A long tête-à-tête between Blaney and Babs on a park bench. His claims of innocence she does believe, but "thousands wouldn't." And, "I must be soft in the head letting a suspected strangler put his arms around me" as mockingly he wrings her neck[20] and they warm even more to each other. But now materializes an old friend, Johnny Porter (Clive Swift). From the height of his hotel-room balcony across Park Lane, where his wife Hettie (Billie Whitelaw) remains surveilling, we watch the mime of the conversation, then Johnny leading them up. Hettie knows Blaney well enough, thank you. In her committed belief, he's a murderer and can give no mollification. But our Johnny will be a master of geniality. He's opening a British pub in Paris; Blaney and Babs should come over and work for him there. Against Hettie's protests, Blaney stays the night in the Porters' suite:

> HETTIE (with scathing bourgeois virtuousness): Thank God we're off to Paris tomorrow morning, that's all I can say. That is, if we're not in jail. I'm going shopping!
>
> (A short while later:)
>
> BLANEY (to Babs, who has agreed to meet him in the morning at Victoria Station): Mum's the word, heh? Don't tell a soul I'm here.
>
> BABS: Cross me heart and hope to die! (*They kiss.*)

Hettie is taking the opportunity to poison Babs's taste for Blaney. The vicious divorce petition, says she, alleged on the wife's behalf extreme mental and physical cruelty. Blaney protests, with a tone of distinct sanity, that it was the lawyers who put all that language in, since he and Brenda wanted to be separated quickly and not have to wait the regulation three years. Hettie's churlish reading will have resonance soon.

[3] Chief Inspector Oxford's office, where under Sgt Spearman's eye he sits savoring a "full English" at his desk. He does think he's got Blaney nailed, but Spearman is fixated on the ham and egg:

> OXFORD (to Spearman): My wife is currently taking a course at the Continental School of Gourmet Cooking. Apparently they've never heard of the principle, to eat well in this country one must have breakfast three times a day, and an English breakfast at that. I don't mean a *café complet*. (*Spearman is mystified.*) It's a cup of coffee half an inch deep in floating bits of boiled milk and a sweet bun full of air. That's what I had this morning.

A subordinate brings more ammunition: the ten-pound note found in Blaney's jacket "bore traces of the face powder found in Mrs Blaney's handbag." Well it would: at the club she slipped him the money unobtrusively, out of her handbag. But how alarming to see the finality, the rapidity, and the unquestioned certainty with which these agents of the law, even decorous and well-intentioned Oxford, leap to conclusions that are unfounded. A delicious little instant of audience-character separation.

About these "psychopath" types Oxford can see his sergeant is baffled:

> OXFORD (instructively): The important thing to remember is that they hate women and are mostly impotent[21]—don't mistake rape for potency, sergeant; in the latter stage of the disease it's the strangling not the sex that brings them on. Above all, of course, they're Sadists. And you know what they are, sergeant, I'm sure.—'Course if you don't you can read all about them in there—Mrs Blaney's divorce petition. Tells you a great deal about the habits of our hero.[22]

The Blaney divorce petition, available, like other legal documents, to the police, details all those cadges solicitors foisted upon the court, phrasing them as truths.

[4] At The Globe, Forsythe is whinging to the police by telephone that his barmaid is missing. Rusk stands nearby, idly drinking with a chum who deals in a business he himself is glad to be far from: potatoes—

> RUSK'S CHUM (Richard Wyler): You're not a bad judge, Bob. Potato business is poison, always was. It costs a fortune to dig 'em up, another fortune to transport them, and what do you have at the end? Hardly any money for them.... I'm going to send a truckload back up to Lincolnshire tonight, and what will they do with them? Plough them back in... And they say there's people hungry in this world.

Enter Babs. Forsythe leaps, berating her for sticking with that "murderer" Blaney—for her the last straw. She strides out livid. But on the sidewalk outside, a pause to consider her position. Very close facial shot of Anna Massey, weighing reality, at a loss: a full two seconds. And now from just offscreen Rusk's plummy cello voice. How it must be hard for her. How he will help. Stay at my place until you can figure out what to do. I'll bring you there, and then go back for your things. And yes, he does bring her, escort of escorts. Up the stairs. To the door...

[5] Rusk lives above Duckworth and Co (publishers in 1915 of Virginia Woolf's *The Voyage Out*). Just as they pass out of view we hear his voice: "I don't know if you know it, Babs, but you're my type of woman...." A celebrated cinematic gesture is here opened. We do not approach Rusk's door, but instead back away down the stairs. Hesitation? Modesty? Foreknowledge? Fear? A surfeit of imagination, to be sure. The camera retreats around the landing, down the first flight, through the red-carpeted atrium, past the Duckworth and Co door sign, out into the street, across the road, until it stands "catching its breath" on the opposite sidewalk. Rusk is in there now, isn't he, settling himself upon Babs. Street traffic noisily passes in the sun.

[6] The Chief Inspector is now fighting his appetite back home. To illuminate their table and what is served upon it the Oxfords have warm table lamps, *but to illuminate that illumination* one lamp stands directly in front of the camera, slightly obscuring our view so that we must move to join the feast. Keep up respectful good cheer. She has prepared a *soupe de poisson* including, as he discovers to his gray dismay, "smelts, ling, conger eel, john dory, pilchers, and crawfish!" this potion to be followed (as soon as he secretly manages to dump his bowl back into the tureen) by "A simple roast bird—*Caille aux raisins!*—*Quail with grapes!*" On the Staffordshire dinner plate the quail does indeed look simple, possibly because it is almost inconceivably small and by this point in his day our dear Chief Inspector is ravenous. When one's hunger builds to a frenzy one's rationality dissolves.

Not long later, an odd little contretemps, also at table:

MRS OXFORD: How long did you say he was married?

OXFORD: Ten years.

MRS OXFORD: Well, there you are! A *crime de passion* after all that time? Look at us! We've only been married eight years! And you can hardly keep your eyes open at night!

Married eight years, but still at table taking tea with the queen, or *soupe* with Louis XVI.

[7] The night is dark. Rusk packs away and fully dispenses with Babs on the Motorway, hiding himself at a pull-in. Details of this escapade just below.

[8] Morning. Back at the Hilton, Hettie screams at the awakening Blaney for killing Babs. He is gutted. Babs!? To help his pal, Johnny would like to testify that he was here at the hotel with them when Babs was slain, but Hettie is convincing that he'd be arrested for harboring a fugitive. "I'm all right, Jack, and dump the ladder!" shouts Blaney scornfully, as he leaves.

[9] Blaney finds his buddy Rusk at the fruit market. Cheery offer of a place to kip—Rusk has found his perfect double!—Dick to head off

by the long way round while dutiful Bob schleps his bag. A chummy welcome to the flat, and Rusk departs. But no sooner does Blaney pour himself a drink there than the police barge in, arrest him, and cart him off. In a cutaway at Rusk's stall we see a favorite bobby grateful for his tip—there's no reward on this one, though. "Virtue," says Rusk, "is its own reward."

[10] At Scotland Yard Blaney's bag is opened to reveal Babs's clothing and purse. He explodes in realization. It's Rusk!!!

[11] Trial, verdict, and sentence in swift succession. Blaney hauled down in wails:

> It was written that those who had tortured, humiliated, and chained me would receive, promptly and plain for me to see, high wages for their crimes, as though Providence was bent upon showing me the futility of virtue. (Marquis de Sade 101)

In the empty courtroom, however, the inspector cannot leave his seat, lost in thought, replaying his memory of Blaney being dragged off at the top of his lungs, "It's Rusk! Rusk!!!" *Should he listen???* Back to the Blaney Bureau and Monica. About a man in a photograph she is very precise. Mr Robinson. He was a very difficult one. He made *certain* demands we did not feel we could satisfy. Nose lifted (away from the vulgar stench of even a photograph). Angular shot of her gaunt face. Very thick eyeglasses, stylish but also defensive. A pronouncement: "Men like this leave no stone unturned in the search for their disgusting gratifications."[23]

[12] Dinner at the Oxfords' again, when Spearman interrupts. Yes, he reports, the lady at the highway pull-in did positively identify Rusk, and said his clothes were dusty and loaned him a brush. *This* brush. He unwraps a gift.

[13] Blaney has attempted in the prison to flee from some guards and has crashed down a steel staircase, injuring his head. Off by ambulance to the infirmary, where other inmates soon help him to escape. He steals and hot-wires a car, grabs a crowbar to use as weapon, heads to Rusk's.

[14] The Chief Inspector's wife is still serving food and opinion:

> MRS OXFORD: I told you it wasn't Blaney, didn't I. I told you you were on the wrong track. Women's intuition is worth more than all those laboratories. I can't think why you don't teach it in police colleges.
>
> OXFORD: What does your intuition tell you I want for dinner tonight?
>
> MRS OXFORD: Steak. And a baked potato. But you're getting *Pieds de porc à la mode de coq.* I put it in the same sauce the French use for tripe.

As she serves, and he stares in trepidation, a chat about the case. How Rusk got the body out of the sack because he wanted to find something she was clutching in her hand. He had to break her fingers—Mrs O. snapping a bread stick in glee. "What do you think it was? A locket? A brooch? A cross!" But no, "Not a cross, I think." He doesn't see why not a cross. "Religious and sexual mania are closely linked. Anyway, whatever it was he found it." They had one stroke of luck, he says. Rusk stopped at a pull-in somewhere out of London. "A *pull-in???*" Moving the fork and knife on the plate with a mouthful sitting in his cheek. "A café frequented by truck drivers, dear. They serve humble food like bacon and egg sandwiches, sausages and mashed potatoes, cups of tea and coffee." The melody of lost hope. Not only may he have wounded the innocent Blaney but his favorite cooking has sailed away forever.

[15] Oxford races to Rusk's place and finds Blaney standing in the middle of the room, the crowbar dangling from his hand. On the bed, head partly caved in—because, certain he'd caught Rusk snoozing, he struck the blanket fiercely—is the naked body of another murdered girl, tongue out, eyes bulging, necktie around her throat. "No...!" Blaney pleads hoarsely, but Oxford raises a finger to his lips. He hides behind the door. Someone is coming and hauling something heavy. The door opens. It is Rusk, his shirt open, a massive steamer trunk in his hand. "Mr Rusk! You're not wearing your tie!"

Note the darting around, the skulking. The darkness and the faux brilliance. Extremities of personality, rushes to judgment, impotency, divorce, calculation for profit, smarmy judgmentalism, cooking up stories and quails. How fully *Frenzy* captures the tremulous spirit of the great, urban, modern machine that is London. David Kynaston quotes P. F. William Ryan, for example, on formative conditions before the turn of the twentieth century:

> At eight o'clock the roar of the City has gathered strength and fullness, approaching the din of noonday. At nine o'clock *every man, woman, and child in the Metropolis seems to be going somewhere*. Crowds bubble intermittently from the underground stations. Buses in endless procession converge upon the Bank. The pavements are black with people. (qtd. in *City of London* 192; emphasis mine)

That constant rush of movement, in all directions, geophysically and psychologically, permeates every scene here. The goods trundled iconically around the market. People's employment, relationships, pasts, anticipations all vibrating and changing moment by moment. The trucking and exchange of merchandise: vegetables, opinions, odds at the track, hellos and goodbyes. And the fury of flight, since refined and genteel as Hitchcock manages to make it here the police presence nevertheless mobilizes a quest for escape. In all this hubbub Richard cannot pause and reflect. Too many attitudes and angles to catch quickly, weigh, position on an internal map. And always checking the getaway route. He has become in his essential identity *the hunted man*. Understandably he does not grieve for the death of Brenda; or grieve for the death of his affectionate chum Babs. Grief is for those who can feel safe enough and empowered enough to take the time.

POTATOES

The aftermath of the Babs Milligan murder (elided in the film) is a full-blown ballet for potatoes, handled with a comedic touch to dampen the viewer's genuine—but for engagement potentially obstructive—shock at the death. She was, after all, only wise, helpful, charming, straightforward, and noble. Rusk is hauling a loader's cart down his steep staircase and into the street (the camera's route earlier). Sweaty, painful, tricky: the cart bears a huge, fully stuffed potato sack.[24] Across Henrietta St and into the market, a shady line of parked lorries with back ends to brush past. Now:

- Rusk is disguised in a tweed cap low on his head and a marketer's apron, necessary because everyone in this neighborhood, even the bobby who prowls by night, has learned to recognize him by his nappy attire, his gleamy neckties, his carrot-red hair, and his smart diamond pin that glistens like stars. The weight of his "potatoes" becomes evident when having found the right lorry he must strain mightily to hoist it into the back. Some canvas tarpaulin material is stretched there, not unlike theater curtains. He's "getting the show on the road."

- Away with the loading cart: stand it in a queue of others. The apron and the noxious hat: bin them. Home, breathing like a human being!
    Have a tranquil lie-down on the sofa.
    Gulp some wine and chomp some meat pie.
    But——
    Arousal as by electric prod. Something missing! Something vital! Where can it be? Where is it? He tears open the drawers of his dresser, riffling through Babs's clothing and handbag. Now under the bed... and on the bed... and in the bed. No no—it's gone. It's gone it's gone it's gone it's gone it's gone!!

- For the viewer a merciful flashback "inside" Rusk's striving mind and Babs's in a silent scream (see Weis)... necktie wrenched tight... her face, and her hand crawling up to his... her hand hunting, hunting, frenzied... the hunt of the final breaths... until it finds—the tie pin. Finds, seizes, clamps, and then death. All this in macro-close-up for two reasons: Hitchcock needs us to concentrate on minute details, the traditional use of the close-up; but he also wants the murder memory to swell in proportion to the commonplace action of the moment, to dwarf Rusk and dwarf our consciousness as we follow him into the nocturnal market. The tie pin: an elegant encrusted "R." (Reflection of Bruno Antony's pin in *Strangers on a Train* [1951] and the monogram in *Rebecca* [1940].) As narrative invention the flashback stands for the character's experience but also for his (and our) education: he is teaching himself: That's where it is! She's got it! Back outside, racing now. Don't go pulling that lorry away! Don't leave!

- Inside the back of the lorry he tries desperately to undo the sack but immediately the driver has started up and the vehicle, with ancient springs, throws him around. Working the knot, fingering the knot. He can't get it open. The lorry bumping along (a studio set upon a hydraulic mechanism so that Foster can really be jostled and lose balance). Balance lost, he stiffens and goes red, becomes more frenzied (the true phallic moment). The knot still won't open. The jerking lorry. Rusk suddenly stunned by klieg light but no, it's only car and truck lamps as they follow or pass. The Motorway. Tucked behind potato sacks he's mercilessly thrown about. Can it really be true that all these potatoes wouldn't sell, that in London there's no market for potatoes? Of course!—potatoes are Irish![25]

- Now some potatoes are scattering onto the motorway and a passing driver yells up to the lorryman that he's losing his load. He pulls over, adjusts the twin clips on the tailgate. *Don't* let him see you!!!—driver as potential audience peeking into the wings because the tarp is Rusk's proscenium. On the road. The lorry has him bouncing around again, jerking, red in the face with fear and urgency, panicking. But the sack is open!

- Except that he packed her head-first! A foot sticks out, bumps his face (a premonition of the downhill drive in *Family Plot* [1976]), catches under his chin. He's still losing balance—the suspension couldn't be worse (suspenseful suspension)—and he has to finger his way up the body (down into the sack), past the knees and the thighs and the unmentionables (the untouchables?) until he can discover the hand.

- But Babs's hand is clenched because rigor mortis has set in. (Of course: he killed her mid-afternoon, it's now gone past eleven at night.) He can't get the pinky to move, prying with all his might, straining almost to bursting. Killing was easier. Sweat layering his red face. There's a little pen knife hidden away somewhere, where is it? oh yes. Use your mouth to pry out the blade (but don't use your mouth to pry back those fingers). He sticks the blade between two fingers and pries, but the blade snaps off. Now what?

- Truck still jerking. He applies himself to that pinky, pulling back until—a bone-chilling snap. (At the Oxford table, the bread stick.)
    Two more fingers now.
    The fist open.
    And yes, there it is! There it is!!! He has it in hand, yes yes! he has it!!!! Hand to hand. Visible sigh of relief. Mop the brow, a hard night's work.

- The truck shows mercy and draws into a pull-in where, treasure cached inside his jacket, Rusk escapes. Hide in the "Men's" until the driver gets his drink and drives out again. Creep over to the café yourself.

- Soon enough, farther up the road, as the truck speeds past, two constables parked on the shoulder notice a naked body in the night. "Do you see what I see?" A chase. The siren. When the trucker brakes, Babs goes tumbling out and onto the road, waxen as a mannequin at Madame Tussauds. Her body glows with pallor against the night.

This sequence plays for fourteen minutes and twenty-two seconds, twelve percent of the film. Putting Babs into a sack of potatoes is to make of her, essentially, a load, certainly an objective weight instead of a human presence. In effect, this is Bergson's "momentary transformation of a person into a thing" (28), the *momentariness* derived from the very few seconds at Rusk's door when Babs was visible in place of her metaphor, the sack. Hitchcock is careful to show her body on the road, gleaming in the police head lamps. Dead, Babs is lit like a thing in a Still Life with Potatoes. But this is not a lone irony.

Dramaturgically the film is made of contradictions. Take the necktie killings, for example. At one moment, by the Embankment, we find an attitude of disruption, shock, if also wonder and ironic humor: the nude corpse polluting the river exactly where a *mavin* has proclaimed pollution will be gone. At another moment, we find salacious entertainment on the front pages of newspapers, things become their own sellers; no more "vendors shouting out the afternoon headlines" to spike the local "gossip about lurid crime cases" (McGilligan 12). In the toff's conversation we learn how the "fearsome" necktie killer is a buried treasure, a contributor to the local economy:

> LAWYER IN PUB (to his chum): Well, we haven't had a good, juicy series of sex murders since Christie.[26] And they're so good for the tourist trade. Foreigners expect the squares of London to be fog-wreathed, full of hansom cabs and littered with ripped whores, don't you think?

Foreign tourists will bring movement. Movement will bring collision. Collision will bring criminal charges. Criminal charges will bring profit. Have another pint!

Contradictions or sanctity: At a culminating moment we find the murderer in the heat of his passion, terminally rude. There is nothing comic here at all, not even his "cute" little move of finishing up Brenda's apple. The action of the encounter is beyond journalistic or surgical remove, philosophical analysis, aesthetics—beyond all of what is civilized. But in the throes of the rape, while his penetrations race, Brenda is murmuring verses 5, 6, and 11 from Psalm 91 (in the King James version):

> Thou shall not be afraid for the terror by night.
> Nor for the arrow which flieth by day.
> Nor for the pestilence which walketh in darkness.
> Nor for the destruction that wasteth at noonday.
> He shall give His angels charge over thee,
> to guard thee in all thy ways.

The destruction that wasteth at noonday. It is noonday now.

RUSK OF LONDON

Rusk, a toasted piece of sweet bread. Bob Rusk's hideous sweetness merits particular attention, unpleasant as attending may feel.

First, that his charm is a persistent, cheap veneer, outvaluing our knowledge of his actions. He is never less than rakish except when preoccupation dilutes his concentration. This is dramaturgically essential, because only some attraction or other will nourish audience attention, and even repulsed we must find him, minimally, not unattractive.[27] We must not decline to peek at Rusk: we would be lost to the film and thereby to the filmmaker. Even the man's galling discomposure *in extremis* must lure our eye.[28]

Hitchcock never avoided the idea that appearances cover (even when we have seen what they cover). This presentational problem of surfaces and interiors is complex. Viewing a character through the lens of contradiction could prove confusing, or at least unclear enough to interrupt or fully take over attention to a film's flow. Therefore, in presenting his characters Hitchcock cheats the surface-to-interior ratio to one side or the other, appropriately for the action of the moment. Each may have two sides, but the viewer always knows which side she is looking at, and can look while holding knowledge of the other side in abeyance. The portrayal of Rusk is a model of this approach.

Further, Rusk is a kind of *generality*. Victimized by him, Brenda and Babs are brief focal concerns, their deaths staged as productions that absorb attention deeply and thoroughly: Brenda by conversation, Babs by transportation. But beyond the dramatic "star moments" these two victims are only "anyones," that is, all of us potentially—all of us / all women / all of us women—and the film cedes only the scantiest information about either victim before her termination. Mere *char à canon*, they cannot differ from any mortal viewer. They gain narrative substance retroactively as victims remembered more than as creatures heading into darkness, selected from the vast multitude of beings in the Great City, their lives certainly touching upon our central characters' but hardly the only lives to do so. They lack centrality, *as everyone in the film does*. Our memories of them have no centrality either, as though from the streets of Covent Garden one could choose an award-winning corner! All of London is without centrality: it is a thoroughfare admitting traffic, and traffic—of potatoes, of souls—is its action. We all become less than ourselves when we go into the city. It is only through watching in silent frenzy the silent frenzy of Londoners fearing the Angel of Death that Rusk can seem the grain around which the crystal of the film forms. But he is not the grain. Like everyone else we see, he is traffic. Any viewer could be, or become, Rusk.

Eric Rohmer and Claude Chabrol note in Hitchcock's touch a "constant ambiguity of form—which once again proves that technique is nothing in itself; what counts is the use one makes of it.... Hitchcock is one of the greatest *inventors of form* in the entire history of cinema" (151–52; emphasis original). Where is the form in *Frenzy*? Where, in *Frenzy*, is the form?

In the hunger for form, surely.

Frenzied hunger for elusive form. Not just searching but posing the question that provokes the search. Consider the many hungers on display:

[1] Brenda and Babs hungry for life, cut off; [2] Rusk's hunger for satisfaction; [3] the Chief Inspector's hunger for the "real"; [4] Blaney's hunger for luck; [5] the politicians' hunger for cleanliness and approbation; [6] the hawker's hunger for potato sales; [7] the Porters' hunger for success in Paris; [8] Forsythe's hunger for Babs; [9] the toffs' hunger for one-upmanship; [10] The Coburg bellman's hunger for propriety (and fame); [11] Mrs Oxford's hunger for the smallest compliment; [12] Sergeant Spearman's hunger for his boss's bacon and eggs; [13] Monica's hunger for others' punishment; not to mention [14] Brenda's hunger for her lunch; [15] the Chief Inspector's hunger for normal cooking; [16] Blaney thirsty for his morning drink; [17] Johnny Porter hungry to show friendship; [18] the Coburg desk clerk's hunger to imagine the salacious.

All the scuttling millions of London are hungry—some are cannibals.

One hungers for a radiant point of contact, a "true voice of feeling" in Herbert Read's phrase, where we might pause and reflect. But there is no place for pause, no peace, no glorious perspective, nothing but traffic. A murderer we cannot befriend, a wanderer who won't be befriended, Scotland Yard overwhelmed, the ecologists overwhelmed, the fruit and vegetable sellers overwhelmed, the workers overwhelmed by limits, the middle class overwhelmed by insatiable ambition. The storyline, as far as it stretches, is just sufficient to carry us through the space of the film by stationing us—and only briefly—with types, none being "our type": from The Globe to the market to Brenda's office to Rusk's rooms to the Chief Inspector's table to the motorway to the courtroom to the prison to the hospital, wandering like Blaney, unsatisfied like Rusk, in daylight and in dark, and in company with millions of others on the same route of the cross. Rusk's cross is a sexual wound. Blaney's is misfortune. The Chief Inspector's cross is the fear of missing a crucial fact. And our cross is being caught up in a modern labyrinth where every step takes us in a wrong direction. All we can be sure of is that we are in the middle of the road, as it were with traffic of all sorts blaring and screaming all round.[29] The middle of the road, of the great road; the middle of our experience.

DIRECTED MISDIRECTIONS

Until his climate-altering second thought, late in the film, the Chief Inspector is convinced Blaney should be hounded, in the name of protecting civilized life in London and thus the moral order. His wife, who favors her instinct over laboratory data, is committed to Blaney's abject innocence. The dinner table is thus an altar for the naked presentation of opposition: the guilt of Rusk, the accusation of Blaney. Note that in the build-up of accusations against Blaney, starting with Forsythe's reprimand for "stealing" liquor and ending with the murder charge "legitimated" by the divorce petition based on extreme cruelty ("extreme cruelty"), we see him always under a weight he cannot lift. He and Rusk are alter egos, in that every "certain" call against Blaney is a direct avoidance of certainly pointing to Rusk, whom *we know* as the guilty party. Blaney is Rusk's social mask, his "beard."

Viewers must confront these two men and the chains of action and characters with whom each is involved as a single construct, a dramatic unity. London must somehow seem a world in which a Blaney and a Rusk could be uncovered, as it were, together. As to cinematic seeming, our aide and companion is the camera: here is the artful camerawork in three shots that immediately follow Brenda's death:

> [SHOT A]
> Forty-five-degree angle on the bureau's street doorway, a FRIENDSHIP & MARRIAGE wall sign posted above right and three painted white arrows pointing off-. Rusk emerging, tidying his hair, pacing leftward and frame centered (as we pan to follow). Passing closely, and walking all the way down a slim corridor to Oxford Street (our pan is more than ninety degrees by now). Turning right, disappearing (we may think, into the crowd).

[SHOT B]
Continuous action. Panning back rightward to discover a narrow walkway just left of Brenda's entrance (but unnoticed in [A] because the focus was on Rusk's passing body). Blaney heading toward us. Swiveling to his left (our right), noting the doorway, entering and mounting the stairs, knocking politely on the outside door of the offices. (Monica forgot to lock the door when she went to lunch, this being Rusk's "entré.") "Anyone there? Brenda, it's Richard." Pause pause pause. Turning to leave.

[SHOT C]
Outside again, same camera position as in [A]. Stepping our way along the route Rusk took (note, *not* the route Blaney took), and in reverse of Rusk's heading, is Monica returning from lunch. Complacent. Self-satisfied. Even sashaying little. At some distance squinting and frowning to see Blaney emerge and, oblivious to her, duck into the little walkway that brought him here. She enters the building.

Monica as the visual relay whereby guilt and innocence "collide."

Blaney and Rusk missing each other—being both together and separate—is dramatized *in the image alone*, the viewer tensely worrying if they will collide (if Blaney will come to know Rusk as the murderer, in the way that we do). The "togetherness" of Rusk and Blaney onscreen (same camera position) is optically naturalized to our view. Guilt and innocence stride the same streets, along with the third who points a finger.

LOST SOUL

Court adjourns. Court vacated. Blaney hauled away screaming. "It's Rusk!!!!" Now the room is but an empty cavern plied over with the gleamy wood of officialdom. The Chief Inspector occupies a bubble of silence, a man of delicacy and honesty who deserves a moral redemption. Silently breathing. Silent in the space that now, it seems for the first time, has air. Still hearing the Blaney rant, the echo chamber of memory. The still strong voice. "Out of the depths I called to You." Is it possible all his computations were wrong? Memory amplifies voices in experience, especially in a room's yawning emptiness. Was it not evidence but mere trappings covering over a falsity that he found and showed? Has he been trapped by trappings? Or: what is the reality in which all of these people are trapped? Tom Cohen sees the displays of fruit at Covent Garden as "icons of nature" (149), but in this film nature is everywhere. It is London that is nature. *Frenzy* asks what life has become, now that this is the nature in which we find it.

"London was everywhere, but it had lost its soul," Iain Sinclair writes (7), that being London the endlessly visualized: look at William Henry Fox Talbot (1800–1877) and Alvin Langdon Coburn's (1882–1966) photography and find a telling difference. Talbot, defining urban space, especially architecture, shoots what would today seem postcards: idealized views of "important" places. Coburn, fixed upon civic life within urban confines, shoots even London landmarks so as to reveal their connection with, even foundation upon, hard economic realities. Ideal views or bare essences, withdrawals into conception or engagements with experience. David Bailey (b. 1938) follows from Fox Talbot, exaggerating by idealization. Don McCullin (b. 1935) follows from Coburn. Hitchcock's films often show urban scenes by way of postcards, idealizations that convey immediately the placement of action in a recognizable—previously accepted—view. Nob Hill in *Vertigo*, Vermont in *The Trouble with Harry*, Rio in *Notorious*.... Every image correct, but for the viewer also expected. *Frenzy*, however, has only one "postcard" moment:

As the director's name flashes onscreen the split roadway of Tower Bridge has been raised, not unlike a pair of receptive legs. (So that when she raises her legs, Brenda becomes a bridge.) As we penetrate the opening, the camera, which was three hundred or so feet in the air, now swoops down like a gull, navigating the river.

What should we make of that quasi-bestial, that provoking maneuver, the lifting of the bridge's "legs"? The helicopter could have soared over Tower Bridge as it soared over Rotherhithe. Could Hitchcock not be preparing us—always he prepares his demonstrations—to see a depiction that strays from received subject matter and angle, that eschews idealization in order to focus on the unadorned (Coburnian) truth of things? In terms of London the city, shie away from Big Ben, from Buckingham Palace, from

St Paul's, from the Union Jack, from the black bowler and brolly. Back off, retreat into the street to show things in their vernacular, no paint or monumentality but only the detritus of civilization. This could apply as well to characters and story. Cut through the gilded presentations of affect, the prettying up, the swank or shabby habiliment that is an instant giveaway, the omnipresence of the "received" British speaking style. Once we lose beautification—entirely a capitalization of the body, treatment of the body as commercial product—we have the unfettered presentation of biology. Gustave Courbet took an approach like this in "L'origine du monde" (1866). The subterranean secret, that held such allure, evaporates when it comes to the surface.

Here, then: beneath the decorous bra the helpless breasts. Beneath the etiquette the release. Beneath the gleamy haberdashery raw spleen. Beneath *haute cuisine* a sack of potatoes. Beneath gainful employment the doss house. Beneath the friendly hello the angry goodbye. Beneath the marriage bureau, marriage. Beneath glamour the autopsy. Beneath serenity, agony. Beneath the smiling personality, social class. Beneath philosophy the street.

CHAPTER FOUR

FOR THE GRACE OF GOD
The Wrong Men

> I entered along the deep and savage way.
> —Dante, *Inferno II*

When on 26 March 1956 Hitchcock started filming *The Wrong Man*, what he considered a documentary-style story based somewhat strictly on certain events of 1953 in the life of Christopher Emmanuel Balestrero, Henry Fonda, who played the protagonist, was fifty years old and Balestrero himself was forty-six.[1] Fonda did not have to act the experience of a man experiencing what in the 1950s was thought "middle age," as Manny was with his steady enough if not high-paying job and a sincerely felt responsibility to support his wife and family and pay the mortgage on his little house at 40-24 78th Street, Queens. Fonda had more money, to be sure, but not more responsibility and no less a family to be concerned about. It is hardly surprising, then, that there is something penetrating and honest about this piece of performative work, even though Fonda brought honesty to his work always; his "Chris" (as the police impolitely call him) is true to the bone, a man not only placed in Jackson Heights but emergent from the

mentality, propriety, and modest taste that the Borough of Queens cultivated, and in his private, measured, and ritualized daily life a New Yorker through and through: "There is always an idea of neighborhood" (Goodman and Goodman 142). Manny's work is at Manhattan's Stork Club, East 53rd Street, just steps away from Fifth Avenue (at what is today Paley Park). He must commute back and forth every day on the E train. He works late, most likely coming into town in the late part of the afternoon if not around dinner time and returning home in the small hours of the morning when everyone in his family is peacefully asleep. The word *peaceful* nicely describes the Balestrero routine, and Manny's manner in playing it out.[2]

    Manny's "day" would amount to a series of repeated actions, placements, and duties. He would still be asleep when the children went to school, would wake up late in the morning, have a light breakfast and coffee, do fix-it-ups around the house or small household chores such as buying groceries nearby, perhaps sit and read, give Rose (Vera Miles) a loving kiss, walk the four blocks to the Roosevelt Avenue–Jackson Heights station, descend the dark, grimy, metal-capped stairs to the platform, wait for the Manhattan-bound E train. Must be on the correct (inside) platform, this is an express stop and his E, along with some F trains, will have sped through a number of stations before coming in here. Ride through Queens Plaza, then 23rd Street, then Lexington/3rd Avenue–53rd Street, to Fifth Avenue–53rd Street, the right stop. Up the long, long, long echoing staircase past the blazing whitewashed walls, onto the street close to the corner, walk straight ahead fifteen paces, and you're there. At night reverse it, step by step. Every day of the working week just the same, without a rush, without an attitude, without comment and without despair, just inhabitation of the channels of the city one has made one's own. At night, heading home, if he misses the E train at the Fifth Avenue station he will have something of a wait for the next one. The train at that hour will be close to empty, but there'll be loners on board—at 3:00 a.m. the Warner Bros. researchers estimated "about 30 to a car" (Points 1). Perhaps people going home after a late night in the City, perhaps other workers. He will nestle in his private world behind his newspaper, figuring the crossword as a religious ritual and a private devotion.

A routine, all routine, nothing but routine: sleep in after the boys go to school, wake up late, have breakfast, do some chores, give Rose a loving kiss, walk to Roosevelt Avenue–Jackson Heights, descend the dark, grimy, metal-capped stairs to the platform, wait for the E train. There won't be too many people heading into Manhattan in the late afternoon. Ride through Queens Plaza...

Sleep in, have breakfast, a few chores, maybe read a little, give Rose a loving kiss, walk to Roosevelt Avenue–Jackson Heights, the same route, the same sidewalks, passing the same house fronts, the wrought iron fence with the plaster Jesus, the red-painted mock veranda,... descend the dark, grimy, metal-capped stairs to the platform, wait for the E train. Ride through Queens Plaza...

Every step on the sidewalk countable, always the same count. Every newspaper the same as every newspaper the same as every newspaper: just a container for the crossword. The long long long steps up and down at Fifth Avenue, the silent platform, the smell of dust, the gray rats scampering across the gray trench below the grimy-gray tracks. Every rat scurrying on the same arcane path as yesterday...

Routine frees Manny to think. Think about what? Think about how he'll manage the future.

By the E train you can almost set your watch. Roosevelt to Queens Plaza, thundering on the express track, about four and a half minutes. Queens Plaza to 23rd Street, about a minute and three quarters. Under the East River to Lexington, a good four minutes, unless there's some kind of hold-up and you can stare out the window into the unforgiving blackness of the river bottom as imagined, praying the tunnel will not collapse. Lexington to Fifth, twenty-five seconds. Every day, all the days, these exact timings, just like this, and you can tune your body to these timings, and your body knows when to stand and get near the door and how many steps from the door to the staircase, and how many steps on the staircase before you are in the world.

At Roosevelt–Jackson Heights, the station is situated beneath the Victor Moore Arcade (where some of the film was actually photographed). This is a two-story bricked structure (named after the Broadway and movie star Victor Moore in the early 1940s) with very narrow corridors, offices upstairs, tiny shops on the street level, as well as a small bus station, fronting on Broadway, where one can get the Q47 to La Guardia. Past the turnstiles one is met by two stairways, one to JAMAICA and one to MANHATTAN. Or stay inside and find Bickford's, a tiny coffee shop, perfect icon of Hemingway's "clean well-lighted place," where there is always a soulful helping of toast. This particular coffee shop, one particular table in it, is Manny Balestrero's temple, the Real Temple of His Real Body in the Real Everyday. He can mark up the racing form for Belmont, or scan the paper: THE NEW YORK SAVINGS BANK DIVIDEND EXTRAS. He will shuck off the oily skin of cosmopolitan glitz in which he performs his labor—he plays double bass in the house band at Sherman Billingsley's establishment (in the mid-1950s one of *the* go-to nightspots for the New York and tourist bourgeoisie)—breathe now without tempo and without the rolling pulse of the subway wheels, stare off once in a while toward the vague, pleasant, commercial light, and eat without some dutiful concern about who else might be here and what they might be doing.

An island of peace in the great city. It is being a New Yorker to seek and find one's island of peace.

Manny Balestrero's routine both structures and emblazons daily life in the capital of mid-twentieth-century modernity. From the perspective of population density, New York of the 1950s is an epitome of the crowded metropolis, a place in which one can be lost in many different ways. The physical state of life in the five boroughs, Queens and Manhattan most especially, involves self-placement in the crowd. There is a crowd on the sidewalk, a crowd in the subway car, a crowd in the elevator at work, a crowd in the department stores, a crowd at the meat counter in the market. One's personal routine is a kind of adjustment to the Crowd, a way of protecting the body against incursion but also protecting one's navigation against the pressuring waves of human movement. Routine is also a way of thinking, quite necessary in New York unless one would have one's mental capacity diluted and eroded by the constant chatter on all sides and the New Yorker does not wish his mental capacity diluted in the least. It is a question of directing one's consciousness, not losing it, albeit crowds, wrote Gustave Le Bon in 1897, "are always unconscious, but this very unconsciousness is perhaps one of the secrets of their strength" (ix). What the *unconsciousness* means in effect is that the crowd does not have a will to obliterate the individual mind, nor does it require a will; it merely overwhelms by pure magnitude, and the personal routine is a surehanded method of finding or making a chain of nooks within that magnitude, a quiet resistance.

Once one has come to know the passing details of it well, a route becomes one's own, even a personal territory. The metropolitan crowd, such as one finds in New York yet observes always only in fragments, most closely resembles Le Bon's "electoral crowd," which is a vast and imperceivable entity configured in people's minds as a congregation yet materialized only through its product; the metropolitan crowd has this distant, imagined horde form but is always, in a localized and limited way, materially manifest. One sees a "them," and "they" inevitably "belong to" the crowd, yet also remain unidentified and unidentifiable. In a subway car, at least theoretically, given the multiple interlinkages in the system that permit the movement in every direction of anybodies from anywhere, one could easily be sitting next to an anybody; indeed the person, the actual, real person sitting adjacent does in fact become converted into an Anybody by virtue of the subway car as container for the crowd. Georg Simmel writes of the metropolitan condition:

> With each crossing of the street, with the tempo and multiplicity of economic, occupational and social life, the city sets up a deep contrast with small town and rural life with reference to the sensory foundations of psychic life. (410)

And,

> There is perhaps no psychic phenomenon which has been so unconditionally reserved to the metropolis as has the blasé attitude. (413)

This quality of being distanced from, being unaffected by the jarring eventualities of the everyday is something of a stimulus shield, as Freud put it, a way of warding off excessive stimuli that without a defense would saturate consciousness to the point of drowning it.

To secure him in all this, owing to his musical talent, his hard work, his perseverance, and, perhaps, his strength in competition, Manny has found a job.[3] At the Stork Club a jazz combo occupies the customer's night, and Manny has what seems a long-term commitment there since, as we learn, the band is part of Sherman Billingsley's establishment. The numbers themselves Manny has played so many times that he could easily work in his sleep, yet he has a rapt concentration, a tidy manner, a smiling devotion not only to the music but also to the customers and their delights. Tonight the group is in the midst of a charming *Cubano* theme by Bernard Herrmann, token of the effortless Sybaritic delights of the well-to-do, and we are about to discover that we have come upon him at the very end of the night, when the dancers have trailed off the floor and the tables are being cleaned off by waiters eager to get to bed. Hitchcock's research team was asked to determine whether

> [w]hen the band stops played [*sic*] does it sign off or does that only happen when there are a lot of people dancing. If there are a few people dancing and it is 4.00 a.m., should we say, do they stop or do they have to continue until there is only one couple or so on the floor? (Questions).

To which an answer was speedily forthcoming. "Regarding lateness of hour at Stork Club and quantity of people usually found there at closing time, there are 2 to 3 couples dancing – 4 or 5 people at bar – closes around 3:30 a.m" (Points 1). Also of concern, the "types and number of people that hour in morning" at Bickford's coffee shop in the Victor Moore Arcade:

> Regarding Bickfords Victor Moore Arcade at about 3:30 am – quantity of people – types, etc., there are about 20 moderately dressed people and lower types. (Points 1)

The very casualness of the music, its roteness, its being part of the musicians' bodies like muscle tone—all this suggests, in still another way, the power of routine. Routine work, a routine gig, a routine instrument, routine numbers, a routine audience eating a routine dinner and whispering routine nothings in their guests' ears.

Power players, showoffs, the curious, the hungry, and the restless flocked to the Stork Club in the mid-1950s, sitting to a dinner served with "class" and cooked to what at the time were up-to-date chi-chi American standards—it wasn't until February 1963 that French cuisine became the rage in America, thanks to Julia Child, even if French chefs were in the kitchens of the great New York restaurants cooking the way Americans liked it. At the Stork Club while Manny played, diners could have a Shrimp Cocktail for $2.25, Sole Almondine for $5.25 or else Lamb Chops for $5.50, either served with Mashed Potatoes, $0.90, or String Beans, $0.90, and capped by Crêpes Suzette, $3.50. Then, as the evening warmed they could be dancing the night away, perhaps nibbling some Camembert, $0.95, and settling into coffee (with cream), $0.60, to preface some serious drinks. Though Billingsley and Hitchcock were friends, the Stork wasn't Hitchcock's New York grotto *de rigueur*, notwithstanding that it sat very close by the St. Regis, 55th Street just east of Fifth Avenue, where he routinely stayed and where at luncheon, the day we catch Manny playing, he could have nibbled (at an astoundingly cheap price, since at Hushy's deli on Times Square it was going for almost three times the price) half a grapefruit for $0.25 and then a Special Luncheon Steak for $1.45 and Ice Cream for $0.20 to polish it off. If the Stork was just two short blocks below the hotel, "21" was just two short blocks below that, with Beluga Caviar for $6.00 and a full dinner for five or six dollars more. For patrons who wanted a night to forget their realities, the Stork was high dining in New York, even if not as high as "21" or Le Cirque or The Four Seasons. Manny is routinely smack in the middle of what insiders and outsiders alike recognized (and Charles Walters contemporaneously filmed) as "high society."[4]

In the middle of, but not part of. Encountering such luxury at close hand but through an impermeable veil could be chafing. A truly potent resentment could be harbored by blue-collar workers who only heard fables about and never directly encountered such luxury. Two cops pounding the beat on 53rd Street as we watch Manny leave the club, for example. The New York working class, in their apartments or bungalows in Harlem, the Bronx, and Queens—commuters on the Long Island Rail Road, such as populate *The Man in the Gray Flannel Suit* (1956), are working in finance and advertising uptown—kept the mercantile establishments well oiled and running, making daily surgical infiltrations into the body of pleasure without stimulation of their own,[5] and for the most part could not treat nightclubs and other such establishments as their own tickles. Because Fonda brings a characteristic grace and nobility to Manny's poise and stance, a grace to his slow but progressive pace as he walks, and a notable professional concentration to his bass playing, our protagonist seems to possess a certain dignity "above" what we would expect from a menial laborer. Yet a menial laborer he is, and when the night is wrapped, and the band leader gives a signal with his hand on a culminating downbeat, Manny just closes up shop plain and simple. Standing up straight, leaning away from his instrument, gathering it into its case, stowing it in his locker, all with practiced moves and scarcely a flicker of attention, and then in his topcoat and hat heading into the lonely Manhattan night. Now in the vehicle of his Being, he glides away from the dandy life and into the shadow, down below the street, onto a pathway that will lead him a very long way off, that is, home.

A long way because the little house in Queens that Manny walks into, squeezed and elbowed among dozens of other little houses just the same—a homely crowd, indeed—isn't like the effete Stork Club at all, or like blazingly lit and sumptuous midtown shops and cafes, or like any place that dreamworld Manhattan's late-night denizens think they genuinely inhabit for the price of their ticket. To arrive here in his little retreat in quiet Queens he has shifted gears, locating his every moment as if by blind instinct. In the house he will move with not only familiarity but also system, a private and singular system, touching this, touching that, checking this, checking that. His choreography is known so intimately, and through so much repetition, that action flows out of his musculature as though without command.[6] Initially he moves with a quiet and efficient delicacy: it is the middle of the night, but there are things that must be done and that fall to him alone. As we presume his wife does when he's not here, now that she sleeps our Manny keeps this little world going—the lone spirit under the small light in the sacred dark silence of the everyday. His routines, and other people's, are not rudely impressed upon some natural freedom of the spirit (such as Rousseau invoked) but have been themselves naturalized, fitted into a pattern that has all the earmarks of inevitability and correctness. For Manny, this is not just his idiosyncratic life, structured in the context of, and against, an urban universe of equally idiosyncratic if contradictory lives, this is *life itself.* That vast, punishingly white, tiled wall in the subway, harshly illumined. Those regular iron pillars on the platform, a rule for measuring one's space. Now, the soft bed where Rose was asleep but now sits up to greet him with predictable affection. The boys soundly dozing in their beds. The refrigerator where the quart of milk from the front stoop is stored (Hitchcock's researchers wanted meticulous description of the type of milk bottle one would find on a stoop in Queens). The peculiar silence of continuity. Through camera placement, lighting, and performance Hitchcock and his team offer us a portrait of the small life, mid-century New York, quite as punctual as anything painted by Edward Hopper.

To be sure the small life, the modest life, the life of the everyday is open to criticism, such as what we read from Henry Miller:

> My people were entirely Nordic, which is to say *idiots.* Every wrong idea which has ever been expounded was theirs. Among them was the doctrine of cleanliness, to say nothing of righteousness. They were painfully clean. But inwardly they stank. Never once had they opened the door which leads to the soul; never once did they dream of taking a blind leap into the dark. After dinner the dishes were promptly washed and put in the closet; after the paper was read it was neatly folded and laid away on a shelf; after the clothes were washed they were ironed and folded and then tucked away in the drawers. (11)

Manny is surely an exemplar of the "painfully clean." But taking and offering a view of Manny's life Hitchcock must show the reassuring, the sedate, the pacific, the earnest, and the unassuming side for the time being, since he will be bringing on a tidal wave to smash all the beautiful elements into shards.

INHERITOR

Manny Balestrero does not work as a slave, though he works with a slave's disenfranchisement and a slave's reserve of energy. He is one of ancient Greece's *demiourgoi*, those whom Hannah Arendt describes as the workmen of the people at large, who moved freely outside the private realm and within the public. A later time even changed the name for these artisans, whom Solon had still described as sons of Athena and Hephaestus, and called them *banausoi*, that is, men whose chief interest is their craft and not the market place. It is only from the late fifth century onward that the *polis* began to classify occupations according to the amount of effort required. (81)

Yet at home, Manny is safe from the *polis* in his way, abstracted into a much later social form, the worker's own private domain separate from that of the factory owner and financier. His craft is his chief interest, but for him the true craft is a mixed business involving music on one hand and family shepherding on the other. We are going to come to need to sense all this, if not recognize it in these terms: Manny's loyalty to family, his embodied link to his music and his band job, his place in the social hierarchy, and the solid routine by which he proceeds through his life. That Manny is not now, nor ever was under a master, yet also that he must be bound to labor. He is in the working class.

And Rose has been having a tooth problem and needs some dental help. But how to pay for it? A perfect example of the family responsibility as it falls upon the head of the family who was, very much in 1955–1956, the father. Betty Friedan's explosive *The Feminine Mystique* was published only in 1963:

> No matter how much she had wanted that husband, those children, that split-level suburban house and all the appliances thereof, which were supposed to be the limit of women's dreams in those years after World War II, she sometimes felt a longing for something more. (18)

Notwithstanding the tender, subtle look of longing that Rose bears, there is also the agony of the mouth, and that is why money is needed, *extra* money, money the call for which was hitherto unanticipated, money over and beyond the regular (the ruling) family budget. At the Associated Life of New York (since 1897), in the Moore Arcade, Manny makes a polite inquiry: could he cash in part of his insurance policy to the extent of three hundred dollars? The clerk, maintaining a smile from her previous customer—but looking awkward behind the bars of her grille—straightens her face when

Manny walks in. Hitchcock made a special point of using Laurinda Barrett, a family friend, as one of the principal clerks; the other was Doreen Lang, who would appear again, signally, in *North by Northwest* and *The Birds*. The clerk is discernibly and inexplicably nervous. She will have to just check something. In a back room a hasty conference, this one with two others, who gaze at the document Manny has handed over as though it is one of the Dead Sea Scrolls. They are pondering, they are wondering, they are surmising, they are estimating, they are thinking that yes... maybe... yes, yes... Could it be?

More consultation will be required, sorry. He goes away. The employees consult with their manager. Much consultation, but the tooth needs fixing. Rose is in pain. As a civilian member of his class, Manny has the most ineffectual of citizenships; he can only beg.

That night when he comes home from work there are visitors, and the chain of happenstance that is the film's primary concentration is now set in place. The events of *The Wrong Man* begin with a little surprise because like the tender shoots of spring they rise up from nowhere; become dismaying; transform into producers of anxiety; flower into aggrievement and fear; and as an anti-climax throw off breakdown and despair. Only the finale, slashingly swift and potent, brings both release and a slim ray of hope.

[1] Their personalities tucked under growling fedoras and inside long coats, two men wait in a car outside Manny's house, then confidently interrupt his passage as he walks up to the front door, key in hand. Two workers in the police force. Members of the working class, too. They have some questions they'd like to ask, could he join them? That awkward and imperial status of the *question* in Western culture, the motor of the Quest; that sacred utterance by posing which one gains the *open sesame* to all caves of privacy and personality! Only a few questions begging answers; because when a question is asked an answer is thought by everyone to be properly forthcoming. I will return to these two policemen but the machine has started to run...

[2] Sitting in the dark rear seat of the men's car. Then, escorted by them to the police precinct, and inside. He walks between them (they are not quite bookends; and he is not quite a book hiding behind its cover) to a

pleasant enough room that has... bars on the window. "Sit, Chris," the taller, younger one says (Charles Cooper), the one, as we notice, not yet quite softened into the resignation of a long career here but perked up by aspirations to jump to something better. "Chris—," a name also out of nowhere. Straightforward questions, as they at first seem. The shorter, older cop (Harold J. Stone) explains why Manny is here:

[3] A man has been committing robberies in the area, for several months, and an accusation has been made that this man is Manny. The police merely need to check things out.

Merely. Only. Just.

Just to be sure. Nothing more than. You can't just claim to be innocent, after all, if there's nobody to say you are. This last is of course one of the great themes of Western literature, age-old, and one of the foundational inspirations of Eric Rohmer and Claude Chabrol's revelatory *Hitchcock: The First Forty-Four Films*. You cannot claim to be innocent if there's no one to say you are. And if you are alone, untouched by the polluting friction of society, uncorrupted by contact, alone in the middle of the night munching your buttered toast, who will say you are innocent then?

[4] Let's take a ride (it's mid-1950s, we all love the automobile).[7] Manny is chauffeured to a liquor store, the young hungry one driving with a smirk of anticipation. Every success is a rung on a ladder.

OLDER COP: What do you do at the Stork Club?

MANNY: I'm a bass player in the band.

YOUNGER COP: Suppose you have some pretty high old times there.

MANNY (at a loss): What d'you mean?

YOUNGER COP (with a grin Manny cannot see): Well, women, drink, dancing, that sort of thing.

MANNY (affirming): I don't drink.

"Been here before?" the old one asks, referring to the liquor store and totally oblivious that Manny just said he doesn't drink. This won't be hard. All you have to do is go in, walk to the back, look around, turn and walk out. Easy as ABC. (Police infantilization as a routine.)

MANNY (wanting to get it right): I don't *say* anything?

OLDER COP: You can if you want to, but to do it isn't necessary.

As he stands inside near the door, behind Manny hangs a sign partly visible: "By The Case." Later we see all of it: You Can Buy WINES AND LIQUORS By The Case. But Manny is already in a case. Being examined By The Case.

[5] Let's go for another ride. This time to a delicatessen. He will go in, walk to the back, turn around, walk out. On the way a genteel talk with the older cop:

COP (casual): Your wife ever go to the Stork Club with you?

MANNY: Nah, we have two children. Even if we didn't...

COP (curiosity aroused): Even if you didn't...?

MANNY: Costs money!

COP (genuinely not knowing): Well, what costs so much, admission?

MANNY: No, there's no admission price, but the people that go there... well-to-do, they wear expensive clothes, everything y'order is expensive.

COP: Oh, but you got lots of money at times.

MANNY: No. I never have.

The truth for Manny. But *the wrong thing to say.* Manny acts out the routine as directed, while the deli proprietor and his assistant finish serving a customer. They would like him to repeat the "take," so he obliges. Does the assistant recognize him? "Gee. I dunno!"

[6] Meanwhile, Rose has been on the phone to Manny's mother. "It's been over an hour... must be an accident. This isn't like Manny. You know if he couldn't make it home for dinner he'd—" Mama is all reassurance: "He's so steady, you never expect him to be late." At both ends of the line, we see a solitary woman holding a phone next to a warming table lamp. "I've always dreaded being alone more than anything else" (Friedan 515). The phone, a cold agency of systematic and essentially anonymous communication, anybody talking to anybody. The table lamps, domestic, safe, homey, personal. No thing or person of moral value enters to address the aloneness.

[7] Back at the police "shop," the questions begin to amass. Are they the building blocks of an institutional architecture?—

> OLDER COP (to Manny, matter-of-factly, as though it is beyond doubt that he has the right to ask): What do you make at the Stork Club?
>
> MANNY (forthright): Eighty-five.
>
> COP: That's the take-home pay?
>
> MANNY: Yes.

Then pick up speed and rhythm, a kind of drumbeat: "You play the horses?" — "How often?" — "You go to the track regularly?" — "Ever borrow any money?" — "When was the last time?" — "Pay it back?" — "Was it difficult to pay it back?" — "How much do you owe?"

> MANNY (calculating): Oh... forty-five dollars.[8]
>
> OLDER COP (not really listening): Maybe a hundred?
>
> MANNY: No no, couldn't be that much.
>
> COP (strangely devious): Less than a hundred?
>
> MANNY (wavering some): It's less than fifty, I'm sure. Probably less than forty, maybe less than thirty, I don't know, it's hard to say when I'm not—

COP (sharply): WHEN YOU'RE NOT WHAT?

It is not difficult or strange to wonder what the cop figures he'll get from these questions, other than a clue spilling from nervous Manny's mouth. Owing money doesn't mean you would steal for it, and claiming you owed wouldn't work anywhere as evidence you were a thief. If he's searching for motive, his search works only if Manny is expressly lying—that is, harboring a compounded motive, to steal and to cover the stealing. The thief has taken a lot more than thirty or forty dollars, and if Manny is lying these questions aren't going to be able to show he's guilty of that.

[8] Broadly speaking the older cop has been wearing a Helpful Chum mask. He isn't as brash or ambitious as his young colleague, he's been here before, he's been everywhere before, he knows guys like Manny and every other kind of guy, he knows what it is to be put through the wringer, especially this wringer, and he wants Manny to taste his sympathy. People are going to come in and try to identify him. "You'll be confronted by the witnesses. If you haven't done anything you have nothing to fear." Very straightforward, very simple, very anxiety-allaying. And all as though the assurance is true, is real.

If you haven't done anything you have nothing to fear.

[9] Through the film so far, Manny has been confronted repeatedly with people who eye him. His wife when he comes home, lovingly; the clerk (behind bars) at the insurance company, with a forced application of neutrality covering unease; the young cop, with cocky assurance he has helped nab the right man; the older cop in the back seat of the car, his eyes focused ahead at the back of Manny's head and yet seeming to be looking at the rule book which is in another universe. In the question session, there is a palpable sense of optical confrontation, especially as the two cops, standing, lean over the table to "examine" Manny's person. Yet all of the police rhetoric skips connections—bluntly, not artfully—admitting the possibility of error, analytical and perceptual. Everything really and truly *is as we see it*; thus everything *is as we say it is* because *we saw it*.

Perceptual acuity is in the very root of blooming police procedure. Even when a police officer has been present at a crime—unusual in the extreme, since criminals, who know about the police, tend to hide their activities (see McIntosh 114ff.)—in follow-up there is no escape from reliance on something seen or something heard, that is, an account of a seeing or hearing which is tantamount to a claim provided by someone who purports to have been the seer or hearer (a "professional" claim the verity of which will usually escape testing). In this "perceptual context," the officers are relying on eyewitness identifications, and relying, too, on their own optical and auditory detections as unimpeachable and evidentiary. When Manny is told (with agonizing sloppiness) that he can't claim to be innocent if there is nobody to say he is, by inversion he is also being told that if there is somebody to say he is, he can; and this logic is, of course, fraught. The "everything-is-as-we-see-it" attitude morphs temporally: "everything-*was*-as-we-see-it-*now*," and at the center is not only the police officer's sight, that is, state of knowledge as informed and spurred by a perceptual act but also his retroactive certainty, that everything was, at an earlier time, what his present sight is suggesting to him now. We behave the same way in the theater when we watch a film. *Everything as we see it now.*

[10] The cops would like a little help "seeing it"—a polite invitation to torture. The thief handed the girl at the window a printed note, Manny. "You could go a long way to showing if you're the same man." Paper and pencil are provided. "Now, you say you're not that man." — "Certainly am not." — "Well, you certainly won't print the way he does," a comment to which we will have to return. "An innocent man has nothin' to fear, remember that." Obediently now, even diligently, Manny takes dictation and in block caps prints the note. The cop looks hard at it, shows it to Young-and-Ambitious, and then looks Manny in the eye. In all this sequence Hitchcock pays more than considerable attention to the optical gaze (the arrogant gaze of power and the reticent gaze of powerlessness), and the lighting is geared to give the greatest lambency to the eyes. "Now I want to be entirely fair to you, Manny, so I'll tell you right now there's a rough similarity between

your printing and the note." If Manny has been feeling calm and self-assured—we have certainly seen him keeping his cool—this little piece of information will rile him.

A second chance is offered, with the same dictation, the same diligent penmanship hard at work, and we can hear the pencil clicking through the paper on the wooden tabletop, like a telegraph key.

"Hmph!" exclaims the cop, "It's one of the most remarkable things I've ever seen...!" (Ever: in my long, long career facing my many, many perpetrators.)

[11] "This looks bad for you, Manny." He has a right to know, so our friend the cop will tell him, our friend is a decent fellow, he'll keep nothing back. "First— now there's a kinda similarity in the printing of course but that doesn't mean much—most people print alike when they use capitals." If Manny doesn't register for us at this instant that he's picking up what is boldly there to be picked up, we surely are: that the cop is offering a direct contradiction to a claim he made with blunt confidence only a minute or so before, that if Manny isn't the thief he won't print the way the thief prints. Because now there is a rough similarity that's *entirely discountable, because when they print in capitals people print alike*. Which is it, then, people all print differently or people all print alike?[9] But now comes a clincher. The thief demanded of the clerk that she give him the money from the cash drawer, and this final word, drawer, he misspelled "DRAW." And Manny has done exactly the same thing. (Write it as you hear it.)

When Manny speaks now, he gives us a Hitchcockian moment truly unlike any other, in that he says precisely, verbatim, and in the same tone as we could reasonably expect, what we must surely think he is going to say: in effect, we jump to the finish line before he does. "I meant to write drawer, I guess I was in a hurry, I left off the er. I made a mistake." To err is human. Everyone makes mistakes. Nobody's perfect![10]

The hold-up man made a mistake, too, the cop says, and "it happens to be the same mistake." *Happens to be:* in one way, a casual usage of its time, a way of formalizing the simplicity of a strange coincidence; but in another way a marginally sarcastic, surely dubious brushing aside of happenstance and a subtle allusion to a hidden pattern that has nothing to do with chance. *Happens to be*, as in *damned well is*. As to happenstance: could an identical error of spelling be committed by two different people who have no relation to one another? Eliminate words in the message that are simple and tiny and obvious, like *gun*; see how very few words there are that might look the way they sound and get misspelled; imagine the population of a fifty-square-block zone in Queens and narrow it down to tall, slender men. The number will still be great (Manny's is no abnormal body type for New Yorkers), and the greater the number the more random chance there is that one *might* find a similarity with the handwriting of a stranger, there being no underlying pattern to the spontaneous appearance of chance similarities in a population.

For that matter, stand in your bedroom three thousand mornings and refer to that thing in the bureau as a "draw" when you speak, and soon it will be transformed into a "draw." ("Draw" for "drawer" is normal pronunciation in parts of the East Coast.)

Lineup time.

[12] Manny will not be surprised to see marching in for a lineup (what the British like to call an identification parade) a group of men all wearing more or less the same fedora as he, and the same long coat. That is, a group of other men *who resemble him*, this grouping being part of police procedure itself! There are plenty of other "identicals," then; moreover, there are plenty who can be assembled on call! This is nothing strange, and should not befuddle the policemen. The blitz in product differentiation that we have seen since the 1980s, with untold variants of every conceivable item, was not to be found in the 1950s.[11] A man would not say he was wearing, as I described above, a "long coat" and "fedora"; he would say he was wearing a "coat and hat." But even Manny could have been unsettled a little to see all these almost identical coats and hats gathered together and on show, to notice how many other men could be found on a moment's notice who might be seen as looking vaguely like him. I suspect any of us would be somewhat shocked to see on exhibition, as though by mathematics, how many other people could be our identical twins. Another way to state this, and one more

germane to the proceedings onscreen and to Hitchcock's intention in framing them this way, is that inside the urban metropolis, which is highly and densely populated, and in which the human figure is in constant motion, we invent a sanity and repose by treating ourselves as discreet individuals, each in her or his bubble of security and peace, each responsible for the self or for the family attached to the self, each knowable in a unique and original way; yet at the same time this blazing individuality, this Marquee of the Self is a myth and we all know it. A worker bee is a worker bee is a worker bee. One middle-aged man living in Queens is like many others. The police officers themselves are more than likely to be "working men living in Queens." How, then, can the police justify to themselves placing such weight on the similarity between Manny's "mis"-spelling and the crook's, except by positioning themselves *above justification*. This particular middle-aged man named Manny, centered in a row of similars, is observed by two of the three insurance clerks from a room across a corridor, in short from a good fifteen or more feet away. They are asked to number the faces, and to stop at "the one you know," which cannot possibly be a hard task, of course, since Manny was in the offices of the company only hours before.

[13] Perhaps Manny is gradually coming around to seeing himself not as a person but as an instantiation of a type, and in this way picking up the policeman's categorical attitude toward identification and labeling, one that goes all the way back to the mid-nineteenth century and Alphonse Bertillon (see Gunning "Tracing"). The police operation is incessantly binary: guilt, yes/no; innocence, no/yes. The similarity in typifications (that all assembled "members" of a set must in some respect be interchangeable) is both utile to and invisible from the investigators—in this particular police lineup, as we will only after a grueling ordeal learn, all the men standing are innocent. Nor in the modern city is any individual, guilty or innocent, discreet and irreducible. Gunning quotes Peter Finley Dunne:

> A cow goes lowin' softly into Armours and comes out glue, gelatine, fertyzlizer, celooloid, joolry, sofy cushions, hair

restorer, washin' sody, soap, lithrachoor, and bed springs, so quick that while aft she's still cow for'ard she may be anything fr'm buttons to pannyma hats. (17)

Manny may remain a feelingful self aft, but for'ard he'll be habits, facial expressions, clothing, hunger, gambling history, bank account, audacity, method, gambling, and guilt.

[14] Identified now, by his hand and by the voices of others remembering "what they saw," Manny is brought back by his bodyguards the older of whom now brings in his captain. "Well, Manny?" An accusatory stare that reaches out and embraces the tall, dignified body of the quiet man who cannot believe all this, a stare that embraces, stamps, catalogues. "Can't you see I'm just trying to tell the truth?" Manny has not yet come to see that no one can see what anyone is trying to do. The captain is pushing the button, however. "Given the evidence, there's nothing to do but lock him up." For a full—that is, utterly bitter—understanding of this action we need to see how the captain is operating according to the stipulated guidelines of a system that does not recognize human feeling, potentiality, sincerity, individuality, or history. He has (we have) the comparative notes of threat. He has store operators not refusing to accept Manny as the robber. He has Manny's answers, equivocal as they may sound, to the police questions. And to cap it, he has the positive identification from two witnesses. This police captain is not wholly to be blamed for having no loopholes by which to pass the personality of a man who could easily seem meek and innocent, an inheritor of the earth.

DIGESTED

With the two detectives Manny will pass through a door and then a second door, and in this passage he will discover a new world—that is, he will discover his world changed, even drawn away, even removed. All this in an echoing silence. Some of our greatest writers have pondered and expressed the horrifically subtle, even matter-of-fact transformation of the free man into society's slave, say, the ease with which it is possible for an accusation to take hold if only it is made in the right voice by the right kind of person at the opportune moment. Committing a crime is hardly a requirement for the Guilty pronouncement. Committing a crime may even be outside the purview of a person's mind. Hitchcock wants to continue showing us—both pointing backward to indicate that he *has* been showing us; and moving forward to new, profounder revelations—the inner workings of the justice system, the systemic routine. The justice system or to call it by a righter name, the punishment system, since the *justice* it proclaims itself (so proudly) to attain in so pure a state neither exists nor is sought out by those whose more primordial thirst will be slaked by nothing less than enforced penury. Punishment: reserved for those who are deemed to merit it. We must bond with Manny and believe everything he says and denies; in short we must fully, wholly, unequivocally, and aggressively disclaim his guilt and responsibility, Hitchcock knows, in order that the operation of the machine upon his body be made more visible. "The machine was freshly polished and glistening," wrote Kafka:

> I used new replacement parts for almost every execution. In front of a hundred eyes—all the spectators stood on tiptoe as far as the hills—the commander himself placed the condemned man under the harrow. Something that a common soldier may do today was assigned to me, the presiding judge, and it was an honor for me. And now the execution began! No jarring note disturbed the running of the machine. Some people stopped watching altogether; they lay in the sand, closing their eyes. Everyone knew: Justice was being done. In the hush, all we heard was the condemned man's sighs, muffled by the felt gag.... How profoundly we took in the transfigured expression from the tortured face, how intensely our cheeks basked in the glow of that justice, attained at long last and already fading! What wonderful times, my friend! (210–11)

Rather than through dramatic excess, the shock of an angle, the express pointing to an elaboration of action, the System must be seen to operate as a complex interweaving of impersonal and routine threads of accomplishment, this in order that the personality of the accused be altered, as though by chemistry, into a mere chain of reflexes independent of any individual biological history. When he lights the system, Robert Burks knows, it must shine uniformly, all the parts in their relations. The cinematographer

> never before had been faced with such difficult lighting and camera problems.
>
> He credits a comparatively new lighting unit for easing much of the way for him on this assignment. A dinky little lamp, no larger than an automobile headlamp, but far more powerful, proved the answer to his lighting problems. This is the Garnelite, a small, lightweight unit that takes a 300-watt PAR 56 lamp and puts out as much light as a 5K.... Burks used Garnelites exclusively for lighting all location interiors and night exteriors. He used them for key lights, for front lighting and for just about every other set-lighting need.
>
> "These lamps have tremendous range," said Burks, "and they carry to great distances ... We actually lit streets a block and a half-long with this equipment." (Foster 113–14)

The very powerful lights presented special problems in tight interiors, where they had to be reduced by diffusers custom-made for the moment by the grips (114). A good example is Manny's fingerprinting episode. Just before he is taken to his future, he is given a little taste of what's to come as the younger detective inks his fingertips and uses his hand on Manny to turn them into stamps to be pressed onto the record card. Manny looks down and sees his prints (for the first time), seems to see his hand becoming no longer his own but now nothing other than a physical specimen that can be registered through the action of inking a bureaucratically marshaled form. So evanesces his feeling of self.

"There's nothing in the world more difficult than candor," wrote Dostoevsky. As with his Parasha, "She, in her innocence, did not foresee any perfidy and succumbed inadvertently, without knowing, without thinking, and so on and so forth" (476). *And so on and so forth:* we all know this so I don't have to tell you. But did you know that I am noting that we all know this and I don't have to tell you? Because *that* is why I'm telling you: I'm telling you because you think I don't have to tell you, because you know already, because we all know. But we all behave as though we all don't know. For Manny in the lock-up, every gesture, every breath, every memorable moment simply happens as for the bodies trapped in here it has always happened *and so on and so forth.*

There is a history to confinement as penury, one that imbricates the prison in an elementary way with the dissociation of the person from the body. Michel Foucault describes France of the seventeenth century:

> Jurists held firmly to the principle that "imprisonment is not to be regarded as a penalty in our civil law."... Its role is rather that of holding the person and his body as security: *ad continendos homines, non ad puniendos*, as the tag has it; in this sense, the imprisonment of a suspect has a role similar to that of a debtor. Through imprisonment, one has security for someone, one does not punish him. (*Punitive* 118)

To confine persons, not to punish them. And this holding "the person and his body"—the two entities joined—is coming at a time before capitalism helps divorce the brain from the hands, the personality from the labor. In the era of which Foucault writes, the person *was* the body, but we are very capable today, for example, of inflicting demeaning and excruciating agony on the body while disingenuously claiming, "Nothing personal."

The initiation procedure requires no particular language from Manny: it is by no means an avenue by which he may express a self. Erving Goffman writes of total institutions, and the prison is surely one, that on admission

> the individual is likely to be stripped of his usual appearance and of the equipment and services by which he maintains it, thus suffering a personal defacement.... In addition to personal defacement that comes from being stripped of one's identity kit, there is personal disfigurement... loss of a sense of personal safety is common and provides a basis for anxieties about disfigurement.... On the outside, the individual can hold objects of self-feeling—such as his body, his immediate actions, his thoughts, and some of his possessions—clear of contact with alien and contaminating things. But in total institutions these territories of the self are violated. (*Asylums* 20–21; 23)

The Manny who had a territory of the self at the Stork Club and on the E train and at Bickford's and at home must now become a Manny whose self and self-territory are designed and owned by the City of New York. Yet here in Hitchcock's story, the transformation will conform to a matter of arraignment, not trial, conviction, or sentencing, and so steps will be taken doubly, in a preliminary, even equivocal way, every gesture toward incarceration coupled with a matching gesture of liberation either possible or probable or certain. This rather tentative foray into the loss of self has particular dramatic value for its very tentativeness; what it is that Hitchcock needs to state and emphasize is the minuscule size of the actions committed upon Manny, their effortlessness, their routineness, their belongingness to the matter-of-fact everyday. Routines are the compositional blocks of *The Wrong Man*.

Manny is guided forward out of the interrogation room:

[a] An empty corridor with overhanging lights, with every footstep echoing quite as though a beat is being kept for his progress by some invisible drummer;

[b] The sergeant at the booking desk, politely asking questions again, receiving straightforward answers. Manny says he is thirty-eight (!). He lives on 78th Street, Jackson Heights. "Search him."

[c] The young detective, who is handling Manny's person now with his older colleague a quiet observer, takes from Manny's pockets some loose change, a comb, and a rosary. Manny looks at this merchandise with a cold and chilling kind of distance, not as though he is surprised to see what he has but as though he is surprised and thrown off guard to see that what he has is now *what he had, and it belongs to them*. Manny is asked to retrieve from his inside pocket what else there is, his wife's insurance policy. There is $6.17 in bills and coin. The accusation is that he took seventy-one dollars and change from the Associated Life. He is given permission to retain the rosary.

[d] A door opens at the side, with a policeman in blues. Inside this, unmistakably, another door with bars. Manny's jaw drops and he freezes staring at it. "But my wife—" The young cop: "That's been taken care of," with a smile of small kindness. Hitchcock frames several compositions here showing Manny in close profile moving against bars, and

when he is put in his cell and the door drawn shut we see him look out with the shadow of the vertical bars dividing his face. (This sectioning by shadow goes all the way back to *The Lodger* [1927].) The good from the bad, the light from the dark, the promise from the vacancy. William Rothman gives it an ample discussion in *The Murderous Gaze*.

[e] Definitely stunned, definitely confused, Manny sits and ponders. At home Rose and Mama stand in stunned silence while the brother-in-law (Nehemiah Persoff) speaks on the phone with his wife listening closely. He gives off a report: Manny has been arrested for robbery; he will spend the night in jail. A jump cut to the two boys peering through their bedroom door to hear this sentence in wonder.

[f] Manny is pacing his cell. We are watching his legs and feet. Manny is a tall enough man, with long enough legs—inhabiting Henry Fonda's 6′ 1½″ body. Even working to keep his paces modest, he can step only two paces in any one direction in this cell. Two paces, turn, two paces, turn. His musical hands change into fists: endure, endure, endure. It is clear enough that this holding cell for Manny is roughly what an iron cage is for a lion, if not considerably smaller; more like a dog cage.

[g] Manny must spend the whole night. He stands against a wall, a look of forlorn desperation on his face, and slowly at first, then more and more quickly to Bernard Herrmann's trumpet obligato, the camera swoops up left, around over the top of his head and face, down on the right, left under his chin, up and above him, over, down, below, up, over... until it is circling Manny's face like the hour hand of a clock running not on Greenwich time but to the rhythm of his speeding heart. This spin is a moving way of expressing time's passage, of flagging the morning on approach, at least in Manny's expectation. But it is also a way of portraying a blunter fact: that this Manny we recognized and lingered beside is already being converted into a nameless man in a cell. A creature of somebody else's clock. In short, Manny is becoming systemic: is beginning the process of routine digestion by the system.[12]

DEPOSITED

The police system and Manny's domestic system both work in a kind of silence, since no one pauses at their margins to note and comment upon them. We see it all in our own enforced silence.

Foucault establishes a very interesting fact about the early use in Europe of imprisonment as a social retribution. A separation is made between the accused as a taker of property (a false possessor) and the accused as a shirker. Thus, the theft is at one and the same time (i) meritless appropriation, the removal of some good from its "proper" place (proper ownership), and (ii) evidence that someone who has not paid society with his labor is now in debt to a specified amount. Since jailing a person does not necessarily return to victims what has been taken; or even if such a return can happen does not completely enough fulfill the felt need for retribution and balancing, the guilty is made to secure his person to the state for a length of time long enough to account for work that should otherwise have been done (offered) in lieu of stealing. Even if the victim is fully paid back, that is, beyond retrieving what was stolen and putting it where it "belongs," there is seen to be reason in locking someone up to "do time." The world in which work could and should have been done must be addressed, a balance is to be achieved, so that, literally, the body held in a cell is performing a substitute work there. The long empty day is a labor. "Wealth is, after all, an apparatus of production in relation to which the worker's body—now directly in the presence of this wealth that does not belong to him—is no longer merely the locus of desire, but is now the source of labor-power, which must become productive force." The illegalism that "essentially exists in refusing to apply this body, this force to the apparatus of production" might come from idleness; or the worker's irregularity; or festive revelry; or refusal of family (Foucault, *Punitive* 187)—no matter; of no concern; without interest.

In an important way, then, stealing—of which Manny stands accused—is "the refusal to offer these arms, this body, this strength on the labor market" (Foucault, *Punitive* 187). The implication of "refusal to offer" in a context where offering is both regular and mandatory would help us grasp the import of the two detectives' guarded yet quite evident *attitude* regarding Manny and their charge upon him. For them, as would seem, this is not merely an issue of seventy-one dollars putatively in Manny's pocket that should be in the insurance company's cash "draw"; it's that they are themselves, in their own view, hard workers in their serious (if menial) jobs and this man thinks (apparently) it's okay to just take things without putting in the labor. Ultimately, *ressentiment:* degrading others for apparently having done what you deeply believe everybody should ideally be able to do (in a Utopian vision) but you too distinctly aren't. By not being at home with his family, Manny's body as person is being held "on deposit" in the cell.

In the morning, a bright day, he is taken with others in a police van across the 59th Street Bridge into Manhattan where there is a Metropolitan Police facility collecting arrested persons from all five boroughs. Manny is "Queens No. 1." He stands on a stage before a microphone (that we see obscuring his face) and against a vivid whiteboard with height markings. The young detective affirms to the master sergeant that Manny is being "held for questioning by the District Attorney's office," at which point Manny goes off with him, again by van and now back in Queens, to a small police holding area where he is cuffed to another man and led to yet another van among a group of similarly linked pairs (the Hitchcock tune of bondage, seen already in *The 39 Steps* [1935] and *Saboteur* [1942]). A chain of to-be-detecteds-by-us:

[•] In the van we see a circle of shoes, all belonging to numbered and handcuffed persons heading they know not where. We can think them all guiltier than Manny and in this way single him out for our attentions; or else we can think that in legal fact no one of them is guiltier than Manny is. A round-up, the usual suspects.

[•] An arraignment court, stepping into which he sees Rose and his brother-in-law and mouths to her, "No." He is bound over on $7,500 bail, and when he inquires of the young detective whether he'll be able to see his wife he is told, "If she comes to Long Island City jail." That jail is the next stop. He is uncuffed, moved into a disrobing area. Soon we see him clothed again, necktie undone, marching up to a cell with a bundle of bedding. When the door slides shut on him, Hitchcock arranges that the camera will swiftly dolly forward to peer into the horizontal feeding slot, and, like Manny's nourishment, or his resuscitation, we slide through the slot ourselves until we are in the cell with him. Until we are comfortable in that cell, it goes without saying, since in cinema, certainly Hitchcockian cinema, the viewer is never in danger.

[•] Manny stares out the barred window at a featureless whitewashed brick wall (shades of *À nous la liberté* [1924]).

[•] But swiftly his name is called and he is free.

We have been engaged thus far on a purely police-generated and police-oriented process, and Manny has not, until the moment he walks out of the jail, been outside the direct physical control of one policeman or more. He has been escorted, chauffeured, manacled, unmanacled, stood up in court, borne away, led out of a van, walked down a corridor—all by police officers. The police are marshaling the jail. And this final voice, giving him liberty for the moment, is definitively a police voice.

That the film may be in a position to present a redemptive finale, something on a level of seriousness and causation far beyond the police and juridical systems, far beyond the family, far beyond everyday life, it is necessary that Manny (and Rose) be brought to a condition of true crisis. *Crisis:* "decision," "resolution," "direction." Like Job, they must have lost all hope. They must have been eroded to powder by the system's mechanisms and rigors, arbitrary though these be.

And so, in a kind of prelude to culmination, a descent: to what is for Manny the lowest level of direct experience, his wife sliding off the rails, and what is for us, in our engagement with him, a sudden vacant shapeless sense of indeterminacy that makes all hope evaporate. There is a touching nuance here, elegantly handled by Hitchcock and performed with precision by Miles and Fonda. Manny must be seen to be distraught, even trembling with helplessness by what has happened to Rose, her descent into the limbo of doubt, but this sense he has must differ from the way we in our sympathy are affected, too. We must note her, watch her, feel "concern for" her; yet Rose is never now, nor ever was, as significant for us in the picture as Manny. Manny is the focus of our concern, and our "worry" about Rose is an ancillary worry: she is his focus as he is ours. She descends, at any rate, and whether he senses it as she does, or not, Manny descends with her:

> According to [the Balestreros' lawyer] Mr. O'Connor, Mrs. Balestrero's decline was rather rapid. The first meeting with the Balestreros was on Sunday, January 18th. He noticed a decided change in Mrs. Balestrero by Thursday, January 22nd, and on the following Monday, January 26th, she was in a very bad way. (Points 2)

The steps down the steep ladder, each giving vantage for a peek into chilling corridors of déjà vu:

[a] Reunion outside the Queens City Prison, Manny thanking his sister from the bottom of his heart for the bail, and falling into Rose's arms. "You'll never know how much I needed you!" We do not get a close shot of Rose; she is still at a distance. It is perhaps true, we can see, that she will never know. Or: knowledge can't be counted on.

[b] Walking up the steps to his house when this part of the ordeal is over, Manny sees across the street an empty parking spot and is carried back for an instant to the police car that sat there "about a million years ago."

[c] Embrace from his boys and his mother. As he lies down, the older boy comes in to be with him. "I hope you never go through anything like this, Bob, but if you do I hope you have a son at home who's as wonderful to come home to as you." He confides that he never knew how much his children meant to him until now. In close focus here, Manny's large hand around Bob's head. Back to this hand in a brief moment. But Bob and his brother stand at a distal end of the long corridor of time, beyond Manny's hand altogether.

[d] As he rests, Rose calls a lawyer she's been told about, a Mr. O'Connor. He's gone home. She finds his number in the phone book—macro-close shot of the print, duplicating what we see the same year in *The Man Who Knew Too Much* (1956)—and calls, finding not the lawyer but his wife. The wife is willing to take a message but no, Rose would like to tell the story to her. We fade very gently to black as she begins her narration at the Stork Club, so that there can be a hint of a déjà vu for the viewer, too. . . . In all mysteries like this, which have not yet rounded to a pleasing conclusion, there is a lozenge of tranquility and

reassurance that is afforded the viewer by any scene such as this one, and most especially by an element of absence: Rose's *retelling* suggests the continuity of the tale, so that distal Mrs. O'Connor has every bit of information we do (as much as this is possible from Rose as narrator). Somehow our not meeting the lawyer's wife makes us feel her benevolence, that her powers will extend that benevolence into justice by sharing certain imperceivable touches of meaning or sentiment with her husband who will convert them into battlefield moves.

[e] Manny and Rose are heading to O'Connor's offices—which are, coincidentally, in the Victor Moore Arcade! The quiet coffee shop, the tense insurance office, the patient lawyer, all in the same place. As they stand outside his door, Manny looks off-camera with hesitation and some alarm, because very close by is that insurance company office he is alleged to have robbed. Contaminative exposure.

A MUSICAL HAND

We will surely follow Manny and Rose. But first, what of Manny's hand that cradles the boy's head? The hand to which we always return in one way or another. I would aver, perhaps only on the evidence of the first few seconds of the film, that Manny Balestrero is a good bassist, not just a bass player. His digital and wrist moves, his ease in moving, the tone he produces and keeps up—all very accomplished. To play the double bass, and absolutely to play it well, one must have a large and powerful hand, most especially when working on the fingerboard down near its base (where the high-pitched tones are to be made). The strings themselves can be pencil thick, and one must not only reach across the fingerboard to get all of them but slide up and down as well, sometimes in a massive stretch with muscles hard at work in the hand. More than muscles, indeed. Writing of the "gymnastic training of the hand," given that the extreme pressure borne by the hand could be extensive and severe, Stephen Stratton quoted Sir Charles Bell, the hand's foremost early student:

> If the palms, and inside of the fingers, and their tips were not guarded by cushions beneath the skin, it would be too much for

the texture even of bones and tendons, and certainly, for the blood-vessels and nerves to sustain. (111)

At the end of the century Thomas Dowse adds of these "cushions on the ends of the fingers" that they are useful "in subservience to the organ of touch; conferring a power of receiving impressions, which the utmost delicacy of the nerves themselves could not bestow" (50). In wrapping oneself around the fingerboard by way of wrapping one's hand, in navigating on it, in pressuring the thick strings, all in syncopation and directly to the beat of the leader (in this case Peter Rotonda), one would be a person hard at work yet also exceptionally sensitive. And one would be, in a sense, hearing with the fingers, in that the sound-touch of familiar notes would for each come to be idiosyncratic.[13]

With this in mind—or on the tips of the fingers—travel again to Manny and Rose's bedroom where little Bob comes in to visit dozing Manny and a father expresses how thankful he is for his children. Manny draws Bob to him and in macro-close shot we see Manny's strong, long-fingered hand wrapping itself around the child's neck. Frank Wilson writes of "the rapid adjustment of forces at the fingertip based on mechanical resistances encountered at the fingertip from the moment of contact" with, for example, the string (358). Down on the C-Bout near the bridge, the fingerboard is roughly as thick as a young boy's neck. Bob is Manny's music; and also Manny's instrument in the simple and relieving sense that here and now he is functioning to make Manny feel, through vibration, that his world has returned.

Given that Manny's hand carries importance in his professional work quite as in his family and emotional life, and that Manny's hand gains particular attention from Hitchcock, we may come to conclude that handing, handcuffing, and handling may in some ways be fundamental to the film. Handcuffing always disempowers, and is a frequently employed screen trope in procedurals. But handcuffing Manny Balestrero stymies his body memory of his music making and his affection with his family at once. He is *silenced* when his hands are taken out of the picture. The first half of the story, in fact, is about Manny's distinct inability to handle the environment fashioned by police routine yet at the same time about his distinct ability to handle himself there. When with routines in mind we watch the images

Hitchcock has mounted on the screen, what we see is a careful establishment of Manny's everyday routine, personal and domestic, based in a family history that is moderate, above all considerate and sweet; this against a careful establishment of police routine, demoralizing, anonymous, cold, strangely numerical. As the film proceeds, we examine each of these forms of routine, the domestic and the legal, our experience of the legal routine being apparently as real a representation in the context of Manny's life as the routine at home. As real, but in no wise similar. At home we see preparation for work, dressing in front of the kitchen mirror, then taking the subway, and playing the gigs at the Club, and returning in the wee hours of the morning by way of his favorite coffee shop—all this stepped through virtually every day, and for years. The police routine will be sharply cut off from his life; alien, the way the world is for a tiny child learning for the very first time how to walk toward a chair, how to sit, what to look at, when to speak. Return to the (amazing and beautiful) Fonda performance to see the way his eyes look inquisitively at the world, how every single little situation and aspect of a situation in police custody is a puzzle for him, one he does not want to get wrong since above all he is respectful of authority but one that chafes in an idiosyncratic, marginally nauseating way.

And Manny who handles himself with aplomb and calmness, whose hands cause sound, must now hand over his necktie to the jailer, his freedom to the cell keeper, his innocence to the judge. He is handled, if not man-handled, by the system. His hands become the property of the system, that will work to make the claim he has had idle hands (doing the Devil's work) and must be incarcerated for that.

Of Manny's sojourn in the police system, it can generally be said that, as with Collodi's Pinocchio facing the police, "they instructed him in military tones: 'Forward and quick march! Or else, so much the worse for you!'" (101), with the ironic difference that of course Pinocchio was a naughty fellow and Manny is everything but. Nor is it so much into the care or monitoring of only specific police types that Manny falls, since in practice he is allocated, guided, observed, interrogated, confined, and moved around by numerous different individuals whose individual differences are evaporated in an important sense by their obligations to the police system. This system is a substantial corporate arrangement, ultimately bureaucratic, by which the accused is not only divorced from his own will and determination but separated in a thorough way from his ties to family, community, and self so that his own view of who he is becomes a mimicry of systemic perceptions. Take the fingerprinting. Manny is not so out of touch with reality that he doesn't know what fingerprinting is, but he has never been fingerprinted before—those sensitive, strong, important fingers!—and is therefore an innocent to the actual process in its immediate reality. (An innocent, ironically, observed by a detective who does not affirm the innocence.) We can see Manny's separation if we look carefully at the slight withdrawal (for focus) and slight querulousness in his facial expression as his fingers are grasped by the younger detective and inked. His reaction to being touched that way and inked is evident not only in the moment where the ink is applied but shortly afterward when he is given a paper towel and told peremptorily to wipe his hands—the dirty little boy being corrected by the teacher. A stain is being laid upon Manny's person—hands as person—blotting his immaculateness. (The inkblot motif will be reprised, of course, in *Marnie* [1964].) Not to forget, either, that Manny knows his fingers, knows them intimately, indeed knows himself to have musical fingers, fingers inseparable from music and that are now, in someone else's manipulations, being separated from him. One thinks of Caliban's curse upon the learnèd Prospero: "Burn but his books."

For Manny, the fingerprinting ink, completely functional for the police system, is a foul substance oozed from the abysmal, a sinful pus; exactly the kind of substance he has been spending his entire life stepping carefully away from. In its way the inking represents the moment in which Manny is utterly turned away from the family routines, the moment when he cannot possibly show his hands to mama. What helps make the inking so troubling is the methodical pacing and direction of the detective's moves: it couldn't be clearer that even relatively young as he is, this man has done the fingerprinting routine countless times and makes the moves almost automatically—just as the police system makes all its moves with a kind of blunt automaticity that blots the spontaneity of the human. Here, the family routine is not only dominated but devoured and digested by the routine of police action and discourse, and since that family routine consisted of actions deeply embedded in Manny's being, hands on necks, its replacement by the unrecognized and unrecognizable brings a shock.

BEFORE THE LAW

Mr. O'Connor (Anthony Quayle) is as pleasant and no-nonsense a gentleman as one could hope to meet under any circumstances, but *in extremis* a moment at his side is bliss. Yes, he will take Manny's case, and gently passes along Mr. Billingsley's assurance that the musician needn't worry about his job. When, affecting a routine voice, he asks for some proof of innocence Rose assumes command of the ship. "Proof of Manny's innocence? We've been married for nine years and we haven't been separated for more than two days at a time. If Manny had done anything wrong I'd know about it. And I know he hasn't." Nevertheless O'Connor would like them to dig in memory, to "discover exactly where you were and what you were doing on these two key dates, the dates that the insurance company was held up." Rose again, with a smile of promise: on the first date, "We were vacationing at a hotel in the country—Mr. Ferrero might be able to help." Somewhere upstate; woodsy, wintry, bucolic as in a postcard, with a clapboard lodge. They drive, we accompany. This sequence is in brilliant sunshine, a kind of holiday respite in itself by comparison with the grisly pewtering of the film so far. One sees clear skies to a distance, one virtually inhales the fresh air. Narratively the scene looks and reads like a flashback while actually it is "present time" in which a flashback is the subject of talk and of memory. A utopic peace reigns. And there are extremely long shots where tiny figures move across a bucolic space. But poor Mr. Ferrero and his wife are having trouble thinking back, until Manny steps over to a side cabin and remembers it was raining, he spent the whole day playing cards with three others. The Ferreros grab their guest book and manage to name two of those others, and Rose and Manny race off on the hunt. First, pulling up to an apartment building on West 178th Street just at the city end of the George Washington Bridge, at twilight, and then in a docks area, possibly Long Island City. Mr. Lamarca at the first location and Mr. Molinelli at the second are each, however, dead. At the Lamarca apartment the information is conveyed by two little giggling girls, a pair of antitheses to fearful, then brooding Rose.[14] At the second location Manny has to strain in Spanish to a concierge. "Vengo...aver...a Signior Molinelli." — "A Signior Molinelli! Ooooo. A se tiempo que murio." Rose turns away abruptly into the very dark shadows and breaks into an uncontrolled laugh: "There's an alibi! It's perfect!" One can feel the pressure of her world closing in as the vision of losing her husband step by step becomes clearer. In both Lamarca and Molinelli's apartment buildings, very long, narrow, darkened staircases, a sense of Rose and Manny at first ascending out of the depths but soon later dropping back again, into depths below those depths.

If Manny was battered in the systematic police routine, now as he moves into the systematic justice routine he is battered once again and more cruelly, because much more than him the mantle of trial appears to have covered Rose. She has reached out, into the shadows, and taken it upon herself. He is in their kitchen, fixing his tie for the club, and she is cooking, back to camera. But as she comes into his zone of consciousness it is as a strange figure wearing a thick and binding mantle of guilt:

> ROSE: It's my fault this happened to you.... Wisdom teeth! I knew I shouldn't'a asked you to go down there.... We've been in debt before because I haven't known how to handle things—now we're going into debt to O'Connor, all because I haven't known how to economize.... Truth is, I've let you down, Manny.

This is more than trying to bear her dutiful share of Manny's onus. She is feeling so powerfully the smack of defeat on his behalf that it has come, this nulling and depressing sensation of loss, to be her very own; it is her unbounded empathy lashing back.[15] Now, she piles responsibility onto herself in accreting layers, until she can be found guilty of the whole "thing." In her sorrow, which will darken and grow, Rose neglects to see what Manny is undoubtedly also neglecting to see, although Hitchcock chooses to spell out the effects on her: that Manny's crime, as she has lifted it onto herself, is actually only "crime," a crime as posited—Manny robbing the insurance company (and many other places as well)—that didn't happen. And one of the magics of the film is that without having witnessed anything originally, and without witnesses now, and without evidence, we not only believe it didn't happen, *we know*. He and Rose are neither of them associated with any robbery, albeit Rose avows her own tortured responsibilities before Manny's loving face. The "facts" here are circumstantial, not real. Yet, what is the difference between circumstance and reality? In the province of justice Manny and Rose's circumstantial links to the robbery may become real. Finally, it is in the realization of their vulnerability, their helplessness, that they become sensible of the justice system and its powerful routines, which differ from family routines even more potently than the police routines do. We saw this immediately with O'Connor, when Rose begins her speech with the assertion that she has been with Manny for nine years. Been with him in a marriage; built a family; run a house; lived a family life. Yes, but—...

From O'Connor's diligently furrowed brow we can read that things don't look very good for Manny, and Rose is walking into darkness.

SLIDING AWAY

When one thinks of *The Wrong Man* in terms of the transfer of guilt—this is a motif many observers have found in Hitchcock and *The Wrong Man* is certainly its clearest exposition—one possible "reading," not actually confirmed when we *look*, is that Rose is taking Manny's guilt onto her own "shoulders," affirming herself as the Scapegoat. In Leviticus 16:21–23 are the instructions followed by Aaron, including taking a goat and placing a hand on its head to confer the sins of all the people; and then, by means of a selected intermediary assigned specially for the purpose, having the creature taken into the desert and "exiled" there. Christian tradition often calls up primitive sources in which the animal has the people's sins conferred by one hand upon the head, but is then slaughtered by the other hand, the death of this innocent serving to "remove" guilt from others. Manny Balestrero, however, is *not* guilty in the first place and so Rose is not his scapegoat. The idea that in the first place Manny is *guilty because alive,* that very strict (and purely Catholic) generalization, is not consistent with all the details of Hitchcock's storytelling here, especially not with the portrait of Manny's morally meticulous normality and the artfully revealed pain of its ruin. This is a film about human action, not the human condition; systematization is a form of human action.

As to Rose, however, we may reasonably wonder now whether in the very depths of her mind (even if not in the depths of her heart) she does fear that he is guilty.

She would know if he'd done anything wrong, she affirms; but Vera Miles confers a sharp glow of intelligence to this woman; about herself she must know enough to guess, here and generally, that her "knowledge" about Manny and about life is insecure; that, after all, *all knowledge is insecure*. We can see in O'Connor's eyes when she attests to Manny's innocence that he can see this minuscule ray of the strange light of doubt. She reflects, then, in this very restricted sense—and in this way calls up—the dim, dim, dim hint of suspicion that lies buried under all our confidences. Call it, if you must, the shadow of our doubt. A shadow buried under all our confidences about the earth floating in space; about the destination of the dead; about the origin of morality; about the openness of family; all our confidences about everything, and especially about this man, realizing that in the event we weren't there, and she wasn't there, and the police weren't there . . . a shadow nobody can claim to know. There are so very many nobodies. There are so very many angles of view from which a shadow can be cast.

This self-doubt, which could lead to a person like Rose feeling the obligation to take "guilt" onto herself, is further developed, even exacerbated, as it is bounced back in contradiction, as we notice that the police have become very certain *that they do know*, notwithstanding that they, too, have the intelligence to suspect themselves but do not do so. On Manny's innocent face all through the ordeal, on that face of innocence that we see him wear, wherever he is and subject to anyone's command, that face for photographing which it was absolutely necessary to have Henry Fonda, is just a tincture of uncertainty, too, especially when he proclaims his innocence. As though he knows that even though he knows, and whatever it is he knows . . . it won't be enough. It is not that he fears he is a thief. It is that he is asserting his experience and recognizing how any assertion of experience can, for others, even for oneself—perhaps horribly for oneself—be suspect.

Manny, at any rate, has neither been adjudged guilty nor given us reason to believe he is, and so if there is transference of guilt here it is not from him onto Rose. We must keep this in mind. *Whose guilt* could Rose be transferring onto herself if that is what she is doing, and in what sense can she be considered the figure taking "the guilt of the other" for her own, in some sacred ceremony? Or might a darkness even thicker be looming in her strange, her ethereal movement?

The first sign that Rose is sliding away is manifested when for a second time she consults O'Connor with Manny. She is wrapped into herself now. "Yes—," she replies to a question very clearly not knowing what the question was. As they leave, Hitchcock presents a foreboding view of Rose standing and walking away from the camera toward O'Connor and Manny at the door. The camera is low, shooting her as though she is of monstrous proportion, the flat coat affording not even a ripple of vivacity on her back. But the hair, seen from behind, is dead in her movement, much like a wig spotted on the skull of a corpse. Of course, Vera Miles will be central in a reprise of this image only a few years later.

O'Connor whispers to Manny that his wife is very unwell. A professional voice, from one who has seen many wives in despondency.

One night afterward, after wrapping at the Club and pacing home, picking up the milk bottles, Manny quietly opens the bedroom door to find Rose fully dressed and seated beside the bed, her hands folded limply on her lap. She is only half responsive when he expresses concern. No, she says, she's not unwell, why should she see a doctor? For the last few days, says he, she hasn't seemed to care what happens at the trial. And some vortical chain of shallow-breathed phrases trickles out of her:

> Don't you see it doesn't do any good to care? No matter what you do they've got it fixed so it goes against you... No matter how innocent you are, or how hard you try, they'll find you guilty. Well we're not going to play into their hands anymore. You're not going out. You're not going to the club and the boys aren't going to school.

They will lock the doors. They will stay in the house and "lock 'em out and keep 'em out." When he suggests that the boys might stay with his mother during the trial she rises swiftly, her eyes like beacons. "You want to get the boys out of the house because you think I'm crazy, don't you? Don't you! Well,—" a bomb, we are seeing now, has been on a timer. She has been waiting, has been waiting with diminishing patience: "You're not so perfect either. How do I know you're not crazy? You don't tell me everything you do, how do I know you're not guilty? You could be. You could be!... You went to the loan company to borrow money for a vacation"—she has been walking forward toward him, her shadow moving grotesquely on the wall behind her, and now she faces him in profile, the shadow profile dense and adjacent a framed picture of Jesus—"You did that when we couldn't afford it. You always wanted to buy things on time. I told you not to. I told you they'd pile up and pile up."

O, but there has been a piling up...

Finally a fatal pronouncement: *"You can't win!* They've fixed it so they can smash us, and they will, they'll drag us down!" She reaches down for the hair brush on the dresser, gathers it up and raises it, a silver vengeance ready to descend from the air like a punishing bird. It smashes into Manny's forehead, and in recoil smashes the dresser mirror so that Manny's face is vertically divided in two, one half raised above the other. Two Mannies, the inner Manny and the Manny as visible; the Manny whom Rose once loved and the Manny he might be today, as far as she knows; the Manny before justice, and the Manny ground down by justice. She steps forward and takes his face gently in her hands. "It's true, Manny. There is something wrong with me. You'll have to let them put me somewhere." A *very* slow fade to black.

Note: *for the past few days she hasn't seemed to care what happens at the trial.* No, she doesn't care, a truly believable state of affairs. She looks like someone who cares about nothing in God's world. But we are obliged to offer a complete honesty ourselves. Is "the trial and what happens at it" truly, really, unequivocally the mountaintop of our concern and care? Surely, like Rose, we have already—thanks to Hitchcock's scoring—come to the decision the trial could never be fair, never revealing, and that the justice system is a factory that can produce no good. Why build the machine if not to make sausage?

Until now, if Manny has worried that the horrible police accusation will produce damage, he has been thinking of damage to himself. Damage to his strength and resolve, perhaps. Maybe even damage to his career and therefore to his future. And therefore damage to his family as a unit for which he feels himself bearing full responsibility. But something much worse has become evident. The accusation has wounded Rose, and wounded her seriously. She is only a wreck of the Rose he knows. And further, having withdrawn from the Rose he knows she has achieved a position of startling, ineffable, dazzling clarity, the refractions of which cannot be denied or blocked away; clarity, at least as to the way a vastly empowered neutral system casually regards the quality of any one life. To a psychiatrist in deep shadows she softly cries, "They're after me and they'll get me, they come at me from all sides." She sees how each and every one of us is powerless when *they* conspire to take action against us, *they* being myrmidons of a system inviolate. A system without mercy, without compassion, without feelingful deliberation, without self-doubt. A system in which self-doubt is unthinkable because a self is unthinkable. A non-living entity that can claim knowledge but not doubt it! Because in a circumstantial case like this one—all the witnessing is purely circumstantial—there is no single "fact" that cannot also be seen as a false proposition. Just as the claim of innocence can be thought—as apparently it is thought by the police—"truly false," the thought of "true falseness" can be truly false. If the police system depends on, is built on the foundation of, human supposition and suspicion, then the justice system is built on the foundation of human thought, if not probability. And what Rose is showing that she understands, what she cues all of us to understand on Hitchcock's behalf, is that human thought is finally insufficient and the probable finally inscrutable. That thought can be systematized though life cannot. That life is greater than thought. That the immeasurable silence of life is greater than the ponderous silence of thought.

Things will, yes, go unwell in the courtroom, almost exactly as Rose presages in her (Sybilic) delirium. But at home Manny takes his mother's advice to pray. He stands in front of that picture of Jesus. It is a simple picture, starry night, head and torso of the figure with a brilliant (lenslike) halo behind and the two hands raised in anticipation. We are close to Manny's face as, in silence, his lips move in prayer, and suddenly as though from his lips a second, superimposed, image appears, a man heading toward us on a New York street. Are Manny's words not somehow invoking this man? He is wearing that torturously typical trenchcoat and fedora, and the closer he comes, two visions assault us powerfully, although Manny, praying, sees nothing but the picture on the wall, nothing but Jesus, and we are separated from his consciousness for the first time in the film. The figure in the double image, we see, its posture, its complacent ease, its peacefulness for an instant, seems to ape Jesus and to ape Manny at once. And also this figure, whose face is clear now, starkly—far too starkly—resembles Manny. We will learn that this man has been arrested and identified in a line-up, and the police detectives are able to inform Manny that he is free. Rose continues to be unwell for some time, however.

FLOATING

Hitchcock can be counted on not only to mount to his climax but also to prepare in advance all the scaffolding required to bring us to a height, at his side. We will have to see a gentle musician calmly at work and calmly enjoying the tiny piquancies of his private routine. We will have to see him in the family, with his loving wife and his two charming sons. We will have to see his routine life brutally interrupted by agents of a rational system (*rational*, not *moral*). We will have to see the police system produce, then aggrandize, the problem. We will have to hear Manny identified by witnesses who are sure of themselves but in error: Sartrean bad faith. We will have to see him toggled over to the justice system, in care of his advocate O'Connor and whilst Rose slowly comes apart at the seams. We will have to see the trial, something of a charade in which it could not be more evident that everybody is paying very careful attention to the prosecutor and only the most casual attention to O'Connor (since, of course, why would this man Balestrero be standing accused in court if he were not guilty?). In this Country of the Blind there must be dark passages: the search for the two witnesses; Manny's bringing Rose for medical (psychiatric) consultation. At that consultation we will have to hear the practitioner's confidential assessment that this is a "well-known pattern"; "she's buried under some kind of landslide of fear and guilt... She's literally in another world from ours." Manny knows very well what it is to be in another world. We will have to accompany him as he takes Rose to a restorative institution outside New York, as he is asked to bid her goodbye in the vestibule and as he watches (in long shot) her climb the stairs in the company of medical assistants. Is this bright, happiness-inducing place not, in its way, also for her "a frightening landscape that could be on the dark side of the moon"? We will have to see Manny clutching his rosary during the trial. When the more voluble of the insurance company witnesses (Lang) steps over to identify him, we must watch in aggravating macro-close-up the condemnatory and fearful placement of her hand upon his shoulder.[16] We must countenance the tedious questioning, and countenance especially the bored juror who instead of countenancing stands up to ask the judge if they really have to listen to all this. We must see the judge rule a mistrial and O'Connor explain to Manny that they will have to go through all this again. We have to see

Manny in the kitchen with his mother watching, at once a font of wisdom and a font of belief: "My son, I beg you to pray." We have to see Manny standing before Jesus in the bedroom, staring at Jesus's face and muttering as he stares. We have to see, to witness, in superimposition at first vague and then becoming crisp, another New Yorker walk the streets and stare forward as Manny is staring forward, stare so intently that his eyes and Manny's eyes, in matched overlap, become the same:

> [Richard] Robbins read in Walter Winchell's column that producer-director Alfred Hitchcock was seeking an actor who resembled [Henry] Fonda. He sent him his photograph and 24 hours later was playing the holdup man for whom Fonda is mistaken in the story.
>
> Robbins also has certain facial characteristics in common with Jack Palance and John Carradine. He likes to play heavies.
> (Publicity)

We have to see this man attempt to rob a deli, and the European owners thwart him, man and wife in teamwork, and call the police, who take him to the precinct. We have to see the young detective finishing his shift, stepping out into the night and walking away. Stepping into the night the way, as the film began, Manny stepped into the night, his workday done. We have to see this detective pause. We have to see him turnabout and head back with—what, a new thought? A second thought? Second sight? All of this, everything here, every nuance and jot, links in a chain of preparation, where what comes next always seems a resolution of what was. But now:

Manny is playing at the Club, is in the middle of a number. A house manager steps up quietly and tells him they are asking him to come immediately to the 110th Precinct. We see him enter and find O'Connor waiting. They stand together. O'Connor leads Manny to turn his eyes down the corridor.

And the camera, being Manny now, looks down that institutional corridor, too. Empty, lit flatly, uninviting, unprepossessing, unevocative. There are voices. We zoom forward a little the better to hear.

"... count off from the right and stop at the one you recognize."
"One... two... three... FOUR!"

And a moment later the young detective striding confidently across the hall from one chamber to another. And then the two witnesses coming back down the corridor, coming our way, getting ready to encounter us, then pausing when they see Manny, pausing and walking forward with stiff confidence, that more voluble one, who had touched him in court, making the tiniest oral gesture of shame—or is it a complete failure of recognition? The young detective comes out. "Okay, Manny?"

—Meaning, with a broad smile, "You're free."

As the hold-up man is led out, he passes in front of Manny, and the two matching heads are juxtaposed in the frame. "Do you know what you've done to my wife?" says Manny, but of course his emotions are flooding, as well they ought to be, and it wasn't this criminal doing anything to Rose, was it. Not this criminal, not any mere cog, but something far grander and far more evil.

Now, Manny at the institution, telling Rose everything is fine... yet Rose is still lost in another world, or is it only another space emptied and waiting for a world?

MANNY: This awful nightmare we've been through: it's all over now!

ROSE (blankly): That's fine for you.

MANNY: Can I help you, Rose?

ROSE (flatly): Nothing can help me. No one. You can go now.

We forget, no doubt, what Rose said to Manny only seconds before: "Doesn't matter where I am, where anybody is." But perhaps not what the nurse tells Manny when he confesses he was hoping for a miracle. *They happen. But it takes time.*

Doesn't matter where anybody is is a hefty contradiction of the principle D. H. Lawrence unquestioningly states in *Studies in Classic American Literature*, that place is, in a way, everything; that there is a spirit of place that shapes experience. Rose has come to the point (or to the surface) where she is convinced the forces that shape our lives are both anywhere and nowhere, are without position and vector, without a binding to space.

An end title informs us that two years later Rose was indeed fine, and the family moved happily away. We see them walking peaceably down a palm-lined, sun-drenched street in Miami, in long shot.[17]

To feel one's way, not simply rationalize one's way, through this film is finally to catch that the scene with Rose in the sanitarium after Manny's release, albeit sad, albeit horizonless, is an epilogue. The finale is not Manny's freedom, his innocence, his return to his nature but the fact that since his belovèd has not returned to hers, he has not returned to his nature at all. To see the approach of the stranger... the approach of the stranger in a purely fabular zone... the approach of the stranger in a purely fabular zone while Manny is praying; to see that the stranger is born not in space as we know it but in the reflection from the picture of Jesus; to *see the silence* of the stranger born; and to know him heading toward Manny, toward Manny's head—*but all this in Manny's head*, is to understand an anti-climax. All the structure of the film depends on this half-phantasmal half-spiritual build-up to the mechanical arrest of the stranger, and then this falling away into the ether through the confrontation with Rose. But—

If finding the real robber is the anti-climax, what, then, is the climactic moment? The pinnacle of the ladder. The top of the Tower we cannot quite reach?

As soon as Manny enters the 110th and sees smiling O'Connor waiting for him there he can let go his breath, and we know that just at the instant he does. The lawyer's warm expression. The sense that breathing is possible. But when lawyer and client turn to listen to the corridor/auditorium, we do more than tune in. We position ourselves to hear with the greatest fidelity possible. And in this one tiny moment—a moment another filmmaker would have avoided—Hitchcock is going to pump up the sound just a little, and make the vision swoop in just a little, to cover that augmentation. When we hear "Count off from the right...," knowing—as Hitchcock knows we will know—that we heard this before, we are sharply aware that the Manny with whom we are affiliating, hearing this, has heard it before, too. A speech that in itself is an echo. All of our *Before* happened when the world had turned on Manny (Job) and he experienced the countdown, "One... two...," as did we, from within. *I think I am what they are counting down to, though I hope I am not.* But now, louder for emphasis and even with a tiny echo, we are hearing it from without. We are hearing it the way that, originally, other people would have heard it. The way the witnesses would have heard themselves vocally pointing. Not only with a confidence absolute, but through a magnificent and distancing projection.

A projection and a project: There! Out there! Down the corridor, in one of those chambers. Shhh, you can hear! The lineup, there! there!...

Over *there* is our scapegoat.

Our scapegoat *is over there.*

Take him, take him to the wilderness. He deserves it. He'll get what's coming.

Hearing the countdown now coldly, reverberating with objectivity, aimed at somebody else far far away—not Manny: not Manny: Manny is right here beside us, listening—we are given leave to reckon ourselves and our friend safe from challenge and safe from harm, that is, innocent, untouched, correct. Untouched. Correct. Innocent. And ennobled, too, through the process of a pointer not aimed at him.

That one instead. Him. Not me. *Them*, not us.

We need to be floating in that corridor for this. Hitchcock has placed us floating in that corridor. (Think how many other ways there would have been to accomplish a concluding scene.) Floating. Floating and waiting to be innocent. Waiting to be innocent and seizing that innocence when it wafts our way.

As the women emerge from their act of official witnessing—They are sure! They are absolutely sure!—we can retreat again, not only in order to hear the sounds of the place but to sense and feel how effortless, how invigorating is the superiority with which one can be a pointer and the matter-of-factness of being pointed at. *And so on and so forth.*

We have learned what pointing is, as Hitchcock points his camera.

And look at us, here, pointing, too! Him, the miscreant, whom we saw trying to rob the deli, whom we saw in the policemen's clutches. Him! All while forgetting that we know what it is to be accused, even if one does have a gun in one's pocket. Why does Hitchcock show us the attempted robbery at the deli? So that *we can be witnesses too,* so that we can see, we can be sure, We Can Be Absolutely Sure, and then as the man appears a moment later onscreen we can think and say, Oh yes, he's the one, he's the one we saw. We saw him at it! He's *guilty.*

(There is no evidence presented *to our eye* that this man is the same man who robbed the insurance company. We are *told* he confessed, yet we have seen already how policemen interview those who might perhaps make a confession if guided right.)

"One. Two. Three. FOUR."

In the calling out of FOUR! there is no sympathy, no compassion, no self-reflection. No hesitant pause. No caught breath or choking voice. No fear. And the person one has pointed to is being converted, even as one sighs with relief or even pleasure, into a thing.

CHAPTER FIVE

THE TROUBLE AND HARRY

> There's an expression of melancholy in his face,
> my dear, which is very interesting.
> —Charles Dickens, *Oliver Twist*

OVERTURE: ET IN ARCADIA EGO

Dramatis Personae:

Capt. Albert Wiles, retired and somewhat shy. Is he hiding something? (Edmund Gwenn, the highest-paid cast member at $4,000 per week, five-week guarantee [File 947])

Sam Marlow, a painter, of good intentions. Is his work the work of a genius? (John Forsythe)

Miss Ivy Gravely, a somewhat old-fashioned spinster, love interest of Capt. Wiles. (Mildred Natwick)

Mrs. Wiggs, owner of the local general store. (Mildred Dunnock)

Deputy Sheriff Calvin Wiggs, her son, a serious official dotard. (Royal Dano)

Dr. Greenbow, an extremely nearsighted practitioner. (Dwight Marfield)

Jennifer Rogers, a pretty young mother new to town. (Shirley MacLaine)

Arnie Rogers, her son. (Jerry Mathers)

Harry Worp, Jennifer's former husband, now a corpse. (Philip Truex)[1]

A wealthy art enthusiast from the city. (Parker Fennelly)

An art critic from the Modern Museum. (Leslie Woolf)

A tramp. (Barry Macollum)

Setting:

A quintessentially picturesque small town in New England (the shooting was at and near Stowe, Vermont),[2] at the rich peak of autumn, under blue skies.

* * *

We begin with some landscape portraits, emphasizing the town's pristine white church with high pointed steeple, and the immense, lushly laden oaks, maples, elms, and other trees surrounding the little valley the town occupies, these trees in full leaf, even explosive leaf, since the colors are absolutely vivid red, yellow, orange, ochre, and scarlet. The world is dying. All around are the spectacular colors of the death.[3] "La mise en train en est simple, presque virgilienne," writes Simone Dubreuilh: "L'automne, les feuilles mortes" (The film's set-up is simple, as in Virgil: "autumn, leaves dying.") The white church affirms itself amid all this. The church, standing in the field of blazing color, is like a grave marker.[4]

Originally the script detailed—with an eye almost medical—a complex time-lapse, in-camera maneuver, involving a maple leaf reaching out to the sun,

> growing from tender infancy to a full, broad and deep green maturity. The stem turns brown, and slowly the leaf begins to change color. The tips scarlet with the first frost. The sap retreats toward the stem to find itself blocked off. The palm of the leaf colors down from the scarlet fingers to a paler red, deep orange and into yellow. The veins darken and stiffen, holding the leaf up with Autumn's regal pride before the death of winter (File 945),

but on 10 October 1954 the unit production manager "Doc" Erickson[5] noted a second unit at work shooting the main title backgrounds: "They will not be as appear in script—just trees and scenes. Hitch wants it all scenic" (Production).

We are viewing from high on a hill. Far below, the tiniest of forms is moving across the landscape. Then, closer, we pick up Arnie, climbing our way among the sunny trees. Arnie is four, "an energetic, forthright little male explorer in life" (Script, 27 July 1954). Imagine what a paradise this must be for a little boy, to have such a boundless forest as his private domain. Adventure at every fingertip.

Arnie is carrying a plastic space-travel gun shaped like an automatic rifle: he's ready to make "death." Through the trees, over some stumps, through the fallen leaves. Of the forest and of the human being, let us say, a more natural portrait would be unthinkable. Albert Bierstadt could have painted this, or Fredric William Church. Arnie is doing what little boys do, on a quintessentially splendid autumn afternoon. The autumnal trees of New England: iconic:

> Nature's first green is gold,
> Her hardest hue to hold.
> Her early leaf's a flower;
> But only so an hour.
> Then leaf subsides to leaf.
> So Eden sank to grief,
> So dawn goes down to day.
> Nothing gold can stay.
> (Robert Frost)

Because of the beauty of the landscapes that introduce us to the world of the film; the compositions out of Claude but with a color palette from Courbet's "Still Life with Apples and a Pomegranate" (1871–72) and Cézanne's "Still Life with Apples" (1895); the unearthly silence; the comfy nestling of the little town among the hills; the blemishless sky (Hitchcock believed happiness was a blue sky), one's heart is in meditative rest, and immeasurably remote is the idea that anything could or should happen here. This is already Arcady. If the woods, so vibrant and so rich, are populated it must be by wood nymphs and fairies in the shafts of light, by animals at peace. Little Arnie is going to chance upon a reposing Oberon and Titania....

It would be a mistake to think Little Arnie doesn't know, or isn't learning, these woods by heart. This is the only place, pretty much, that he plays, and he's a playful one. Yet it would also be a mistake to think Little Arnie knows where he's going, except that he wants the snout of his "gun" to find that pesky squirrel. An American tyke. Tousled hair, freckles, a cherubic face, a boundless energy. As everyone knows who knows this film, Jerry Mathers would move on in just two years to play the eponymous "Beaver" Cleaver on a sitcom legendary in American television history. "Beav" would take on a universal usage in America, and along with the intonation of that syllable the image of Mathers, which is to say the idyllic Blue Boy of postwar American culture, Arnie.

But then: BAM!..... BAM!...........BAM! Three sharp reports that a boy like this, already familiar enough with country living, would know instantly as gunfire.

Arnie steps over a little rise and with eyes agog sees, stretched peacefully on the ground, a body. Male, suited with necktie, some blood on the forehead. He runs away.

This little overture gives light to a number of valuable paradoxes:

The paradox of familiar discomfort. Arnie marches through the forest and over the hills as a person intimate with this territory. If he has not spent almost all of his life exploring this place in this way, he has devoured the place quickly. And for a child of this age, a month is a very long time. There is not even the slightest hint of troublesome unsurety in his step, nor awkwardness, nor any nuance other than a thoroughgoing *Gemütlichkeit*. But he is stopped in his tracks by a creature entirely unfamiliar, a being that, dead or alive, does not fit here. The man is dressed for a business meeting in a board room, not a hike in the woods. And Arnie has never seen him before. So the confrontation is not pleasant, is *unheimlich*, and the unpleasantness is only partly due to the man's being dead. Were he alive he would already be strange; dead he is incomprehensible.

The paradox of real play. Arnie's voyage is a play trek in search of a "proper target." That is, not something to actually shoot at but something to "shoot" at, a figment of the imagination, situated here—or "here"—in this glorious forest. If nothing more, a suitable stimulus to the imaginative mind. This is a forest of fable, where amazing stories take place. Therefore the very loud and sharp reports, which Arnie takes to be gunfire, produce displacement because at once they can belong to his imaginary world, a world he can have filled with hunters and beasts; and belong to this real place at this real time, this real place where he is aware of himself walking. In short, someone he cannot see is out there with a gun and is using that weapon, be the "someone" fabular or hyperreal. The real end of the real-fabular axis is terrifying because this has not been identified in the film as hunting season and surely if it were, this little boy would not be wandering alone in the woods.

Paradox of an impotent proposition. Arnie's carrying the gun marks him. From a distance we do not see its toy nature, though soon and sharply it becomes evident. If he is not a tiny killer at heart and by nature, he is a young 'un with "killing" on his mind, and "killing" is not killing of a sort.

As soon as we know the identity of the weapon, and the cinematography makes it very clear—lit in balance with the boy himself—the proposition that he would kill is voided. This is a water gun. He can only, in the event, surprise (just as he has surprised us). We conceive "something that will most likely happen" in the same curve of consciousness with "something that cannot happen at all." Happening married to not-happening.

Paradox of silent declaration. The proposition implicit in the boy-with-gun presentation implies not only action but the perceivable resultant of action. In the case of gunfire, a BAM! And indeed we hear precisely that, three times, yet only from an indeterminate distance. The sound of actual gunfire is not coming from Arnie's pacific, silent gun. Is this boy, through some kind of telepathy mobilizing an action at a remove, a kind of junior ventriloquist? Is he imagining that he is—are the sounds coming from his imagination? With the sounds comes a barking of some indiscriminable exhortation, a verbal bullying, yet little Arnie is a model of silence.

Paradox of magical transubstantiation. Arnie has been invoking for himself a dramatic scenario—play scenarios are always dramatic—the epitome of which is a "death." He has gone into the territory of death to make this invocation, since what he moves upon is a blanket of dead leaves in a forest where everything that was alive is dying, dying its annual death. (One is carried instantly to anthropological studies of ancient tribal civilizations and their regard for, their mythology about, and their reverence for this annual death [and rebirth]). Yet in only a second, Arnie is going to see real death and it will be of an astoundingly different kind, not the substance of a child's dream but a fact on the ground. Play "death" becomes real death.

Paradox of an alien confrontation. Associated here are two blunt facts, both made visually explicit by Hitchcock. First, Arnie's gun is not only a toy, it is a toy invoking the genre of science fiction: space voyaging, star games. (This woods is a planet.) The "ray gun" is futuristic in design, lightweight, in some ways arcane. (Children understand the "weaponry" of their toyboxes more raptly and more swiftly than adults do.) This is clearly a ray gun much more than a rifle. So Arnie has come onto his hike prepared for alien confrontation, and what he meets, in fact, is an alien. Not only a creature that is alien because dead but also a creature who could be, but is not, literally known; a stranger to these parts; some kind of invader of this forest haven, since he is dressed for the city and since Arnie knows with certainty that he has never seen him before. We can add other facts rendered by Hitchcock with visual explicitness: that Arnie is in blue jeans for the wilderness while the corpse is in suiting material; that Arnie is very small and the dead man is extraordinarily tall, since as he stretches away from the camera his head is at f2.8 and his shoes are way down at f11 or f16 (an arrangement that in the film's concluding moment will be reversed). The dead man is a giant, Arnie is a tiny figurine by comparison. Odysseus with Polyphemus. David who is not certain whether he killed Goliath.

To highlight and make emphatic:

[a] These paradoxes are not developed in the surface narration at all, here. No scripted comment is made. No demarcating action takes place in a direct way. Instead, these are all *implied paradoxes made explicit* through the genius of Hitchcock's composition, coloration, mise-en-scène, pacing, cutting, casting, and, in general, presentation. We see all of these paradoxes whether or not we recognize and think about them. We see even before thinking—or: we manage some visual thinking before we manage some verbal thinking. In a sense the scene is constructed out of these paradoxes, these antithetical visual/aural assertions. In discussing them here, I am only, as it were, pausing the image on the screen in order to meditate upon its contingencies.

[b] Underlying the paradoxes, in almost every case, is a discrepancy between what we may take this little boy to be wondering about, imagining, or hoping for as he tramps forward through the trees and what we might say is *actually there* for him. In that sense, the quality of this sequence is distinctly fabular, not journalistic (in the way that we could see, for instance, in *The Wrong Man* [1956]). We are in a world where the dream bounds up against the fact, and where just as fact colors dream, dream colors fact. Dreams and facts: Julio Cortázar, speaking to a group of students at Berkeley in 1980:

A man—in this case, me—has a motorcycle accident, they take him to the hospital, all of this you know. He falls asleep and discovers he is a Mexican Indian fleeing in the middle of the night because he is being chased. As happens in dreams, when we know everything without the need for an explanation, I, or rather the person dreaming, knows that he belongs to the Moteca tribe, a tribe I invented and that a critic thought was derived from the protagonist having a motorcycle, which shows the dangers of purely rational thought when looking for associations in certain ways. (*Literature* 51)

[c] Perhaps most obviously, so very obviously that it is invisible—we have the palpable and dominating presence, as this film begins, of a little boy and his little-boy world (a world interrupted by the chance of reality). We must be close to the ground to see this little boy as a full-fledged character in portrait shots—that is, close, already, to the residential domain of Harry—and we must adopt Arnie's point of view. Nothing will add up here if we are not at first gazing at his domain from above, seeing him exploring in it, then falling to the ground as he approaches, racing to catch up with him, following his steps over the leaves, participating in the excitement of the gleam of his eye. We could ask: is Arnie not only the character through whom we enter this film but the character who guides us all the way through? Are we not always like Arnie, perhaps a friend of Arnie's, someone who remembers being an Arnie, as we watch *The Trouble with Harry*? A child gazing forward at a troubled domain that is his home.

ATALANTA AND MELEAGER

Atalanta the huntress is on the chase with Nestor, Peleus, Jason, Telemon, the fated Ancaeus, and Meleager, as the poet Robert Graves tells it. Killing a pair of ravishing centaurs, she proceeds with the others against a vicious wild boar, which beast, after producing much physical damage upon the men, is finally slain by the heroic Meleager. He flays it, and gifts Atalanta the pelt: "You drew first blood, and had we left the beast alone, it would soon have succumbed to your arrow." On his part this donation is, of course, courtly and loving (to say the least), even a proposition, but as to Atalanta, "the Delphic Oracle had warned her against marriage." Something of a spinster she, then, in company with a hungry—but mannerly—hero; and in the face of death.

Into our woods creeps Capt. Wiles, a brave and stalwart seafarer if ever there was. Now he is to be found in plump retirement, but not so withdrawn from the world that, of a sunny happy morning, he wouldn't voyage with his trusty rifle into the woods in search of rabbit. Since he is British, rabbit is a notable thing for him. As he puts it, man is at his truest when he is hunting.[6] Here, if not still living an aristocrat's life is a British male sufficiently in mind of, even possibly descended from, the aristocracy that held to itself the game hunt as a special preserve of dignity, elevation, removal, even purification. For those in the Captain's class, the aristocratic hunt has been converted to the solitary voyage out. A man in his element. A man chasing after his dinner. He wants his rabbit, possibly for a neat little pie. And his trusty rifle he has made his special friend, to whom he can chatter as he walks, sometimes with a slight indistinctness. Was it this Meleager of the twentieth century we heard shouting a moment before, orating as though the forest were a tackle room? Now he comes upon a tin can with a bullet hole, disappointed at his piffling aim. Then there's a NO HUNTING sign with a bullet hole, too, and his disappointment mounts. Finally he steps over a rise...

The body.

Oh my heavens! Consummate politeness, concerned muttering, confusion. Who are you? You're not from around these parts. Prying into the inside pocket of the jacket to retrieve a letter in its envelope, addressed to Mr. Harry Worp in Boston. Well, Mr. Worp...

And now here on a breath is Miss Ivy Gravely, another epitome of the prim and the proper, yet without the least trace of astonishment (Spirit of the Huntress). If you're going to move the body, Captain, we'd best not chat so much. Is he precise in his language and considerate of her feelings because he has been treasuring a hope regarding Miss Gravely that is unspeakably bold? Hers is a very restrained manner, to say the least, but all the better that way for showing off the little twinkle she has been keeping in her wide eye for him. Grave as Miss Gravely's manner might be, as with a veteran librarian, she makes certain as he hauls Harry into the bushes to issue an invitation for tea and muffins. Nor just muffins—blueberry muffins. And to light the torch: *highbush* blueberries! He feels awful about having killed Harry Worp, but after all it was a human act, an accident not an intended effect. You're not going to call the police? No no no no no.

We have the pleasant old sea captain, then, an abject murderer on an autumn day; and his conspirator Miss Gravely, who while assisting him to hide the body with soothing encouragement is meanwhile unable to block the thought of blueberries. There we are. The forest, the old couple, death, and blueberries. Wiles, a man with wiles, has all the complacent decency of a "decent" person who would not knowingly commit a crime, and Miss Gravely, a woman who behaves with gravity, or as though beside a grave, is observing tranquilly as he lays Harry in a different part of the earth. If he's a killer he's a well-meaning, civilized, avuncular, wholesomely genteel one. A killer without malice or violent desire, like Meleager. How odd to sense her actually effecting a sober evaluation of this man! And if she is an Atalanta, not eager, exactly, to become attached to a man, what could be more innocent, more pleasing, more companionable than coffee with blueberry muffins? Highbush blueberries.

SLUMBER

Hitchcock is here limning onscreen what Amy Freund has found in the painting of Jean-Baptiste Oudry, "the drama of violent conflict and the narrative power of [the] protagonists' bodies" (75). If in his painting Oudry's dog reshapes "human viewers into animals, making space for violence and animality in a supposedly refined society" (78), here in *Harry* the corpse reshapes "human viewers" into bodies without sensation (as well as sensitive and fully sensorial bodies in spectatorship). Perhaps the voyage is toward a kind of erasure. Jean Louis Schefer:

> There is in Christianity a pressure—albeit surrounded by and working with both allegory and mysticism—the pressure of a necessity: that of the interior body, that—in a way—of *anatomy;* and it's

only resolved through the annihilation of the body and of the very symptom that the body represents more than it can figure. (28; emphasis original)

If you cannot hide a body from the world, you can also not prevent the world from seeking a body, even without intent. The Captain has promised to come to Miss Gravely's for tea early in the afternoon and she has shaken his hand most nobly. Now, grabbing the feet of this thing and making ready to haul it away, he hears Arnie, off-, telling his mother about it and the pair of them approaching. He tucks himself behind a thick trunk (this and all subsequent medium shots in these "woods" being made at Paramount).[7] Jennifer instantly recognizes the corpse as Harry, someone she seems entirely unchagrined to see dead. Arnie wants to know how the man got hurt. "By sticking his head where it wasn't wanted" tells volumes, mostly about her. As they trundle off, mother and son, the Captain mutters to himself, "She won't care what I do with him."

This is a wonderful Hitchcockian moment far too easily raced past. "She won't care": we're going to hear it reprised at a very signal moment in *Vertigo* (1958). The old man is saying, surely to himself, that Jennifer will not take a care, that she is not caring for this man and was not; and that it will not be in her care(s) whether he lays where he is or is carted off. The Captain is *not* saying to himself that she wouldn't be interested or curious; or that she wouldn't have something to say about it if pressed; but that her *care* would not be attached to the corpse of Harry at this point. A certain attitude toward mortality is expressed here, essentially that *care is for the living*. Origin before 900 A.D. in the Gothic *kara:* lament. That death being only death—as the Captain imagines Jennifer seeing it, because he sees it that way—no lament is required, because no lament can be helpful to the dead.

Now another passer-by approaches (a Hitchcockian joke is the *passer-by* character in the middle of a forest), this one being the prodigiously hyperopic Dr. Greenbow with a book held up very close to his face as he walks. Greenbow was envisioned as "a man slightly detached from the realities of human life pursuing more energetically, as he does, the elusive prizes of entomology" (Script, 27 July 1954) but on the soundstage the entomological interest was dropped. The doctor's book is his mask. He trips on the corpse—of course!—but picks himself up unwaveringly: this happens to him all the time, he can never see where he's going: and continues on his way blithely swimming in his text. "Couldn't have had more people here if I'd sold tickets," the Captain marvels to himself, still behind the trunk. But then, "This could turn out to be the luckiest day of my life," as a tramp makes his way onto what is now, apparently, the well-trodden path:

> The surface of the earth is soft and impressible by the feet of men; and so with the paths which the mind travels. How worn and dusty, then, must be the highways of the world, how deep the ruts of tradition and conformity! (Thoreau 358)

Sack over his shoulder, big hat shading his brow, a stick to help him over the terrain:

> Mine are the night and morning,
> The pits of air, the gulf of space,
> The sportive sun, the gibbous moon,
> The innumerable days.
> (Ralph Waldo Emerson, "Song of Nature")

He sees the corpse, gives it a kick, moves down to the feet clad in very glossy brown leather shoes and kicks them, then sits and trades these dead man's shoes for his own:

> I am dumb in the pealing song,
> I rest on the pitch of the torrent,
> In slumber I am strong. (Emerson)

Observing all this action as closely as we are, the Captain has now slid into resignation: "Might as well sit here until the rest of the world comes paying their last respects. Sooner or later one of them has to turn out to be the Deputy Sheriff." Roman comedy, to be sure. Fade.

LEAPS

An elevated view across the meadow again. Another figure is marching purposefully along, singing Mack David and Raymond Scott's "Flaggin' the Train to Tuscaloosa" as though all the world vibrates at his fingertips.

His are active fingertips, too, because this is the painter Sam Marlow, now heading down the lane toward Mrs Wiggins's post office and general store, outside of which Emporium of Good and Sundry she has set up a stand with a cigar jug and a number of his (roughly abstract expressionist) paintings on display in the glazing sun. Sam is "carved it seems, from solid gold.... His eyes are blue, if you can see them, but usually they are screwed up as though viewing a distant sunset" (Script, 27 July 1954). For his part, Capt. Wiles is asleep back in the woods, the body nearby with its gigantic feet stuck into the camera. Two feet in the face, as it were; feet as principals.

"Wiggy Wiggy—you haven't sold a painting! All my pictures are in the same place." Across the little road is a pasture with happily mooing cows. The two begin to invoke the city, in particular Fifth Avenue, she with some nostalgia.[8] But Sam lets his cynicism show: "Hundreds and thousands and millions of people, but what breed? They're little people, people with hats on." (Thoreau's "monkey in Paris" putting on a new hat.) In an adjacent garage Wiggy's son Calvin is tuning the idle on a vintage car. This one, not exactly a fool if slow and methodical, "heard shootin' a while back.... There shouldn't be any shootin' around here."

"Why not?"

"It's posted land, that's why."

"Why's that?"

"'Cause I posted it."

Ironically scoffing: What has Calvin got against people doing a little shooting now and then, letting off a little steam? (As though the Law can trouble to have an attitude.) Hitchcock speaks through Calvin now, never holding back from stating the moral principles upon which his architectures stand: "Bullets and guns are dangerous. They kill things." New England is for life, not killing.

As Calvin gets into the car and drives off in it—the thing purrs like a panther—a sleek black limousine passes him on the road, coming our way. It halts at the roadside stand and an elderly man steps out to examine the paintings. The sleek elegance of the town car signals the wealth of this personage, his ability in a flash to become Sam's patron. But before we come to his opinion of the art, let us wonder, as self-aware viewers, how we came from a body in the woods to a body of painting at a roadside stand; from one outsider lying dead on the ground to a second outsider ready, perhaps, to spend a good deal of money for pictures abstract and blazing. After all, we have been watching all of this in pictures, pictures that, as we see them, blaze with freedom—surely, as Wilhelm Worringer predicted and, I think, our Sam supposes, freedom from intellectual supposition. Abstract art is not "the production of reflection and calculation" but instead, "purely instinctive creation." For Worringer, as "intellect had not yet dimmed instinct, the disposition to regularity, which after all is already present in the germ-cell, was able to find the appropriate abstract expression" (19). Worringer concludes with what could be a testament to Sam's spirit: "These regular abstract forms are, therefore, the only ones and the highest, in which man can rest in the face of the vast confusion of the world-picture" (19).[9] If Hitchcock's pictures of the body in the woods seem mysteries—who on earth is this man, how did he get here, how does he come to be dead?—Sam's pictures on the roadside are mysteries, too. What do they picture, if indeed something whole? How does the abstract form come to have meaning? In *Suspicion* (1941) a young police detective stared hopelessly at a painting formally not so unlike these, framed on a wall, and clearly could come to no resolution about it. Is the oddity of these canvases intended to make detectives of us all, fugitives from instinct? Made into detectives, might we head in the wrong direction attempting to arrange or rearrange the pieces of this little community puzzle so as to explain that corpse and its at once bizarre and entirely natural placement? Tom Gunning writes that Hitchcock's work depends on "the creation of depth effects and a sense of illusionist representation. In this sense modern paintings open up a different scene, another space and perhaps another story" ("In and Out" 42).

In conventional narrative practice, a thread or tie binds any sequence to any adjacent sequence, even if the tie is indistinct or invisible at first and becomes accessible only somewhat later, a fundamental conceit being that beneath the level of the narrative organization lies one single coherently woven "reality stream." Visible to us now only in aspects, it is so large that every one of the aspects will by nature partake of the same fundamental essence as all the others (since they emerge for us from that coherent singular stream). At the level of human discourse, one argues for establishing at some base level the fundamental human nature of all the characters, every disparate one of them. But in this film Hitchcock eschews opportunities to do that. He wants us to see these people in "another space," each quite distinct from the other; each having a set of life motives very different from anyone else's, each heading in a different direction with a morality guided by Worringer's instinct. They come together, if at all, only as assemblages, not unities. If one could but imagine an abstract canvas in which every form seemed to come to fruition of its own volition, or of the artist's distinct volition: this artist a person who is many persons, whose personality involves wavering and shifting, who does not accomplish the entire surface of the work in a unitary frame of mind because beneath the frame of mind, clear at any moment perhaps, flows an instinctual stream that defies what we in our rational thought choose to call clarity. The artist as incoherent. So, this semi-circular blotch in the upper right, what could it mean? But then this curving swooping swath to the left, in olive or lime green, or some shifting color combination? And this large blue-black thing.... The eye seems to hop with indistinct instinct from piece to piece, from aspect to aspect, but between the pieces there is no connecting system of paths other than the biography of Sam Marlow (of which we are told nothing). If the painting is powerful enough—Sam's paintings are very powerful as visual allures[10]—the canvases will seduce the eye of the viewer directly into proximity, a position from which the movement from one spot to another spot will have to be by discontinuous and arbitrary leaps.

A corpse lies stolid in the woods... A happy man strides down the road humming... An ancient vehicle glides away... A new town car glides forward... The sun glitters through the trees. As to linkages, we can make a beginning to sensing some that are coherent, or that might promise coherence to the uncomfortable mind, but:

[1] *Miss Gravely and Capt. Wiles.* These two share an old-fashioned etiquette that might somehow serve to bind them: they will certainly not be chafed apart. But from the corpse, from little Arnie, from Arnie's mother, from Sam, from Wiggy, from the Tramp, from Calvin, from Dr. Greenbow, from the rich man staring at the canvases they are disconnected.

[2] *Dr. Greenbow.* By what book is he so entranced, and where is he headed with it? His urge to move forward finds no abatement, and his urge

to turn the page is the same: Dr. Greenbow and his unspecified project, linked to nothing in his surround.

[3] *Wiggy*. What is she hoping for with her roadside stand and with those paintings, though she admires them without comprehending? She works a kindly but inexplicable project. Did she make a deal with Sam? Is she attached to him? She seems fond of the paintings, or is trying to decide whether she could be; are the paintings her substitutes for him?

[4] *Calvin*. Whence his deep fascination with tinkering, since, as his mother says, he never makes a great deal of money selling those restorations. Not unlike a boy with his meticulously assembled model car (instead of a ray gun), now grown large. Calvin has Arnie's insatiable curiosity but since he wears a badge that curiosity raises trepidation. At the same time, Arnie is always regarded with some distinct caution, as though he raises trepidation, too.

[5] *Harry*. What was Harry hoping for when he entered those woods? To see Jennifer? To bring back the past? Then why the woods? She seems resolved and in place upon her veranda; the woods are Arnie's haunt, not hers. Harry's project is defunct at any rate; we can afford to join the characters in having no real care for what it might have been, but also sense trouble in trying to link him in.

All these wonderings about all these projects, including little Arnie's play project to nab something in the woods, would fail to "add up" in such a way as to make the contents of one single mystery. There is always a *meanwhile*.

Meanwhile, just over here . . .

Does the eye not stand and penetrate an apparent object, a space bounded, until the energy of seeing wanes and for revivification the eye craves to move on. Does the eye not tramp across the canvas? Beyond placement a change of placements, progression from placement to placement, as though on a journey, yet without a map, without a trajectory. The many incoherent visitations of the corpse in the woods seem to resolve, or hint at resolving, only in the body itself, and this body is at present a meaningless glyph. Go to something else. Go *on*. And in silence. If the viewer would like to hope or believe that in this "going forward" a promise of some resolution is on offer, some understanding, so be it, although it might also be the case that *the going on* is itself the meaning. At any rate, we mimic, and are mimicked by, Wiggy staring at these canvases and trying to put the pieces together. The most recent one she ogles intently, until Sam gently takes it and flips it upside-down: she has been seeing it "in the wrong direction."

Will the body in the woods lead us to look at *The Trouble with Harry* in the wrong direction? He is death positively manifested, nothing less, nothing more. All around him, as far as the eye can see, here in New England on this sparkling day, is death, too. To concentrate on the corpse is to zoom into the canvas, to choose one notable form as root and promise, while all around is vibrant life and vibrant death. Life at the edge of death, here, everywhere. "Bullets and guns are dangerous. They kill things." And killed, things take on an eerie, a challenging silence.

Were the narrative more classical, this woodland corpse would provide an "Aha!" moment (the "Aha!" goes back very far indeed, appearing originally in Jeremiah) to bring all the separate narratives together as organic parts of a single and fully unified whole. But for such a purpose Hitchcock would not have needed to include abstract paintings. We will see Sam sketch the corpse and note that, as with other abstract expressionists, he knew perfectly well how to make a conventional artistic rendition of a face. Our Sam could have been displaying nice little landscapes, the sort of kitsch Jerry exhibits on a wall, for selling to ignorant tourists, in *An American in Paris* (1951). But our Sam has made his proclamation: those tourist types are city folk, who "wear hats."

PAUSE FOR ESTIMATION

Relative to this problem of navigating with some sense of coherence from event to event; this problem of discerning binding continuities or seeing and appreciating discontinuous space-time, we have exemplary moments of characters working to estimate, idiosyncratically, the nature that is before them. To find some perspectival method. To decide whether a work is or isn't finished. To compose a frame. *What could this look like in the work of art I envision making?* Or adjunctively, *How would I proceed to make a work of art from this?* Consider tendencies to isolate, highlight, privilege, and organize—to make a perspective instead of swallowing an abstraction:

- Little Arnie squinting forward past the camera at something he must find a way to estimate before he can approach it; *what can I know that thing to be* before *how close can I come to it?*;

- Capt. Wiles taking the liberty of withdrawing that letter from the corpse's inside jacket pocket, and actually reading the address to himself (and us) aloud; *Who are you, where do you come from, what are you doing here?*; how through some magical integration can I fit you and your world together with me and mine?

- Miss Gravely refraining in politesse from staring at the body, instead giving her friend Capt. Wiles some genteel glances; *Even in the presence of this absorbing item, it is you in my focus instead*;

- Jennifer walking around the body to get a look at the face *from the correct side*—that is, rightways-up—and giving it a name, this calling up an untold history, which for her is a perspective, but which is also, at this point, entirely unknown to, and unrelatable by, others;

- The wandering Tramp kicking to estimate the corpse's likeness to a corpse, then ogling the shiny shoes before making the decision to reconstitute himself by wearing them; of all possibilities the shoes, center of a frame for him;

- The extremely emphatic way that Dr. Greenbow gestures to estimation by patently withholding from it, by being so absorbed in his private bubble he does not even see the body he is tripping over: a negative perspective;

- Mrs. Wiggs checking out Sam's paintings as she puts them out on display—will they sell?;

- Miss Gravely in the general store examining a coffee cup to see if it might be perfect for a use she has in mind, and going so far as to involve Sam in her estimation by asking him to put his finger through the handle to see if it fits; she is imagining a scenario and this moment is a rehearsal—rehearsals are perspectival, they center key moments, key gestures;

- The old stranger from the city standing outside the emporium trying for a "view" of canvases that have potently struck his interest, but then driving away when nobody will talk to him, it being only dialogue that can make his perspective come real;

- Sam standing back to estimate Miss Gravely's age (and getting it wrong by eight years too many!), then standing back to gauge her hair and decide how, as an artist, he will cut it and reconstitute her "look."

Not to mention:

- Calvin flummoxed as he stares at Sam's sketch of Harry's face, and hyper-flummoxed gaping at Sam taking the thing in hand and "tampering" with "evidence" by masterfully opening the eyes. *Opening eyes as evidence tampering!* (crucial importance of perspective), or: *eyes open as evidence ruined!*

What is this estimation, this act of observation-evaluation we perform as we sit as an audience for Hitchcock's film, and that his characters appear to be performing upon one another and upon their world? What can we say it is, that we are looking at and focusing upon? And what are we trying to accomplish in trying to say? (Calvin Wiggs's profound enigma.) Study nature, Da Vinci cautions. And:

> The organ of sight is one of the quickest, and takes in at a single glance an infinite variety of forms; notwithstanding which, it cannot perfectly comprehend more than one object at a time. For example, the reader, at one look over this page, immediately perceives it full of different characters; but he cannot at the same moment distinguish each letter, much less can he comprehend their meaning. He must consider it word by word, and line by line, if he be desirous of forming a just notion of these characters. In like manner, if we wish to ascend to the top of an edifice, we must be content to *advance step by step*, otherwise we shall never be able to attain it. (2; emphasis mine)

To a young painter (Sam would take himself to be Da Vinci's pupil, but also perhaps Da Vinci's *inventive* pupil) he gives this advice:

> In order to acquire a true notion of the form of things, he must begin by studying the parts which compose them, and not pass to a second till he has well stored his memory, and sufficiently practiced the first; otherwise he loses his time, and will most certainly protract his studies. (3)

To note: in "advancing step by step" one may surely proceed by way of a continuous path but that will not always be either necessary or possible; a path may break off and a second point of relevance appear only across a chasm of sorts. (Arnie's challenge trekking through the woods; indeed, the ultimate pedagogy of nature.) This chasm, as I term it, is what modernism discovered. We may think of the space between electrons in motion inside an atom of some substance, even the space between the orbits in which electrons move—orbits that are probabilities. The little town of Highwater is constructed for us as a kind of "atom" of American society, and all its inhabitants and visitors concocted as moving electrons, each—or each pair—in a separate orbit. And we must study them all if we want to know the place. But once again for emphasis: the "orbits" aren't places, they are probabilities, which means uncertainties. "The ghosts must be appeased, the Spirit of Place atoned for. Then the true passionate love for American Soil will appear. As yet, there is too much menace in the landscape" (Lawrence 60). To attain some sense of "true form" may be a real challenge in watching a film, as all the elements shift into the past very swiftly, every one of them, always.

Perhaps if we stay with the painter he will give us a clue.

He goes ambling in the woods (this walk seems by now something of a local habit), equipped with a giant sketch pad and some chalks. He sits when he sees a natural growth and begins a very quick sketch. But then, standing back and looking at it (his critical moment) he sees what looks like two feet. Feet in the forest? He walks over and speaks to the man who is evidently lying down, only then discovering him as a corpse. Sam finds the body by way of his sketch pad, then. Sam draws first and interprets afterward. The parts of the picture that came to be identified as feet—we knew them instantly but he didn't—were not feet as he drew, they were parts of a form. When one can name a thing one is not regarding it, not in the sense that Sam Marlow would think of the regard; one is taking it as having already been regarded. Sam is giving us a lesson in looking-before-knowing; at knowing guided and formed by sight.

(Stop listening to the dialogue so obsessively; watch the picture.)

Of the torso Sam makes yet another sketch, somber and clear.

It is in Sam's sketch that we notice for the first time how very *somber* Harry is, how this thing is not merely a human form without an expression but instead a bold expression itself: gloom, shadowiness, as though without the application of shadow the colors will not take form. This *autopsy* being performed by the painter, this seeing with his own eyes, directly, plainly, shows us the corpse as it really is, not as we might like to fashion it to satisfy our privilege.

The corpse is of course a fountainhead of silence:

> To die, to sleep—
> To sleep—perchance to dream: ay, there's the rub,
> For in that sleep of death what dreams may come
> When we have shuffled off this mortal coil
> Must give us pause. (*Hamlet*, III.i.64–68)

And silently, accompanied by the corpse, and behind his tree, the Captain still sleeps.

A VISION OF FORMS

I suggested earlier that *Harry* could be thought of as Arnie's film. It is so early we are introduced to him that he could be considered our narrator; or, if not precisely a voice at least a sort of consciousness through the aperture of which the proceedings are taken in and wrestled with. The child can see without language; language follows experience. This boy-narrator lives a life margined very closely with the finite and equally closely with the phantasms of the unreal. The object he carries—any one of us could easily see it's an inexpensive, plastic toy—is for him a bona fide ray gun and can do whatever he imagines a ray gun can do. As long as any object can do *whatever we imagine it can do,* we are satisfied with it as a useful tool; the issue isn't the thing, it's our imagination of the thing, and when we begin to imagine uses that the thing cannot fulfill it becomes antiquated, part of the decor. Arnie knows full well that he is stalking the woods near his mother's house, but as he moves what he experiences, what he sees, are not woods but an alien planet. Imagine that he does not understand the things and events of the film in the way that any of the adult characters would, in fact he does not understand the things and events clearly at all, insofar as we would grasp what it means to understand clearly. That is partly, I would argue, because he has an abstract vision of happenings and does not select relevances to feature and frame in discourse. Thanks to the model of his consciousness, when we watch we do not get a clear picture either, of motive, of gesture, of possibility, of likelihood, of history, of desire, of direction. Force we understand, we can see it by outcome. Light we understand, it shines. Form and the adjacence of forms we understand through presence. Trees and rivulets and squirrels and red and yellow and orange and the veranda and the sky. Let us say Arnie gifts us a very formal vision of this universe, a vision of forms: forms gathered. When forms gather there is no king or queen of forms.

Yet to claim of him that he, especially he, doesn't grasp the connections between lines of action would make no sense, because it is we who fail to grasp connections. With Arnie we are flooded—Hitchcock's full intention—with expression, much of it barely discernible in a broken context. Here is why Sam's canvases can be taken as a kind of analogy to the flood: expressions, cataloguing, personalities, tones of voice, facial gestures of the most superficial sort, words of command, simply posed questions, the color and shape of automobiles, the whiteness of the clapboarding of a house and of the church, the length of the fields we traverse, the gray and red socks on the man in the woods—gray with red tips where the toes are—all of this universe we must wander through. Our most imaginative approach, our looking, "expels us furthest outside ourselves," Julio Cortázar wrote in "Blow-Up," "without the least guarantee" (119). The Tramp who took the shoes: of him we know only that he has been rambling. Whither, and why? If he is wandering these woods so is Arnie, and so is Capt. Wiles, and so is Miss Gravely, and so is Dr. Greenbow, and soon later Sam. All wanderers. In the woods of Highwater. In silence. In their various unique silences.

The many projects of the film do not conveniently harmonize:

[1] The Captain delighted to be, as Sam confides with a conspiratorial male-to-male wink, "the first man to... cross [Miss Gravely's] threshold." If he is an aging Romeo, does not this body in the woods function as an obstruction to the furtherance of the romance—"one hand beats / Cold death aside" (*Romeo and Juliet*, III.1.163–64)? What can he do to disconnect himself from this victim he thinks he has shot in order to brush aside any roadblocks to his approach to her?

[2] Miss Gravely asks Sam in the general store how old he thinks she is, and he says, easily enough, "Fifty." But she is forty-two. For her, the body in the woods is a reminder of Time. To see the world as she does, carefully step over the body (respect, after all) but then put it out of mind. If you can. Make coffee. Make blueberry muffins. Highbush blueberries.

[3] Sam seems to involve himself in other people's lives: the Captain freed of guilt; Miss Gravely adorned; Mrs. Rogers reborn. Is he a kind of angel? (Is his painting from Another Sphere?)

[4] Dr. Greenbow confronts again and again the functional blindness of the self. Outside his book breathes the body of life, or breathed; but for him the body of life is a block to trip over.

[5] For the Deputy Sheriff the body will be sufficient reason for a criminal investigation, which for him would be tantamount to a promotion in the offing, if his "evidence" didn't dematerialize.

[6] For Mrs. Rogers Harry is an unwanted memento of the past she eagerly left behind before moving to this town with her son. The body, the past; the past, the riddle and turning that brings us here.

To see any of this with some *clarity* one steps back for a point of view, favoring one tale (of the moment) over all the others; but then the eye shifts. And in shifting, the eye seeks meaningful links between the characters, beyond that they are the inhabitants of this place. A troubled eye, then; an eye for a trouble. In the sense of what the word "trouble" has long meant, these people constitute the *trouble* with Harry: *trouble* originates in the Latin as "small group of people." *A trouble with Harry*, with trouble afloat, to be sure. When he got up this morning, reflects the Captain, "right away I knew somebody was in trouble—what I didn't know was, that it was me." In trouble. In *a* trouble. He didn't know himself as being a part of this community as he knows himself now because of the intercession of the stranger.

SHADOWS

Sam and the Captain are conversing beside the corpse—that is, as happened in *Rope* the corpse has become the altar beside which cultivated conversation can, and ostensibly should, take place. Having seen the rifle, Sam is a little chiding: "Stands to reason they can't touch you for it." But Capt. Wiles won't stop fretting, so Sam elaborates, in a telling way, a possibility: Heaven's decree was that this man was to die, but somehow the Heavenly mechanism didn't work:[11]

> SAM (meditating): It was an act of God, perhaps. In a way you should be grateful that you were able to do your share in accomplishing the destiny of a fellow being.... Heaven's will is done, and Destiny fulfilled.

Perhaps Destiny is only the name we give to a grand abrogation of responsibility, not unlike a scapegoat. Or perhaps, as Cortázar taught, fate is "a mode of the fantastic" (*Literature* 65). A "mode of the fantastic" is the art of Sam Marlow, each canvas a destiny. The Captain isn't worried about destiny, however; he's worried about the police "and their suspicious ways ... You're guilty until you're proven innocent ... I want nothing more to do with them."[12] *Nothing more* to do: has Capt. Wiles had to "do" with the police before?

But Sam is no servant of bureaucracy, police or other. Asked the time, he answers by looking up into the sky to see where the sun is. The sun, timekeeper and all powerful, the sun center of the universe. Martin Jay reads Bataille for a case possibly more supreme than Sam but nevertheless of the same blood: "At the moment Van Gogh introduced the sun into his work, 'all of his painting finally became *radiation, explosion, flame*, and himself, lost in ecstasy before a source of *radiant* life, *exploding, inflamed*" (225, quoting Bataille 59). Sam is of course not Van Gogh; and he is *not* not Van

Gogh, too. If, as Jay argues, "disillusionment with the project of illumination is now so widespread that it has become the new conventional wisdom" (592), Sam has fought disillusionment (as has Hitchcock the illusionist); he is a man of the Enlightenment, who believes that art, illusion, will show the way and that light will make art. If instead, slave in the darkness, one credited happenings to an all-knowing, all-foreseeing Fate, if one adopted cynicism, one would have to conclude that all the events perceivable in Highwater are organized from beneath or above into a coherently integrated whole (of whatever questionable moral worth). But with cinema, the fountain of light, this is vexingly (and joyously) difficult because, per Da Vinci, "The organ of sight...cannot perfectly comprehend more than one object at a time." To go from object to object here: here in this little hamlet, here in this hamlet bordered by woods and merry lanes and noble trees, here in this warren of thought and worry and activity, one jumps; even jumps through fades. To the general store, to the Rogers house, to Miss Gravely's sedate veranda. The eye cast up to the sun and back into an old face. Up to the cosmos and back to the human race.

And what is so easily forgotten in the eye's frenetic thrust is this:

That when we leap from one object of interest to a second, anything anywhere, *during* the movement of the leap the world in all its complexity and urgency *does not stop*. What we have leapt away from tails off in a way we cannot judge; and what we are heading toward tails upward into life, as it were, with similar inscrutability. And in between...? In between we were in motion, so we could not clearly see. A quick example: while we stand in the general store watching Sam assessing Miss Gravely for a hairdo, what is the Captain busy doing? (We know now—afterward—that he is still behind his tree, sleeping, but we will not actually see that until later, when Sam goes up into the woods.) What is Mrs. Rogers doing? What, Arnie? What, Calvin? What, the doctor? In fact, there is only one current resident of the community whose doings can always be known from any position of interest, and that is Harry, who isn't doing anything or going anywhere. He is to the form that is this film what the Stone of Milyon in Istanbul was to the Byzantine Empire, a pillar at the very center. What we see as we move around this narrative universe is—can only be—fragments of numerous different ongoing and silent occupations, arbitrarily seamed together by us, perhaps so that we can artfully neglect the brutal fact that they are fragments. Different ongoing silent occupations with different people, all gathered into the *trouble* of Highwater. To these fragments, the camera obediently delivers us seriatim (in *Rear Window* [1954] this delivery is openly declared). As a believer in illumination as a source of experience, what Jay notes as an oculocentric, Sam knows there are also areas of shadow, sometimes very dense shadow: *somber* areas.

And Arnie, our guide, knows the *somber* even more faultlessly, because less thoughtfully. For him the world simply is highlight and shadow, color and texture and shape and presence: the world is moment. He hasn't learned yet to put things in proper places and give them proper names.

MORTALITIES

Will Jennifer Rogers fall in love with Sam Marlow, the man who sees without knowing what he's seeing? Will Calvin Wiggs arrest somebody for murdering Harry Worp? Will the old sea captain and the brave spinster join hands in some holy union? Will the doctor ever finish reading that book? Will Wiggy be rewarded, on earth not in heaven, for her unstopping kindness in supplying everyone in the universe with everything they need? Will the little boy—?

Will the little boy what?

Would we have the little boy grow up, and become another deputy sheriff or painter or doctor or man in a gray suit? Would we have him become preternaturally wise, as so many children are onscreen, able to spout home truths to much older people who can't see what's in front of their eyes? Would we have him be forgotten as, in the busy world of adults, children are so often forgotten in one or another of a thousand ways? Perhaps he will be himself, on and on.

One grasps *The Trouble with Harry* only superficially if one takes it as a comic murder-melodrama, and concentrates on trying to figure out who did what when where to whom and why. This would be tantamount to making a serious list of all the blotches and swirls on Sam's canvases. Or to cataloguing all the leaves dropping from all the trees. With surety, all those who deserve happiness will find it, possibly in a startling and fabulous way. But something else is here. What if—Sam says to the Captain—what if in Heaven it was determined that this man was to die today? More helpful, possibly: what if on earth it was determined that this man was to die today? Because Hitchcock has made that determination, his offices being the only heaven near his films. What he has given us, through his masterful controls, and directly through the eyes of the little boy who will be suitably astonished, is:

A body.

And that body is the object of veneration around which the figures of the film dance their holy dance. The body not really as a presence, because very often here it is *not* present but instead is invoked as *having been* present, or as *being present elsewhere:* invoked through a language formula that has the power to draw it near to the conversation, quite as though it resides between the conversants when they know and we know that it does not. Early in the film, plenty of face-to-face conversations take place over the corpus itself: see those joinings, overhear the noises, but also see people more distally, worrying in the town about *that thing*—a look from above at the scurrying that is never for an instant not polite. Here is an old formula, and in the early 1950s one very popular with filmgoers at least in the United States: some civilized huddle suddenly broken into by the penetration of, and thus the distinct presence now of, a *thing*. Nobody really knows much about the person who was living in this body, Jennifer being the closest if still somewhat in the dark and everyone else merely picking up straws. Since we cannot really say things about Harry we need to say things *of* him, that he is dead, that he is there, that someone might try to hide or bury him, that someone else might dig him up and bury him somewhere else—the dog-and-bone scene of Hawks's *Bringing Up Baby* (1938) comes vividly to mind. That he exists; that his existence is already a value. The irony (or, if one must insist, the joke) is that just as he is, he isn't. But the corpse is certainly a thing to be done with, perhaps to be informed about but surely to be touched and placed, rendered properly to whatever elements call for it.

The motor that makes *The Trouble with Harry* dramatic, however, moving, pulsing, forward-going is a question of who should take responsibility for the corpse, and how, and why. *This thing of darkness I / Acknowledge mine.* Who in trouble—who in *the* trouble—will claim legitimate ownership of, or control over this thing, and what transformation of the self will result: that is the nub. Because here in yeoman New England, very little comes to supremacy above responsibility. What in the world is one obliged to claim, tend, place, move, refurbish, clean? More deeply, who is responsible for the flesh itself, for mortality? The mortality is suddenly (on a child's whimsical movement) here, but who is to tend it?

Before he is our character, before he has any identity tags at all, Harry is a body, our most highly valued form. Stripped of identity tags (which in this film are fashioned to be very telling and emphatically characteristic), every character here is a body, too, a particle in the stream of mortality. All of what we do, we do as bodies. I write these words with fingers that played Debussy on the piano (like my late friend Stanley Cavell, actually); the fingers are under muscular and nervous control even as they are also my ten ways of reaching into and having relation with my world, and even as they constitute my responsibility. We live as bodies when the bodies are in time, when the bodies age, were young, can be eager for the flame of feeling. Against that kind of background it becomes possible to see every engagement here as a quaint gavotte or a stride in a hoe-down or a thrust forward and backward at the same time, as in modern dance. The little courting story of the Captain and his Miss Gravely, and that she would make *highbush* blueberry muffins for him, not just blueberry muffins (anybody can get blueberry muffins, but unless you live near blueberry bushes you don't get highbush blueberries), or search for the proper coffee cup (when coffee will fit into *any cup*), or that he might hope blissfully for a sip of elderberry wine: a *pas de deux* that our dead man in the forest will not perform with anyone.

Or the conversational dance, as with the two women in the store and their direct, succinct, no-nonsense politeness, the spinster a little more melodic (one can imagine that she was once a music teacher) and Wiggy polite as the wafting breeze. And that warped little conversational dance between a young mother and her very young son as she both teaches him about life and refrains from teaching him. The blunt, almost invasive talk of the law. The arias of the painter, full of wit, full of high and low pitches, a life-view of someone who sings his way forward (and who probably sang his way through making those paintings).

Or the elegant shuffle that happens when people walk this way, walk that way, approach, recede, creep behind a tree trunk, emerge and take hold of Harry's shoeless feet, trip, pull themselves together, walk this way, walk that way, walk away. Although a limousine has brought what we can take to be a man from the city, who stops and looks and drives off, perhaps going nowhere, it is true, too, that all the people we meet are going nowhere, just as Harry is going nowhere. They are fixtures of the town, this town is a fixture of the countryside, the countryside is a fixture of the Northeast. Meanwhile, beyond the polite requests and timid smiles time is passing by (like a camera on its dolly). Every autumn colossal death, then the snows of winter, then the rebirth of spring, then the burgeoning of summer which leads to colossal death. Year by year until there are no more years left. (Alfred Hitchcock died 29 April 1980, in Bel Air, at 9:15 a.m.)

Harry as a person for whom there are no more years left.

Harry with his temporal status confronting us over and again, just in the way that autumn comes over and again, until, of course, this film is dead and there are no more revolutions left for it (until the last frames of the final reel zip through the projector and please our eyes).

TOMORROW

Following Kenneth Keniston, think of *morals* as

> the socially learned, largely unconscious, relatively specific and apparently self-evident rules of right conduct in any community. When an individual violates his moral code, he feels guilt, the pangs of conscience experienced as a part of the "not-me," as an alien force that acts upon the conscious and experiencing self. Moral codes tend to be specific and situational: they tell us how to behave ourselves (or how not to behave ourselves) in defined kinds of situations.

Ethical behavior differs from moral behavior, however. *Ethics* are:

> the individual's thought-out, reflective and generalized sense of good and evil, the desirable and the undesirable, as integrated into his sense of himself and his view of the world. When an ethical man violates his own ethic, he feels not guilt but a sense of human

failure, a kind of existential shame that he has not been who he thought himself to be. (628)

It may be useful to consider *Harry* as revolving around moments in the lives of a number of locally gathered people, a "trouble" *with* Harry, only two of whom have an ethical self, that is, only two of whom attend, in their behavior and reflection upon their behavior, less to what would be seen as appropriate, accepted, and approved by relevant social others and more to the cloak of principle they have taken upon themselves. The ethical two are Sam and Arnie, the first because in spirit all the way through he is an artist and the second because in spirit all the way through he is a child. Each of the others has learned how to seem "right" in various specific situations, how to give the proper impression (as far as medical condition will permit). Telltale examples: Miss Gravely seeking Sam and Mrs. Wiggs's blessing as to the "right" coffee cup that she wishes to buy for "someone"; does it look like a nice coffee cup to offer, a coffee cup appropriate as a gift from a woman such as she would be taken to be? Is the handle big enough to fit a finger, *but not her finger?*—Sam must test it, a good male hand with a good male finger—because if it is not big enough she will seem a crude hostess. Or Capt. Wiles railing against the police (the police here, and almost universally elsewhere in Hitchcock, being sources of moral pressure yet entirely lacking an ethical sense).[13] Heading back into town happily enough at one point, the Captain suddenly spies Calvin leaning over the driver's window of a state police car parked outside the Wiggs Emporium, chatting to the cops inside. Suddenly panicked by the presence of these moral imperialists, he tucks his rifle under his jacket and lets it trail down his leg as he hobbles past the car. The Captain did make it expressly clear to Sam, too, that it was the police who bothered him, in regard to the dead body and his responsibility; not some "heavenly" (read ethical) judgment.

The corpse in the woods sparks ethical crises, in Arnie a new patch of darkness in his generally sunlit confusion and in Sam a vibrating tension between the body as a figure in space (an artistic form) and as the remainder of a person who had an independent life. Others have moral concern with taking "proper" responsibility for the dead man's death—every death is an Action; every Action must be placed in the Ledger—and with clarifying and rectifying the social disorder produced by Harry's intrusion into this tight, vivacious community. Georg Simmel discusses the Stranger as "the person who comes today and stays tomorrow" inside a spatial configuration that both engenders and gives intelligibility to human relations (402).

A conversation takes place between our two dreamers, living in disparate but equally ethical universes founded upon a sense of the relation of the self to the world as directly apprehended, not the world as "correctly" interpreted and learned. Sam crosses the road under some splendid old trees, golden as sunset, and on the porch of the Rogers house meets the young mother, whom he finds exceptionally beautiful—"Paint you in the nude!" For her part she is cool but not unfriendly: "Some other time." She goes inside to make some lemonade: "You're not only beautiful, you're considerate, too." Out storms Arnie, a deceased rabbit slung trapper-style over his shoulder (numbers in parentheses refer to discussion immediately below):

ARNIE: Hello Mr. Marlow!

SAM (holding a paper bag): Hi! Whattaya got, a rabbit?

ARNIE: Yes. What've you got?

SAM: Oh. I got me a little frog. *(Squats down, opens bag, and the frog leaps out onto his palm, then onto the floor. He, Arnie, and Jennifer try to nab it.)* There he is.

ARNIE: Whoop! It's hungry. I'll trade ya.

SAM: (v) Your mother for mine?

ARNIE: The rabbit for the frog.

SAM (Putting the frog into the bag again and handing it over): It's yours, Arnie.

ARNIE (Handing over the rabbit): I think you got the best deal. Dead rabbits don't eat. *(Jennifer takes the frog into the kitchen to give him some lemonade. Sam and Arnie occupy the wicker settee, Sam holding out the dead rabbit to view. He folds his arms. Arnie leans over and pets the creature.)* Pooooor rabbit, four rabbit's feet and he got killed. He shoulda carried a four-leaf clover, too.

SAM (rabbit on lap): And a horseshoe.

ARNIE: Say— (vi) how do rabbits get to be born?

SAM: Same way elephants do.

ARNIE: Oh, sure! How come you never came around to visit me before?

SAM: I didn't know you had such a pretty mother, Arnie.

ARNIE: If you think she's pretty you should see my sling shot.

SAM: Hm. Perhaps I'll come back, tomorrow.

ARNIE: When's that?

SAM: Day after today.

ARNIE: (ii) That's yesterday. (i) Today's tomorrow.

SAM (a little perplexed): It was.

ARNIE: (iii) When was tomorrow yesterday, Mr. Marlow?

SAM: Today.

ARNIE: (iv) Oh sure. Yesterday.

JENNIFER (coming with lemonade): You'll never make sense out of Arnie, he's got his own timing.

Jennifer might be right, but it would be relieving if at least we could make sense of Arnie, here, now, today, for just a moment. When Arnie says (i) today's tomorrow, he must mean by "today" what today would have been, looked forward to the day before (we would say "yesterday"), in short, that yesterday his mother promised him something "tomorrow"; today is the tomorrow discussed yesterday. Sam's "It was" is a kind of confirmation. But when Arnie replies to "Day after today" by saying (ii) that's yesterday, either he has leapt into a future, some point beyond the day after today, so that "yesterday" is seen as such by looking back; or else by "that's" he is linguistically pointing to Sam's pointer to "today." Tomorrow, the day Sam is calling "today" will be yesterday. In the query (iii) when was tomorrow yesterday, however, Arnie assumes a stance yesterday and asks when from that stance "tomorrow" was thought to be (as though he were saying,

"Tomorrow, when was it yesterday?"), and the answer to that is, today. It may seem that time is being played with, but grammatical construction is really the toy: words and their arbitrariness. Arnie caps it all with (iv) Oh sure. The complication involved in pointing to the present moment—present as past, present as future: that no matter what you point to, you point from where you are standing; but where are you standing? (At the Equator, the Earth is moving round and round at roughly a thousand miles per hour, so where are any of us standing, indeed?)

Further, the integrity of the two universes of Arnie and Sam, their gaping separateness, their distinctness from the practicalities of the everyday ([v] "Your mother for mine?") as well as their slippery surfaces along which one easily falls out of one subject and into another ([vi] "How do rabbits get to be born?") shows the energizing power of a "useless" regard, call it an artistic approach to life. The eye, seeing much at one time, moves like that frog from point to point, "hungry" for other points.

This delightful but seemingly offhand little passage gives an excellent example of how a film is not somebody's text about itself, regardless of how zealously the texter tries to be faithful. If we pause, reading the page, to go over and over this conversation, we may find ourselves swirling into Wonderland and never quite coming into clarity, save that Arnie talks one language and Sam another. But when we watch the film, all this goes by with a perfectly even tempo, and a rhythm that is unbroken, two voices merely speaking and without emphasis, in a kind of follow-up to the frog-rabbit trade—a frog; a rabbit; an exchange. What a charming, friendly little conversation this one is! The dialogue is complete before we can wonder about it, so that what we must find ourselves wondering about, sitting in the dark, is our own desire to wonder, now curtailed by Jennifer's reappearance.

As to Arnie and Sam's sense of time, here is Albert Einstein to the rescue. He is writing about simultaneity, which in the terms of physics is roughly analogous to mutual agreement in language. Take it, he tells us, that

> you offer the following suggestion with which to test simultaneity. By measuring along the rails, the connecting line AB should be measured up and an observer placed at the mid-point M of the distance AB. This observer [why not imagine it to be Jennifer] should

be supplied with an arrangement (e.g., two mirrors inclined at 90°) which allows him visually to observe both places A and B at the same time. If the observer perceives the two flashes of lightning at the same time, then they are simultaneous.

I am very pleased with this suggestion, but for all that I cannot regard the matter as quite settled, because I feel constrained to raise the following objection: "Your definition would certainly be right, if I only knew that the light by means of which the observer at M perceives the lightning flashes travels along the length A >> M with the same velocity as along the length B >> M. But an examination of this supposition would only be possible if we already had at our disposal the means of measuring time. (26–27)

There we are: veranda removed from beneath the feet.

Jennifer Rogers very easily persuades the casual and relaxed viewer that her Arnie is on his own clock, and that Sam will never quite get him. But the irony is—and through her quizzical expressions, halting comments, and general aura of doubt we are going to sniff it again and again—Jennifer is not actually equipped to make the judgment that Sam and Arnie presently do not agree; nor the judgment that they do. And because she is not equipped, neither are we. Nor is Jennifer, or anyone, equipped to make judgments about anything we see here. She comments to Sam, for example, that she thinks— *that she thinks*—Capt. Wiles shot this rabbit. She also comments about Harry that he was her former (now deceased) husband's brother, who married her but then on their wedding night (her second) left her alone (because his horoscope told him to!), so she walked out and now he has followed her and she smacked him on the head with a milk bottle (a nice explanation for the blood we saw). But hitting someone's head could produce a death either directly or subsequently, and so perhaps she is transferring the Captain's guilt onto herself, but this seemingly without recognition, since she is smiling happily all through the recounting. Or else she is a ghoul in disguise.

For another tiny conundrum: what was Calvin talking to those state troopers about? Was it connected to any business that could have appertained to the creeping Captain, or was it about something wholly unrelated but temporally contiguous?

Or, how does Wiggy find that new canvas of Sam's so positively and fully alluring, so captivating, given that—Sam's declaration—she has it upside-down? First, he doesn't seem to care a whit about the misorientation. Next, she is truly captivated, and the question is: if with an "incorrect" orientation she finds a pleasure that carries her away, what is the function of orientation?

And why is old Capt. Wiles so very shy about women, that Miss Gravely must extend herself to make the overtures? Is his every present encounter with her dragging up something from his past?

And what *is* that book Dr. Greenbow is reading so obsessively?

And if, for a language, one has been restricted (by youth? by invention? by memory?) to three words only of temporal reference, *today*, *yesterday*, and *tomorrow*, how, indeed, can one possibly answer the question, "When was tomorrow yesterday?" With a comma inserted an answer pops up, but Arnie does not use his little voice to insert a comma. No one in cinema inserts a comma.

THE NOW

If not following his lead precisely and to the full extent, let us at least take a hint from Merleau-Ponty regarding embodiment, since we have agreed that the presence of Harry-as-body in the film is the "main event," the understructure of our experience of others' experience in Highwater. Merleau-Ponty confesses himself "obsessed with being," and writes:

> I consider my body, which is my point of view upon the world, as one of the objects of that world. I repress the consciousness that I had of my gaze as a means of knowing and I treat my eyes as fragments of matter. From then on my eyes are placed within the same objective space where I attempt to situate the exterior object and I believe that the projection of the objects upon my retina brings about the perceived perspective. (73)

My eyes and the things my eyes see: all a trouble in the same objective space...

This is very close to Ortega's point of view about "distant" vision. For him, the object can become "an unbodied spectre composed only of light"

(111). He adds that in "pure distant vision, our attention, instead of being directed farther away, has drawn back to the absolutely proximate, and the eye-beam, instead of striking the convexity of a solid body and staying fixed on it, penetrates a concave object, glides into a hollow" (112–13). In Impressionism, sensations "are no longer things in any sense; they are subjective states through which and by means of which things appear" (124). What if, viewing the world of the film in and through distance, it is the eye-beam that is with us and that emerges from us that makes up the world, and instead of touching the world with the eye (Ortega would say, making it real) our eyeing is itself the touching: looking at the world as though it is all touch, as though every look is a touch, we touch the world by the way we look at it. If Harry is the token of the film, the Eternal Resident, every enacted moment of perception, navigation, sensation, decision, recursion, and repetition is achieved upon the substructure of that body whose ocular gaze is no longer a means of knowing but has become, like that corpse, a part of the world. Merleau-Ponty as Harry.

Everything of sweet Jennifer is a flight from Harry, for example, an evasion of Harry, a remonstration of Harry, a mocking of Harry—Harry being for her even more than an ex-husband a trace memory of the beloved brother who died shortly after she married him. Arnie is from the beloved brother, and thus a reference obliquely to Harry. Sam Marlow, to whom Jennifer is clearly attracted, is curious about, and therefore centrally involved in perceiving, Harry. Harry who would not be here in Highwater were it not for her presence; she who would not be here in Highwater had she not fled the presence of the demanding Harry back home. It is not living Harry who obsesses her now; it is this dead Harry, whom she is quite happy to regard in that state since already before the film began he was "dead" for her. Having no use for him, she finds him dispensable, in the way that ultimately the body itself is dispensable. He is to be thrown out: out, away from the civilization of the town and into the surrounding woods, where the wild things are. The savages of the woods, the woods as savage. The woods as salvation. Savage • *salvaticus* • salvation • (Lat. wild).

For Sam, at least initially, Harry as body-in-the-woods is a perfect subject for drawing, an aesthetic form par excellence. Nothing could be further from his concern than Jennifer's account of this body as having once belonged to a person with business in the world. Harry's personhood as a consciousness is not part of the Harry who becomes for Sam an aesthetic subject. And it is Sam's conviction in making pictures, his ethical self-identification as a picturer, that gives him the aesthetic regard he turns upon Harry. In a similarly focused, if quite opposite way, Calvin's self-identification as a law-keeper makes him regard corpses in terms of crime; if there is a body in the woods it is a detective-style mystery to be solved. Sam does not solve mysteries, he paints them. Calvin does not picture mysteries, he undoes them. He undoes a mystery in the same way he undoes the mechanism of an antique car, taking out the parts, cleaning them, putting them together in a rational way. Sam does not assemble the parts of his pictures in a rational way, and this is why rational Wiggy, who would like her customers to pay their bills (Sam takes just about everything on credit), does not have a straightforward time making sense of them. If she can relax and stop trying to make sense she can be released.

Think of the Wiles-Gravely "romance" as taking place under the sign of the body. Ivy thinks she looks younger than others think she does. The Captain feels ripe, even overripe, and nervous at being so long out of touch with the world of women. Will his plump, weary body be acceptable to a woman he considers magnificent? Will his body fit into the cup she has collected in order to impress him? Looking at these two with Sam and Jennifer in the background we cannot but find them older, wiser, and more fragile as lovers, nor can we stop hoping they will connect before mortality strikes; whereas the younger lovers seem to have all the time in the world.

Arnie is living in, and recognizes, only the now.

EMBELLISHMENTS

The turgid, unprovokable silence of the corpse contrasts against the ceaseless flow of conversation all around, and *The Trouble with Harry* is surely one of Hitchcock's more conversational films. It bears some similarity in that way to *Blackmail* (1929), another film in which the arc of development is given over verbally. If we contrast *North by Northwest* (1959) or *The 39 Steps* (1935), we find movements indicated pictorially, whereas in *Harry* the pictorialism, to be discussed below, is not principally about dramatic movements.

For the most part the conversations are long and crisply polite, very often with much verbiage that is decorous without being probing, salutary without coming on, genteel without being precious. We can think of Miss Gravely's extreme etiquette with the Captain in the woods, over the body. Or the long, involved discussion in the Wiggs Emporium about refashioning Miss Gravely. We have the complex little phenomenology between Sam and Arnie, and also some much more suggestive (while completely innocent) chatter between Sam and Jennifer in which she reveals Harry's backstory and says a great deal about herself, too, and he rhapsodizes over how beautiful she is (keeping us in the dark as to whether he means, as a subject for a painting or as a subject for a love affair, or both). We have the Captain visiting Miss Gravely for coffee and their utterly macabre liturgy about forms of death and how guilty the Captain may be. Arnie interrupts to scarf some of the highbush blueberry muffins and also to affirm that the dead rabbit he is carrying was shot by the Captain—that is, one of the Captain's bullets went here. The Captain is traipsing into the woods with Sam, both with shovels, and there follows a short series of conversations, each fading into the next, about what to do with Harry, whether the Captain does, after all, have a conscience or is merely petrified at the thought of being caught by the police, where to dig a grave, who should do the bulk of the work. They get Harry into the ground and pat the earth down over him and at that point, then and only then, launch into a conversation in which Sam emphasizes to the Captain something the Captain was already told, but did not carefully absorb, namely that the rabbit was his prey. He glows with delight at having bagged his rabbit, the hunter's joy, but is sharply taken aback when he realizes he shot only three bullets, one into a hunting sign, one into a can, and—"And one into Harry," says Sam, but now this calls for correction: "No, one into the rabbit." So the Captain's guilt can evaporate, more or less as Harry's life has, and now they had better dig Harry up—why? Because he's not the Captain's corpse to be concerned over and, as Sam had said archly, it would look much worse for him to be burying a body he didn't kill than hiding a body he did. Bodies again, *the* body, the principal body and the twisting pathways of conscience and consciousness it reveals. Talking about this body with such verve, Sam and the Captain seem disembodied themselves.

Sam also takes the liberty of informing the Captain that Miss Gravely's handsome new looks were created by him (indeed, her hair was not only cut but also colored; and makeup was applied to her face). Soon later, having chauffeured her in his canoe—the Powhatan canoes being weighty, young Pocahontas "would not have been able to handle" one herself (Custalow and Daniel 26)—the Captain is escorting Miss Gravely to his house (where, in a trope Hitchcock will repeat a few years later in utterly different circumstances, there is underwear hanging in view, that he must snatch away). Here, in halting, nervous, yet always decorous tones, the good lady confesses to her new beau that the body in the woods is . . . *hers*. With more and more twisting, more unexpected turns, we continue to hear pitter patter about how the body came to be where it is, who put it there, why it is dead, what to do about the fact that it is dead, who might or might not have reason to be personally concerned about the death, whether the authorities (Calvin) should be informed, and, consummately, where, if it rests at all, guilt should properly rest. (Guilt as body.)

As to the conversations and conversational topics in this film, are they not, perhaps, as well as invocations, masks? If we think of Harry once again, that locus of embodied silence at the heart of things; and if we refresh our thoughts about the corporeal essence he invokes and advertises, the essence that resides in all things; and if we refresh, too, our own entirely corporeal way of seeing, we can think of the characters' concerns as superficial embellishments of the pervasive mortal fact of Harry. Harry not only dead but *as Death*. There he is, and everything else is marginal. In taking such a stance, we might see by analogy how the conversations of the film are also superficial embellishments of its persisting identity as a film, that *Trouble* is, to quote V. F. Perkins's well-known phrase, "film as film," and not film as a container for a chain of expressive happenings that might bear informative weight.

MELODY IN LIGHT

A Place in Nature

Watchers and lovers of Hitchcock will immediately recognize that one of his supreme talents as a visualizer of dramatic space is to establish, with the camera as his only mapmaker, a distinct sense of where things are in relation to one another, in an n-dimensional universe that holds his people, their places, and their things. Since we participate in the drama, this orientational issue is crucial: where can we think things are in relation to each other and to us? He adjoins pieces to each other in such a way that a territory is knowable. In *A Dream of Hitchcock* I have wondered about spatial orientation vis-à-vis the city of New York in *Rear Window* (1954). In *Psycho* (1960), if we were to track away from the shower, still looking at it, and turn about-face to make way into Marion's bedroom, where would the little bedside table be, where she tucked the folded newspaper—to our left and forward, to our right and forward, directly forward, or behind us near the wall and near the framed bird print? There is only one clear answer, *ahead and to the right at the corner*, and we can virtually see the room. Hitchcock is especially facile at making space intelligible not merely in the design on the soundstage but in the camera frame, particularly when people are having dialogue; there he sometimes dotes on playing with the "conversational" distance between two interlocutors, different as felt by each, by placing his camera not halfway between them but cheating to one side; see the conversation between the blind hermit and the fugitive in *Saboteur* (1942) for a good example. Hitchcock always has the power to render his dramatic space tellingly, in a way that participants and viewers would find rational and consistent within the rectangle of the screen; he does not guess; he does not stab in the dark; he does not make mistakes.

It is therefore worth consideration that in *The Trouble with Harry* the space as rendered may seem peculiar:

Dispositions

[A] *Size*. The story space, generally, is vast yet also wholly confined, both at the same time: confined because we repeatedly know ourselves to be in a tiny hamlet, where the population is less than a dozen—this village confined among the low hills of a lush countryside where the nearest neighboring hamlet is outside the limits of perception. But at the same time the vegetation is vastly spreading, further by far than the eye can see. We have numerous pictorial long shots in which we see ranges of richly colored trees dropping away from the focal center, with the tiniest of human figures striding across a dwarfing landscape. It could be argued that landscapes always dwarf the human figure (see, for example, Albert Bierstadt) but in Hitchcock this is actually often not so—the fleeing figure at the beginning of *Vertigo*, Marnie on horseback. Walking into the woods here, our characters enter a greater territory: greater than the little town; greater even than the arching trees that adorn the houses of Highwater, yet the characters are always whole and idiosyncratic. The arching trees are forestial, says the color palette. And the forest is encompassing, mystifying, endless. It is a place where Destiny and Conscience and Fear and Responsibility and Concern and Wit and Amusement all commingle. (Imagine the forestial glades of Watteau's *fêtes galantes*.)

From the film's very outset we see the tiny boy wading through the immense trees, then his confrontation with an alien more than twice his size. Arnie's small stature gains emphasis when he talks to Sam and his mother and when he stands at Miss Gravely's tableside. One also senses a young, relatively small wisdom (at least state of information) up against the age-old wisdom of the trees that parade through the cycle of nature fully cognizant. Hitchcock offers "size flags," too: the coffee cup, is it *big* enough?; the little frog traded for the big rabbit, that rabbit being a two-muffin, not a one-muffin rabbit; the long gaunt extension of the corpse's face in Sam's sketch; the fact that in all the photography of him where he is seen full-bodied, the Captain is clearly a very short, rotund man, physically *smaller than* Sam and Harry and Calvin, closer in size to Arnie than anyone else in the film—even smaller than Miss Gravely. Sometimes the camera shoots up so as to mask this difference, sometimes the camera shoots him full-on so as to reveal the Captain's "tininess" in the greater context. Even hairdos have size relations in the film, with Miss Gravely's hair being "too long" and getting cut and shaped; Jennifer's hair being more than notably short and a good match for Sam's.

[B] *Indeterminate Positions*. But in establishing his space Hitchcock goes further than playing with size. Where are things relative to one another? The charming New England clapboards of Highwater seem *nearby* the forest whereas Boston, for example, is *very far away*—this signaled through Boston's being referenced by only an address on an envelope in a dead man's pocket. But where are the houses in relation to the spot where Harry lies? In which offscreen direction? And where is Harry's resting spot in relation to the little hillock Sam and the Captain climb with their shovels—directly facing it, a little way off, a real distance off? When Calvin drives off down the country road and the millionaire in the limousine comes forward, where is it that we can imagine Calvin is headed? And from where is this limousine coming our way? When the millionaire gets irritated at not finding anybody in the kiosk and instructs his chauffeur to drive away, and we see the car turn and head down that road again, to what destination are they headed and in what compass direction? I don't mean to posit that these destinations have diegetic significance; what has significance is that the cars, moving off in so-called real geographical space in a world that looks very much like our world, travel in a vague—if glorious—ether.

We never see the point in "map" space where Harry lies, or the point where the rabbit is shot, except in relation to the limits of the screen; we wouldn't know where to head if we had to wander through this forest to find either, presuming we could find an entrance to this Arden. And where is this Arden, anyway? We see the corpse stretched on the ground, no more, and the dead rabbit commences on Arnie's shoulder. How did the corpse come to be where it is? What is the relation in space between (a) the Captain's tin can, (b) the hunting sign, (c) the rabbit, and (d) the corpse—this being, for the Captain at least, a critical question to engender fear.

[C] *Points and Surrounds.* In argument, our characters invariably reveal themselves to have definitive positions. Moral, amoral, nervous, complacent, coy, canny, guilty, tickled: because of this crisp definitiveness they are black and white in personality. But their surround is surely the most sumptuously composed and vividly colored of all the surrounds in all of Hitchcock's oeuvre. Indeed, while he and team were finishing up *To Catch a Thief* (1955) in Nice they worried considerably about getting to New England in time to catch the autumn foliage.[14] One has the sense of the trees not only richly and liberally spreading out but reaching, too, past the limits of their frame; as this tale reaches across the surface of the Northern Hemisphere, the annual time has arrived for all the rich verdure of the world to be drying and dying and for (eternal) winter to be coming on. The landscape shots have perspective and distance, a sense of an always-receding horizon, but not position. The colors of the trees are a puzzle never to be solved. If this narrative "place" is Arcady, residence of Pan and his followers, and if, as in Guercino and Poussin, death is here, too (*Et in Arcadia ego*), the gist of the paradise is the final unknowability embedded in its enchantment.

Where else but Arcadia, indeed, could we be, here in Highwater? There is no instant in the film when we receive a clue as to the whereabouts of this town, except that the architecture screams "New England" (and perhaps beckons us to consult, for a tonal guide to attitudes and pieties, de Tocqueville). Does Hitchcock intend us to sense, actually, a *nouveau England* here? Is America—after the Puritans a *new England*—entirely symbolized, synopsized, and surrendered in this place? Had the filmmaker, born in London, resident later in Surrey, made a new home in a second, a "new" England? The quaint and delicate mannerisms of the characters in *Harry* are overfilled with a strict civility, a characteristic of behavior (and personality) appropriate to a tiny, cramped island where collisions are relatively likely, much more than to a vast uncultivated space, the "West" that Henry Nash Smith describes, where one does not see one's neighbor among the trees.

Here in the forestial kingdom of *New England* we watch this film by finding ourselves lost: lost on the compass, lost among strangers however polite, lost in the spectrum, lost in time as well as language.

A Ghost

Our friend Harry—we are intimates now, he has been so present in body or word—has been buried and dug up and buried and dug up so many times, even by poor, delicate Miss Ivy Gravely getting dirt all over her face while the Captain waits patiently by his tree, that by the time Sam and Jennifer are summoned into the fray, standing with the digger and her beau under that great oak, it is really difficult to say where the fellow is now and where he will be next. Dr. Greenbow chances up and agrees—now that he sees a corpse for a corpse—to give it a diagnosis if they will bring it into the light and clean it up. He will soon enough pronounce in a way that surprises them all, but for the moment Wiggy has run up screaming for Sam because the man from the city is back, and he's definitely a millionaire, and he wants to buy all of Sam's paintings. The deal concluded, our magical foursome retire to the forest and carry Harry in an eerie parade to the Rogers house. While the Captain dozes, the other three make haste cleaning up Harry's clothing and making him proper for the doctor. But in the Wiggs Emporium earlier, after Sam does his business with the millionaire, lanky Calvin, suspicious of something going on and trying to phone the State Police, glanced down and saw Sam's sketch by his feet; now, as we learn, he's had what seems by his happy face the joy of running into a tramp and taking from the man a pair of new leather shoes; and this tramp described the dead man from whom he took them; and that description fits this picture. Quite a syllogism.

At Jennifer's, drawing in hand, the deputy sheriff is convinced it was made in the meadow where the tramp says he saw the body. Sam is outraged at such an affront to his artistic sensibility, claiming with some ferocity that the picture sprang from his creative imagination. To prove his point, he seizes the sketch pad and quickly alters the pastels so that now the figure's eyes are wide open—all just to show how inspiration can be turned into graphic action in a flash. Calvin stomps away in a huff—that was evidence!—but not before little Arnie opens the bathroom door and we see Harry's feet sticking out of the bathtub. In the midst of Hitchcock's overriding elision of spatial detail in the film, here, suddenly, a very tight composition showing how we can see the body, and so can everyone else, *except* Calvin. When he leaves, the doctor goes into the bathroom only to emerge soon later with the announcement that Harry died of a seizure. Everyone is innocent. And innocence is everywhere. As Jennifer attempts to tell him about Harry being buried and unburied all day, the man leaves in disgust.

There is barely a breath in the film when someone or other is not panicking about Harry, turning over guilt about Harry, wondering what the best thing is to do with Harry, worrying that the police will find out about Harry, fretting that Harry "belongs" to them. Yet this "Harry" is a spatial marker, his placement articulated in the screen rectangle but mystified as regards the broader geography. If everybody here is innocent, including the corpse, *where is here?* Or: *where is innocence?* The riddle of bodily presence and spatial disconfiguration, all the while the forest glows with color, needs resolution. Miss Gravely will plant some highbush blueberries on Harry's grave. Little Arnie, made subject of a cute little plan, will bring the film to an end: go into the woods again, he is urged, and this time when you discover the body run back and report it to your mother, who will call the police. But for all of these charming people, all of this *trouble*, their troubles seem centered even in innocence upon the impossibility of getting away from Harry; that Harry has infected them, or has infected their bucolic community; that Harry or the memory of Harry will disrupt the peace of this paradise.

So many scenes *point off to* a Harry who is not present in the space. Thus, a ghostly figure invoked, yet in the pleasantest, most eloquent, most courteous tones. Watching Harry's *trouble*, this happy gang, no matter the pairings or couplings or joinings or gatherings they display, we find Harry an invisible presence. A blaring silence. An American Godot. And we conceive him visually, as we watch the others sit peaceably and chatter his name. He is up there stretched out on the ground. He is four feet under. He is dug up. He is lifted around. He is put back in the ground. But he never ceases to be there, wherever we could say *there* is. By virtue of his endurance in the diegesis, he is set apart from the dead rabbit, another corpse but one that is finally dispensed with and forgotten. Nor is he like Jennifer's first husband, spoken of, dispensed with, forgotten. Harry has an eternal presence, even less as thing than as reference to a thing, a word that means a thing. And all around, by day and also by night, are the windblown dead leaves, the forest going into hibernation, and beyond this moment: hibernation for eternity. This is an eternal Autumn. Harry is *always* present: in the room, under the oak tree, in the shadows of memory, waiting for the snow.

And so we can come at last to see a most marvelous Hitchcockian construction. In scene after scene a collection of interesting characters *in conversation:* leaning on a veranda bannister, sitting on a plush sofa, sitting on a porch to coffee, standing in the Wiggs Emporium, shuffling around a living room with a man's clothes, gathering by an oak tree, and so on: and while the talk trickles on, and with an idiosyncratic royal etiquette, the macabre ghost as both figure and invocation waits in the air between the faces. More: all the conversations are framed onscreen to give room between the conversants for invisible Harry to wait and observe—all the conversations except the brief one when Sam kisses Jennifer (and Harry is banished). Artfully, Hitchcock returns us again and again to the burial site, the giant spreading oak, just so we have enough of a vision of the corpse itself to mobilize the memorial. Harry: with Sam and the Captain as they trudge into the forest with their shovels; with Jennifer, Sam, and the Captain as Miss Gravely explains how she killed him; even with Arnie trading the dead rabbit for muffins since that rabbit is something the Captain does not believe he shot because he shot Harry instead.

This *thing* that is Harry undergoes continual metamorphosis, being a different creature for everyone who takes him up in talk. Yet he cannot vanish, surely for the citizens of Highwater but also for us, posing as our friendly giant, feet in our face, still in the final shot of the film, as we read "The Trouble with Harry is over."

A Provocation

Dialogically Harry is silent, a cipher, either the conversational subject of every scene or a tactfully avoided subject, which means a subject by negativity; or else a provocative interruption of what begins as a scene about something else but is now waylaid by his inert concerns. In short, Harry is always "there." The little scene in the Captain's house, whither he has invited Miss Gravely after their return from the tranquil lake, gives a telltale example of civil, even incipiently romantic, if ineffably courteous conversation broken into by the ghost of Harry rather in the way that a thunderclap in the street outside could invade a chamber concert of Schubert's lieder:

> CAPTAIN: I'm a man who can recognize the human qualities in a woman. When I first saw you, down where Harry was—
>
> MISS GRAVELY: Captain Wiles—
>
> CAPTAIN: Yes, ma'am?
>
> MISS GRAVELY: Before you make your killing thoughts known to me, I should like to offer you some explanation of my sudden invitation to coffee and blueberry muffins this afternoon and my... and my sitting with you here now...
>
> CAPTAIN: No, ma'am, you don't have to explain anything. You came to my aid at a moment of crisis for which I am truly grateful.
>
> MISS GRAVELY: Thank you. But it's just that... I owe you some reason—
>
> CAPTAIN: Ohhh no no, I won't hear a word of it. You saw the predicament I was in with that body on my hands and all, and you shut your eyes to it in the most sporting fashion that I've ever seen.
>
> MISS GRAVELY: Captain Wiles—
>
> CAPTAIN: Yes, ma'am?

MISS GRAVELY: I'm trying to tell you that the reason I asked you to coffee and blueberry muffins was because... I felt—

CAPTAIN (helpfully): Sympathy.

MISS GRAVELY: Gratitude.

CAPTAIN: Gra— but *I'm* the one who should be grateful!

MISS GRAVELY: No I was grateful, I—I *am* grateful, I—I'm grateful to you for burying... *my body.*

CAPTAIN: *Your* body?

MISS GRAVELY: The man you thought you killed was the man I hit over the head with the leather heel of my hiking shoe.

CAPTAIN: You?

MISS GRAVELY: And with a metal cleat on the end of it.

CAPTAIN: Then why?—

MISS GRAVELY: He annoyed me! I was walking towards home when he suddenly came at me with a wild look in his eye and insisted ...we were married....

CAPTAIN: Oh, then you'd known he'd done it before.

MISS GRAVELY: Believe it or not, Captain, I'd never seen him before in my life and...if I ever had I never would have married *him.*

CAPTAIN: He must have mistaken you for someone else.

MISS GRAVELY: No, he very definitely pulled me into the bushes.

CAPTAIN: Yes?

MISS GRAVELY: I came out again.

CAPTAIN: Go on.

MISS GRAVELY: He pulled me back.

CAPTAIN: Twice.

MISS GRAVELY: He swore at me—horrible masculine sounds—I didn't understand them, of course—

CAPTAIN: Of course. Of course you didn't.

MISS GRAVELY: We fought.

CAPTAIN: Then what?

MISS GRAVELY: I won. My shoe had come off in the struggle and I hit him, I—I hit him as hard as ever I could.

CAPTAIN: You killed him.

MISS GRAVELY: I must have done it.

Several aspects of this chit-chat intrigue me (aspects replicated in many chit-chats of this film). First, partly out of an overwhelming sense of self-doubt stemming from a realization of how complex even the simplest human acts can be; and partly from a truly profound sensitivity to others and a sincere hesitation to cause pain, both conversants move forward by only the tiniest of steps, so that it takes time for the facts to emerge (the "facts" as given). Not exactly timidity but a gentle patience with one's listener, and a fear of causing upset by dropping a weight too heavy too soon: pure Hitchcock. Second, the formality. The talk may come across as stiff, particularly Miss Gravely's. Yet there is a twinkle of something frivolous, devil-may-care in her eye; and the Captain, we know, normally all bluster and impulse is here marshaling that under the cape of The Decorous Gentleman. There is also a nervousness, perhaps excitement, about the relationship itself, that these two are in the man's house talking, that an intimate scene has been invoked, because each of them hesitates to reveal the full energy of the self to the other until a moment of dramatic potentiality—dramatic not in terms of the film and its structure but dramatic in terms of the human association and its probabilities. And of course there is the (inevitable) intrusion of "horrible masculine" Harry into this space where Miss Gravely is confiding a personal moment to a second person who seems half a winking suitor and half an old codger.

When I first saw you, down where Harry was: He may be referring to "first time today," that is, "earlier, back then," or he may be indicating openly that although these two have been residents in this town for some time they have never met. Not "first saw you *when*" but "*first* saw you." In the American small town, such social distancing is quite normal.

Offer an explanation for my sitting with you here now: A woman with Miss Gravely's propriety would not simply invite a man to her house for muffins, and would surely not simply enter that man's abode because he opened the door for her: post-Victorian. This in addition to the fact that he must snatch down and tuck away the underwear drying on a line, while she stares agog and hypnotized.

Eyes shut in a sporting fashion: The Captain does not for a moment want tender, possibly delightful Miss Gravely to suspect or believe that he believes her tale: that she "turned away" from his business with the corpse because she already bore a connection with it. No no. No such thing could be true of her, or accepted as truth. She is too pristine, too proper. She was being *only* a good sport.

Reason and gratitude: Miss Gravely tries hard to make the Captain know that there was method behind her invitation to coffee—no, not an invitation to coffee, an invitation to coffee and blueberry muffins. Highbush blueberries. I picked them myself. (From, as happens, a bush near the spot where Harry lies.) She tries hard, at any rate, against his polite demurrals (she is so pleasing to be with that no explanations are required, *at all*). She tries to show she has method but does not immediately succeed (this leading the viewer's suspenseful feeling to build). And then the two of them have what amounts to an unctuous debate about who owes gratitude to whom? But clearly they both feel grateful. They are two people possibly going on a first date, but already, each, grateful for something that isn't clear.

Grateful for burying my body: She will be meaning, of course, the body of Harry for which she is here and now claiming responsibility; but what she is patently saying is that he did bury, or is in the process of burying, her own actual body. My body, that should be hidden away from our moment of delight together: thank you for burying it (disregarding it). She has been self-conscious about her body, but this Romeo is boiling her self-consciousness away. And, too, she is about to absolve him of his guilt most powerfully.

With a metal cleat: When she goes on a hike, Miss Gravely has no intention of slipping or tumbling to the ground. That is, she keeps a distance from the ground by way of a protective cleat. Soon, she will be digging *into* the ground.

I never would have married him: Miss Gravely is about to hand the Captain a list of characteristics she would shun in a suitor. Don't be like him, Captain...

He must have mistaken you: On the surface the Captain is trying to clear up what might have become muddied waters for this splendid lady who deserves to be kept free of mud. But he is also putting a motive on this metadiegetic Harry so as to inform Miss Gravely what he would be most likely to suspect: not that she attracted Harry's interest because she seemed, or even could have seemed, available but that she attracted Harry's interest because he mistook her for another woman.

Pulled into the bushes: He pulled me into the bushes—Yes?—I came out again. How delightfully succinct a tale-telling, cutting straight to the action. She could be Alfred Hitchcock cutting shots together (Hitchcock wrote or dictated memoranda to his editors with extremely meticulous requests for shot shortening or lengthening: a few frames here, a few frames there). We may surmise that his conversational partner caught the flicker of the Captain's salacious thought and decided to dampen it without delay. With her claim that Harry pulled her back, a little (invisible) film within the film is building to its own little climax, a climax that will be, for Miss Gravely, a dire necessity because it will explain her having done something no lady such as herself would ever do.

I didn't understand them, of course: For Miss Gravely not hearing bad language is not enough, she must hear garbled sound, incomprehensible sound. To say it was bad language one would have to have heard it and recognized it. But Miss Gravely would not fully recognize such stuff; it would not be part of her habitual usage. Shall we expand our horizons and think that the country air has kept Miss Gravely in alabaster purity, and the city has besmirched horrible masculine Harry?

I must have done it: How surprising, yet how unsurprising a conclusion: she recounts the happenings in the indicative, but slides quickly, however briefly, into the subjunctive as a way of not actually indicating.

We should note that it is not until she thanks him for burying her body that Miss Gravely is participating unequivocally in a conversation about death, although clearly she has been thinking of the ghostly Harry all through. He is named, however, only here, and this is some way through the scene. Until then, it has been all melodies about decorum and blueberries, blueberries and decorum. Now it becomes a news report. And in this film the news is always about fatality.

ARTIST AS HERO

Jennifer Rogers being a charming sprite who is missing love, and her little son needing a father, Sam brings a double salvation when he proposes to her. But Sam, the artist hero, is a savior far more generally. To Calvin he gives benefit of a lesson in the power of the creative imagination that will, we can reasonably hope, be transformative someday. For the others, a moment of what can easily read as self-sacrifice. The millionaire wants to buy all the pictures, and if he comes back next month there will be more. He believes in Sam's genius. Sam has come up with a very innovative price, and won't take a lot of money. He asks everybody, one by one, what they would most like in the world and with each answer calls upon the rich man to make notes; fresh strawberries delivered every month, a smelly chemistry set, a new cash register, a new gun and hunting outfit, a hope chest, and for himself something that is one of those secrets that cannot long remain unrevealed (but that onscreen, because in 1955 the Production Code is still in effect, must remain silent until a moment when the pointer can be embedded in a joke).

Sam wants a double bed. And Jennifer, who thinks this would be useful, warns him, with her very short flaming hair, that she has, of all possibilities, a short fuse. We may have wondered how something as simple as Harry missing the wedding night could have motivated her to run away. And how with her spontaneity and good nature, her resemblance to the flaming trees and her chirrupy good sense, she might be confounded between yesterday, today, and tomorrow. For that matter, who could assuredly not be confounded that way, given the pacific simplicity and stability of the landscape and climate, the clock seeming to stop or race or stop again every time Harry gains a new position above or below the ground. When was tomorrow yesterday, indeed.

And Then...

There is one more turn of the screw in our friend Harry's coffin, now that, more than a burial, he will have a funeral, too. And that turn is, that there is no funeral for us to attend. The plan to have Arnie rediscover Harry is likely put into action, but we have to imagine it. One persists with the feeling that, storyline be damned, for all our involvement in the shenanigans and intimacies of this bucolic paradise we are not getting to its real heart. Not, that is, until the very end, which is—so typically with Hitchcock—the end that comes after what we would take as the end. Sam and Jennifer and Arnie seem on their way to becoming a family. The Captain and Miss Gravely seem on their way to a marriage of true minds. Wiggy's emporium will thrive, Calvin will tinker with another car, the millionaire will show up once a month and add to his very signal collection. But what is given to us, here as the colors radiate and the breeze brings time forward, is the body of Harry still on the ground. Mortality at the center of the wheel of fortune: both meaningful and meaningless as an object, both the center of our concern and utterly marginal to vivacious social happenings, both enduring and unchanging and also a token of an abandoned past. Harry as riddle. *The Trouble with Harry* as a story about this civil *trouble* and Harry, a story full of intent and energy, promise eternal, yet also a carnival revolving around an unknown.

Harry himself: his face is shown not once, except in an artist's rendition viewed by an agent of the law. There is no revelation. "Surely some revelation is at hand." We muddle on without, as the colors of the trees blaze in the sun.

CHAPTER SIX

THE DIRTY TRUTH OF *TOPAZ*

> Were they all to die here, lying in a road, while a machine gun worked from body to body, seemingly never satisfying itself that the body it was striking was dead?
> —Norman Mailer, "A Calculus at Heaven"

PROLOGUE: TERRIBLY MORE TERRIBLE

The Cuban missile crisis of October 1962 was generated by Cold War tensions that had been mounting since World War II's aftermath in the late 1940s. In October 1949, considerable fear spread among America's top nuclear scientists about what a leading journalist to be, David Halberstam, would come to call "a weapon of the unknown," being developed in Russia. Halberstam quotes James Conant, chairman of the National Defense Research Committee (and president of Harvard University, 1933–53): "The Russians will soon do the Super, and...we had better beat them to it." And the attitude in Congress was described by J. Robert Oppenheimer: "We must have a Super, and we must have it fast." This so-called "Super"

(finally unsupported by Conant) was not the atomic device that had been exploded in August 1945 upon Nagasaki and Hiroshima but something on another scale, of which Oppenheimer, head of the Los Alamos Laboratory, had hinted on 16 October 1945 when he concluded his tenure with the Manhattan Project. Oppenheimer, Halberstam reports, told a reporter that day, "If you ask, 'Can we make them [atomic weapons] more terrible?' the answer is yes. If you ask, 'Can we make a lot of them?' the answer is yes. If you ask, 'Can we make them terribly more terrible?' the answer is probably" (qtd. in Halberstam 34). This terror of the near future was a hydrogen bomb, a device of such magnificent power it would require an atomic device as its trigger. The atomic race was on. It was called in the popular vernacular "the arms race," and it is still on today, with no visible finish line. Zeno in Purgatory.

For the American hydrogen bomb project, paternity was awarded to a Hungarian scientist named Edward Teller, who somewhat contentiously presided until computing was available to help with the necessary mathematical computations. The fusion device was detonated at Eniwetok on 1 November 1952 without Teller attending. It weighed some 65 tons, Halberstam writes, "and yielded some 10.4 million tons of TNT, or a force a thousand times greater than the Hiroshima bomb" (98).

The Cold War, begun as the postwar world was carved up and Russian and American politicians saw themselves in conflict, now rested under an ominous threat that could be pictured: even the 1945 mushroom cloud would be nothing by comparison. But in the early 1950s, movement sped up. On 12 August 1953 the Russians tested their own version of the fusion bomb.[1] In August 1957 the Russians were testing an intercontinental ballistic missile

(ICBM), capable of being equipped with a nuclear warhead and of flying six thousand kilometers to deliver it. In January 1959, the Americans tested theirs. And on Tuesday morning, 16 October 1962, the "gun" was cocked.

Robert F. Kennedy describes the American center of power at that vital moment:

> Shortly after nine o'clock, President Kennedy called and asked me to come to the White House. He said only that we were facing great trouble. Shortly afterward, in his office, he told me that a U-2 [spy plane] had just finished a photographic mission and that the Intelligence Community had become convinced that Russia was placing missiles and atomic weapons in Cuba.
>
> That was the beginning of the Cuban missile crisis—a confrontation between the two giant atomic nations, the United States and the U.S.S.R., which brought the world to the abyss of nuclear destruction and the end of mankind. (27)

On their (little) television screens, Americans (and Canadians) by the multitude saw the cold faces of their favorite news commentators intoning gravely about threat and response, about John F. Kennedy's ultimatums to Nikita S. Khrushchev, about the clock ticking, and finally, for gasping viewers, about the Russian withdrawal. His biographer and speechwriter Theodore Sorenson says that he sat with Kennedy calmly discussing the possibility of nuclear war. All of this in an era when for most Americans Cuba was little more than a nearby foreign territory, albeit its (capitalist-friendly) Batista regime toppled by Fidel Castro who was now vociferously in power. The world of the everyday could easily seem, even to the young and uninitiated, a garden surrounded by encroaching, growling, horrifying machines of destruction. Schoolchildren were occupied practicing bomb drills and imagining what they would bring to the fallout shelter, not that most families had one. All of culture, all of the economic flowering, all of civility —everything[2]—could be reduced at any second to ashes; and so one lived one's local life, surrounded by one's friends and familiar places, with the thought that outside the perimeter of lively everyday sensation, and not so far outside, was the poised, fully antagonistic International Community, policed by politicians, fraught with endless negotiations, following a body of law entirely unknown. The "World" was born.

FIGHT AND FLIGHT

To spur excitement for a Cold War espionage tale, *Topaz* (1969) begins with what is probably the most *stirring* credit sequence in all of Hitchcock. To the bristling snare-drum tattoo of Maurice Jarre's march, we pull back from a huge scarlet poster of Marx, Engels, and Lenin, the Soviet trinity—"FORWARD TO THE VICTORY OF COMMUNISM — *VPERED K POBEDE KOMMUNIZMA*"—to a long view of Red Square in the middle of a military parade. The titles are flashing smartly, that is, precisely on the downbeat from a kind of conductor, and beneath them we see carefully selected archival shots of guided missiles gliding past on their launchers and platoons of Russian soldiers marching left to right with punctilious piston rhythm. Of the soldiers there are thousands. Of the missiles, more than we take time to count. And guns. And more soldiers, eyes right, eyes forward. Salutes, tanks, and-one and-two and-three and-four, a beat that might go on forever. The faces without expression... the faces without expression... the faces. In the background banners read, "LABOR FREEDOM EQUALITY BROTHERHOOD — *TRUD SVOBODA RAVENSTVO BRATSTVO.*" What is it that is not being proclaimed here, not being proclaimed explicitly except in the silence of a vision? The answer is: Russia has produced and enforced a major military build-up, and is demonstrating to the world its capacity to challenge and defeat an enemy. Highlighting *missiles* is essential to a vivid, secret case, that from afar (afar, as hinted in the present extra-long set-up shot) much damage can be produced *upon you by us*, only flicking our finger: these are ICBMs. A brutal, aggressive, thoughtless apparatus for destruction gilded as "conquest," acquisition.

Watching the parade is an innumerable crowd—unidentified strangers all. We find ourselves among them, because we are watching this watched parade. And now, as the drumbeat sounds fade, a screen card:

> Somewhere in this crowd is a high Russian official who disagrees with his government's display of force and what it threatens. Very soon his conscience will force him to attempt an escape while apparently on a vacation with his family.[3]

Segue to an aerial view of an entirely contrasting urban space, the sunny Kanal of Copenhagen, tidy and blue, with the busy Knippelsbro supporting a civilized and richly capitalized flow of traffic. Now another aerial view, a house with a Russian flag aflutter in front. A family of three are departing under the observation of a stern-looking minder, presumably KGB. Strolling the broad streets—some of the streets in Copenhagen are *very* broad—they are soon picked up by a tail. Father is guiding his flock and using his arm to protect them from passers-by. A pair of city buses gives cover and they disappear. We pick them up in the regular visitors' tour of the Royal Copenhagen porcelain works. From a stockroom loaded with fired but unpainted figurines, they shuffle in an attentive little crowd between artisans working at decoration. One worker intrigues both this family and Hitchcock's camera, a woman using a palette knife with meticulous care, and prodigious fingertip control, to lift up an unpainted rose, apply some glue to it, and place it among others upon the base of a still unpainted figurine. Hitchcock gives a macro-close view of the rose figure held at the tip of the artisan's fingers. A flower of hope? A flower of sacrifice? We will see other flowers in this film.

Soon we come to a painter adding color to a plate, his specific concentration being still another flower, this one at the end of a long stem, which is being touched with yellow and ochre. Close on the daughter of the family, Tamara (Tina Hedström), a girl of perhaps eighteen years, with attractive features and very long hair, as she leans forward in fascination at the skillful application of paint. There is something genuinely magical about this tiny brush manipulated by a knowing hand as it touches the design with the silent, unknowable mystery of color.[4]

But the girl must pull back in fright, because one of the KGB team is almost next to her, staring her way. Secretly she whispers to her father. The family splits up three ways, vanishing in this warren of artistic activity. The entire sequence openly declares a conflictual state of being: we have a chase, albeit quiet and slow-moving, because the three fleeing Russians are being pursued; yet this takes place methodically, calmly, inside a shop where people of the highest training work with the greatest delicacy to make objects of beauty (and estimable value). The Russian thug is a literal embodiment of a bull in a china shop.[5] Hitchcock's selection of the china workroom not only shows off a tourist's delight in Copenhagen but also, by contrast, points out a coarseness we are to take as typical among the myrmidons of a society this defector desires to leave behind.

Russia as a military and political power is dramatized here as stereotyped in Western conceits of the 1950s and 1960s, which envisioned Moscow society as monolithic and dull, brutally confining and cheap, a culture of bread lines. Here was the domain that threatened American postwar prosperity (perhaps, as we will soon see, threatened from far too nearby, on the Cuban shores). The three members of the defecting family are dressed plainly, tidily, respectfully, but entirely without pizazz. They exhibit no smiles of pleasure, only studious interest, just like their minders who are of course studiously interested in them. Heading off into a different area where finished dinnerware and figurines abound, Tamara sees that her thug is now within arm's reach. She calculatingly takes up a figurine—macro-close shot of the article in her gloved hands—and with deliberation "accidentally" drops it to the floor where of course it smashes and draws the sharp attention of a woman at a desk in the alcove that adjoins. She rushes over, figurine shards in her guilty hands,[6] and, as from a distance we see in mime, expresses sincere regret; also in mime the saleslady graciously refuses to let her pay. But now she has opportunity to ask an innocent question—it seems probable she is looking for a washroom—and is momentarily led to an official backspace into which the Russian thug cannot penetrate. There, with the woman's assistance, she uses the telephone. With an immediate cut to an exterior shot of the American Embassy (a match structurally with the previous Russian embassy shot, the stars and stripes waving but in front of a much more expensive, newly built structure) we navigate to an office where, John Fitzgerald Kennedy (a figure Hitchcock admired [McGilligan 684]) watching in full color over his shoulder, a friendly agent type (John Forsythe) has the phone to his ear. This, we will soon learn, is our CIA man Mike Nordstrom, efficient to no end, swift, precise, but also handsome and gracious and smooth—a real operator. They should meet him at precisely 5:15 at Den Permanente (at the time, American tourists' favorite shopping spot for local pottery and creative art, in the Vesterbrogade district).

As realized onscreen by Hitchcock, and as it is in reality, Copenhagen is a city overflowing with bicycle traffic, this very artfully managed with reserved lanes adjacent the sidewalk on many of the avenues. The Russian family is departing Den Permanente at closing time. Nordstrom has had a car pull up to receive them. But Russian minders are on their tail. American agents posing as passers-by now cagily block the chasers, as the defector and his wife race into the back seat; but poor Tamara is stranded on the bike lane and hit by a biker. It is only because Nordstrom rushes back to help her that she manages to join her family in the escape. As they drive to safety, the girl with bruises blossoming on her knees, the father gives the American a sneer of rejection: "It wasn't the way *we* would have done it!" *We Russians!*

An aircraft taking off into a glorious sunset, then a snub-nosed Boeing military transport gliding into a docking space in Washington. A small motorcade across the Potomac to an isolated home in the Maryland woods.[7] But what is this! Here in the land of the free there is a minder, too, this time a pleasant middle-aged woman (Mrs. Forsyth [Ann Doran]) who radiates an aura of knowledgeability and skill but who doesn't miss a flinch. Life on the American side, in its minute day-to-day aspects, may turn out to be very much like life in Russia, except that the quality of the settings, the furniture, the clothing, presumably the food, and the conversation will be friendlier and designed for accommodation rather than naked use. Perhaps the truth of life in America is more covert, more artfully covered by modernized neo-European social graces that distract attention from the brutality. Had he not wished to point to this prospect, Hitchcock need not have shown us the Russian's eyes opening with some surprised dismay.

MUDDLES

In this opening defection sequence, the Chase After Kusenov, there are some interesting muddles:

> *Human guidance is unnecessary.* Albeit it is (only) a credit sequence, the Red Square military demonstration exercises a curious power onscreen, given the precise selection of shots (many originating as stock footage), the thrusting syntax in which they are edited, and the fact that the forward cutting is sharply on the downbeat of the 4/4 march. The effect is that the missiles and other machinery, brute, enormous, and cumbersome, start to march onscreen themselves, even, if one can say it, dance, and then the aggregates of soldiers are composed as dancers, too. The music works like a motor.[8] The world as it is conventionally understood, with the machines of war kept separate from the arts of peace, is muddied and confused, the war machines not so much being *put on* parade as—given the

shot angles that feature their urging forward—springing ahead of their own "volition." Human guidance is not only missing; it is unnecessary, once an arms build-up of this sort can be set to the triumphant music of progress. The future that humans hope for has been placed in the care of machines—one of physicist-dissident Andre Dmitrievich Sakharov's strongest complaints.

Familial, strange. Our little Russian family—papa bear, mama bear, and baby bear—has the strange (and enticing) quality of not radiating family warmth at all (at least not in the way American viewers of this film would have come to recognize "family warmth" on network television).[9] For all the world can know, three semi-talented actors (agents) have been suborned to appear *en famille* to push the Americans into engineering a defection: defection as KGB ploy. Directness, expertise, method, and obedience are all on show, but not affection. If these Russians are not who they claim to be, perhaps this defection is not what the Americans think; in espionage fakery is central and absolute. One way or the other, for this family, or "family," posing is vital; as a trio they will make for good cover but also work for the defector as arguments against rough treatment once he has sold himself over the border. Not that Hitchcock means us to suspect this father, mother, and daughter team; or that, diegetically speaking, they are anything but what we take them to be; but a glow of relation is decidedly lacking.[10]

The painted "real." But fakery and naturalness are bluntly before us. To see a painter brushing color onto a drawn flower that we are now to see as a real flower in full bloom, for example: see or quickly imagine. The flower looks like a picture of a flower, realistic but not real. So, we are watching an artisan making a rendition while at the same time watching a motion picture made of renditions. That little bisque rose: it is in three dimensions, glued onto a pure white, still unpainted figurine. It has bulk. It has reality. The Prince (Burt Lancaster) in *Il Gattopardo* (1963): "Beyond what we can touch with our own hands we have no obligations." It is easy to predict that once paint has been applied to the little rose, in its three-dimensionality and weight it will have an even more powerful effect than the flower image painted upon the dish; it will seem like a perfect noisette rose.[11] We are being offered opportunity to see the difference between what seems substantial and what does not, and perhaps more crucially between what *is* substantial and what only *seems* so. The viewers' ability to catch these fine distinctions in visual representation indicates an adult audience (see Gombrich).

Industry. Here in the cloistered territory of the ceramics workshop, by way of the meticulous gestures of extremely disciplined and talented craftspeople, we watch—like tourists ourselves—an industrial process,[12] ironically one that models itself upon nature in an explicit way. Here is Jean-Paul Sartre in 1952 on industry's *antiphysis:*

> As soon as the worker asserts his rights, the realm of man ceases to be natural. In producing, man forges his own essence; in consuming, the consumer recognizes himself and reappears *as producer* in the object consumed: he consumes what, in other circumstances, he could have produced, and what appeals to him in merchandise is the indubitable mark of human labor: a polish, a softness, a roundness, a sharpness of color that cannot be found in nature. With the advent of a manufacturing society, aristocracy, taste and naturalism disappear together, as is foretokened by what is happening in America. (*Genet* 361–62)

One might discern here a vision of the transitional phase between cottage industry and factory capitalism, the former based in and grown out of the worker's own fashioned world and the latter grounded in a space owned by someone else, lit by someone else, warmed by someone else, and opened to labor on someone else's idea of a schedule. The prevalent myth in the 1960s was that, its open-faced denial of capitalism notwithstanding, the Soviet way of life drew away from the personality of cottage existence into a kind of factory sensibility. The defector's utopian hope in flying to the U.S.A. could have been that he and his family would find there a culture based on the dignity of the individual personality—a culture in which personality leaches into the machinic rather than the other way around.

Purity. In the car driving through Washington, Tamara asks one of the CIA shepherds if "that" is the White House and he replies, no, that is the Capitol. A tourist's-eye view. Thanks to the girl's innocent question we can note the sparkling whiteness of the building against the sky. In only a moment, just as he promised, he shows her the White House and we get a tourist's view of that, too. Equally white, virginal, gleaming. A blue sky. She is utterly enchanted, seeing for the first time in actual space something of which she has carried only an image before. Hitchcock has diegetic reason for these shots, but he transcends diegesis in catering to the curiosity of a widespread audience in which would sit many who had never been to DC. How curious that these buildings are white in the way that the Royal Copenhagen porcelain was white as we looked, after its (industrial) baking but before the artists got to it.

Re-troping. The opening chase sequence offers Hitchcock opportunity for a beloved pastime, what I would term "re-troping," his use in one work of a device borrowed, transposed, and renovated from another. Viewers of *Topaz* who are familiar with Hitchcock's work will know that we have been in Copenhagen before: in *Torn Curtain* (1966) the American scientist Michael Armstrong used this city as his jumping off point for a defection to Communist Germany and now the city is the jumping off point for a key Russian dissident planning with his family to defect to the United States. There is on-the-ground intrigue in both cases but the directon of defection has undergone a sea change.[13]

Axis. There are strange angular transitions in the early part of the film. After the takeoff in Copenhagen we transition to a brief scene in the French Embassy in Washington, where André Devereaux (Frederick Stafford), a spy posing as a commercial attaché there, is told of the Kusenov defection and given to know, too, that this news *came from Paris*.

From Paris—?? The man is a *Russian* defecting to *America* by way of *Copenhagen*; where does Paris come in? How did the French come into the knowledge? Were they, possibly, informed by Moscow? If so— we're getting a quick hint only—is somebody in Paris in conversation with Moscow, secretly, continually, pithily? Repeated conversation on a clandestine channel: if that were possible, anything the Americans said to their French allies, or that the French (Devereaux) whispered to the Americans (Nordstrom), might leak. Now we jump to André's Bethesda home as he walks in, proceeding away from the camera along the hallway to the kitchen at the rear, where his cook is at work. We view him from directly above, the camera tilting to follow his action as he moves into the distance. He looks like a clinical subject under review.

Looking down. But this downward-peering vertical view is a familiar one in Hitchcock, generally used to set the viewer's consciousness *away from* the character on display, or to suggest that the character has been set away from someone or something else; and to bring to the viewing a tiny modicum of consciousness about that viewing itself. We will be seeing Devereaux as a friendly force, chummy with Mike Nordstrom; but the camera angle on his entrance, a prelude, pulls us back from amity some. We saw the Kusenovs from above, too, leaving their embassy. We will soon later look down upon Devereaux pushed to a sidewalk in New York. Later still, we will look down with Devereaux and his daughter, first as they race up an expansive staircase and then as they peer at a body that has "fallen" from a window. We will look down upon a woman collapsing to a floor in a spectacle. At a conference in Paris we will look down on a huge empty space with a French cluster huddled at one end and an American cluster near us (I address this later on). At his interrogation in Maryland, we look down on Kusenov's broad forehead as he calculates how to answer vital questions, our view made both diagnostic and anxious. Ongoing, persistent anxiety; Cold War anxiety; what will turn out in retrospect to have been the anxiety of the 1960s.

SCHOOLED

With his daughter happily engaged at the piano and his wife happily trying on a new dress under Mrs. Forsyth's kindly eye, Boris Kusenov is being grilled by American intelligence officers in a boardroom where every breath is being taped. About his position in the KGB, he asserts, he will have nothing whatever to say, this line of questioning not being part of the understanding he gave before coming over. But has he heard the word "*topaz*"? A group of close portraits of the man pondering hard before saying no, shots from slightly above his left side detailing the receding hairline, the sharp eyes cast aslant, the calculated (and sonorous) voice. *Topaz*... heard of it in relation to what?

In relation to anything: a codeword... *topaz?*

"Nohh!" The simulation of graciousness in a delivery that is patently supercilious. And also, with some clarity, deceit. The man's pronunciation is memorable: *kneh-uwww.*

We are sharply poised. This man is: (a) naturally reticent with strangers, (b) a gambler holding back his ante so as to increase the value of his chips, (c) a kind of "tourist" willing to answer American questions as long as the answers don't preclude him seeing the sights. As to *topaz*, however, his blunt denial can be only an affirmation that he surely does recognize the word. He surely does know. The negativity is a palpable signal—to us if not to the intelligence agents around the table, because in any film about intelligence the viewers constitute the real agents in place—that he is not to be fully trusted. A real possibility: this isn't a defection but a concoction of Russian Intelligence to plant an agent deep inside the American power structure. In such a case, Kusenov would answer questions evasively, just this way, stretching the game for several vital days. In an interrogation, make the questioner hungry by saying, "I deh-uw-nt kneh-uwww."

We cut to a newspaper headline informing the public of present concern about military build-up in Cuba, invocation, with the help of a memory flash to Kennedy smiling out from his photograph in Mike's embassy office in Denmark, of the missile crisis. Something big is going on; bigger than Kusenov and his little family. Or has Kusenov come here to open Cuba to American oversight and action...?

A breather in the comfortable sitting room. Kusenov irritated at the questioning, so much that Mike has to pitch a forceful rejoinder: if you agree to help, you and your family will be given new identities and even a start-up business so that you can earn a living. You will never be bothered again. Your daughter will be given entrance and tuition coverage for the best music school of her choice... or else you will be left to fend for yourself. "Fend for yourself": read the silence between the words. Swiftly the Russian leads the way back into the board room. A man devoted to his family, surely, but also, as we see now, very serious about the idea of schooling. Targeted with the overriding question, "Cuba?" he becomes eloquent in a wholly professorial way. "Cuba!" a pleasing smile. And then intonation...: This is Politics 101, and here's the Official Mouth. The esteemed scholar with the international reputation and umpteen books under his belt, every one about Cuba. He is going to give a lecture, take out your notebooks.

And here Hitchcock makes what is for him an extremely strange structural move:[14]

This erudite, supercilious Kusenov, *dorogoy, lyubimyy, uvazhayemyy Professor*, by way of his answers to the Americans' questions, more or less dictates not merely information for the delectation of the CIA but, as though on an itinerary, the events of the plot-to-be for the next several sequences of the film. He spiels the story, as it is about to come our way. Everything Kusenov points to with his words in this scene will be pointed to dramaturgically as the film unwinds; every name will be attached to a body, every body to a place. It is quite as though Hitchcock is warning, "I am telling you what you must look for." This is the espionage business. Follow my words and see what you will find:

[1] The important Cuban government official Rico Parra is about to address the United Nations.[15]

[2] Parra traveled to Moscow and had a meeting there with Russian authorities, who gave him

[3] a memorandum of understanding the contents of which I, Kusenov, am unable to describe. *However!*...

[4] Parra has an aide, a man named Uribe, and this Uribe carries this document:

> KUSENOV: The KGB is carefully divided. Cuba was never in my field. I cannot give you facts.
>
> NORDSTROM (exploding in anger): Kusenov—you made an agreement with me!!!
>
> KUSENOV (far from happy): Yes, I know, I made my bargain with the devil! Facts!
>
> NORDSTROM (serious): Well, what are the Russians doing in Cuba?
>
> KUSENOV: They came bearing gifts from Russia to Cuba.

Kusenov's sly remark will gain attention here soon. But—have the Russians brought offensive weapons into Cuba?

> KUSENOV (stubborn): I told you, I cannot give you facts. (Then, as if flicking an ON switch:) But Rico Parra has the trade pact,

he has the aide-memoire. It's all there for you to read. *If you can obtain it....* So now I have given you my information—what will you do with it?

If only it were possible to get to Uribe! Because then,

[5] it might be possible to see the memorandum. The CIA men can see far too clearly that if there is a build-up of military materials in Cuba, "gifts from the Russian people," this puts a military threat within easy targeting range of the United States.

From all this talk emerges a kind of map:

- We (the CIA) will go to New York and find Rico Parra, wherever he is staying; then,

- We will pressure the man Uribe, in order to extract the Moscow memorandum for examination; and

- If the information warrants, we will advise Kennedy on mobilization of a military defense.

This is quite a lesson for a single session in class! (We can see gravity registered on the faces around the seminar table.) Perhaps, wait for next week's seminar when Kusenov might tell us all about—

But who can wait a week when the Russian ships are ninety miles offshore?

We will not forget Devereaux's curiosity as to how and why the defection—Kusenov's presence here—could have come to attention *in Paris*, but that curiosity is going to be overwhelmed at present by Devereaux's friendship, both professional and personal, with Mike Nordstrom. Time flies, and that memorandum of understanding is screaming to be seen. Maybe friends can help friends secure it...?

MIME

With his background in silent cinema (*The Lodger* [1927] is one of the great silent films), Hitchcock understandably esteems the possibilities of mimed action.

In order to facilitate a mime, to focus a silent display of gesture on the viewer's mind, it is ideal that the mimer not be so stereotyped a figure that the behavior will be readable in advance. To be sure, one must gaze at and see the display. The mimer defines a self by way of the gestural outplay of action, instead of being known already and perpetrating just the moves we expect to see. Casting and design are crucial here. Hitchcock's search for the "look" of a CIA operative and his somewhat unexpectable casting of Forsythe, this prototypically smiling and wittily cagey American type—"For casting and wardrobe purposes we will need photographs of an important CIA official" (Research Needed)—his assembly of the Russian family, especially the intellectual broad-browed professorial type as defector; the oh-so comfortably furnished, welcoming CIA house in Maryland:

> We would need photographs of estates in the Maryland countryside. It is important that the estates photographed have a long driveway leading up to the house. If possible there should be a high iron fence and gates surrounding the estate but we could put up our own if necessary. It would be ideal if there was a stream or river adjacent to the house. It would be very important to photograph the entrance and interior in great detail, especially paintings, objects of art and furnishings. (Research Needed)

—all this helps us to *see into* the interrogation's silences, to take the session, exactly by way of gestures and placements, as both pressing and real. Hitchcock's casting I find meticulous and exact, because it refuses the "already known." As to casting for film and how it can play to, cuddle against rather than refuting, the already known, here is Michael Arlen regarding a "Marlboro Man"-cowboy type needed for a commercial:

> On the little screen, as they step into camera range to begin the videotaped audition—eyes straight ahead, arms at sides, no particular expression on the face beneath the cowboy hat—each man looks like a cowboy; or, rather, he looks like what one is accustomed to seeing on the movie or TV screen as a cowboy. (58)

What people were accustomed to before they came into the theater was not what Hitchcock wanted to show. So, if Nordstrom the iconic American is a cowboy of sorts, he is a country-club cowboy, used to good martinis. Henry Nash Smith had noted the American ethos bound to a move westward, the West being the undiscovered, untamed land, so that the cowboy figure, at least in myth and in the popular imagination, was the American type par excellence. Mike is advertising—without speaking it—the New West, the America that John F. Kennedy is striving to save from Russian missiles so near to its heart.

Kusenov brings our attention to the main object of concern, the trade pact. Nordstrom must possess it to read it, and reading it is essential. We must get to Parra in New York, but by way of what will seem a diversion (yet, in true Hitchcockian fashion, is not). Idlewild: André and his wife, Nicole (Dany Robin), are welcoming their daughter Michele (Claude Jade) and her artist-journalist husband François Picard (Michel Subor) for a blissful five-day family holiday in New York while the United Nations Assembly opens. They all arrive at the St. Regis on East 55th Street and proceed directly to suite 801-2, where, as the door swings open, their gay smiles fade because standing in wait for them (and having just delivered a massive bouquet of chrysanthemums) is Mike Nordstrom. A guarded frown pops onto André's face—oh no, my holiday is ruined!—and a grander frown, partly condemnation, partly disgruntled resignation, decorates Nicole (who in an earlier scene at their home, when Mike was over for dinner, bantered about this intelligence work with emphatic wifely dismissal). Michele tenses and guides François into the privacy of the next room. Mike makes eloquent apology to Nicole. Departing, she thanks him for the flowers, *over her shoulder*, quite as though to say, very beautiful bribes. Mike must now in whispers explain to André about the Cuban papers and the secretary, Luis Uribe, who detests Americans. Could André not act on his behalf today, tonight, and secure the papers? Urgent! Dangerous! Secret! André demurs at first, but Mike makes it plain how critical the situation is for the United States. André beckons his son-in-law to come out and show Mike his collection of diplomat portraits, and the three men pore over François' sketchbook until Uribe is found. Mike lifts out the page. André will take it, and Mike's money, and see what he can do.

André is now aiding Mike on a hunt for the aide-memoire (an aide for an aide). Don't take your eyes off the ball.

He taxis to 125th Street, Harlem. Parra and his retinue are at the Hotel Theresa.[16] Opposite is a floral shop called Martinique, where André confabulates with the owner, Philippe Dubois (Roscoe Lee Browne), an old contact *and photographer*. Philippe has plenty of fake journalist IDs and will pose as a reporter from *Ebony* or *Playboy*, which? André chooses *Ebony* over Philippe's mild protest ("Oh man, are you square!"). Importantly, the explanation given to Philippe by André is unheard—by anyone else in the shop and by us—since the florist has led his friend into his glass-doored walk-in refrigerator: we are in the Territory of the Gesture, and we must interpret only by virtue of what we see. The men's lips are moving and their eyes are zoning in on each other's.[17] A directorial ploy, this, since we think we know the gist of what Philippe must learn here, and having the scene in mime elides a need for repeating a tedious explanation, as well as carrying us beyond what we know and focusing us on the men themselves. Further, as the actual conversation is inaccessible to us *we presume* what André is saying but could never attest to it. A reprise mime now follows, from Devereaux's lookout down the street, among the crowd and across from the hotel, which helpfully has a huge plate-glass façade. Philippe enters and gestures to the desk man. Soon a bespectacled gentleman emerges from the elevator. This, we recognize from the sketch, must be Uribe (Donald Randolph). Gestures ensue between the two of them as they speak—we hear nothing. Philippe guides Uribe outside, where the screaming crowd presents a second wall to block us from hearing. More gesturing, then suddenly Uribe pulls back in horror and shoos Philippe away. He retreats. But Philippe follows close behind, catches him at the elevator, and indicates the bulge (the payoff) in his pocket. Uribe perks up. He disappears upstairs to get the document case. Philippe signals Devereaux with a hand held up: 5 minutes.

Suddenly Philippe makes the choice to ascend himself and meet Uribe in the bathroom of his suite, under a glaring lightbulb: an assignation if ever there was. He is going to deflect Parra (John Vernon) while Uribe pilfers the briefcase.

Parra's suite: Dubois lures the Cuban onto the balcony to take some shots "for his magazine." Uribe deftly withdraws the case. Dubois takes the elevator down, but then circles back up through a stairwell and creeps into Uribe's room, a second assignation. Meanwhile Parra is working at his desk, distracted and smoking his fat Fidel Castro-style cigar. He discovers the missing case. A young soldier is typing for him. Where is my case? Oh, Uribe took it. "Uribe? But there's only one key, and I have it!" He takes his bodyguard/henchman Hernandez (Carlos Rivas) down the hallway and they crash into Uribe's room.

A vision of two men caught in a sort of *flagrante*. Their embarrassment and fear manifest a perfect simulation of sex discovered, but it is far from sex of the conventional kind. What has been pried open is the red attaché, and Philippe is still photographing. In less than half a second he is out onto the balcony and into the air, as Parra fires on him. Onto an awning, onto the sidewalk, into the massive crowd screaming even more because of the gunshots. Police stirred, on foot and on horseback. Cubans rushing out of the hotel. Dubois racing down the opposite sidewalk, crashing into Devereaux and pushing him down. A quick hand movement. Devereaux helped to his feet, ironically by Hernandez on the chase. André looking down to find Dubois' camera. Dubois, meanwhile, has deftly found sanctuary back in his flower shop, mounting a fuchsia ribbon on a wreath: REST IN PEACE.

This Dubois-Uribe sequence is structurally fascinating as well as dramatically central, the latter because it contains the most elaborately choreographed complex action in the film, and because it is framed around the secret document that is tantamount to hard evidence of what the Russians are doing. Yet almost all of it—certainly all the phases directly involving access to Uribe and then access to the attaché case and then photographing the document—is performed silently, mime again, so that the only access available to witnessing characters and to us is by way of interpreting gestural expression, body alignments, and facial expressions in context—that is to say, in terms of the context as far as we are able to apprehend it through silence. We have seen the Americans roused by a "hint" that something is going on in Cuba, seen Kusenov speak out substantiation, seen André go into action persuaded by Mike's words and voice, seen Dubois persuaded by André... but the actual events of 125th Street all happen at a distance, as it were both openly and secretly at once. We "understand" what we see partly because Kusenov's "itinerary" readied—also led—us. This central action of the film is produced as pure cinema, the onflow of movement in space as recorded in light. Hitchcock's films must be seen to be believed.

There are at least three chases proceeding in series here, each morphing into the next: (i) conversational—Dubois after Uribe's psychology; (ii) criminal—Uribe stealing the document; (iii) violent—Parra after Dubois. Uribe is a catalyst, facilitating but swiftly disappearing from the action. Hitchcock attended carefully to this character:

> Mr. Hitchcock wishes Don Randolph (playing the part of 'Uribe') to wear eye glasses [*sic*].
>
> Actual lenses must be used—they are to be those worn by a very myopic (short-sighted) man.
>
> The lenses must not be tinted.
>
> The frames must be thick steel. (Robertson)

The triangle of Devereaux, Dubois, and Uribe is given to us almost entirely in silence, quite as though, being voyeurs, we peek from a distance to steal the intimacies of their action. There are other instances of mime in this film, crucial to the watching experience:

- The entire opening sequence in Copenhagen is without dialogue until the vital telephone call to Mike (which is peremptory).
- Parra's confrontation with Uribe and Dubois has him gazing at a soundless relationship.
- André will leave DC for Cuba and Nicole's "farewell" at that point will be all mime. She mounts the stairs of their house, coldly silent, her manner intended to convey not only her feeling as he leaves her but the abject tension of the moment.
- In Cuba, a man sent off to photograph the Russian ships being unladed gazes through his telephoto-equipped camera to witness action at a distance beyond the range of hearing. The telephoto makes our acoustic withdrawal clear in itself.
- The Americans have aerial photography of Cuba, this having led them to suspect a military build-up. The pictures show still frames of physical relationships between structures, with no sound.

- Returning from Cuba André will make a discovery in the toilet of his aircraft—pure silence. There is no one there for him to talk to, and in any event he would be secretive, but the event has been structured for camera that way.

- A man and woman will eye each other outside a Parisian pied-à-terre—signally silent. The eye tells all, for each.

- A climactic confrontation will take place in a gilded Parisian conference room. Here, from far up near the ceiling and out of hearing range we observe keenly. A tiny interruption with up-close dialogue, to punctuate; then more mimed action at a distance.

"Watch and Surmise" is the motto here. Watch and calculate. Watch and, if you can manage to, remember. But whatever you come eventually to think, you will have to found it upon what the eye could see and the mind surmise. As to that, the detail of the secret memorandum, that aide-memoire (aid to memory), is never for an instant shown, and Philippe photographs it desperately, but in silence. All the business of *Topaz* is of the kind that words do not (adequately) describe, an edifice grounded in secrecy and built up out of secrets carefully posed. One could go so far as to say that espionage is silence; and in this film the silence provokes for the audience a speculative seeing.

FAMILY PLOT

While Nicole Devereaux is perfectly willing to be gracious to Mike Nordstrom at her table, there is something about him she doesn't like, or better, affiliate with. On the surface he seems an interloper working to dissolve her marriage. And her marriage to André may be a pillar of her temple. When she finds Mike present to "welcome" her at the St. Regis, her distaste could hardly be more palpable, and we must begin to wonder what faux pas could produce so tendentious an unpleasantness. No slouch, and air-brushed to the hilt, Mike clearly picks up the vibrations, with the linguistic precision of his apologies to her indicating sensitivity and graciousness—neither of which she trusts. He must not mar the friendship; André is useful to him. Indeed, as in a marriage, they are useful to each other. But she knows very well how the CIA is all about using people, in myriad ways and for purposes that almost never become clear. Is Nicole's prickliness coming from this secretiveness, that everything Mike ever seduces her husband into is a silence? A problem in gender politics? Only six years before this film came out *The Feminine Mystique* had roused public consciousness to gender politics, especially within the bounds of the family; it was in essence a book about melodrama (see Elsaesser), and notes of melodrama perfume parts of this film. But if mere gender were the problem, Michele would share Nicole's attitude and she seems not to. Nicole possesses André, and perhaps the intimacy of male-male espionage operations is a threat. Or perhaps the threat is altogether different...

A reading of the Devereaux family as microcosm of the missile crisis could clarify *Topaz* some. But to clarify the film a great deal more, notice something pointed out *only subtly* in the early scene at the Devereaux residence, the fact that Nicole *la Parisienne* speaks English far less fluently than her husband does, and far, far, far less fluently than the eloquent Mike Nordstrom. She is not only with the French; she is not only French herself; she is, by her manner and clothing, her style, and her wit the very quintessence of the sophisticated Parisienne: she has been drinking Puligny Montrachet since childhood, knows *quenelles de brochet*, has schmoozed with French intellectuals about the special value of George Sand and Simone de Beauvoir and Marguerite Duras. If we listen beyond what anybody says here to how they say it we hear Mike's gracility, André's wariness, and Nicole's hauteur. She knows how to read a situation, and sees now what she has seen too many times before, that the Americans are quite willing to use the French to do their dirty work anytime they please. The French are the good servants of the house. This of a nation that boasted Versailles, that boasted the Eiffel Tower, that includes the City of Light. For the Americans, as she sees it, suave and eloquent and apologetic and generous as they may seem, the French are but maids and valets.

THE CUBAN MACHINE

"Let the Americans do their own dirty work," Nicole warns André in their Bethesda bedroom. There is something ambiguous in her tone, resentment or gravity. She fears for his life on this upcoming trip to Cuba, but perhaps also regrets what her life is becoming at his side and certainly wishes she knew more than she does about Juanita de Cordoba (Karin Dor), the beautiful Cuban woman he has gone so many times to meet. "She is the leader of their underground," he confides, perhaps unwisely. And he must help the Americans because now, after the Bay of Pigs disaster,[18] their organization in Cuba is shattered. "Those papers we photographed in New York scared the hell out of me. I've got to see what the Russians are up to." Not only do Nicole's eyes moisten in her silence but Hitchcock arranges for a macro-close shot of her face, which fills the screen just as pallidly as it fills André's thoughts.

On the plane a close-up of the *New York Times* front page in André's hands: CAPITAL'S CRISIS AIR HINTS AT DEVELOPMENT ON CUBA; KENNEDY TV TALK LIKELY.[19] The film means to access the backstage area of the missile crisis. The phrase "crisis air" hints that Kennedy still lacks vital information he'll need if he plans to talk on TV; André is presumably after that information. Because in espionage stories securing information is the organic center of the plot, drama is infused when gleaning is perilous. André will be clever, but he is too gracious, too tall, too distinctly well dressed, too distinctly handsome, and at the same time too physically clumsy to be able to act efficiently on his own. Another chain of interwoven actions is now required: the Cuban machine, something like a second family.

To dramatize the Cuban episode Hitchcock uses temporal curtailment, incisive editing, and actorial pantomime. At the center of the kaleidoscope: ships, a camera to photograph them, photographs from that camera. André arrives at Juanita's sumptuous villa to find her in... Rico's arms. She is not only the Frenchman's confidante, then, but the Cuban leader's lover. If she is sleeping with both of them she is nothing short of dangerous herself. Rico and André can exchange pleasantries but they don't exchange trust. Soon André's lovemaking brings us back, sharply, to his flat denials to Nicole. Perhaps a man like this is not the genteel and honorable sort he's been pretending to be. He hands Juanita some American spy technology—gifts from America—the sine qua non of espionage fiction written or filmed, since apparently information can be procured only by way of penetrative devices, human perceptivity being axiomatically insufficient. If the technology grabs our eye we should be warned: human perception is not at all insufficient, as will become apparent. Some of the vital technology here—a Geiger counter—is put to use out of our sight; but we will watch some of it—a camera with an especially long lens, for photographing Russian ships at Imias—get the user into the worst kind of trouble. To do her dirty work Juanita involves her servants: Señor and Señora Mendoza (Lewis Charles, Anna Navarro) will photograph the Russian ships, her houseboy Thomas (John Roper) will process the film to negatives and hide the negatives. She is balancing on a very thin wire.

But what unravels the Devereaux scheme in Cuba is a character's tiny, silent observation made without the aid of technology.[20] Fidel Castro is giving one of his famously long-winded speeches, with Parra, his assistant Hernandez, and Juanita in cap and uniform near him on the podium. In the crowd watching all this is Devereaux. But Hernandez is the one who, by utter happenstance, helped André to his feet on the 125th Street sidewalk during the chase after Dubois and now, gazing into the crowd with an eagle eye, detects him. A whisper to Parra. Parra's thick eyebrows lifting (a screaming silence). Rico must now suspect Juanita and wastes no time before having the Mendozas, caught after their photographic escapade, tortured. Señora Mendoza is at death's door as in macro-close shot she whispers into Rico's very proximate ear, "Jua...ni...ta." Rico very much wishes not to believe it.

He threatens André and declares him a spy. Leave the country in the morning, and if at the airport you are found to have anything on you, you are going to suffer greatly. (We know already that Uribe was killed, and that the Mendozas are in little better condition.) Thomas brings André a special razor and blade injector (containing the film) and Juanita gifts him with a small green notebook, token of their mutual affection. As soon as André has left her abode for the airport, up rides Rico with his soldiers. They barge in and search the place, finding Thomas's darkroom hidden in the kitchen. Utterly infuriated but at the same time utterly deflated, his delirium of love fully converted to a lesson in realism, Rico takes Juanita into his arms and in a torturous little whisper of combined menace and adoration shoots her in the heart.

André sails through security at the airport. They found nothing on him, especially in the razor and blade injector! Telephoning to Juanita to assure her he's safe, he learns that she is dead.

All this vortical action, building and spinning from Moscow to Copenhagen to Washington to New York to Cuba, races us through an investigation aimed at the Russian ships docked in Cuba and the merchandise they are delivering there. This is the American aerial-photography target to be used in the White House Situation Room. Those grainy, grainy, too grainy photographs are perfect motive for photographing better and up close. Will the CIA get the proof America needs (thanks to Kusenov's shopping instructions)? Will handsome Devereaux escape some future torture or insoluble dilemma? A tight weave, for fans who adore to find story weaves in movies, that is, who think of movies as packages to contain woven stories. But so far, nine elements beg for special consideration:

ANOMALIES FOR THE EYE

[1] *Purple.* Juanita de Cordoba is in a luscious imperial purple gown when she dies, and we watch her body collapse to the marble floor from high above, so that the purple swirls out and turns her into a flower. But in New York, in our chum Philippe Dubois' flower shop, the REST IN PEACE ribbon he was finishing was intensive fuchsia purple, a premonition of Juanita's robe. Flower shop... the flowers of death... death as a flower. But death also as a signal of the unreal and invocation of the problem of realism and artifice: the little flowers in the Royal Copenhagen factory, introduced before we had any reason to think of flowers as important, or of floral purple. The flowering gown is tropical, something like a purple hibiscus, short-lived the way Juanita was short-lived.

I think it possible that Hitchcock arranges for the gown to become a flower at Juanita's death for yet another reason. Let us focus on the issue of her loyalty. Because we have seen her (artfully, and of dire necessity, we may decide) flirting with Rico, we can find ourselves poised on a knife edge (as she is) between believing she is only pretending to be a revolutionary but is a secret CIA asset; or believing she is pretending to be a CIA asset, friend of Devereaux, but is secretly true to Rico. She is poised between Rico and André, knowing how to curry André's favor by making him her lover or to curry Rico's favor in the same way. Which side is she on? Love, at least in the context of a story such as this, is not a foundation for an architecture but a show, within a circus filled with shows. And as Nicole and André's relationship makes plain, the claim of love is but one of the many shows for catching and holding interest. Perhaps André, unfaithful to Nicole, is unfaithful to Juanita, too—flying back to America he does seem tranquil after her demise, a little rueful but not devastated. As a player in the spy game, Juanita can be putting on a face, too. And given this conundrum about her, this balanced pair of possibilities—that she leans left, that she leans right (leans toward red; leans toward blue)—something must throw the weight a little to one side. While any woman could be equally faithful to two men on opposite sides of the Iron Curtain, spy fiction would have us believe such a contingency incredible; if she is loyal to Rico, her behavior with André must be false. Consider, then, how linking her through purple with Dubois, who almost lost his life in straining himself (indisputably) for André's benefit; putting her, as it were, under Dubois' banner by having her die under the sign of purple just as he, making a wreath to decorate a death, lives under the same sign—how these purple moves tilt the scales and allow us to hope, with the best of reasons, that it is the Americans she trusts and that her death will somehow be to their benefit. The purple flower is a dramaturgical tool, ballast for one particular conviction about Juanita de Cordoba.

[2] *Gulled.* Juanita's staff have prepared the duteous Mendozas with some special Cuban sandwiches, the fresh (and tantalizing) crusty bread neatly picked out on the insides to make room for a camera in one and a telephoto lens in the other. Now they are off on a grassy rise spying the docked ships and ready to go to town. Señora Mendoza hands her husband the notably phallic telephoto lens to screw onto the camera—Hitchcock's signal to us that even from this distance the pictures will be accurate, telling, and easy to read, appropriately an improvement of the U-2 photographs and thus legitimation for André's trip—and

he snaps away. But at the docks down below is a moment of genuine—and, because of its placement here, bizarre—comedy. One of the Cuban soldiers guarding the access gate to the security compound is having a lazy gaze into the tropical sky and sees a seagull winging by. But this gull is carrying a huge piece of bread in its beak. Oh well—gulls are all thieves. But a moment later, still gazing upward, he sees a second gull carrying another piece of bread, and now he starts thinking. Following the bird's trajectory he moves his eyes and catches sight of two people crouched far up the rise. He begins a pursuit. A chase-within-the-{chase-within-a-}chase follows, with shots fired and the couple running away through some trees. Their car pulls off. Soldiers race after them in a jeep. On the road, a car is stranded with the man trying to fix something under the hood. Soldier: "Did you see a car go by?" Man: "Yes, yes. That way..." But walking over to the woman, our sky-gazer sees suddenly that she is bleeding.

Beyond casually quoting *The Birds* (1963), with its significant avian marauders; and regardless of its benefit as quick relief; what serious reason can Hitchcock have had for staging this discovery sequence with, of all possibilities, flying gulls? There are plenty of realist answers that all depend on taking the gulls' presence for granted: gulls because they scavenge, and if the Mendozas have been careless enough to throw away their bread these crooks will snag it; gulls because we are near the water, there would be gulls there; and a sandwich-bearing gull because such a creature would be noticeable, attracting the guard's eye. Yet will it not seem as though some indefinite force from afar, call it a fatality, has taken control of the action and sharpened attention in a particular way, since it *just happens* that these particular gulls (who have stolen the bread) should fly past at the same moment that the guard *just happens* to be gazing into the sky? If all the machination of the espionage, all the manual carrying, can so easily seem an organized, purposive, meticulous product of little people's concentration upon a giant lethality, we also have... happenstance. "Happenstance" as diegetic manifestation: what cannot be planned for, cannot be built into the choreography, though of course Hitchcock plans carefully for the happenstance he shows.

[3] *Confession.* When brutal Rico questions Señora Mendoza as to the origin of her photographing activity with her husband, she answers with so little remaining breath—the Mendozas have been severely tortured—that he can make out her words only if he comes very close and places an ear next to her mouth. This technique of framing of course brings the attention of the viewer very close to the syllables the woman emits. We have a profile shot showing a mouth at left reaching over to an ear at right, these in macro-close-up so that nothing else is on the screen. Narratively, we are put inside the woman's voice, quite as though her mouth and larynx constitute a kind of auditorium and we are positioned within, just so as to hear a solo utterance from the "stage" of her tongue. But then, to show us the registration, Hitchcock cuts to a second macro-close shot, this time of Parra's face as he hears the woman with the rear of her head nestled against his head. The proximity helps with shot composition, surely; but its value is interpersonal touch, something we see but do not hear. Rico's tautly focused eyes tell the story of his (a) hearing and (b) response. I think this is a particularly interesting case of what we might term a "re-troping *en passant*," where the self-quotation (from *The Man Who Knew Too Much* [1956]),[21] without ever losing its distinctness and visibility to the knowing viewer, nevertheless speedily evanesces, since the secret here being confessed will help turn the story directly, "now." Typically with Hitchcock there is dramaturgy whenever there is aesthetic design. Approaching Mrs. Mendoza so closely has the secondary benefit of bringing her within our proximal space as well as Rico Parra's, affiliating us with her agony, negating any wisp of potential suspicion on our part that she may *wish* to give Juanita away. Often long or medium shots of tortured people have a cold neutrality that lends the victims motive.

[4] *Chicken.* That the telephoto lens of Mendoza's camera is shown initially as a phallic object—it is indisputably more phallic than the train in the final shot of *North by Northwest* (1959), which is so cavalierly pointed out by fans and critics—helps frame a bizarre (also somewhat comical) little routine as the camera and lens, retrieved earlier, we guess, from the stanchion where the Mendozas hid them at roadside, are now

"delivered" from a gaping and wholly vaginal opening between the spread legs of a chicken being dressed in Juanita's kitchen. Close shot, with an obstetrical hand reaching in to withdraw the camera (in plastic wrap) and then, for a punch line, the (phallic) lens. Just as in *Psycho* (1960) Hitchcock had found delight in opening with a *reverse* sex scene, in which two lovers get dressed instead of getting undressed, here he gives us a reverse penetration, in which a phallic object is pulled out of—is born wholly developed from—the carnal opening. Certainly the camera and lens needed to be hidden somewhere in order to make their way in secret to this kitchen (there are prying soldiers' eyes all around Cuba), but why the splayed legs, the unmistakable opening, the framing of the shot? Again, method. Hitchcock needs us to see how even when detailed plans have been made and efficiently carried out, still, results are surprisingly born, emerge from the dark, present themselves without announcement.[22]

[5] *On the stairs.* At the Devereaux house, as he departs for Cuba from the front vestibule with Nicole on the staircase nearby, he turns at the door to say something but... she is already gone. Looking up (up into Hitchcock's zone of the sacred) he discerns her shadow mounting the last few steps to the second floor, where it (and she) will be out of sight. In her movement she is like a bird slowly taking off, and in gazing up at her André presages the Cuban soldier who will gaze up at the gulls. Nicole's shadow is on the staircase, and again, as with the chicken to come, a reverse re-troping: Marnie's mother limping downstairs, cane in hand, from outside the girl's room, out of frame while *her shadow* is flickering on the wall. Here, then, not the Shadow Mother, as much dead as alive, descending into the Underworld but the Shadow Wife, ascending into the *au-delà*. While he is in Cuba, she will be on an aircraft ascending toward Paris.

[6] *Servitude.* Should we be listening with ears attuned to matters of class, as Hitchcock's always were, Nicole Devereaux's offhand remark to her husband that he should stop doing "other people's dirty work for them" would have a characteristic ring. It is not merely engagement in servile behavior she is commenting upon but that such behavior involves work. Nor is she frowning upon work per se, the application

of the body to a labor for which it is called (a vocation). It is quite specifically *dirty* work she does not think André should be doing: menial work, application of the body as though the body is the only value the worker possesses to offer and the offer is made to someone else who commands. She seems snobbish, giving André (and us) to know that her own sense of class is offended by his doing dirty work at all, any dirty work but certainly dirty work on other people's call and, it seems, most certainly if the other people are Americans. She sees herself as being above that sort of thing (we can have every reason for suspecting André married up) and he is an embarrassment to her pretentions. Of course the French, breathing a culture much older than the American one, might frown upon America in general, but Nicole is making a broader reference, to slave labor itself. The queen is showing signs of sophistication; the husband is a worker bee. Nicole could easily tell André, "Stop going out of your way to help Mike Nordstrom," without invoking the term "dirty work" at all.

André will employ others to do the dirty work of his "dirty work," of course. His principal servant will be his "love," Juanita de Cordoba ("de Cordoba" suggesting a Spanish heritage, possibly nobility, but something of no importance to the dignified Frenchman even if her heroic late husband's name holds sway in Cuba). For her part, Juanita has other people doing her dirty work, too, Thomas and the Mendozas. We will even see an old horseman who appears after the Mendozas are carted away and withdraws their hidden camera; he is a peon doing dirty work for them. A vertical hierarchy in which one feels not only empowered but also natural in suborning those lower on the ladder to do one's dirty work.[23] It may be that Nicole Devereaux is accustomed to having her husband do dirty work for her, and resentful that he would stoop for anybody else—especially Mike. On the military side, things are mirrored, if within a more brittle structure. Castro has Parra to do his dirty work; Parra has Hernandez and also the slimy Muñoz (Roberto Contreras), who will do the groveling labor of connecting with the airport authorities to instruct them in searching André's bags and who was undoubtedly responsible for torturing the Mendozas. The soldier who saw the gulls bearing bread away is one of the legion at the bottom of that hierarchy.

I think it inadvisable to wander far from Nicole Devereaux and her sensitivity to matters of service. The wife of a diplomat would hardly be innocent to the "dirty work" her husband does routinely, after all. Perhaps she is speaking in marital code: "I don't like Mike Nordstrom. Stay away from him," but *dirty work* is the code for Mike, and the country he stands for.

[7] *Automaton below.* When Kusenov is thinking under fire how, whether, and to what extent to provide answers to the jabbing American questions, Hitchcock frames him from above his head and to his left, so that in slightly turning his head one way or the other, in casting his eyes askance, in slowly forming his words (a Russian fairly articulate in English) he begins to simulate an automaton. This is a way of casting the character in a silent, subtle, unaffirmed way as typical of an "automatic" society. But it also calls upon a very frequent tactic of Hitchcock's, to select out a brief instant of extremely provocative, usually tense action, action that is very often a silence covering thought, and film it from above. Vandamm confiding to Leonard about Eve Kendall being brought to fall from a great height, but confiding in a shot in which we look down upon the pair of them; or in *The Man Who Knew Too Much* Ben and Jo being seen from high above as they endure the chilling conversation with their kidnapped son by telephone. Let us say the look downward produces a certain *frisson* of silence. The figure of Kusenov here connotes horror, fear, darkness, the scathing blade of the future.

Kusenov's positioning "down there" is meant to imply that no matter his august position in the KGB he has become at the moment nothing but a tool useful for digging the dirt.

[8] *Pietà.* Brutally tortured, the Mendozas are covered in blood. We see them in medium shot, draped upon a bench against a stone wall. Their fate is no surprise but the postures awaken vision. Here is a variant of Scottie in Midge's arms as he tumbles from her stepladder in *Vertigo:* nothing less than a pietà, with the male(-child) nestled against the would-be protective, but now hopelessly impotent, female's body. The direct line of narrative attachment is to the photography from the crest

of the hill, thence to the camera itself and its birth out of the chicken, this very camera's possession and presentation by Devereaux an echo of Dubois' tiny camera confided to Devereaux silently on the 125th Street sidewalk. Any camera is finally a reflection of its user. Dubois uses his camera with a certain skill and astonishing rapidity; Mendoza and Thomas operate with André's camera in their own way, calmly, deliberately, but also, in the end, torturously. "Watch the camera," Hitchcock is saying in "mime," a classical mime that equates the "visionary" with the son of Mary.

[9] *Home*. Airborne out of Havana, André withdraws the little green notebook from Juanita and reads on its title page her inscription signed to him with love. Again, no particular reaction. Stafford is notably less expressive than Hitchcock's many other leading men, a functionary, a switch puller. We have to watch the actions in which he is involved, not his handsome figure in involvement. His finger is haphazardly sliding back and forth over the front endpaper, where now he feels something: a final trace of Juanita de Cordoba. He rises, walks back to the toilet, locks himself in, delicately moistens and carefully pries back the endpaper. Waiting there . . . Thomas's film. (The razor-blade injector was invented as a ruse.) This clandestine film is of course utterly silent, but once it has found its correct home it will speak volumes, becoming the *fact* (the repository of fact) that turns the tide on the missile crisis, giving Kennedy the ammunition he needs (!) to frighten off Khrushchev and his now-visible missiles. Kusenov has led Mike into the dirty work of asking André to ask Juanita to ask the Mendozas to ask Thomas to get something for John F. Kennedy, supreme aristocrat, who will now appear triumphant. The plane ride as we see it is quiet, even beautiful, composed in beiges and golds and delicate shadow. It could easily give us the restful impression that the chase has been resolved, and indeed we have every reason to think that the long chain of torturous events, all the way from marching soldiers in Red Square and the fleeing Kusenovs to Cuba, has come to its end. The secret film finding its way home, we will be able to back away.

But:

HOMEWARD BOUND

Entertaining Mike back in Bethesda, where a chilly vacancy blares Nicole's absence, André is interrupted by his contact at the French embassy who now complains that his Cuban mess has made waves in Paris. He is to return immediately, tonight. (Now he is a material that must find its way home.)

Before the City of Light, however, Mike wants André to make a stop in Maryland. Come to the safe house and hear with your own ears a revelation Kusenov has been offering while you were in Cuba: "I want you to listen to him before you face those people over there," before, that is, you show your face to, and look at the face of, the baroque Parisian bureaucracy. Russia-Paris again, the deep puzzle reinvoked and still unexamined.

A decorous little moment at the safe house. Four men (Kusenov, Devereaux, Nordstrom, and his boss McKittreck [Edmon Ryan]) are couched in what resembles a mid-twentieth-century Mayfair sitting room done up American style, an ornate coffee table and service between their knees. Juanita's mansion was by far the more modern, architected by a name, no doubt, the more capacious, and airy. This place is all upholstery, oil paintings, crystal, and bone china. We have Kusenov's minder-now-chum Mrs. Forsyth serving the coffee. "Mrs. Forsyth makes wonderful coffee!"[24] Kusenov is feeling at ease, even a little masterly, with a handsome cigar and a soothed, even amicable manner:

> KUSENOV (to André): These gentlemen have asked me to repeat to you about Topaz. Why?!
>
> MCKITTRECK (holding his cup and saucer in the air): Please, uh ... do us a favor... tell him what you told us.
>
> KUSENOV (eyeing André): Then you have succeeded in getting them the information from Cuba! *André looks to Mike; Mike gives a nod.*
>
> ANDRÉ (nodding): Yes.
>
> KUSENOV (to André): And now they are afraid that you will be obliged to pass it on to your government...

That is, the CIA is afraid that André will be called upon to allow the French government vision of (their) evidence of what the Russians are doing in

Cuba. France is an ally of the United States, after all. But it may not be apparent yet why the French government would benefit from seeing this evidence, or why the CIA might reasonably be wary to share it.

> ANDRÉ: And, uh... what is Topaz?

What is Topaz, indeed! This oblique thing, mentioned now several times, not to say the main title of this motion picture, yet we know nothing of it nor, more importantly, why we should wish to know. What is this thing that it could be connected to the Russians in Cuba, to the United States, to André, to anybody? Hitchcock has worked to be especially secretive about Topaz, and it is possibly at this moment that his audience comes to recognize that fact, and to wonder about a structure in this film far more deeply buried than Rico Parra with his cigar. Perhaps about this Hitchcock has been even more than especially secretive, even charged with silence.

> KUSENOV (professing again): Topaz is a code name for a group of French officials in high circles who work for the Soviet Union.
>
> ANDRÉ (looking dubiously at Mike and McKittreck): I don't believe there is an organized ring.
>
> KUSENOV (ultra-professorial): The head of the ring has a code name, Columbine. I do not know him but I know he is important and powerful. The second man in line is Henri Jarré.
>
> ANDRÉ (astonished): Jarré!
>
> KUSENOV: Yes! Henri Jarré. He was my direct contact. Any vital documents that passed across his desk came to me.
>
> MIKE: Do you know him, André?
>
> ANDRÉ: Yes. He's an economist at NATO.
>
> McKITTRECK: Do you know him *well*?
>
> ANDRÉ: Yes.
>
> MIKE: And it is believable?

ANDRÉ: It's... possible.

KUSENOV: It's more than possible. *Raising his cup as in a toast.* It's true.

Pronounced *tree-oo*.

This gush from taciturn tight-lipped Kusenov with the graceful spout of the Sterling silver coffee pot jutting up in front of him and a rosy afternoon light behind—opulence, tranquility, the peace of mind in which those with a philosophical bent can sit over their beverage and explore a thought. The mantlepiece, upon which André is leaning, is covered with small, gaily painted Revolutionary War figurines. "Our government is prepared to take any action against Cuba, or Russia, that circumstances demand," announces McKittreck, his arm extended casually upon the back of the sofa. "Any leak to the Russians of what we know at this time could be fatal." Mike fills in the silent lacuna: "The Russians could make those missiles operational, pointed at every big city in America."

Someone in Paris could help attack America! Now!

America will be informing Paris officially in three days. Meanwhile, André has seventy-two hours to uncover Topaz, at the "risk of my own skin." The cloak of silence is now lifted from André Devereaux and his nationality. There is a leak in the pipeline, a Parisian leak, but Parisians will take seriously only other Parisians. (The Parisian can love the American without taking him seriously.) André must plug the leak. André *le campagnard*.

In the duration of a cut, invisibly, André is being chauffeured from Orly by Michele and François, after a seven-hour flight delay. They are rushing him to a cocktail party he wanted very much to attend. "Mother will be there. Will you speak to her?"

"Of course I will speak to her. She left me. I didn't leave her."

A sumptuous, ornate residence (on what would likely be the Right Bank: one easily imagines the Avenue Foch). Jacques Granville, the host here (Michel Piccoli), is a monied man, with another house on the Côte d'Azur and a third in Switzerland. Uncountable twinkling bulbs in crystal chandeliers and wall sconces, pleasing powder blue walls with rich snow-white mouldings up and down, wallpaper by Zoffany, somber guests in business attire. In a glamorous gown (the color of a topaz!), Nicole is rapt in conversation but looks up and freezes as she sees André. Diamonds twinkle on her ears. Each knows the formalities, and the importance of performing them:

NICOLE (sweetly): I'm sorry you have been recalled.

ANDRÉ: It is not the way you meant for me to come to Paris.

NICOLE (half-smile): No.

ANDRÉ (straightforward): Hello, Nicole.

NICOLE (genuine smile): Hello! *They kiss each other's cheeks tenderly.*

While André is chummily waylaid by the fabulously successful Jacques, Michele whispers aside to her mother, "He's in terrible trouble!" But Nicole keeps cool: "There's nothing I can do." This moment is a miniature show of a broader doubling: on which side does Michele stand, André's or Nicole's? A hall of mirrors, this film, with doublings everywhere, without end. Jacques would very much like André to confess the fool he has been. "You've raised a hell of a fuss, you know!"

Another guest steps up, the rather sanguine Claude Martin (John Van Dreelen), playfully asking André if he has been having an affair with the Americans, to which comes the staid reply, "It was purely Platonic." It is hardly difficult to catch the undertone of the *affaire de coeur:* that, typically French, André is not above *la recherche de la femme perdue.* But beneath that undertone is another undertone: that here in Paris it is *known* that he "has been having an affair in Cuba." Affection, loyalty, even lust, perhaps, and *extrêmement typique,* but was there something deeper and more involving? Was André linking through Juanita to the Russian secret, and possessing the Russian secret to serve the CIA? Someone high up in Paris is more than miffed that André's information is not coming to them directly. "You're in trouble," says Martin, "You want me to help you."

The invocation of the word *affaire* may help us recollect Mike as a loner. No wife, no girlfriend, nobody. Only, if you will, André. America operating on the world stage without much confidence, and man to man.

André wonders if Claude and Jacques could arrange a small private luncheon tomorrow. Jean Chabrier. Émile Renault. And Henri Jarré.

CLAUDE: Jarré—You know him well?

ANDRÉ: Yes. And I respect him.

Meanwhile, social butterflies thrilled to attend a real gathering of the French elite, we spy a tête-à-tête as Jacques confesses to Claude how sad it was that Nicole left her husband. We've been together, the three of us, since the war, he adds. "People wondered which she would marry, André or me. She married André." A gentleman who has never relinquished a much earlier dream of happiness, and a staunch friend of the couple. Or else: Jacques cached inside the Devereaux palace. *We've been together since the war.* And *people wondered whether she'd marry André or me.* Was Nicole ping-ponging, one lover before the other—or both simultaneously, in a cute *ménage?* Our only snatch of backstory for Nicole Devereaux, the most thoroughgoingly authentic French person we know here. Beyond this snatch, silence.

Lunch the next day, *Pierre*. This is a Michelin-recommended and rather old establishment in the Palais Royal (residence of Philippe, brother to Louis XIV), where our little party may devour *Foie gras en terrine* or *Boeuf à la ficelle*. Private upstairs wood-paneled dining room containing a lovely arched window. Chabrier (Roger Til) is a somewhat gaunt and anxious one, he wants to make it explicit that nobody up high is to know that they are in this room with André (André the reprobate, André the CIA's man, André who has not had the courtesy to see the Directeur-général, a matter of protocol. *André prodigue*).

Jarré (Philippe Noiret) arrives in good spirits, taking André's hand warmly with his left since with his right he must handle an aluminum cane. When they sit, Jacques introduces André's problem and his need for advice before he confronts the board of inquiry that will demand a full report of his activities working on the Americans' behalf. The punchline: it is true he procured information for them, gentlemen, but he cannot share it with his own government (read, with us) *because there is a leak*. The cloister of diplomatic secrecy is mimicked by this lunch in the private dining room.

Chabrier leaps up in outrage, but while he is calmed by Jacques— "Slowly, slowly, let André tell us in his own way"—André peeks down the table at Jarré, who is serenely sipping his wine. Too serenely, if there really is a leaker, possibly dining in this room.

André pops the question. "Have any of you in your official work had any hint of a spy ring called Topaz?" Looks of suspicion, disturbance, fear, awkwardness around the table. A spy ring, here in Paris? In *our* circle?!!! With another peek André sees Jarré calmly chewing and having more wine. "A number of officials... working for the Soviet Union."

Again Chabrier jumps up, but "Jean! Sit down! I need you!"

Claude desires calmness, efficiency, clarity above all things, "What is the name of the defector?" since it can only be by way of a defector to America that such a spy ring could have become known, and also since (as we know) it has become evident in Paris that there is a defector, though obviously no more than that.

"Boris... Kusenov."

Jarré leans over with eyes wide open. "But André—that is not possible! The KGB official of whom you speak, Boris Kusenov, has been dead for over a year." Pressing a morsel of baguette into his mouth, "This man who has been planted on the Americans is obviously a double agent. And he has taken in the Americans. And he has taken in you." In French films, there is a characteristic enthusiasm with which the authentic *Français* chews his morsel of bread, and for this signal moment Philippe Noiret, long practiced at film acting in France, gives a summary performance. We can taste the baguette by way of which he tells us that Kusenov is not Kusenov. Are we shocked? Jarré chews calmly.

The man has now stood with some difficulty and limped over to the sideboard to help himself to more food, puckish Hitchcock rubbing it in that we are trapped in cinema seats and unable to eat at *Pierre*. André's face is cloaked in doubt. "How do you know that? What makes you think that?"

Jarré: "It's a matter of record. I have it in my file!"

Now we are outside an apartment block on the Left. Jarré limps into a taxi that brings him to the very tiny Passage de la Visitation in the 7th arrondissement, a half-mews at the end of a half-block, perfect hideway. Here is a line of quintessential pieds-à-terre, at one of which he rings the bell to have the door opened by... Jacques Granville.

The CIA mansion in Maryland... the Cordoba mansion in Cuba... the ritzy pied-à-terre in Paris... The film may have seemed to center upon Cuban happenings, but the resolution is occurring in France.

INFORMATION

Jacques paces around in a brilliant scarlet robe, posing in front of arranged white carnations and smoking a substantial cigar (a Cuban cigar, no doubt). Jarré's anxiety—we should get rid of André!—must be tranquilized; Granville seems the perfect therapist. No "final solution" just yet, though Jarré presses for one. After a brief cognac, a polite inquiry about an interview Jarré has promised to give a reporter about NATO. Then the door, *mon cher*, because "I am expecting someone." As Jarré limps away, a scarlet taxi passes him, disgorging a super-chic Nicole Devereaux who, as departing Jarré cannot avoid noticing, bubbles with delight to be in Granville's arms: "I am a free woman!" (Nicole with André and Mike at dinner... Nicole at the St. Regis... Nicole on the staircase... Nicole at Granville's party... Nicole now: the briefest of glimpses in every case.)

It is night. Bounding up the interior limestone stairway to Jarré's apartment is the journalist to whom he promised the interview: François Picard, trusty sketch pad in hand. That sketch pad: in Hitchcock one sees again and again an object in one place at one time, and then much later, as though on legs of its own, the same, or a matching object making a curtain call. François will sketch Jarré as they talk about NATO's internal structure, while Jarré gives off a gracious smile, then a little hesitant frown, then the gracious smile again: trying on masks. "You have access to all decisions that are made, military as well as political." A cold look from Jarré: "I did *not* say that." But François is on the hunt for a traitor, not information about NATO, and he's the son-in-law of indomitable André and Nicole Devereaux: "We can assume, can't we, that in your position you have access to confidential files?"

JARRÉ : I don't see how that can be of interest to you.

FRANÇOIS: Ohhhhh, Monsieur Jarré! The readers of our newspaper find such things... fascinating! For them, to know that a civilian like you can have access to military secrets—

JARRÉ : You cannot print... that I have access to military secrets.

FRANÇOIS (converted into a terrier): It is a rule for a journalist not to be dull. Surely I can print that files marked TOP SECRET cross your desk every day.

JARRÉ (calmed): Why do you stay on this subject? What are you trying to find out?

FRANÇOIS: Well, everyone knows that there are leaks in NATO.

JARRÉ (fierce): What. Has. That. To do. With me?

FRANÇOIS (huge smile): I'm just trying to clear up a discrepancy for my article.

JARRÉ: What... discrepancy?

FRANÇOIS: Well, you see, sir, it is our information that the Head of the Russian NATO desk, Boris Kusenov, has defected and he's now in Washington. But we are also informed that you claim Boris Kusenov is dead. Could you clear up this discrepancy?

François has been holding his slender pencil vertically, a pendulum, or a stiletto; Jarré has his much bigger, heftier cane. From the side we see Jarré pensively pull open a drawer in his desk, sternly consider the contents, then slowly push it closed. Taking cane to hand he rises, limps around the desk, paces behind François in total silence, and removes to the other side of the long room.

JARRÉ: This is not a newspaper interview.

FRANÇOIS (brave and brash): No, but I wouldn't mind publishing it.

JARRÉ: Who sent you?

FRANÇOIS: My father-in-law.

JARRÉ: Who is he?

FRANÇOIS: André Devereaux.

JARRÉ (giving a little nod): He sent you because I don't know you...

FRANÇOIS: And because I'm a journalist. I can probe.

JARRÉ (with definition): There is nothing to probe for. Your mission has failed.

FRANÇOIS (his voice gaining a kind of broadcast power): Oh no, sir. This cannot be escaped. Boris Kusenov is alive and has stated you were his direct contact. The Americans have NATO documents that you gave to him. With your name on them. Your initials on them. Even notations, signed by you. (*Jarré has dropped his head in despondency.*) Those documents can be on the desk of the head of our government in eight hours. I do not think I have failed.

JARRÉ : What do you want of me?

FRANÇOIS: Information.

JARRÉ : And in return?

FRANÇOIS: You'll be given time to disappear.

Jarré proudly lifts his head then drops his chin in cogitation. He takes a chair and fingers his shiny aluminum cane. "I'm not going to talk to you."

We float in toward his pensive face. He will talk to Devereaux, only. "I'll talk to him here. Alone."

As François dials to inform André, two men enter the Jarré apartment, and leaping to André at his end of the line we hear the conversation suddenly cut off. André races with Michele to Jarré's place. In a double-speed recapitulation they mount that same stone staircase. The apartment door is open. All André can find is the sketch pad, in which there is a splendid—and splendidly equivocal—head of Jarré in pencil. (Pencil as guillotine.) But out a window Michele has seen the body of her husband splayed across the top of a car in the courtyard below. "I want to go down! I want to go down!" At triple speed they tear down the staircase until at the vehicle itself André can take the victim's head in his hands and turn it so that we can see the face. It is Jarré. Because of the precise camera angle, and the black suit on the body, and the almost black hair, the head looks as though decapitated.

Now, Nicole's ultra-pink Parisian apartment. The doorbell is violently ringing. André and a teary Michele rush in. François has disappeared. "He went to do a job for me." Distraught Nicole falls into her husband's arms and François appears on the scene as if by magic. He has been shot in the arm, and he wants a drink. André gives him a snifter of cognac, just as Granville gave Jarré. Bad cognac to energize evil; good cognac to cure the honest and sincere.

ANDRÉ: I must have shaken Jarré at that lunch.

FRANÇOIS: Then Columbine must have been there, too.

The assumption being that Jarré's murder was ordered by his superior, as a safety measure.

ANDRÉ: Yes. But who?

Here is a structural echo of the much discussed "reveal" scene in *Vertigo*, often thought a "too early" giveaway. We are placed ahead of André, knowing by now, because we visited that pied-à-terre, what he must strive to learn later. The fact that the pulsion of the film is in no way slowed or interrupted by this foreknowledge of ours might cause us to wonder if finding Columbine, and then Topaz, is really the issue at hand here.

A HARVEST OF DETAILS

On the story's surface informational tidbits are being dropped with exquisite precision; we both assemble puzzle pieces and watch ourselves doing so. Many (a) questions to which we may frame (b) answers.

Questions:

(1-a) Why must Granville be wearing a robe when Jarré visits, and why is it scarlet?

(2-a) Why must Granville have vases of flowers in clear evidence, flowers in one sense more alive and in another sense less alive than the ones we saw at Royal Copenhagen?

(3-a) Why are François' report of his interview with Jarré—a sketch—and the revelation of Jarré's corpse handled in terms of decapitation?

(4-a) Why is Nicole's Parisian apartment pink?

(5-a) Why is it François' *left* arm that has been shot?

(6-a) And why did Devereaux send his son-in-law to do his dirty work?

Speculations:

(1-b) *The robe.* It is the late 1960s and Jacques Granville is a man of considerable means and taste. To be at home and receiving *une amie* is no casual trifle (nor was Hitchcock ever a man for casual dress on his own part or that of any person working on his set; jackets and ties for the men). Jacques will have a house robe and it will be sumptuous in its way. *Must it be scarlet?* If a somewhat proud man, who (i) deceiving his country and (ii) pleased with his successes so far, wishes to make an announcement, indeed to only the very rarefied audience who will find him in his pied-à-terre (we saw his more regal, glittery city residence [on the Right Bank] earlier), why not boldly? Red for passion, when *she* will be at the door. Red for a silent courage Jacques' calmness has hidden. Hitchcock understands a particular problem for actors: that conveying inner states such as excitement or eagerness requires a visible signal, something like a red robe.

It should go without saying that Granville's somewhat cumbersome confederate Henri Jarré (civilian, not really governmental) is hardly the person Jacques expects to see when that doorbell rings: red to accentuate surprise. Jarré's presence is not only unannounced and unbidden but against the "rules": he is never to meet Granville there unless summoned. Apology, but this will have to be swift. Cognac is poured liberally, red cognac.

- Red cognac drunk in private, by associates of the officials watching that parade on Red Square.

- But this little apartment partakes of *le décor* (as the powder blue walls and snow-white plasterwork in the Granville home whispered earlier). Pristine cleanliness. On the walls only sufficient pictures in pleasing frames that a person cogitating would require for easeful distraction (lighting his cigar Jacques poses in front of a Guardi). Not one but two vases of flowers, sparkling white carnations and some soothing yellow roses. The *cul-de-sac* itself is both fabulously enchanting and wholly hidden away, so that robed Granville is in a secret lair where he can play out his intimate silences official and unofficial. Perhaps in scarlet he is a dandy, with sensibilities dating back to the nineteenth century when cinema was invented and the avenues of Paris bristled with grandes dames and gentlemen of importance. If Jacques is a Baudelairean dandy, he has elevated his aesthetics as his religion, and we can see that all of the art of his commitment and secret action is undertaken and enunciated in dedicated fervor, as though no...other...life...were...possible. He has stance; he has dress. Michel Piccoli adopts a languid way of speaking, utter relaxation in the face of the abyss. Jacques secretly triumphs over Devereaux in having Nicole secure in his arms. How long has his little *tête-à-tête* with her been going on, anyway? Very soon, at Nicole's apartment, we will see a photograph of her with Jacques and André from long ago, dressed as French Underground with Jacques bearing a rifle. All the way back to the war? Back to another silent secrecy...

- Does Nicole know who Jacques really is? When André and Michele come bursting into her apartment, a man and his child entering the pink enclosure, with duteous François on their tail; and when François tells how he was shot, the blood goes out of her face: "You could have been killed!" Is her cognition of things "like this" coming only from her long reconnaissance of André's activities, or is she getting briefings from Jacques? Jacques, whose red passion is worn on his sleeve.

- If the scarlet robe is not central in the dramatic action it is optically magnetic, a part of Granville's body. It goes where he goes, poses where he poses.

(2-b) *The vases of flowers.* Jarré utters not one syllable about Jacques' flowers, doesn't even nod. They cannot be for him, so for whom might they be? But then, what silent, buried, thrilling ectoplasmic impulse can he be feeling in this little house; in coming here at all; in proposing to Jacques so carnal a thought as that they terminate André; in having as his "find" of the moment Jacques Granville's peculiar intimacy? Because for us there is no missing Jacques Granville's intimacy. Does Jarré bring himself here because that intimacy is what he truly desires, espionage aside? When on the street outside he swivels to exchange glances with Jacques' unnamed guest, is he showing the kind of possessiveness, just a little, that Nicole showed in clinging to André in the presence of seductive Mike? Any Hitchcockian work is made up of overlapping nuances like these, hinted at only vaguely in the pictorial context, never openly declared: hinted in an actor's performance; announced by some fillip of décor, in some angle of view or street location or the color of the sky or of flowers. "Intimacy," sing the flowers.

- And how would this Granville-Jarré scene have played out (with these two giants of twentieth-century French film performance playing *ensemble*) had there been no flowers? The space would have been dampened and flattened. The cognac would have seemed abrupt and terminal. Totally and only a business meeting, this. Perfunctory. Dry. But how to integrate so cozy a place into the vision? With flowers there lingers an undertone that keeps silence until it can "sound" whenever Granville steps in the direction of a vase. "Decorated, dressed up, showing form!" the flowers say, and we are quickly offered opportunity to remember how much décor was "speaking" at the Granville house when André first got to Paris. As Michele informed her father at the door there, Jacques made a real success of himself: that is, he is not a man who was born to the money he has now but one who found a way to amass it. The flowers are not natural to him, they are show.

- Also: if Jacques has long been depressed because Nicole did not marry him, he has gracefully covered it.

(3-b) *"Decapitation."* Not one or two but three intimations of decapitation indicate possible or actual punishment for arrogant Jarré. While he asks Jarré compromising and challenging "questions," François sits serenely relaxed with his pencil dangling gracefully from one hand: a "blade" and a head. Soon later we see François' sketch in André's hands: a head-and-shoulders portrait distinctly emphasizing the head. For François, Jarré *is* this head, calculating and treacherous: Guy Davenport notes how the heroic spirit survives in our time as intelligence. "The head as fate takes on new meaning, not as the ancient seat of a noble nature and a stoic rectitude of behavior, but as cunning and intellectual sharpness" (*Objects* 33).

- Then, down in the courtyard, the exact way André takes that head in hand to verify whose it is, and the sense that the thing itself, streaming with blood, is independent of the dark body that recedes from our eye. The short-focus shot helps inordinately.

- But why decapitate Jarré? To clarify that he is committing a capital crime. If he is caught and found guilty the guillotine would be his destination. French society is more than brilliance and gauze. Too, the Jarré head makes us gaze more intentfully at all the heads in this film. François' earlier sketch of Uribe was preface.

(4-b) *The pink apartment.* Nicole's blush-pink apartment perfectly sets off the healthy, invigorated, even stimulated blush of her skin, here in the city that is her home. She is epitomized here. DC was never her place, never the hearth of her commitment. There things were green. Pink vigor will help keep up François' spirits, too, as with his bloody arm (a recapitulation of Señora Mendoza's bloody arm by the roadside) he sips his cognac; he will be in the pink just as Michele is in the pink to see him and as Nicole is in the pink to have her anxieties relieved. In this luscious pink place, only pedestrian André is not in the pink.

(5-b) *A grazed left arm.* Fate has entered the frame. While François will be in a sling he will still draw as notably as before, since he works with his right hand. In two senses, then, François has *only* been grazed. First, the bullet is not inside him, he will heal; and his talent has not been impaired. Jarré also had a strong right arm, with which he kept himself from falling down until, with no cane in sight, he did fall, all the way down. How can this small focus, François' arm, have importance in the context of an analysis of the film? It signals the ability to keep going with one's images, a little recursion of Hitchcock's. Dramaturgically: what happens to this scene, and to the film, if our François sustains a very serious injury, this beloved husband of charming Michele, beloved daughter of one of our heroes and a very intriguing woman? Serious attention is drawn to François, and the film has to lean his way. But François is in the picture only as a factotum to help André help Mike: it is his drawing we care about. This isn't a play toward viewer callousness, it's a vital aspect of Hitchcock's way of drawing and maintaining focus, within a field that is deeply and unremittingly interesting, and in every direction potentially distracting if we aren't somehow oriented and held.

- The problem is establishing and balancing *character weight*, the scenic value of every character balanced against that of others, value being the character's call upon our attention. Hitchcock has already been establishing relative weights, and extends them in line with arcs of development already initiated and planned. He is controlling the viewer's attachment and concern, working to avoid a moment in which viewers' concern could slip out of his preferred alignment. François is a very nice fellow, but we aren't to be watching him instead of watching Jarré, for example, or watching André. François is a charmer, but we must not miss something André is doing because we've concentrated on François instead. Even remembering to confide a telephone number he heard from his attackers, Babylon 8583, he is less central than André, or Nicole, down whose face tears are streaming, because she recognizes it: Jacques Granville. "Horrible! Horrible!!"

(6-b) *Dirty work.* In light of the aristocrat's not being obliged to work, Tom Conley remarked to me that any actions he commits spring from his desire to contribute, in effect his generosity; in that way André Devereaux looks consistently aristocratic, nothing but generous with his labor. If it is out of the generosity of his spirit that he gives labor, its "cleanliness" or "dirtiness" will be both irrelevant to and unnoticed by him. Nicole's aversion to "dirty work," and her desire that her husband should eschew it, reflects her concern for embarrassment. This would be one manifestation of the anthropologist Mary Douglas's "purity rule," in which "unintended or irrelevant organic processes should be screened out" of normal social intercourse (*Symbols* 80–81): André is coming into contact with the wrong substances. Or we could consider Douglas's observation in *Purity and Danger* that in some cultures women were obliged to clean their husbands after sexual intercourse and then clean themselves before touching food; if Nicole thinks or understands cultural obligations this way, she may regard André's doing dirty work a gender slippage, an act of "going to bed," as it were, with the Americans—whom she epitomizes in the figure of Nordstrom. More to follow on this, more dishing of dirt, shoveling dirt, sharing the dirt, discovering what's the dirt, seeing who might have some dirt on someone else. Think of dirt as the darkest fact, in this case the one that will bring on nuclear war.

CURTAIN

Let me ring down a curtain by observing that my reading of the film so far is fairly conventional. I believe such a reading is incomplete. Tested through a crisis, America emerges victorious. Yes, but. . . . If one takes the *target* of espionage—here, The Great Russian Secret—as the subject of entertainment, one fails to catch at the most chilling aspect of the espionage system, namely, its posing an expressive puppet show upon a cavern of dark and impenetrable silence. If we were to think of the film in terms of *what is not given*, the centrality becomes perduring secrecy, a hush riding beneath the show of bravery, daring, danger, and thrill. There is a truth *Topaz* does *not* express. In Hitchcock's work, then, however explicit the imagery, the expository analysis that attends to what is revealed to be happening onscreen and to the chaining of such happenings will not yield as rich a lode as an approach based in what is not said.

Here, then, a wholly different reading of Alfred Hitchcock's Cuban missile crisis, a reading pointed at the strange bifurcation of the film, that after the Cuban escapade the missile crisis business seems virtually completed and yet we progress to Paris and the lingering, itching question of a French traitor. How might these two movements be unified, how might they cohere?

Suppose the following, all of it wholly possible, rather like a carefully shaped lacuna, or silhouette, around which the delicate edges of the construction have placed themselves both without pointing-at and without pointing-away:

[A] The Kusenov defection is actually false, just as Jarré pronounces, notwithstanding that he may not really know this, and may be only bluffing or jesting; false, but not in the way many of us may have predicted. Kusenov *is* Kusenov, and his "defection" *is* a defection, but the puzzle into which it fits as an integral part is not the puzzle so many who have watched this film believe. Take it that the man is a working agent of the Russian government, always was, and continues to be "to this day," and that everything he does in America he does on assignment. Therefore,

[B] The Americans and their ally, their *allié amical*, André Devereaux being set on the trail of Uribe, and thence on the trail to Cuba to find the "secret gifts"—all a result of Kusenov's engineering—are to serve a plan of which the Americans are entirely unaware and thus of which they are entirely unsuspicious. Center on those Russian ships and their lethal cargo, the *thing* at the center here, and note that:

[C] No evidence is ever presented that the as-yet unloaded Russian ICBMs are in fact loaded with nuclear warheads; the word "warhead" doesn't come up near the pier; the ships docked provocatively in Cuba are part of a drama being staged by Nikita S. Khrushchev through his puppet Kusenov (a matching K). By way of, and then resulting from this secret plan, this elaborate silence,

[D] President Kennedy is *intended* to do precisely what he does do: "discover" the missiles through his own spy apparatus, then as a consequence threaten precisely the kind of action he does threaten; and finally see, with a trademark Kennedy smile of success, the Russians pulling back (tails between legs). Thus he *wins* this particular Cold War faceoff (undoubtedly uncorking some champagne...). A significant triumph, one that gives off a sign, because he was intended to be a winner all along and the withdrawal of ships from Cuba is a marquee sign of his victory, glowing to the world. All this to what conceivable end?

[E] To the end that Kennedy's victory will make it appear, to him, his advisors, his cabinet, his Senate and Congress, and the world, certainly to America, that "The Americans" are stronger than "The Russians." A tour-de-force demonstration of American strength, vitality, reliability, and power. Americans will surely then come to feel with certainty that they are superior. And in this way the United States will have been lured into an entirely spurious sense of "military superiority."

[F] The Cuban government, namely Fidel Castro (here represented by Rico Parra), must be lured into this plan, they are crucial supporting players, since the idea of launching against the USA from an island so close by is central to the choreography of the Kremlin's "threat." And here we have a bribe (of some undisclosed sort) paid out by Moscow to Havana, some "gift" nestled in Castro's back pocket. Kusenov's phrase "gifts from the Russian people" is the giveaway. In Soviet Russia, the word *gifts* (*podarki*) is code for *bribes* (*vzyatki*). "Gifts" are given all over the place, in order that routine business can be done. The ships and/or missiles that Kusenov calls "gifts" aren't gifts themselves, as he suggests, but stand-ins for the real gifts that Khrushchev is giving, in silence and behind the scenes, to Castro (and Parra and comrades) to go along with the missile ploy. Go along by not questioning, by not inspecting, by basically lying back. The Cubans are paid supporting actors. But there is more:

[G] Kusenov himself is, less than an actor, an agent, as in, even, a theatrical agent. He is not in charge of the show he moves in. Whoever is in charge of the show wants more than to play the missile card. Even more pressing is opening the CIA's attention to the secret cabal in Paris, specifically to Columbine, who will now, as per this secret Russian elaboration, this final draft of a script, be ferreted out along with his clumsy helper Jarré, and this in an especially tidy way: Jarré will be dead; Granville's fate will be in train. Who was Jacques Granville, after all, but a Russian agent who wormed his way into intimacy with André and Nicole, "fell in love with" and almost married her? A decent placement for a Russian agent wanting access to insider American knowledge by way of their favorite French intermediaries. Yet there are perhaps too many unstable links to this chain of arrangements.

[H] What if Nicole Devereaux is not one of the dupes here, not a svelte attachment to her puissant husband, but the Russian agent in charge? During the war Granville did not approach her, she approached him. This current subterfuge stands upon a foundation laid many years ago—we must ask ourselves why Hitchcock should have felt it necessary to include reference to the war (presumably the war in Algeria or the Second World War) in a contemporary story. She planted seeds of love in Jacques, either love or "love," she cultivated them, and later she lured him with a promise of André's pillow talk, only the most saccharine phrases of which she actually delivered. Jacques thinks he is a Russian plant, and he is, but again, not in the way he supposes; he doesn't work for minders in Moscow, he works for Nicole, who works for *other* minders in Moscow. (Again, the film artfully dances around all these possibilities.) The Kusenov "defection," that was designed to turn the spotlight on Granville by way of his flunky Jarré: her plan all along. He was never her love object. Or, he *was* her love object once, but Nicole thinks of love as a weapon.

[I] No one will even dream of surmising that Russian Intelligence ran so complicated and secret an affair, in effect an affair-within-an-affair.[25] The missile crisis will nicely focus attention on "missiles"; and "missiles" will distract attention from a personnel maneuver.

[J] In the end, a Russian agent will be comfortably nestling near America's forebrain. Her problematic underlings in France will have been tidily eliminated. In Bethesda she will now have almost direct access to the CIA.

Beyond that there is no definite clue in *Topaz* to bear out my choreography of this dance and Nicole's role as prima ballerina—and here, I think, we come close to the heart of *Topaz*—in the espionage business, which is very closely related to Hitchcock's business making this film, the absence of clues, the silence, is not a sign of the presence of nothing. As we accept the value of silence we come closer to knowing espionage, the silence of international affairs, and Hitchcock's method. There are no certain clues in the film about this proposed plot but there are also no certain clues in the film about anything: about Kusenov, about Granville, about Devereaux, about "Topaz"... about any of those other lucky men who went to lunch. We find bodies, what Bill Krohn shows Hitchcock wanted to put forward (with Samuel Taylor's rather benign adaptation of Leon Uris's novel) as the horrible, brutal result of the Cold War; bodies, not explanations (270). This is not a film about a "terribly more terrible" spy caper. It is a film about how one doesn't really learn about spy capers, how there is more to the reality of things than meets the eye. *Topaz:* a lesson, too, that appeals to Hitchcock's sense of irony since of course in cinema everything meets the eye—everything, that is, except what doesn't meet the eye.

ENCORE: CLEAN-UP

An elaborate conference room somewhere, one easily presumes near the Elysée Palace, with French and American representatives ready to meet. Huge, gilded, fin-de-siècle and Louis XVI design combined to slay the attention. We gaze from near the ceiling, the diplomats down below in their self-protective huddles—except that Jacques is standing near the far doors more or less by himself. The Americans at the camera end confabulate—a silence from which no words pass our way. Nordstrom walks down to the other end and speaks to the French, "Gentlemen...," and another silence, this time even without lips moving. Then back to his people. Then back to the French. The camera is absolutely frozen in place. The camera is in a trance. A French official addresses Jacques in a sudden close-up, apologizing profusely and graciously, but... finally to break the silence, "The Americans would prefer that you are not present." No explanations, no decoration of tone. Jacques stiffly leaves.

And then a jump to one of three different endings!

[A] Hitchcock's favorite (see Krohn 270). A very complex duel between André and Jacques in an empty soccer stadium at break of dawn. Pistols awarded. Paces taken. As he points at André, we are given: (a) Jacques' grave, stone-cold face and the gun barrel directed right into the lens (slightly wide-angle to make it bulge)—homage to, but improvement on *The Great Train Robbery* (1903); then (b) a reverse shot showing his hand holding the gun pointing away (homage to *Spellbound* [1945]). At the critical moment, however, a rifleman hiding in the grandstand plugs Jacques in the back. André walks under the stands and meets Nicole briefly. A newspaper now, near the Arc de Triomphe, with a MISSILE CRISIS OVER headline, and over it, superimposed, the Mendozas posed in death, Jarré's head ditto, and Juanita's as André purses his lips on the plane. All this carnage!...

The cut was far too lengthy and so this ending had to be dropped.

[B] Or the "cynical" one (Krohn 270): Orly, a bright day. Flight to Washington. A few steps behind Nicole on the gangway (pathway to a better world) André sees not very far off, with remarkable focus, Jacques climbing up to another plane, Moscow bound. Jacques doffs his hat and smiles in the full truth of friendship: "Bon voyage!" Nicole scoffs. Then the newspaper, the headline, a man tossing the thing into a trash and walking away toward the Arc de Triomphe.

[C] Or: Jacques' pied-à-terre, early morning, exterior. The door is just closing. Three seconds later a gunshot. Then a cut to the newspaper. With the carnage montage from [A] above, this end was shown in the United States.

About Nicole Devereaux there is a great deal not to neglect:

When we see her in DC, decorous as she seems, there is a faraway cast in her eye, as though she isn't fully there. One could say she is dreamy, or restrained. Or calculating dance steps. When André *en famille* meets Mike at the St. Regis, and Nicole disappears with Michele, we know that François can, and probably will, tell her what his tête-à-tête with Mike and André was about, this handing over of his sketch of Uribe. Of what André will be up to in Cuba, and with whom, she certainly has a good idea. But does she know precise details? A pertinent question, of course, but one never knows in life or in narrative what details are in the ken of a person or a character. She could know much more than she lets on, either to her husband or his pal or for our delectation. She certainly does know enough to synchronize her flight to Paris with his being away, indeed with his being "on the job." As to Paris, how far back do Nicole Devereaux' connections there go, how varied are they, and at what level of society—or government—does she mix, have a history of mixing, have the talent and knowledge to mix? We know nothing. Indeed, it may seem alarming to realize how little we know about her, altogether. At Granville's cocktail party she appears a little shocked to see André arrive; or is it that she is surprised to see him arrive alive?[26] If she is at home in Granville's "court" and fully engaged, how did she come to be this way given that she has been, for some years, in DC?

The "romantic" Jacques-Nicole-André triad, confessed by Jacques to Claude: easy to apprehend it as a puzzle or a titillation (Truffaut's *Jules et Jim* dates from 1963), but was Nicole in fact very close to Jacques Granville once upon a time, and if she was, has she remained that way—we think we see when she visits him what the answer is, but what sort of liaison do they have in point of fact, after she tells him she is free? And what on earth does she truly mean by "free"? They most likely have sex (Hitchcock would not be showing it) and sex, after all, is a gateway. We are certainly not included in their conversation. Nicole catches sight of the departing Jarré; is she allowing the departing Jarré to see her? Or if this link is accidental (accidents happen), what could she be thinking that Jarré now wonders about her and her connection to his pal, the traitor? Does Jarré think, as we do, that it's only sex, or is he imagining something darker? And while it is perhaps convenient to accept Granville's power in Paris, power over Jarré, power over his lunch companions, could such acceptance block our view of another person's power, even power over him? He may have been Nicole's subordinate, or her equal, either way a person she schemes to eliminate. She facilitates a plan with Kusenov and the whole Cuban missile affair, that affair being but a charade established by Moscow with her in the captain's seat.

We can note that in the soccer stadium ending she is silently present, ostensibly out of fear for dear André's life but conceivably because the marksman was her employee. Perhaps she realizes (the look on her face shows possible realization) that keeping André alive and by her side in DC is the smartest move. In an alternate ending she is with André on the gangway at Orly, looking coolly at him looking coolly at Jacques (who will receive a welcome she has prepared in Moscow).

Since the duel in Paris was Hitchcock's preferred ending for *Topaz*, it is worthwhile to consider what would have played out for us there, had he been able to use it.

Jacques wants to shoot André dead (the close-up of his targeting eye makes that plain), this enemy who has been working with the Americans and who on the Americans' behalf has been dogging his tail. André will be dead and out of the picture. Meanwhile, the wife, Jacques' secret lover, will be all his, and her words, "I'm a free woman!" will come to have, at least for Jacques, luscious new meaning. He will continue at his position (his secret position) in Paris, and she will decorate his charming residences. So he thinks.

He will continue not to know what he already does not know: that she is likely his controller, and that she is "free" in a way he cannot imagine.

For his part André is willing enough to kill Jacques. The *topaz* business will be concluded, Columbine terminated just as Jarré was terminated, and he will be able to go back to America feeling successful, noble, and heroic. His wife will be with him, in at least the identity he knows how to recognize.

The duel fails because, I would argue, Nicole has made plans that it should. She loves neither Jacques nor André, but has come to live in the presence of both of them with some secret but genuine success. She knows Jacques is no slouch with a gun and that the likelihood is, if there's a shot, André will be killed. Her long game being to arrive in America with free access to André's world and a free line for communicating to Moscow, she would like to preserve him. Jacques will be outed in any event, his usefulness expired.

If it would give us comfort, we are still in a position to think that capable Mike Nordstrom will ferret Nicole out one day, sooner perhaps, or later. His every encounter with her, fabulously polite, even gallant, does not cure him of the need to squint some when he looks her way, or to dress himself in a smile. Does Mike trust Nicole? And does he truly trust the man to whom she is married?

It is very reasonable to imagine that Hitchcock would have put all these cards on the table, had not the film already become larger than Universal was willing to distribute. But what is most fascinating is the simplicity of the duel scene as scripted and, even more, as shot. How each gesture, each minuscule twitch, adds to the weight of each powerful moment, and how in sum, so very elegantly, and so tersely—a kind of musical cadence, no more—all the deeply buried tendrils of the film are brought to the surface, given place, and unified into a whole.

With the oh-so-summative newspaper headline, MISSILE CRISIS OVER, we may sigh with satisfaction that the fever of danger has passed. Or else, seeing this woman heading to Washington with a new strength we may wonder, at the edge of our seats, what's next.

○

What's next: the greatest silence of all.

NOTES

INTRODUCTION

1. In my *An Eye for Hitchcock* (41–43) there is a long discussion of this sequence.

2. My BFI monograph *The Man Who Knew Too Much* (1956) was published on the fiftieth anniversary of that film's release, in 2016, thus not so long ago. It mercifully saved me from feeling—as I would have, had it not existed—the utter compulsion to include it somewhere in these volumes (and in the process lose another masterpiece).

CHAPTER ONE

1. For use in the much-celebrated post-chickie-run confrontation scene of *Rebel Without a Cause* (1955).

2. On the drama of the everyday, see Erving Goffman's *The Presentation of Self in Everyday Life* and other works.

3. On Hitchcock as a wanderer, consider only the locations where he set (and traveled to shoot) his films. He makes analogy to himself in *North by Northwest,* having Vandamm (James Mason) list George Kaplan's itinerary.

4. A somewhat hilarious account is given by Ludwig Bemelmans of the participation of the husband of the decorator Elsie Mendl, in this film:

> Everybody prophesied a great future on the screen for Charles, and in a few days he had puffed himself into Churchillian Britishness. He pronounced everything the way a telephone operator does numbers. He walked about wearing the mantle of empire, and he spoke of his career at luncheon, cocktails, and dinner. (107)

On set he was given to wait in Bergman's dressing room and she rehearsed him: "She told him he was perfect."

5. Floating in the "alphabet soup" the benevolent Professor will mention to Roger at Midway Airport in *North by Northwest* (1959): it was cooking already in 1946.

6. With the ocean scene and road matted in.

7. See Assheton Gorton's comments about skirtings in my interview with him.

8. For a 1936 epitome of this judgmental type, similarly stern and forbidding but without the touch of evil, see Maria Ouspenskaya's Baroness Von Obersdorf in William Wyler's *Dodsworth*.

9. And see Ohler.

10. Hitchcock confiding to Truffaut:

> The producer said, "What in the name of goodness is that?"
>
> I said, "This is uranium; it's the thing they're going to make an atom bomb with."
>
> And he asked, "What atom bomb?"
>
> This, you must remember, was in 1944, a year before Hiroshima. I had only one clue. A writer friend of mine had told me that scientists were working on a secret project some place in New Mexico. It was so secret that once they went into the plant, they never emerged again. I was also aware that the Germans were conducting experiments with heavy water in Norway. So these clues brought me to the uranium MacGuffin. (168)

11. When he made *Topaz*, Hitchcock wanted "espionage with an emotional relationship," like *Notorious*, Patrick McGilligan reveals (685).

12. In *To Catch a Thief* (1955), Grant will wear a French striped *maillot* that vibrates optically in a similar way.

13. Reprised in the final shot of *The Birds* (1963) with a different enemy.

CHAPTER TWO

1. "Accompaniment" as in the simultaneous presentation of mutually regarding acts, what we find in a musical concert. See Moore.

2. *Suspicion* (1941) will begin with a postage stamp, too.

3. One is reminded of Curly Howard of The Three Stooges (who was in the group since 1932; suffered a stroke in 1946 and died in 1952).

4. In the 1930s, the twenty-four-hour clock was used in England militarily, not by civilians. Railways began it in 1964.

5. In a garble reminiscent of the lyrics to the Tramp's nonsense song in *Modern Times* (1936).

6. In regarding Hitchcock, it is easy, perhaps too easy, to take an early moment and "see" it in a direction or point of arrival the film itself doesn't make clear until much later; as though the film syntax can be separated from its accretion of meaning.

7. We are not given a way to tell whether these two are exemplifying typical English gentlemen or middle-class vacationers pumping themselves up in front of strangers.

8. In a reprise of Ginger Rogers's routine with tap-dancing Fred Astaire keeping her awake in *Top Hat* (1935).

9. Clearly one pair of pajamas has been washed. But critics who have been somewhat harsh about "gay villains" in Hitchcock have neglected the way Anna's (and our) presumption of homosexuality works to foil the men's stuffy priggishness about sexual matters (homosexuality is sexuality, after all) and thus the priggish stance of English people in general. Anna's smile of delight makes plain how if the two men are lovers the situation is nothing but entirely positive: she does not snigger or mock, though they are densely incapable of noticing, or of understanding her approval.

10. Straight out of *Nosferatu* (1922).

11. Note to the reader: I revised this little section in September 2021, several weeks after suffering a concussive head trauma myself, thus feeling somewhat sympathetic to dear Iris and the predicament Hitchcock prepares for her.

12. For North American readers, "test match" = "cricket game."

13. Hitchcock's elaboration of story *fragments* will be well developed in *Rear Window* (1954); see my *Dream*.

14. Not unlike a neon sign flashing in the night. See *The Lodger* (1927).

15. Concussive head traumas vary in their severity and duration and even with a medical examination, short of a brainscan (impossible under these conditions; the CT scan doesn't arrive until the 1970s) there is no way to know or predict their outcomes precisely.

16. I paraphrase Lermontov (Anton Walbrook) in *The Red Shoes*, as he comments upon Vicki Page's talent.

17. Gertrude Stein: "There's no there there."

18. The most often-cited case is *Vertigo*.

19. From the glare on the face we may recollect the glare of the jester in the artist's painting in *Blackmail* (1929).

20. For Redgrave an eerie premonition of his performance in *Goodbye, Mr. Chips* thirty-one years afterward.

21. In the decades that followed this film, and most surely after 2000, the doctor's words have been bluntly realized onscreen (by way of make-up effects); it is interesting that in 1938 spoken language alone could conjure the horror.

22. I had not, then, seen Josef Von Sternberg's *Dishonored* (1931), a film with which Hitchcock would surely have been familiar. A spy played by Marlene Dietrich attempts to cache a secret in a handwritten musical score, parts of which are played on the piano.

CHAPTER THREE

1. Of the likes of William Hitchcock, Alfred's father.

2. On cooking and Alfred Hitchcock, see Foery 58; Truffaut 320; and O'Connell and Bouzereau.

3. My thanks to Jason Jacobs for suggesting this link.

4. I am grateful to Alex Clayton for conferring on class in London.

5. *Stage Fright* surely bears intensive discussion, which I do not give here. I have treated it in some ways elsewhere (see "Plague").

6. Recollect the hardware-store scene in *Psycho*, where a customer wonders if there is a way to kill [insects] with no pain. That is, killing is one thing, hurting another.

7. The murders of women almost fifty years after the Hitchcock film (2019) still constituted a notably grave phenomenon: in Great Britain for each million of population, roughly four hundred; and if—just for rough estimation—we apply this rate to 1972, when there were ten million fewer inhabitants, we would find about three hundred and thirty killings that year. Femicides constitute about twenty percent of the murders in Great Britain today.

8. But with patience and sensibility. In 2019, Prof Mulvey noted this

early idea of hers as one with which she has subsequently "been saddled" as though it is all she ever had to say.

9. A condition not very far removed, I would propose, from Gaston Bachelard's observation of the child in regard to "fire"/knowledge—wanting to know more than the teacher knows.

10. *Monty Python's Flying Circus* began on the BBC in 1969 and appeared in North America first on the Canadian Broadcasting Corporation in the fall of 1970. Americans saw it as of September 1974.

11. Nor has it abated as I write in September 2021.

12. The local ethnocentrism, virulent at the common-man level, had also infiltrated the British banking system, where international trade was considered unthinkable, until the 1971–72 period when Barclay's and National Westminster began to think of becoming proper international banks. There were British firms that "frankly feared infection" (Kynaston, *Club No More* 450), but changes in (male-dominated) British banking did follow (British brokers operating as principals in North America) and were what David Kynaston calls "the beginning of the end for the old, ring-fenced order" (450). See *Club* 448ff.

13. The image of the ship at the end of Bernice Edgar's street in *Marnie* (1964) is based on the London docks area but does not represent it. The criminal coven in *The Man Who Knew Too Much* (1934) is in the East End, to be sure, but not Leytonstone.

14. On movement, traces, and detection in modernity see Gunning, "Tracing."

15. My thanks to Matthew Solomon for conversations about type.

16. Hitchcock may be nodding his father William's way: a fruit and grocery seller in Leytonstone, he would have been a shopper at Covent Garden.

17. Or at least the gaoler. The last hanging for murder in England was in 1969.

18. On moral entrepreneurs see Becker.

19. See *Hamlet*, III.2.116.

20. Reflecting charming Mrs. Cunningham (Norma Varden) in *Strangers on a Train* (1951).

21. "The [impotent] man almost always feels his sexual activity hampered by his respect for the woman and only develops full sexual potency when he

finds himself in the presence of a lower type of sexual object; ... his sexual aims ... he does not like to gratify with a woman he respects," writes Freud. "Full sexual satisfaction only comes when he can give himself up wholeheartedly to enjoyment, which with his well-brought-up wife, for instance, he does not venture to do. Hence comes his need for a less exalted sexual object, a woman ethically inferior, to whom he need ascribe no aesthetic misgivings, and who does not know the rest of his life and cannot criticize him" (*Sexuality* 54–55).

22. Note that what may seem the inherent logic of Chief Inspector Oxford's assessment is contradicted by a very close reading of the murder scene as played (and as I have discussed above). Hitchcock intends the logic here to be "police logic," which is to say, a kind of "mathematics" in which the numbers add up, albeit they are the wrong numbers. This trope of the erring detective is a very popular one (with this and other filmmakers) since well before *Frenzy*. The systematization of police labor produces professional preferences, as will happen in any regularized form of work, but the irony of police error is made piquant by the stringent outcomes it can produce.

23. Was Monica among the humble congregation at Ambrose Chapel?

24. To note: Rusk's sack is not as heavy and cumbersome as was the camera used for that retreat shot.

25. So in part were Hitchcock's parents.

26. John Reginald Halliday Christie (1899–1953), necrophilic serial killer (born the same year as Hitchcock), hanged at Pentonville.

27. A different use of the word "attraction" regarding cinema than one would find in Tom Gunning's analysis. See "Cinema."

28. The varying camera angles call up, more than the shower-scene design in *Psycho* (1960), Hitchcock's multi-angular deconstruction of the musical forces at play in the Albert Hall (*The Man Who Knew Too Much* [1956]).

29. My thanks to William Rothman for this canny observation.

CHAPTER FOUR

1. "Since the picture was to be shot on original locales, Hitchcock told [Robert] Burks at the very beginning that he did not want it to look arty in

any way. 'I want it to look like it had been photographed in New York in a style unmistakably documentary,' he said" (Foster 85).

2. Having used the E Train with great frequency in the decade after *The Wrong Man*, I can attest that no matter what time of day or night one rode, the cars were occupied by commuting workers, not tourists. The businesses of Manhattan work very substantially on labor that moves in from Queens and back out again, and most of these workers eschewed the automobile: Robert Caro notes that "postwar traffic congestion was congestion escalated to an entirely new level" (914).

3. The growth of opportunity in musical employment that followed the rock 'n' roll explosion of the 1950s and the continuing strength of jazz, not to say the various theatrical venues around the city where musicians were needed, did not necessarily mean more jobs *for more people*, since the cost of living was rising and the musician's take-home pay was for most not enough to preclude moonlighting. Manny has one job only, and the film details the financial constraints within which his family lives.

4. Walters's *High Society* (1956), with Grace Kelly, Bing Crosby, and Frank Sinatra, was a remake of *The Philadelphia Story* (1940).

5. Referring to an adjacent decade, and stunningly acerbic in its description of the workers' lives in high-class establishments, is George Orwell's *Down and Out in Paris and London* (1949).

6. I recall having been taught by the economist Kenneth Boulding what Pierre Teilhard de Chardin was referring to in his concept of the *nöosphere*, the "sum total of human knowledge." Yes, said Boulding, knowledge *and its artifacts*, such as the milkman's horse, who knows the route so well there is no need to use the reins at all and the creature will stop at every precise delivery point and then move on. As our milkman used a horse-drawn vehicle when I was a child, this example, unbeknownst to Boulding, struck home.

7. In middle-class families at the time, purely for entertainment people went "for a ride."

8. In 2022 dollars, as this is written, more than $437.00. For Manny a cup of coffee would have cost about 5 cents.

9. But when Manny was being questioned in real life I was in elementary school, and we were taught a uniform penmanship. "Make a capital-Q like this!..."

10. Billy Wilder will sell this line powerfully in *Some Like It Hot* (1959).

11. See as well the use of the "similar" gray suit in *Vertigo* (1958).

12. Michael Mann's *Thief* (1981) presaged the Internet Age, echoed by *Ozark* (2017) and then sprung into reality with the Jamal Khashoggi murder of October 2018: the body endures "routine digestion by the system" with extreme rapidity by being dissolved in acid, becoming, more than a cipher, a nothing.

13. I am grateful to Jonathan Wright for consulting about performance on strings.

14. Antitheses and echoes: we found the little girl pair, one of them with thick-lensed spectacles, in *I Confess* (1953); and would very soon find them again, ogling the visiting prime minister in the lobby of the Royal Albert Hall in *The Man Who Knew Too Much* (1956).

15. An empathetic boundary is like Freud's stimulus shield, a guard against self-annilihation through sensitivity. See *Principle*.

16. A shot in David Lean's *Brief Encounter* (1945) may have been an inspiration here.

17. After receiving Henry Fonda's express permission, the production made this shot on location using stand-ins.

CHAPTER FIVE

1. Whose pay for lying down was $100 a day in 1955 dollars, roughly ten times as much at this writing.

2. Autumnal leaf changes were monitored vigorously, including at Peterboro, New Hampshire; Wolfeborough, New York; Bretton Woods, New Hampshire; and Crittenden, Vermont (Production). On 2 September 1954, unit production manager "Doc" Erickson wired Frank Caffey at Paramount, "Leaves plentiful and green."

3. Made especially spectacular through Paramount's VistaVision process, which was projected to cost the production $137,519 as opposed to $95,233 for regular Technicolor (Grosser). On VistaVision, see Pomerance "Gamble."

4. Put before the camera in the fall of 1954, *Trouble* was one of the last films photographed in Technicolor three-strip. To have used Kodak's Eastmancolor negative would have cost $56,265 less (Caffey), but the screen

value of Technicolor three-strip shown in VistaVision was worth the investment to Paramount.

5. Clarence O. "Doc" Erickson (1923–2017), a fount of information about Hitchcock's films.

6. Hitchcock had given specific concentration to the hunt as a social organization in *The Farmer's Wife* (1928), had hinted it in *Suspicion* (1941), and would join it by camera, dramatically, in *Marnie* (1964).

7. On 9 August 1954, Herb Coleman telephoned "Doc" Erickson at 10:40 a.m. to say, among other things, that he was airmailing "to coast today 1953 foliage chart for New England area plus weather forecasts and reports for past years in same area" (Coleman).

8. Like the farmer's wife invoking Sauchiehal Street, Glasgow, on a Saturday evening in *The 39 Steps* (1935) (see my *Voyage*).

9. Similarly, the abstract expressionist I. Rice Pereira saw that "one of the dilemmas of the twentieth-century man is finding a position in relation to frames of reference in space and time; otherwise he will be driven from pole to pole, only to be lost or overwhelmed by the infinitudes of anxiety as the picture of the universe opens up to the human mind, displaying more and more grandeur" (4). Her son Hal, a fixture at Paramount, was an art director on this film.

10. The Marlow paintings are by John Ferren (1905–1970), who would collaborate with Hitchcock on the dream sequence of *Vertigo*.

11. A trope Harry Segall had devised for his 1938 play *It Was Like This* (later retitled *Heaven Can Wait*), filmed as *Here Comes Mr. Jordan* in 1941 and later as *Heaven Can Wait* in 1978; and also a trope central in a less comedic way to Michael Powell and Emeric Pressburger's *Stairway to Heaven (A Matter of Life and Death*, 1946).

12. The screenwriter here, John Michael Hayes, honorably borrows from Lewis Carroll, whose White Queen is thoroughly accustomed to "living backwards": "There's the King's messenger: he's in prison now, being punished: and the trial doesn't even begin till next Wednesday: and of course the crime comes last of all" (chap. 5).

13. A sterling exception is Inspector Hubbard in *Dial M for Murder*. See my *Voyage* 189ff.

14. The establishing landscape shots were made in time before the leaves

fell, but all the footage in the forest was shot on a Paramount stage. In 1954 dollars, the cost for the nursery on this picture was $9,724.99 (about $100,000 today) (Production Cost).

CHAPTER SIX

1. Andre Sakharov was shaken to such an extent that he declared, "May all our devices explode as successfully as today's, but always over test sites and never over cities" (Halberstam 99–100). Later, he wrote, "We, the inventors, scientists, engineers and craftsmen had created a terrible weapon, the most terrible weapon in human history; but its use would lie entirely outside our control" (100).

2. In 1962, Beatlemania was born; John Frankenheimer released *The Manchurian Candidate*; *Who's Afraid of Virginia Woolf?* debuted on Broadway.

3. Peggy Robertson wanted TV journalist Eric Sevareid to be asked "what he would charge to write approximately 100 words regarding the position in which a man finds himself in disagreeing with his government's policy—as in the case of a Russian who defects on that account" (Robertson to Horton).

4. Hitchcock's team was made up of skilled artisans and technicians, reflected in this character.

5. Nathan Holmes finds it notable that for many commentators chase sequences are "given to collapsing space, abolishing distance, and constructing synthetic geographies disconnected from reality." I believe he would recognize Hitchcock's films, and notably *Topaz*, as something of a refutation.

6. There is a key figurine-smashing moment in *Rebecca* (1940), with an even more expansive gesture of sincere regret.

7. Hitchcock's research team had requested "permission to use an Air Force 707 taxiing to a stop at Andrews Air Force Base at dawn" ("Research Needed") but were informed 1 August 1968 by John F. Horton, "The Aircraft would be Air Force KC-135's or VC-137 operating under Special Air Mission (SAM). The subject aircraft would not be one of four Presidential Air Force 707's" (Horton).

8. Sergei Prokofiev sometimes thought of the percussive element in his compositions as a "motor" element.

9. For example, their personalities are very much not in the style of Rob, Laura, and Ritchie Petrie's from *The Dick Van Dyke Show* (1961–1966).

10. As with Hannay and Pamela at the inn in *The 39 Steps* (1935).

11. A rose stolen from Madeleine's nosegay in *Vertigo* (1958).

12. Royal Copenhagen dates from 1775, sixteen years after Josiah Wedgwood's pioneering factory in England.

13. See the morning-on-shipboard sequence of *Marnie* (1964), when the ocean rippling outside the porthole has changed direction; and, in my *Voyage*, the discussion of *Rich and Strange* (1931).

14. In *North by Northwest* (1959), with Vandamm's snide comments to George Kaplan about where he has already been, hotel by hotel, city by city, we have a reverse, summative form of this trick.

15. Along with Nikita S. Khrushchev, premier of the Soviet Union, Castro addressed the United Nations General Assembly in September 1960. It is reported that these two men warmly led the applause for each other there.

16. A summary of Jim Westman's review of newspaper files revealed to Hitchcock that on his celebrated visit to address the United Nations, Fidel Castro stayed at the Theresa Hotel, 9th floor, at 125th Street and 7th Avenue. "Castro and party occupied forty rooms." The details proliferated: "Theresa's lobby is small. Has two elevators (only one was operating at time of interview).... Progressive jazz in coffee shop.... Cuban group charged $21.00 per day each for forty units—five of which were two-room suites.... Guests were annoyed that Cubans were monopolizing the elevator and telephone lines, as well as the bathrooms on 7th, 8th and 9th floors." As to Castro's room, "Policemen, Detectives, and Cuban Security Agents stood guard among cigarette butts and folding chairs.... Before the Premier left via limousine for the United Nations, he sent down to the kitchen for a steak for lunch. Three Cubans, one in uniform, gave the order to the Chef and supervised its broiling. A reporter asked the Cubans whom the steak was for. The uniformed Cuban looked at the reporter's press card and sneered, 'I tell you nothing. You spy'" (Results). Almost all these details given here are replicated in the film in some fashion.

17. *Topaz* was filmed between November 1968 and December 1969, and released in December 1969. Kubrick's *2001: A Space Odyssey*, involving a

celebrated key scene of HAL 9000 "listening in" on Dave and Frank's conversation about it by reading their lips, had limited releases in Washington, D.C., New York, and Los Angeles, as well as a limited release nationwide, in early April 1968. The film did not get a full general release in America until 24 June 1970.

18. A failed CIA-based attempt to unseat the Castro government in April 1961.

19. "Not the victory of might but the vindication of right" was what Kennedy called the American goal, in his televised address about the missile crisis on 22 October 1962.

20. The "observation" trope occurs often, and pithily, in Hitchcock. Reflect on Rupert Cadell in *Rope*, Scottie in the gallery in *Vertigo*, and the ballerina in *Torn Curtain* for just a few cases.

21. In *Man*, Hitchcock had benefit of Jimmy Stewart's sapphire blue eyes, while John Vernon's blue eyes are less tender and more metallic. Stewart's eyes make us think of his ears; Vernon's in this sequence shift aside to make us think of the thoughts racing in his mind. *Man* was shot and produced at Paramount in the mid-1950s, so Hitchcock had benefit of VistaVision for the facial shot there—it would have been literally gigantic on theater screens—whereas here he does not.

22. Perhaps one should note: as in Christian mythology, the infant Jesus is born immaculately, perhaps even as a surprise.

23. The dirtiness of the dirty work is inevitably cloacal.

24. In 1955 Ann Doran was the mother in *Rebel Without a Cause*.

25. That in his scenario Hitchcock does not include, directly or through substitution, Vasily Arkhipov, the man who prevented a nuclear submarine near Cuba from initiating a nuclear war on the day before the end of the crisis, is unsurprising since information about that part of the affair came out only on 22 October 2012. Nor would prevention of the debacle have changed in any way the deft placement of a Nicole Devereaux type in DC.

26. Modeling Eve Kendall at the Ambassador East in *North by Northwest*.

WORKS CITED

HER = Margaret Herrick Library, Academy of Motion Picture Arts and Sciences, Beverly Hills

Ackroyd, Peter. *London: The Biography.* New York: Vintage, 2001.
———. *London Under.* London: Vintage, 2012.
Alighieri, Dante. *Inferno.* Trans. Charles S. Singleton. Princeton, NJ: Princeton University Press, 1970.
Arendt, Hannah. *The Human Condition.* 1958. 2nd ed. Chicago: University of Chicago Press, 1998.
Arlen, Michael J. *Thirty Seconds.* New York: Farrar, Straus & Giroux, 1980.
Bachelard, Gaston. *The Psychoanalysis of Fire.* Rev. ed. Trans. Alan C. Ross. Boston: Beacon Press, 1987.
Barr, Charles. *English Hitchcock.* Moffat, Dumfriesshire: Cameron and Hollis, 1999.
Bataille, Georges. "Van Gogh as Prometheus." *Verve* 1, no. 1 (1937): 20.
Bazalgette, Joseph William. *On the Main Drainage of London, and the Interception of the Sewage from the River Thames.* London: William Clowes and Sons, 1865.
Becker, Howard S. *Outsiders: Studies in the Sociology of Deviance.* New York: Free Press, 1963.
Bell, [Sir] Charles. *The Hand: Its Mechanism and Vital Endowments as Evincing Design.* London: William Pickering, 1837.
Bemelmans, Ludwig. *To the One I Love the Best.* New York: Viking, 1955.
Benjamin, Walter. "The Work of Art in the Age of Its Technological Reproducibility." In *Walter Benjamin: Selected Writings Vol. 3, 1935–38,* ed. Marcus Paul Bullock, Michael William Jennings, and Howard Eiland, 101–33. Cambridge, MA: Harvard University Press, 2006.

Bergan, Ronald. "Jon Finch Obituary." *The Guardian* (13 January 2013), online at theguardian.com/film/2013/jan/13/jon-finch. Accessed 21 June 2021.

Bergson, Henri. *Laughter: An Essay on the Meaning of the Comic.* Trans. Cloudesley Brereton and Fred Rothwell. 1911. Mineola, NY: Dover, 2005.

Binet, Alfred. *Animal Magnetism.* New York: Appleton, 1888.

Brown, Norman O. *Life Against Death: The Psychoanalytical Meaning of History.* Middletown CT: Wesleyan University Press, 1959.

Cachin, Françoise, Isabelle Cahn, Walter Feilchenfeldt, Henri Loyrette, and Joseph J. Rishel. *Cézanne.* Philadelphia: Philadelphia Museum of Art, 1996.

Caffey, Frank. Memorandum on Film Costs, 24 August 1954. Alfred Hitchcock Collection, HER.

Caillois, Roger. *Man, Play and Games.* Trans. Meyer Barash. Urbana: University of Illinois Press, 2001.

Caro, Robert A. *The Power Broker: Robert Moses and the Fall of New York.* New York: Alfred A. Knopf, 1974.

Carroll, Lewis [Charles Lutwidge Dodson]. *Alice's Adventures in Wonderland.* New York: Macmillan, 1920.

Clayton, Alex. *Funny How? Sketch Comedy and the Art of Humor.* Albany: State University of New York Press, 2020.

Cohen, Tom. *Hitchcock's Cryptonymies: Vol. 1—Secret Agents.* Minneapolis: University of Minnesota Press, 2005.

Coleman, Herbert. Notes of telephone call regarding foliage and weather in New England, 9 August 1954. *The Trouble with Harry* production file. Alfred Hitchcock Collection, HER.

Collodi, Carlo. *The Adventures of Pinocchio.* Trans. Ann Lawson Lucas. Oxford: Oxford University Press, 1996.

Corbin, Alain. *The Foul and the Fragrant: Odor and the French Social Imagination.* Cambridge, MA: Harvard University Press, 1986.

Cortázar, Julio. "Blow-Up." In *End of the Game and Other Stories*, trans. Paul Blackburn, 114–31. New York: Pantheon, 1967.

———. "The Daily Daily." In *Cronopios and Famas*, trans. Paul Blackburn, 67. New York: Pantheon, 1969.

———. *Literature Class: Berkeley 1980*. Trans. Katherine Silver. New York: New Directions, 2013.

Crary, Jonathan. *Suspensions of Perception: Attention, Spectacle, and Modern Culture*. Cambridge, MA: MIT Press, 2000.

———. *Techniques of the Observer: On Vision and Modernity in the Nineteenth Century*. Cambridge, MA: MIT Press, 1992.

Custalow, Linwood "Little Bear," and Angela L. Daniel "Silver Star." *The True Story of Pocahontas: The Other Side of History*. Golden, CO: Fulcrum, 2007.

Darwin, Charles. *The Expression of the Emotions in Man and Animals*. 1872. Oxford: Oxford University Press, 1998.

Davenport, Guy. *Apples and Pears and Other Stories*. San Francisco: North Point Press, 1984.

———. *Objects on a Table: Harmonious Disarray in Art and Literature*. Washington, DC: Counterpoint, 1998.

David, Elizabeth. *An Omelette and a Glass of Wine*. London: Lyons and Burford, 1997.

Da Vinci, Leonardo. *A Treatise on Painting*. Trans. John Francis Rigaud. London: Printed for J. Taylor, 1802.

De Beauvoir, Simone. *The Second Sex*. Trans. H. M. Parshley. London: Vintage, 1997.

Detail Production Cost for *The Trouble with Harry*. Alfred Hitchcock Collection, HER.

De Tocqueville, Alexis. *Democracy in America*. 1835. Trans. Henry Reeve. New York: Alfred A. Knopf, 1948.

Dewey, John. *Psychology*. New York: Harper, 1886.

Dickens, Charles. *Oliver Twist*. London: Richard Bentley, 1838.

———. *The Personal History of David Copperfield*. London: Bradbury & Evans, 1850.

Doane, Mary Ann. *The Emergence of Cinematic Time: Modernity, Contingency, the Archive*. Cambridge, MA: Harvard University Press, 2002.

Dostoevsky, Fyodor. *Crime and Punishment*. 1866. Trans. Richard Pevear and Larissa Volokhonsky. New York: Vintage, 1993.

Douglas, Mary. *Natural Symbols: Explorations in Cosmology*. London: Routledge, 2003.

———. *Purity and Danger: An Analysis of Concepts of Pollution and Taboo.* London: Routledge, 2002.

Dowse, Thomas Stretch. *The Treatment of Disease by Physical Methods.* Bristol: John Wright, 1898.

Dubreuilh, Simone. "Review of *The Trouble with Harry.*" *Libération*, 22 March 1956.

Dumas, Alexandre. *The Count of Monte Cristo.* Trans. Robin Buss. 1844–45. London: Penguin, 2003.

Einstein, Albert. *Relativity: The Special and General Theory.* 1920. Trans. Robert W. Lawson. Mineola, NY: Dover, 2001.

Ekman, Paul, and Wallace V. Friesen. *Unmasking the Face: A Guide to Recognizing Emotions from Facial Expressions.* Englewood Cliffs, NJ: Prentice-Hall, 1975.

Eliade, Mircea. *The Myth of the Eternal Return.* Trans. Willard R. Trask. 1954. Princeton, NJ: Princeton University Press, 2005.

Elsaesser, Thomas. "Tales of Sound and Fury: Observations on the Family Melodrama." In *Home Is Where the Heart Is: Studies in Melodrama and the Woman's Film*, ed. Christine Gledhill, 43–69. London: BFI, 1987.

Emerson, Ralph Waldo. "Song of Nature." In *American Poetry, The Nineteenth Century, Volume 1.* New York: Library of America, 1993.

Fielding, Raymond. *The Technique of Special-Effects Cinematography.* New York: Hastings House, 1968.

Foery, Raymond. *Alfred Hitchcock's* Frenzy: *The Last Masterpiece.* Lanham, MD: Scarecrow Press, 2012.

Foster, Frederick. "'Hitch' Didn't Want It Arty." *American Cinematographer* (February 1957): 84–85, 112–114.

Foucault, Michel. *Discipline and Punish: The Birth of the Prison.* Trans. Alan Sheridan. New York: Vintage, 1995.

———. *The Punitive Society: Lectures at the College de France 1972–1973.* Trans. Graham Burchell. London: Palgrave, 2013.

Freud, Sigmund. *Beyond the Pleasure Principle.* In *The Standard Edition of the Complete Psychological Works of Sigmund Freud*, vol. 18, 1–64. Trans. and ed. James Strachey. London: Hogarth Press, 1955.

———. *The Complete Introductory Lectures on Psychoanalysis.* Trans. and ed. James Strachey. New York: W. W. Norton, 1966.

———. *Sexuality and the Psychology of Love.* Ed. Philip Rieff. 1963. New York: Touchstone, 1997.

———. "A Special Type of Choice of Object Made by Men (1910)." In *Collected Papers,* vol. 4, 192–202. Trans. Joan Riviere. London: Hogarth Press, 1946.

Freund, Amy. "Good Dog!: Jean-Baptiste Oudry and the Politics of Animal Painting." In *French Art of the Eighteenth Century,* ed. Heather MacDonald, 67–79. New Haven, CT: Yale University Press, 2016.

Friedan, Betty. *The Feminine Mystique.* New York: W. W. Norton, 1963.

Frost, Robert. "Nothing Gold Can Stay." In *The Poetry of Robert Frost,* ed. Edward Connery Lathem. New York: Holt, Rinehart and Winston, 1969.

Garfinkel, Harold. "Conditions of Successful Degradation Ceremonies." *American Journal of Sociology* 61 (March 1956): 420–24. Reprinted in John Beck, Chris Jenks, and Nellie Keddie, *Toward a Sociology of Education,* 250–57. New York: Transaction, 1978.

Gay, Peter. *Schnitzler's Century: The Making of Middle-Class Culture, 1815–1914.* New York: W. W. Norton, 2002.

———. *Weimar Culture: The Outsider as Insider.* New York: W. W. Norton, 1968.

George, M. Dorothy. "London and the Life of the Town." In *Johnson's England: An Account of the Life & Manners of His Age,* vol. 1, ed. A. S. Turberville, 160–96. Oxford: Clarendon Press, 1933.

Goffman, Erving. *Asylums: Essays on the Social Situation of Mental Patients and Other Inmates.* Garden City, NY: Doubleday Anchor, 1961.

———. *The Presentation of Self in Everyday Life.* Garden City, NY: Doubleday Anchor, 1959.

Gombrich, Ernst. *Art and Illusion: A Study in the Psychology of Pictorial Representation.* London: Phaidon, 2004.

Goodman, Paul. *Speaking and Language: Defence of Poetry.* New York: Vintage, 1972.

Goodman, Paul, and Percival Goodman. *Communitas: Means of Livelihood and Ways of Life.* New York: Vintage, 1960.

Graves, Robert. *The Greek Myths, Vols. 1 and 2.* Harmondsworth: Penguin, 1957.

Grimm, Jacob and Wilhelm. *Snow White*. Retold by Jennifer Greenway. Kansas City: Andrews and McMeel, 1991.

Gross, Kenneth. *Puppet: An Essay on Uncanny Life*. Chicago: University of Chicago Press, 2011.

Grosser, A. A. Memorandum to Frank Caffey regarding comparison of shooting process rates, 24 August 1954. *The Trouble with Harry* production files. Alfred Hitchcock Collection, HER.

Grosvenor, Rita. *Eat Like a Lord*. London: Hamish Hamilton, 1973.

Gunning, Tom. "In and Out of the Frame: Paintings in Hitchcock." In *Casting a Shadow: Creating the Alfred Hitchcock Film*, ed. Will Schmenner and Corinne Granof, 29–47. Evanston, IL: Mary and Leigh Block Museum of Art and Northwestern University Press, 2007.

———. "Tracing the Individual Body: Photography, Detectives, and Early Cinema." In *Cinema and the Invention of Modern Life*, ed. Leo Charney and Vanessa R. Schwartz, 15–45. Berkeley: University of California Press, 1995.

———. "The Cinema of Attractions: Early Film, Its Spectator and the Avant-Garde." In *Early Cinema: Space Frame Narrative*, ed. Thomas Elsaesser, 56-62. London: BFI, 1990.

Halberstam, David. *The Fifties*. New York: Ballantine, 1993.

Heisenberg, Werner. *The Physical Principles of the Quantum Theory*. Trans. Carl Eckart and F. C. Hoyt. Chicago: University of Chicago Press, 1930.

Holmes, Nathan. "Highways through the Void: Chase Sequences and the Built Environment." *New Review of Film and Television Studies* 20 (2022): 37–48.

Horton, John E. Memorandum of answers to queries in *Topaz* research, 1 August 1968. *Topaz* File 761. Alfred Hitchcock Collection, HER.

Jacobs, Steven. *The Wrong House: The Architecture of Alfred Hitchcock*. Rotterdam: nai010, 2013.

James, William. *The Principles of Psychology*, vol. 1. New York: Henry Holt, 1890.

Jay, Martin. *Downcast Eyes: The Denigration of Vision in Twentieth-Century French Thought*. Berkeley: University of California Press, 1994.

Kafka, Franz. *In the Penal Colony*. Trans. Joachim Neugroschel. New York: Scribner, 2000.
Keniston, Kenneth. "Morals and Ethics." *American Scholar* 34, no. 4 (Autumn 1965): 628–32.
Kennedy, Robert F. *13 Days: The Cuban Missile Crisis October 1962*. London: Macmillan, 1969.
Kracauer, Siegfried. *The Mass Ornament: Weimar Essays*. Trans. Thomas Y. Levin. Cambridge, MA: Harvard University Press, 1995.
Krohn, Bill. *Hitchcock at Work*. London: Phaidon, 2000.
———. Personal correspondence, 8 February 2021.
Kynaston, David. *The City of London. Vol. IV: A Club No More, 1945–2000*. London: Pimlico, 2002.
———. *City of London: The History*. Ed. David Milner. London: Chatto & Windus, 2011.
———. *Family Britain: 1951–1957*. London: Bloomsbury, 2009.
Laqueur, Thomas W. *Solitary Sex: A Cultural History of Masturbation*. New York: Zone Books, 2003.
Lawrence, D[avid] H[erbert]. *Studies in Classic American Literature*. London: Penguin, 1990.
Le Bon, Gustave. *The Crowd: A Study of the Popular Mind*. 2nd ed. New York: Macmillan, 1897.
Lem, Stanislaw. *Tales of Pirx the Pilot*. New York: Harcourt Brace Jovanovich, 1979.
Loring, Charles. "Natural Source Set Lighting." *American Cinematographer* (February 1957): 86–114.
Mailer, Norman. "A Calculus at Heaven." In *Advertisements for Myself*. Cambridge, MA: Harvard University Press, 1992.
Mallet, Sir Charles. "Education, Schools, and Universities." In *Johnson's England: An Account of the Life & Manners of His Age*, ed. A. S. Turberville, 209–42. Oxford: Clarendon Press, 1933.
Mannoni, Laurent. *The Great Art of Light and Shadow: Archaeology of the Cinema*. Exeter: University of Exeter Press, 2000.
McElhaney, Joe. "The Object and the Face: *Notorious*, Bergman and the Close-Up." In *Hitchcock Past and Future*, ed. Richard Allen and Sam Ishii-Gonzáles, 64–84. London: Routledge, 2004.

McGilligan, Patrick. *Alfred Hitchcock: A Life in Darkness and Light.* New York: HarperCollins, 2003.

McIntosh, Mary. "Changes in the Organization of Thieving." In *Image of Deviance*, ed. Stanley Cohen, 98–133. Harmondsworth: Penguin, 1971.

Meisner, Sanford, and Dennis Longwell. *Sanford Meisner on Acting.* New York: Vintage, 1987.

Merleau-Ponty, Maurice. *Phenomenology of Perception.* London: Routledge, 2014.

Miller, Henry. *Tropic of Capricorn.* Paris: Obelisk Press, 1954.

Miller, Naomi. *Heavenly Caves: Reflections on the Garden Grotto.* New York: George Braziller, 1982.

Moore, Gerald. *Am I Too Loud? Memoirs of an Accompanist.* Harmondsworth: Penguin, 1979.

Mulvey, Laura. *Visual and Other Pleasures.* Bloomington: Indiana University Press, 1989.

Musil, Robert. *Posthumous Papers of a Living Author.* Trans. Peter Wortsman. 1936. Harmondsworth: Penguin, 1995.

O'Connell, Patricia Hitchcock, and Laurent Bouzereau. *Alma Hitchcock: The Woman behind the Man.* New York: Berkley Books, 2004.

Ohler, Norman. *Blitzed: Drugs in the Third Reich.* Trans. Shaun Whiteside. Boston: Houghton Mifflin Harcourt, 2017.

Ortega y Gasset, José. "On Point of View in the Arts." 1948. Trans. Paul Snodgress and Joseph Frank. In *The Dehumanization of Art and Other Essays on Art, Culture, and Literature*, 107–30. Princeton, NJ: Princeton University Press, 1968.

Orwell, George. *Down and Out in Paris and London.* 1933. Reprint, New York: Harcourt, 1961.

———. "Such, Such Were the Joys." In *George Orwell Essays*, 416–59. London: Penguin, 1970.

Panter-Downes, Mollie. *London War Notes 1939–1945.* Ed. William Shawn. London: Persephone Books, 2014.

Pereira, Irene Rice. *The Nature of Space.* Washington, DC: Corcoran Gallery of Art, 1968.

Perkins, V. F. *Film as Film: Understanding and Judging Movies.* Harmondsworth: Penguin, 1972.

Poe, Edgar Allan. *The Narrative of Arthur Gordon Pym of Nantucket.* New York: Harper and Bros., 1838.
Points to Be Checked on "Wrong Man." *The Wrong Man* File 1037. Alfred Hitchcock Collection, HER.
Pomerance, Murray. "Assheton Gorton: A Life in Film." Special issue of *Film International* 13, no. 1 (Spring-Summer 2015): 56–104.
———. "Bells Are Ringing: Rear Projection and Audience Engagement." *Film International* 15, no. 4 (February 2018): 37–55.
———. *A Dream of Hitchcock.* Albany: State University of New York Press, 2019.
———. *An Eye for Hitchcock.* New Brunswick, NJ: Rutgers University Press, 2004.
———. "Michael Curtiz's Gamble for Christmas." In *The Many Cinemas of Michael Curtiz*, ed. R. Barton Palmer and Murray Pomerance, 221–35. Austin: University of Texas Press, 2019.
———. "*Stage Fright* and the Plague of Fascination." *South Atlantic Review* 85, no. 4 (Winter 2020): 203–26.
———. *A Voyage with Hitchcock.* Albany: State University of New York Press, 2021.
Publicity File. *The Wrong Man*, Warner Bros. Archives, University of Southern California.
Questions on Script Dated 6 February 1956, *The Wrong Man* File 1037. Alfred Hitchcock Collection, HER.
Rancière, Jacques. *The Future of the Image.* Trans. Gregory Elliott. London: Verso, 2007.
Read, Herbert. *The True Voice of Feeling: Studies in English Romantic Poetry.* London: Faber and Faber, 1953.
"Research Needed from Washington." Memorandum, undated but likely July 1968, *Topaz* File 761. Alfred Hitchcock Collection, HER.
"Results of Jim Westman's Review of Newspaper Files." 26 August 1968, *Topaz* Locations File 759. Alfred Hitchcock Collection, HER.
Robertson, Peggy. Inter-Office Communication to Bob Flynn, 16 September 1968, *Topaz* Locations File 759. Alfred Hitchcock Collection, HER.
———. Note to John Horton regarding Eric Sevareid, n.d., *Topaz* Locations File 761. Alfred Hitchcock Collection, HER.

Rohmer, Eric, and Claude Chabrol. *Hitchcock: The First Forty-Four Films.* New York: Ungar, 1979.

Roth, Henry. *Call It Sleep.* 1934. Reprint, Paterson, NJ: Pageant, 1960.

Rothman, William. *The "I" of the Camera: Essays in Film Criticism, History, and Aesthetics.* 2nd ed. New York: Cambridge University Press, 2004.

Sade, Marquis de. *The Misfortunes of Virtue and Other Early Tales.* Trans. David Coward. Oxford: Oxford University Press, 1992.

Sartre, Jean-Paul. "The Meaning of 'To Make' and 'To Have': Possession." In *The Self: Explorations in Personal Growth*, ed. Clark Moustakas, 140–46. New York: Harper, 1956.

———. *Saint Genet: Actor and Martyr.* 1952. Trans. Bernard Frechtman. Minneapolis: University of Minnesota Press, 2012.

Schafer, R. Murray. *A Sound Education.* Indian River, ON: Arcana, 1992.

———. *The Tuning of the World.* New York: Alfred A. Knopf, 1977.

Scharff, Stefan. *Alfred Hitchcock's High Vernacular: Theory and Practice.* New York: Columbia University Press, 1991.

Schefer, Jean Louis. *The Enigmatic Body: Essays on the Arts.* Trans. Paul Smith. Cambridge: Cambridge University Press, 1995.

Scheler, Max. *Ressentiment.* Milwaukee: Marquette University Press, 2003.

Schivelbusch, Wolfgang. *The Culture of Defeat: On National Trauma, Mourning, and Recovery.* Trans. Jefferson Chase. New York: Henry Holt, 2003.

———. *Tastes of Paradise: A Social History of Spices, Stimulants, and Intoxicants.* Trans. David Jacobson. New York: Vintage, 1993.

Simmel, Georg. *The Sociology of Georg Simmel.* Trans. and Ed. Kurt Wolff. New York: Free Press, 1950.

Sinclair, Iain. *The Last London: True Fictions from an Unreal City.* London: Oneworld, 2018.

Smith, Henry Nash. *Virgin Land: The American West as Symbol and Myth.* New York: Vintage, 1950.

Spoto, Donald. *The Dark Side of Genius: The Life of Alfred Hitchcock.* New York: Ballantine, 1984.

Stratton, Stephen S. "On the Gymnastic Training of the Hand for Performing on Keyed Instruments." In *Proceedings of the Musical Association for the Investigation and Discussion of Subjects Connected with the Art and Science of Music*, 99-119. London: Chappell & Co., 1877.

Teilhard de Chardin, Pierre. *The Phenomenon of Man*. New York: Harper & Row, 1959.
The Trouble with Harry Cast Pay, *The Trouble with Harry* File 947. Alfred Hitchcock Collection, HER.
The Trouble with Harry Production File. Alfred Hitchcock Collection, HER.
The Trouble with Harry Script, 27 July 1954. *The Trouble with Harry* File 945. Alfred Hitchcock Collection, HER.
Thoreau, Henry David. *Walden and Other Writings*. 1854. Ed. Joseph Wood Krutch. New York: Bantam, 1962.
Truffaut, François. *Hitchcock*. Trans. Helen Scott. New York: Simon & Schuster, 1984.
United Nations Office on Drugs and Crime. "Global Study on Homicide 2019." Vienna: UNODC, 2019.
Vonnegut, Kurt Jr. *Mother Night: A Novel*. 1961. Reprint, New York: Dial Press, 2009.
Weis, Elisabeth. *The Silent Scream: Alfred Hitchcock's Sound Track*. Rutherford, NJ: Fairleigh Dickinson University Press, 1982.
Wells, H. G. *The Invisible Man: A Grotesque Romance*. New York: E. Arnold, 1897.
Williams, Tennessee. *Camino Real*. Norfolk, CT: New Directions, 1953.
Wilson, Edmund. *The Thirties*. Ed. Leon Edel. New York: Farrar, Straus & Giroux, 1980.
Wilson, Frank R. *The Hand: How Its Use Shapes the Brain, Language, and Human Culture*. New York: Pantheon 1998.
Worringer, Wilhelm. *Abstraction and Empathy: A Contribution to the Psychology of Style*. 1908. Trans. Michael Bullock. Chicago: Elephant, 1997.

INDEX

Note: Numbers in *italic* connote images.

À nous la liberté (René Clair, 1931), 199
Ackroyd, Peter, 121, 136
Alfie (Lewis Gilbert, 1966), 121
Algerian War (1954–1962), 318
Alice's Adventures in Wonderland (Lewis Carroll), 91
Alighieri, Dante, 5, 86, 125, 172
Allen, Richard, 10
Alps, the, 67
Ambassador Hotel (Chicago), 141, 336n26
American in Paris, An (Vincente Minnelli, 1951), 234
American military aircraft: Air Force KC-135, 334n7; Air Force VC-137, 334n7; Presidential Air Force 707s, 334n7; Special Air Missions (SAM), 334n7
American Revolutionary War (1775–1783), 303
Ancaeus. *See* Atalanta and Meleager
Andrews Air Force Base (Morningside, Maryland), 334n7
Andrews, Julie, 141
Arcadia, 218, 259
Arcadia, California, 52
Arcady. *See* Arcadia
Arendt, Hannah, *demiourgoi*, 180
Arkhipov, Vasily, prevention of nuclear submarine attack revealed 22 October 2012, 336n25
Arlen, Michael J., casting for a commercial, 284

Arnold, Malcolm, 134
Astaire, Fred, 327n8
Atalanta (the huntress). *See* Atalanta and Meleager
Atalanta and Meleager (myth), 225–26, 227
Auschwitz, 113

Bachelard, Gaston, 329n9
Bailey, David, 170
Balestrero, Christopher Emmanuel, 172. *See also* Hitchcock, Films, *The Wrong Man*
Balestrero, Rose, 173. *See also* Hitchcock, Films, *The Wrong Man*
Barr, Charles, 10
Bataille, Georges, 241
Baudelaire, Charles, 312
Bauhaus, The, 31
Bay of Pigs (disaster, 1961), 291
Beatlemania (1962), 334n2
Bell, Sir Charles, 201
Bemelmans, Ludwig, 325n4
Benjamin, Arthur, 5
Bergman, Ingrid, 7, 12, 20, 53
Bergson, Henri, 164
Bertillon, Alphonse, 190
Beyond the Pleasure Principle (Sigmund Freud), 64
Bierstadt, Albert, 220, 257
Billingsley, Sherman, 175, 177, 178, 205. *See also* Hitchcock, Settings, Stork Club

"Blow-Up" (Julio Cortázar), 239
"Blue Boy, The" (Thomas Gainsborough, 1770), 221
Book of Job, 199, 215
Boreo, Emile, 68
Boulding, Kenneth, 331n6
Breen Office (Production Code Administration). *See* Hollywood
Bretton Woods (New Hampshire), leaf changes monitored, 332n2
Brief Encounter (David Lean, 1945), 332n16
Brill, Lesley, 10
Bringing Up Baby (Howard Hawks, 1938), 244
Britain: banking system in, 329n12; Barclay's Bank, 329n12; British ethnocentrism, 132; British kitchen in the 1970s, 131–32; British stereotypy, 130; Colonel Blimp (British cartoon character) (David Low), 77; Crown Jewels, 134; digestive motif in British wit, 132; English Channel, 133; Establishment, 137; femicide in, 328n7; French spoken in England, 133, 143, 160; House of Lords, 137, 138; National Westminster Bank, 329n12; Pentonville Prison, 330n26; public schools, 137; Received Pronunciation, 153; in Samuel Johnson's time, 138; social class in, 30, 87, 95, 112, 123, 137, 138, 171, 181; upper-class universities, 137;
Brown, Dorothy "Dottie," New York agent of David O. Selznick, in Long Island, 123
Browne, Roscoe Lee, 286
Buatier de Kolta [Joseph Buatier], 88
Budapest (Hungary), invoked in *The Lady Vanishes*, 69
Buddha (Gautama Buddha), 3, 4

Bumstead, Henry, and Hitchcock's American citizenship, 123. *See also* Hitchcock, Personal
Burks, Robert, 193, 330; use of Garnelite instead of 5K, 193

Café Pierre (restaurant, 10th Arr., Paris), 305, 306
Caffey, Frank, 332
Caillois, Roger: luck, 142; mimicry, 15–16; vertigo (ilinx), 16–17
Caine, Michael, 121
Calhern, Louis, 13
Cambridge University. *See* Britain, upper-class universities
Camino Real (Tennessee Williams), 67
Caro, Robert, on New York traffic congestion, 331n2
Carradine, John, 213
Carroll, Lewis (Charles Lutwidge Dodgson), 333n12
Cartesian. *See* Descartes
Castro, Fidel, 272, 287, 292, 298, 318; Address to the United Nations General Assembly (September 1960), 335n15; sojourn at the Theresa Hotel, 335n16
Cavell, Stanley, 245
C[entral] I[ntelligence] A[gency]. *See* Hitchcock, Films, *Notorious*
Cézanne, Paul, 221; letter to Joachim Gasquet, 96
Charles, Lewis, 292
Chartreuse (herbal liqueur made by Carthusian monks), 107
Château de Versailles, 290
Child, Julia, and French cuisine in America, 178
Chopin, Frédéric, 9
Christie, John Reginald Halliday, 330n26
Church, Fredric William, 220
City, The. *See* New York City

City of Light. *See* Paris
Clare, Mary, 87
Claude. *See* Lorrain
Clayton, Alex, 132, 328n4
Coburn, Alvin Langdon, 170
Cohen, Tom, 10, 170
Cold War, 270; and U.S.S.R., 270–71
Coleman, Herbert, 333n7
Collodi, Carlo, 12, 21, 203
"Colonel Bogey March" (F. J. Ricketts), 74
Conant, James, 270
"Conditions of Successful Degradation Ceremonies" (Harold Garfinkel), 128
Congress of the United States, 270, 317
Conley, Tom, 315–16
Connery, Sean, 141
Contreras, Roberto, 298
Cooper, Charles, 183
Corbin, Alain, 95
Cordon Bleu. *See* London
Cortázar, Julio, speaking to students at University of California at Berkeley, 224–25
Cotten, Joseph, 28
"Country of the Blind, The" (H. G. Wells), 212
Courbet, Gustave, 171, 221
Crary, Jonathan, 92, 95, 96
Cribbins, Bernard, 139
Crittenden (Vermont), leaf changes monitored, 332n2
Crosby, [Harry Lillis] "Bing," Jr., 331n4
Cuba. *See* Hitchcock, Films, *Topaz*
Cuban missile crisis (October 1962), 270, 272, 285, 290, 316, 318, 322. *See also* Hitchcock, Films, *Topaz*
Curiosities of London (John Timbs), regarding Covent Garden, Jamaica, and Calcutta, 121–22

Da Vinci, Leonardo, on nature, 236, 237, 242
"Daily Daily, The" (Julio Cortázar), 58–59
Dano, Royal, 219
Dante. *See* Alighieri
Darwin, Charles, 56
Davenport, Guy, head as fate, 313
David Copperfield (Charles Dickens). *See Personal History*
David, Elizabeth, 131
Day, Doris, 5
De Banzie, Brenda, 141
De Beauvoir, Simone, 146, 290
De Tocqueville, Alexis (Alexis Charles Henri Clérel, comte de Tocqueville), 260
Dead Sea Scrolls, 182
Debussy, Claude, 9, 245
Delphic Oracle. *See* Atalanta and Meleager
Den Permanente (Department store, Copenhagen). *See* Hitchcock, Settings
Descartes, René, 98
Dewey, John, 92
"Dick Van Dyke Show, The" (1961), 335n9
Dickens, Charles, 218
Dietrich, Marlene, 328n22
Dishonored (Josef Von Sternberg, 1931), 328n22
Divine Comedy, The (Dante Alighieri), 125
Doane, Mary Ann, 64
Dodsworth (William Wyler, 1936), 326n8
Dor, Karin, 291
Doran, Ann, 276, 336n24
Dostoevsky, Fyodor, 142, 193
Douglas, Mary, 315
Down and Out in Paris and London (George Orwell), 146–47, 331n5
Dowse, Thomas, 202

Dream of Hitchcock, A (Murray Pomerance), 11, 257
Dubreuilh, Simone, 7
Duckworth and Co (publishers), 157
Dunne, Peter Finley, 190–91
Dunnock, Mildred, 218
Duras, Marguerite, 290
Durham University (University of Durham). *See* Britain, upper-class universities

Ebony (magazine, referenced in *Topaz*), 286
Edward, Duke of Windsor, 148
Eiffel Tower, 290
Einstein, Albert, 250
Ekman, Paul and Wallace V. Friesen, 40
Eliade, Mircea, *axis mundi*, 28
Eliot, T[homas] S[tearns], 5
Engels, Friederich, 273
Eniwetok test of the Hydrogen Bomb (1 November 1952), 271
Enlightenment, The, 242
Equator, the, 250
Erickson, Clarence O. "Doc," 220, 332n2, 333n5, 333n7
Evans, Bill, 9
Eye for Hitchcock, An (Murray Pomerance), 11, 325n1

Feminine Mystique, The (Betty Friedan), 181, 290
Fennelly, Parker, 219
Ferren, John, 333n10
Finch, Jon, 121
"Flaggin' the Train to Tuscaloosa" (Mack David and Raymond Scott), 229
Foery, Raymond, 121, 328n2
Fonda, Henry, 8, 172, 179, 196, 199, 203, 208, 213, 332n17
Forsythe, John, 218, 275
Foster, Barry, 121

Foucault, Michel, 17th century France, 194
French Third Republic (1870–1940), 95
French Underground, World War II. *See* World War II
Freud, Sigmund, 64, 65, 76, 117, 126, 129, 130, 177, 330n21, 332n15
Freund, Amy, 227

Garfinkel, Harold, on degradation, 128
Gasquet, Joachim. *See* Cézanne
Gay, Peter, and Weimar Germany, 32
Genesis (Book of), 3
German Expressionism, 31, 32
Gershwin, Ira, 154
Goffman, Erving: presentation of self, 325n2; total institutions, 194
Goodbye, Mr. Chips (Herbert Ross, 1969), 328n20
Goodbye Piccadilly, Farewell Leicester Square (Arthur La Bern), 120
Goodman, Paul, on silence, 3
Goodwin, Ron, 134
Gorton, Assheton, 326n7
Grant, Cary, 7, 8, 9, 12, 20, 38, 55, 141
Graves, Robert, 225
Great Train Robbery, The (Edwin S. Porter, 1903), 320
Gropius, Walter, 31
Gross, Kenneth, puppetry, 19
Guardi, Francesco Lazzaro, 311
Guercino (Giovanni Francesco Barbieri), 259
Gunning, Tom, 190, 231, 329n14, 330n27
Gwenn, Edmund, 141, 218

Halberstam, David, 270
Hamlet (William Shakespeare), 42, 238, 329n19
Handbuch der Physiologie des Menschen (Johannes Müller), 95
Harvard University, 270
Hayes, John Michael, 333n12

Heap, Anthony, reviewing *Look Back in Anger*, 122–23
Heaven Can Wait. See *It Was Like This*
Heaven Can Wait (Warren Beatty and Buck Henry, 1978), 333n11. See also *Here Comes Mr. Jordan*
Hecht, Ben, 33, 37
Hedström, Tina, 274
Heisenberg, Werner, Uncertainty Principle, 42
Helmore, Tom, 141
Herald Tribune. See *International Herald Tribune*
Here Comes Mr. Jordan (Alexander Hall, 1941), 333n11. See also *Heaven Can Wait*
Herrmann, Bernard, 196; *Cubano* theme for *The Wrong Man*, 177
High Society (Charles Walters, 1956), 331n4
Hiller, Wendy, 117
Hiroshima, 36, 37, 271, 326n10
Hitchcock, Alfred: American citizenship, 123; being a loner, 36–37; and blue skies, 221; born in London, 134; casting, 284; comedic relief, compared with Shakespeare, 133–34; contretemps with Charles Laughton, 123; citizenship sworn, 123; and cooking, 328n2; crossing Atlantic, 123; and Dottie Brown, 123; English roots, 66, 123–24, 260; establishing space, 7, 8, 30, 47, 53, 54, 56, 57, 258, 313; friendship with Sherman Billingsley, 178; and Henry Bumstead, 123; home address at birth, Leytonstone, 134, 329; knowledge of social class, 8, 112; in Los Angeles, 123; MacGuffin, 36, 326; and maintenance of focus, 8, 48, 50, 52, 169, 186, 200, 236, 314, 315, 321; and railway timetables, 66; residence in Surrey, 260; and silent cinema, 283, 287; and St. Regis Hotel, 178; use of research, 174, 177, 180, 284, 334n7; working in England, 123

Films: *Birds, The* (1963), 11, 182, 295, 326n13; *Blackmail* (1929), 254, 328n19; *Dial M for Murder* (1954), 11, 124, 333n13, second-unit photography for, 124; *East of Shanghai* (see *Rich and Strange*; *Family Plot*) (1976), 11, 141, 163; *Farmer's Wife, The* (1928), 333n6; *Frenzy* (1972), 11, 120–21, 120–71; *I Confess* (1953), 11, 332n14; *Jamaica Inn* (1939), 123; *Lady Vanishes, The* (1938), 5, 11, 64–65, 64–119; opening date in London, 113; *Lodger: A Tale of the London Fog, The* (1927), 6, 196, 283, 327n14; *Man Who Knew Too Much, The* (1956), 5, 124, 141, 296, 299, 325n2, 332n14; Albert Hall sequence, 124, 332n14, London location shooting during Spring 1955, 124; *Marnie* (1964), 11, 141, 204, 258, 297, 329, 333n6, 335n13; *Mr. & Mrs. Smith* (1941), 108; *North by Northwest* (1959), 4, 9, 11, 141, 148, 182, 254, 296, 325n3, 326n5, 335n14; *Notorious* (1946), 7, 11, *12–13*, 12–63: filming commences, 36; wine cellar sequence, 18, 53, 56; uranium trope in, 36, 37, 326n10; *Paradine Case, The* (1947), 97; *Psycho* (1960), 5, 11, 49, 257, 297, 328n6, 330n28; *Rear Window* (1954), 10, 11, 66, 127, 149, 243, 257, 327n13; *Rebecca* (1940), 11, 123, 124, 162–63, 334n6, not filmed in England, 124; *Rich and Strange* (1931), 11, 335n13; *Rope* (1948), 241, 336n20; *Saboteur* (1942), 11, 198, 257; *Shadow of a Doubt* (1943), 28; *Spellbound* (1945), 11, 320; *Stage Fright* (1950), 124, 328n5, filmed at Elstree, 124, filming dates, 124,

Films: *Stage Fright* (1950) (cont'd) release dates, 124; *Strangers on a Train* (1951), 11, 162, 329n20; *Suspicion* (1941), 11, 124, not filmed in England, 124, 141, 145, 231, 326n2, 333n6; *39 Steps, The* (1935), 11, 74, 93, 198, 254, 333n8, 335n10; *To Catch a Thief* (1955), 11, 141, 259, 326n12; *Topaz* (1969), 9, 11, *270–71*, 270–323, 326n24, 334n5: and Cuban missile crisis, 270–72; filming dates, 335–36n17; release date, 335–36n17; *Torn Curtain* (1966), 11, 141, 279, 336n20; *Trouble with Harry, The* (1955), 5, 11, 141, 170, *218–19*, 218–69; and studio filming, 228; *Under Capricorn* (1949), 124, filmed at Borehamwood, 124; *Vertigo* (1958), 11, 141, 145, 148, 170, 228, 257–58, 299, 310, 328n18, 332n11, 333n10, 335n11, 336n20; *Wrong Man, The* (1956), 8, 11, 141, *172–73*, 172–217, 331n2, 331n3; filming commences, 172

Settings shown or invoked (* denotes real location in use): Arcadia (California), 52; Associated Life of New York (Victor Moore Arcade), 181, 195; Basle (Switzerland), 69, 70, 70; Beverly Hills, 29; *Bickfords (coffee shop, Victor Moore Arcade), 175, 177, 194; *Bloomsbury (London), 124; Boston (invoked in *The Trouble with Harry*), 226, 258; Brasserie Antarctica (Rio de Janeiro), 22, 49; Capitol (Washington, DC), 278; *Charing Cross Station (London), 109, 111, 112, 118; *Coburg Hotel (Bayswater), 131, 141, 154, 167; *Copacabana Beach (Rio de Janeiro), 38, 50; *Copenhagen, 273, 274, 275, 288, 293; *Den Permanente (Copenhagen), 275; Devereaux residence (Bethesda MD), 290, 297, 305; *Drury Lane (Covent Garden), 139; E train (New York), 173, 174; Elysée Palace (Paris), 320; Fifth Avenue (New York), 173, 174, 178, invoked in *The Trouble with Harry*, 230; *Fifth Avenue—53rd Street station, 173, 174; 53rd St. (Manhattan), 173, 178; *59th Street Bridge (New York), 198; *Floriano Peixoto Square (Rio de Janeiro), 22; *40–24 78th Street, Queens (New York), 172; French Embassy (Washington, DC), 279, 301; *Globe Pub (Covent Garden), 131, 157; Hanover Square (London), 71, 75, 118; Havana (Cuba), 300, 318; *Henrietta Street (Covent Garden), 162; Highwater (New England), 237, 239, 242, 243, 252, 253, 258, 259, 262; Hilton Hotel (London), 158; *Hotel Theresa (New York), 286, 335n16; Idlewild (Airport, New York; now John F. Kennedy International), 285; Knippelsbro (Copenhagen), 273–74; Leicester Square (London), 120, 131, 154; Lincolnshire, invoked in *Frenzy*, 157; *Long Island City Jail, 198; Manchester (England), 71, 75, 80, 110; Mandrika (Switzerland), 66, 72, 75, 76, 83, 87, 89, 90, 107, 109, 112, 113, 116, 117; Maryland, 276, 280, 284, 301, 306; *Miami, 17, 39, 42, 48, 59, 82, 214; 125th Street (New York), 286, 287, 292, 300, 335n16; Martinique (flower shop, 125 St., New York), 286; *Nell of Old Drury (Covent Garden), 139, 140, 142; *New England, 219, 221, 230, 234, 245, 258, 259, 260, 333n7; Nice (France), 259; Nob Hill (San Francisco), 170; *110th Precinct (Queens), 213, 215; *Oxford Street

INDEX   355

(London), 139, 168; *Paris, 156, 167, 279, 280, 283, 289, 290, 297, 301, 303, 304, 306, 309, 310, 313, 316, 318, 321, 322; *Passage de la Visitation (7th Arr., Paris), 306; Potomac River (Washington, DC), 276; *Queens (New York), 172, 173, 175, 178, 179, 180, 189, 190, 198, 200, 331n2; Queens Plaza subway station, 174; *Queens City Prison, 200; Red Square (Moscow [stock footage]), 273, 276, 300, 311; *Rio de Janeiro, 12, 15, 49; *Roosevelt Avenue-Jackson Heights subway station, 173, 174; *Royal Albert Hall (London), 124, 332n14; *Royal Copenhagen Porcelain works (Copenhagen), 274, 279, 310, 335n12; *Russell Street (Covent Garden), 139; St Georges, Hanover Square (London), 71; *St. Regis Hotel (New York), 285, 289, 307, 321; Sauchiehal Street (Glasgow, invoked in *The 39 Steps*), 333n8; Scotland Yard, 159, 167; Sebastian wine cellar, 18, 34, 53, 56, 57, 58, 60; *Stork Club (E. 53rd St., New York), 173, 177, 178, 179, 183, 184, 185, 194, 200; Stowe (Vermont), 219; *Switzerland, 66, 303; *Thames Embankment, 137, 164; Twentieth Century Limited dining car, 9, 10; *Victor Moore Arcade (Roosevelt Avenue-Jackson Heights subway station, Queens), 175, 177, 201 (*see also* Bickford's above); *W. 178th Street (near George Washington Bridge), 205; *Washington, DC, 26, 276, 278, 279, 293, 308, 321, 323, 336n17; White House (Washington, DC), 272, 278, 293; Whitehall (London), 109, 110, 119; Yorkshire, invoked in *The Lady Vanishes*, 110

Hitchcock: The First Forty-Four Films (Eric Rohmer and Claude Chabrol), 183
Hitchcock—The Murderous Gaze (William Rothman), 196
Hitchcock, William, 328n1
Hitler, Adolf: admired and "reincarnated," 13; annexes Austria, 113; concentration camps, 113; degradation of Expressionism, 31
Hofmann, Alfred, 31
Hohenschwangau (Castle), 53
Hollywood: Breen Office, 23; Motion Picture Production Code, 23, 268
photographic and screen effects: crane/dolly for *Notorious*, 57; "day for night," 48; Dutch angle, 144; high-contrast lighting, 54, 124; Kodak Eastmancolor, 332n4; matte, 48, 49, 50, 51, 52, 76, 326n6; optical printing, 17, 48–49, 51, 54, 58, 91, 98; rear projection, 48, 49, 50, 51, 52, 54; special prop effect for *Notorious*, 43, 44, 45, 53, 54; stock footage, use of, 49, 276; Technicolor, 332n3, 332–33n4; three-strip process, 332–33n4; VistaVision, 332n3, 332–33n4, 336n21;
studios: Paramount, 228, 332n2, 332–33n4, 336n21; R[adio] K[eith] O[rpheum], 29, 57; Universal, 106, 147, 323; Warner Bros., 174
Holmes, Nathan, 334n5
Holmes, Sherlock, invoked visually in *The Lady Vanishes*, 104
Hopper, Edward, 180
Hotel Theresa (125th St. at 7th Avenue, New York), 286, 335n16. *See also* Hitchcock, Settings
Howard, Curly, of the Three Stooges, 326n3
Hungarian Rhapsody No. 2 (Franz Liszt), invoked with probably inaccuracy in *The Lady Vanishes*, 69

I Know Where I'm Going (Michael Powell and Emeric Pressburger, 1945), 117
Il Gattopardo (Luchino Visconti, 1963), 6, 277
Ilinx. *See* Caillois
Impressionism, 253
International Herald Tribune (pub. Paris), 73, 90
Internet age, 332n12
Invisible Man, The (H. G. Wells), 106
Invisible Man, The (James Whale, 1933), 106
It Was Like This (Harry Segall, 1938, likely unproduced), 333n11
"It's a Long Way to Tipperary" (Jack Judge and Harry Williams), 120

Jack the Ripper (Whitechapel Murderer), 135, 138
Jacobs, Jason, 328n3
Jacobs, Steven, 29, 53
Jade, Claude, 285
James, William, 64, 65, 81, 116
Jarre, Maurice, 273
Jason. *See* Atalanta and Meleager
Jay, Martin, 241
Job. See *Book of Job*
Johnson, Noel, 139
Johnson, Samuel, 138. *See also* Britain, public schools
Jules et Jim (François Truffaut, 1963), 321

Kafka, Franz, machine of punishment, 127, 192
Kelly, Grace, 331n4
Keniston, Kenneth, morals and ethics, 246–47
Kennedy, John Fitzgerald, 272, 275, 300, 317
Kennedy, Robert F., 272
Khashoggi, Jamal, murder of, 332n12
Khrushchev, Nikita S., 272, 300, 317, 318; Address to the United Nations General Assembly (September 1960), 335n15
Klimt, Gustav, 31
Konstantin, Leopoldine, 44
Kracauer, Siegfried, 30
Krohn, Bill, 10, 23, 27, 33, 34, 37, 54, 57, 319, 320, 321
Krumschmidt, Eberhard, 34
Kynaston, David, 122, 161, 329n12

Lady Chatterley's Lover (D. H. Lawrence), 122
Lancaster, Burt, 277
Lang, Doreen, 182
Lang, Fritz, 31
Laqueur, Thomas, on masturbation, 126–27
Laughton, Charles, contretemps with Hitchcock, 123
Lawrence, D[avid] H[erbert], 122, 214, 237
Le Bon, Gustave, crowds, electoral crowd, 176
Leaver, Philip, 88
Leigh-Hunt, Barbara, 124, 143
Lenin, Vladimir, 273
Leave It to Beaver (1957), 221
Leopard, The. See *Il Gattopardo*
Leviticus (Book of), 207
Lockwood, Margaret, 70
Lombardo, Goffredo, 6
London (*see also* Hitchcock, Settings): Akash Tandoori (Irving Street, London; now defunct), 131; Battersea, 121; Belgravia, 124; Big Ben (Westminster), 170; Bloomsbury, 124; Canary Wharf, 134; Buckingham Palace, 170; Cordon Bleu in, 122; County Hall, 134; Covent Garden grocery market (now defunct), 121, 122, 138, 153, 166, 170, 329n16; Drury Lane (Covent Garden), 139; eighteenth- and nineteenth-century London,

123, 126, 138, 140; Henrietta Street (Covent Garden), 162; Fitzrovia, 124; Greater London area, 123; Kensington Palace, 154; Knightsbridge Barracks (World War II) (*see also* World War II; Leicester Square), 120, 131, 154; Leytonstone, 134, 329n13; Lincoln's Inn, 153; Mayfair, 124; National Gallery, 131; 1970s capitalism and, 120; Piccadilly, 120, 131, 138; Raneleigh Gardens (eighteenth century), 123; River Thames, 134–36; Rotherhithe (London), 140, 170; Royal Albert Hall, 124 332n14; Royal Court Theatre, Sloane Square, 122; Russell Street (Covent Garden), 139; St Paul's Cathedral, 171; sewers, 135–36; South Bank, 134; Thames Embankment, 137, 164; Tower Bridge, 170; Tower of London, 134; Westminster, 134; White's [Club] (St James's Street, London), 138
Look Back in Anger (John Osborne), 122–23
"L'origine du monde" (Gustave Courbet, 1866), 171
Lorrain, Claude, 221
Los Alamos Laboratory (New Mexico), 271
Lukas, Paul, 83

Macbeth (Roman Polanski, 1971), 121
MacLaine, Shirley, 219
Macollum, Barry, 219
Madame Tussauds Wax Museum, 164
Magritte, René, 54, 55
Mailer, Norman, 270
Man in the Gray Flannel Suit (Nunnally Johnson, 1956), 178
Man Who Knew Too Much, The (Murray Pomerance), 325n2

Manchurian Candidate, The (John Frankenheimer, 1962), 334n2
Manhattan Project, 36, 271. *See also* Hitchcock, Films, *Notorious*
Mannoni, Laurent, 88
Marfield, Dwight, 219
Marquis de Sade (Donatien Alphonse François Marquis de Sade), 159
Marsh, Jean, 150–51
Mason, James, 141, 325n3
Massey, Anna, 139, 157
Marx, Karl, 273
Mathers, Jerry, 8, 219, 221
Matter of Life and Death, A. See *Stairway to Heaven*
McCowen, Alec, 122
McCartney, Paul, 148
McCullin, Don, 170
McElhaney, Joe, 23
McGilligan, Patrick, 31, 37, 165, 275, 326n11
Mediterranean Ocean, 93
Meisner, Sanford, 16
Méliès, [Marie-]Georges[-Jean], 88
Mendl, [Sir] Charles, 20, 325n4
Mendl, Elsie, 325n4
Mengele, Josef, 113
Merchant, Vivien, 122
Merleau-Ponty, Maurice, 252, 253
Michelin Guide, 305
Miles, Bernard, 141
Miles, Vera, 173, 207, 209
Miller, Henry, 180
Miller, John, 70
Miller, Naomi, on Orsini Park, 125
Modern Times (Charles Chaplin, 1936), 327n5
Monty Python's Flying Circus (1969), on Canadian Broadcasting Corporation, 329n10
Moore, Victor, 175. *See also* Hitchcock, Settings, Victor Moore Arcade
More, Thomas, 136. See also *Utopia*

Mulvey, Laura, on the pleasure of looking, 129, 328n8
Musil, Robert, and Biedermeier Period, 31, 32

Nagasaki, 36, 37, 271
Napier, Alan, 141
Naremore, James, 10
Narrative of Arthur Gordon Pym of Nantucket, The (Edgar Allan Poe), 55
National Defense Research Committee, 270
Natwick, Mildred, 218
Navarro, Anna, 292
Nazi, regime. *See* Hitchcock, Films, *Notorious*
Nesbitt, Kathleen, 141
Nestor. *See* Atalanta and Meleager
New York City (*see also* Hitchcock, Settings): Belmont Park track (Queens), 175; Broadway (Queens), 175; Broadway (Manhattan), 175, 334; Bronx, The, 178; E Train, 173, 174; F Train, 173; Fifth Avenue—53rd Street station, 173, 174; 59th Street Bridge (New York), 198; Four Seasons, The (99 E. 52nd Street, Manhattan; now defunct), 178; Harlem, 178, 286; Hushy's Deli, Times Square (New York; now defunct), 178; Jamaica (Queens), 175; Le Cirque (151 E. 58th Street, Manhattan; now defunct), 178; Lexington/3rd Avenue—53rd Street station, 173, 174; Long Island Rail Road, 178; Manhattan, 173, 174, 175, 179, 198, 331n2; and menus, 178 (*see also* Hitchcock, Settings); Q47 bus (from Roosevelt Avenue-Jackson Heights to La Guardia Airport), 175; Queens, 172, 173, 175, 178, 179, 180, 189, 190, 198, 200, 331n2; Queens Plaza station, 173, 174; routines in, 179, 195, 202, 204, 207; St. Regis Hotel (E. 55th Street, Manhattan), 278, 285, 289, 307, 321; Stork Club (E. 53rd Street, Manhattan), 173, 177, 178, 179, 183, 184, 185, 194, 200; "21" (21 W. 52nd Street, Manhattan), 178; 23rd Street station, 174

Noiret, Philippe, 305, 306
N[orth] A[tlantic] T[reaty] O[rganization], invoked in *Topaz*, 302, 307, 308, 309
Nosferatu (F. W. Murnau, 1922), 327n10

Oppenheimer, [J.] Robert, 36, 270, 271
Orcus, king of Hell. *See* Naomi Miller
Orsini Park (Bomarzo), 125
Ortega y Gasset, José, 94, 252, 253
Orwell, George (Eric Arthur Blair), on public school, 138
Osborne, John, 121, 122, 123
Oudry, Jean-Baptiste, 227
Ouspenskaya, Maria, 326n8
Oxford University. *See* Britain, upper-class universities
Ozark (2017), 332n12

Palais Royal (Paris), 305
Palance, Jack, 213
Paley Park (E. 53rd St., Manhattan), 173. *See also* Hitchcock, Settings, Stork Club
Panter-Downes, Mollie, 113, 148
Paris, 90, 147, 155, 167, 230, 234, 279, 280, 283, 289, 290, 297, 301, 303, 304, 306, 309, 310, 312, 313, 316, 318, 321, 322, 331n5
Parker, Cecil, 97
Passage de la Visitation (7th Arr., Paris). *See* Hitchcock, Settings
Peleus, *see* Atalanta and Meleager
"Perception of Reality, The" (William James), 81
Pereira, Hal, 333n9

INDEX 359

Pereira, Irene Rice, 333n9
Perkins, V[ictor] F[rancis], 256
Persoff, Nehemiah, 196
Personal History, Adventures, Experience and Observation of David Copperfield the Younger of Blunderstone Rookery (Which He Never Meant to Publish on Any Account), The (Charles Dickens), 66
Peterboro (New Hampshire), leaf changes monitored, 332n2
Philadelphia Story, The (George Cukor, 1940), 331n4
Philippe (brother to Louis XIV), 305
Piccoli, Michel, 303, 312
Pierre. *See* Café Pierre
Pinocchio (Carlo Collodi), 21, 22, 203
Pirandello, Luigi, 67
Playboy (magazine, referenced in *Topaz*), 286
Pocahontas (legend), 256
Poussin, Nicolas, 259
Prokofiev, Sergei, 334n8
Psalm 91, 165
Purity and Danger (Mary Douglas), 315

Quayle, Anthony, 141, 205

Radford, Basil, 69
Rains, Claude, 8, 12, 31
Rancière, Jacques, 59
Randolph, Donald, 286
Ray, Nicholas, 14
Read, Herbert, 167
Rebel Without a Cause (Nicholas Ray, 1955), 325n1, 336n24
Red Shoes, The (Michael Powell and Emeric Pressburger, 1948), 327n16
Redgrave, Michael, 8, 73, 328n20
Réproduction interdite (René Magritte, 1937), 54–55
Return of the Vanishing American, The (Leslie A. Fiedler), 93
Rivas, Carlos, 287

Robbins, Richard, 213
Robertson, Peggy, 334n3
Robin, Dany, 285
Rogers, Ginger, 327n8
Roper, John, 292
Rossini, Gioachino [Antonio], 74, 79, 96
Roth, Henry, 60
Rothman, William, 10, 35, 196, 330n29
Rotonda, Peter, 202
Rousseau, Jean-Jacques, 179
Royal Copenhagen (1775), 274, 279, 293, 310, 335n12. *See also* Hitchcock, Films, *Topaz*
Ruysch, Rachel, 30
Ryan, Edmon, 301
Ryan, P. F. William, 161

Saint, Eva Marie, 9
Sakharov, Andre Dmitrievich, 277, 334n1
Salvation Army ("Sally Ann"), 146, 154
Sand, George (Amantine Lucile Aurore Dupin de Francueil), 290
Sartre, Jean-Paul: bad faith, 42, 212; on industry, 278; possession, 58
Schafer, R. Murray, 59, 93
Scharff, Stefan, 54, 61, 125
Schefer, Jean Louis, 227–28
Scheler, Max, and *ressentiment*, 31–32
Schiele, Egon, 31
Schivelbusch, Wolfgang, on coffee, 45, 46; on Germany after World War I, 30
Schneeweiszchen. See *Schneewittchen*
Schneewittchen (*Snow White*) (Jacob Grimm, Wilhelm Grimm), 44
Schubert, Franz, lieder, 263
Schünzel, Reinhold, 29
Selznick, David O., 37, 123. *See also* Brown
Sevareid, Eric, 334n3
Shaffer, Anthony, 150
Sim, Gerald, 139

Simmel, Georg: the blasé attitude, 176–77; the metropolitan condition, 176; the Stranger, 32, 248
Sinatra, [Francis Albert] Frank, 331n4
Sinclair, Iain, 170
Smith, Henry Nash, undiscovered West, 260, 285
Solitary Sex (Thomas Laqueur), 126
Solomon, Matthew, 329n15
Some Like It Hot (Billy Wilder, 1959), 332n10
Sorenson, Theodore, 272
Stafford, Frederick, 279, 300
Staffordshire china, 158
Stairway to Heaven (Michael Powell and Emeric Pressburger, 1946), 333n11
Stein, Gertrude, 328
Stewart, James, 5, 70, 336n21
Stewart, Sally, 70
"Still Life with Apples" (Paul Cézanne, 1895), 221
"Still Life with Apples and a Pomegranate" (Gustave Courbet, 1871–1872), 221
Stone, Harold J., 183
Stone of Milyon (Istanbul), in Byzantine Empire, 242
Stratton, Stephen, 201–02
Studies in Classic American Literature (D. H. Lawrence), 214, 237
Subor, Michel, 285
Swift, Clive, 155
Swift, Jonathan, on education in rich homes, 137–38

Talbot, William Henry Fox, 170
Tales of Pirx the Pilot (Stanislaw Lem), 95
Taylor, Gil, 150
Taylor, Samuel, 319
Teilhard de Chardin, Pierre, *nöosphere*, 331n6
Telemon, *see* Atalanta and Meleager
Teller, Edward, and the hydrogen bomb, 271

Tempest, The (William Shakespeare), 204
Tetzlaff, Ted, 41
Thief (Michael Mann, 1981), 332n12
Third Republic. *See* French Third Republic
Thoreau, Henry David. *See Walden*
Three Stooges, The. *See* Howard
Til, Roger, 305
Top Hat (Mark Sandrich, 1935), 327n8
Topaz (Leon Uris), 319
Travers, Linden, 97
Tremaine, Kathleen, 70
Triesault, Ivan, 18
Trinity test of the Atomic Bomb (July 16, 1945), 36
Truex, Philip, 219
Truffaut, François, 23, 27, 321, 326n10, 328n2
Twenty-four hour clock, use in England, 327n4
2001: A Space Odyssey (Stanley Kubrick, 1968), 335–36n17

Ulyanov, Vladimir Ilyich. *See* Lenin
Union Jack, 121, 171
United Nations (New York), invoked in *Topaz*, 282, 285, 335n15, 335n16
United States of America: White House, 272, 278, 293 (*see also* Hitchcock, Films, *Topaz*); testing intercontinental ballistic missile (January 1959), 272; and U-2 spy plane, 272
U[nion] of S[oviet] S[ocialist] R[epublics] (now Russia): Cold War, *see Topaz:* fusion bomb test (12 August 1953), 271: intercontinental ballistic missile test (August 1957), 271–72; K[omitet] G[osudarstvennoy] B[esopasnosti] (Committee for State Security), 274, 277, 280, 282, 299, 306
Upstairs, Downstairs (1971), 151
Utopia (Thomas More), 136

Van Dreelen, John, 304
Van Gogh, Vincent, 241
Varden, Norma, 329
Vaudeville, 67
Vernon, John, 286, 336n21
Versailles. *See* Château de Versailles
Virgil [Publius Vergilius Maro], 220
Von Goethe, Johann Wolfgang, 31
Von Ledebur, Friedrich, 34
Von Schiller, [Johann Christoph] Friedrich, 31
Von Zerneck, Peter, 34
Vonnegut, Kurt Jr., 21
Voyage Out, The (Virginia Woolf), 157
Voyage with Hitchcock, A (Murray Pomerance), 11, 333n8, 335n13

Waiting for Godot (Samuel Beckett), 262
Walbrook, Anton, 327
Walden (Henry David Thoreau), 229, 230
Walters, Charles, 178
"Waste Land, The" (T. S. Eliot), 5
Watteau, Antoine, 258
Wayne, Naunton, 69
Wedgwood, Josiah: company (Stoke-on-Trent, England), 44, 335n12
Weenix, Jan, 30
Weimar Germany, 32. *See also* Gay
Westman, Jim, 335n16
Wheel Spins, The (Ethel Lina White), 113. *See also* Hitchcock, Films, *The Lady Vanishes*
Whitelaw, Billie, 155
Whitlock, Albert, 54

Whitty, May, 67–68
Who's Afraid of Virginia Woolf? (Edward Albee; 13 October 1962, Billy Rose Theatre, New York), 334n2
Wiene, Robert, 31
Wilder, Billy, 332n10
Williams, Tennessee. See *Camino Real*
Wilson, Edmund, describing 1930s Los Angeles, 113–14
Wilson, Frank, 202
Wilson, Josephine, 98
Winchell, Walter, 213
Winchester College, 137
Withers, [Georgette Lizette] "Googie," 70
Wolfeborough (New York), leaf changes monitored, 332n2
Woolf, Leslie, 219
Wordsworth, William, invoked in *Frenzy*, 134
World War II: aftermath, tension in, 181; women in, 181; American type in, 69; French Underground in, 312; Hitchcock filming during, 33; Japanese surrender, 33; Knightsbridge Barracks (London), 113
Worringer, Wilhelm, 231, 232
Wright, Jonathan, 332n13
Wright, Teresa, 28

Žižek, Slavoj, 10
Zoffany (wallpapers), 303

www.ingramcontent.com/pod-product-compliance
Lightning Source LLC
Chambersburg PA
CBHW031703230426
43668CB00006B/95